Globalization and Third World Socialism

Also by Claes Brundenius

DEVELOPMENT STRATEGIES AND BASIC NEEDS IN LATIN AMERICA (*editor with Mats Lundahl*)

GRÄNSLÖSA AFFÄRER: Svenska Företag i Tredje Världen

NEW TECHNOLOGIES AND GLOBAL RESTRUCTURING: The Third World at a Crossroads (*editor wih Bo Göransson*)

RECONSTRUCTION OR DESTRUCTION? Science and Technology at Stake in the Transition Economies (*editor wih Bo Göransson and Prasada Reddy*)

REVOLUTIONARY CUBA: The Challenge of Economic Growth with Equity

THE CUBAN ECONOMY: Measurement and Analysis of Socialist Performance (*with Andrew Zimbalist*)

Also by John Weeks

A CRITIQUE OF NEO-CLASSICAL MACROECONOMICS

CAPITAL AND EXPLOITATION

DEBT DISASTER: Banks, Governments and Multilaterals Confront the Crisis (*editor*)

DEVELOPMENT STRATEGY AND THE ECONOMY OF SIERRA LEONE

LIMITS TO CAPITALIST DEVELOPMENT: The Industrialisation of Peru, 1950–80

MALADJUSTMENT IN CENTRAL AMERICA

PANAMA AT THE CROSSROADS (*with Andrew Zimbalist*)

RESTRUCTURING THE LABOUR MARKET: The South African Challenge

STRUCTURAL ADJUSTMENT AND THE AGRICULTURAL SECTOR IN LATIN AMERICA AND THE CARIBBEAN (*editor*)

THE ECONOMIES OF CENTRAL AMERICA

Globalization and Third World Socialism

Cuba and Vietnam

Edited by

Claes Brundenius
Associate Professor
Centre for Development Research
Copenhagen
Denmark

and

John Weeks
Professor of Development Economics
School of Oriental and African Studies
University of London
England

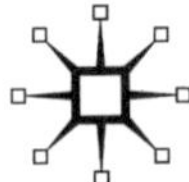

First published 2001 by
PALGRAVE
Houndmills, Basingstoke, Hampshire RG21 6XS and
175 Fifth Avenue, New York, N. Y. 10010
Companies and representatives throughout the world

PALGRAVE is the new global academic imprint of
St. Martin's Press LLC Scholarly and Reference Division and
Palgrave Publishers Ltd (formerly Macmillan Press Ltd).

ISBN 0–333–80043–5

This book is printed on paper suitable for recycling and
made from fully managed and sustained forest sources.

A catalogue record for this book is available
from the British Library.

Library of Congress Cataloging-in-Publication Data
Globalization and third-world socialism : Cuba and Vietnam /
edited by Claes Brundenius and John Weeks.
        p. cm.
     Includes bibliographical references and index.
     ISBN 0–333–80043–5 (cloth)
     1. Cuba—Economic policy. 2. Vietnam—Economic policy–
     –1975– 3. Socialism—Cuba. 4. Socialism—Vietnam.
     5. Globalization. I. Brundenius, Claes, 1938– II. Weeks,
     John, 1941–
     HC152.5 .G55 2000
     338.9597—dc21
                                                    00–065260

10   9   8   7   6   5   4   3   2   1
10 09 08 07 06 05 04 03 02 01

Printed in Great Britain by Antony Rowe Ltd, Chippenham, Wiltshire

Contents

List of Tables

List of Figures

Notes on the Contributors

Claes Brundenius is Associate Senior Professor and Senior Research Fellow at the Centre for Development Research, Copenhagen, Denmark.

Rikke Fabienke is a consultant at T&B Consult, Copenhagen, Denmark.

Miguel Alejandro Figueras is currently Adviser to the Minister of Tourism and former Adviser to the Minister of Foreign Investment and Economic Collaboration (MINVEC), Havana, Cuba.

George Irvin is Associate Professor at the Institute for Social Studies, the Hague, Netherlands.

Ari Kokko is Professor of International Business at Åbo Akademi University, Åbo, Finland.

Dana M. Liu is Research Analyst, associated with the World Bank.

Raymond Mallon is currently Adviser at the Central Institute for Economic Management, Hanoi, Vietnam.

Adam McCarty is economic consultant to international donor agencies, based in Hanoi, Vietnam, since 1991.

Pedro Monreal González is Senior Researcher at CIEI (Centre for Research on the International Economy) and Professor in the Economics Faculty at the University of Havana, Cuba.

Richard Newfarmer is Lead Specialist in the Chief Economist's Office of East Asia Region at the World Bank.

Antonio F. Romero Gómez is Director of CIEI (Centre for Research on the International Economy) Havana, Cuba.

Mona Rosendahl is Assistant Professor in Social Anthropology at Stockholm University, Sweden, and affiliated to the Institute of Latin American Studies at the same university.

Stein Tønnesson is Professor of Human Development Studies at the Centre of Development and Environment, University of Oslo, Norway.

Angie Ngoc Tran is Assistant Professor at the Social and Behavioral Sciences Center at California State University, Monterey Bay, California, USA.

John Weeks is Professor of Development Economics and Director of the Centre for Development Policy and Research at the School of Oriental and African Studies, London, UK.

Acknowledgements

Most of the contributions to this volume were originally presented in draft versions to a workshop at the Centre for Development, Copenhagen, 11–13 June 1998. The workshop entitled 'Globalization, Changing Paradigms and Development Options in the Third World: Cuba and Vietnam', assembled some twenty researchers from Cuba, Vietnam, Europe and the United States. We are most grateful for inputs and comments received by the participants and for the logistic support given to the workshop by the Centre for Development Research.

Claes Brundenius
John Weeks

Part I
Overview

1
Globalization and Third World Socialism

Claes Brundenius and John Weeks

In the 1990s there emerged a consensus that political and economic changes in the relations between countries implied a narrowing scope of development alternatives in low and middle-income countries. Many governments pursued socialist-oriented development strategies in the 1970s and 1980s, but with the collapse of the 'socialist camp' and the end of the Cold War, the remaining socialist countries faced a new reality. They responded to the challenge by opening up their economies, facilitating foreign investment and introducing economic reforms. This book focuses on two of these countries and how their governments have dealt with the dramatically altered external environment: Cuba and Vietnam.

For the purposes of this book, Cuba and Vietnam have several important common characteristics, despite their major differences in population size, level of development, history and culture. First, in terms of the size of economic and social indicators. Table 1.1 shows a series of indicators, ranging from the size of population and GDP characteristics to social indicators such as unemployment, life expectancy and literacy rates. These indicators reveal that Cuba was, in spite of its economic crisis in the 1990s, at the end of the decade, a considerably more developed country than Vietnam in spite of a rapid rate of GDP growth in Vietnam during the last 10 years. One characteristic that both countries share is the commitment to social development; both have high literacy rates, for instance, while Cuba is far ahead in providing health services to the population.

Second, with the collapse of the Soviet Union in the offing, the governments of both countries chose not to adopt the orthodox adjustment strategy derivative from the so-called Washington Consensus (which proved so disastrous in Russia and the other former Soviet states). And, third, both countries suffered from sanctions that the US government sought to impose on them (though Cuba much more than Vietnam after 1990).

To place these unorthodox adjustment strategies in context, this introduction reviews the debate on globalization, the issues, the controversies, the myths and the realities. It is now generally recognized that the blessings of

"

Table 1.1   Cuba and Vietnam: economic and social indicators, 1997

	Cuba	*Vietnam*
Population (000s)	11 059	76 711
Pop. growth rate (1990–97)	0.6%	2.1%
Population under 15 (%)	22.4 (est. 2000)	35.1 (est. 2000)
Population under 25 (%)	35.3 (est. 2000)	54.7 (est. 2000)
Population over 60 (%)	13.6 (est. 2000)	7.3 (est. 2000)
GDP (US$ millions)	18 862	24 008
GDP per capita (US$) (ER[1])	1 706	313
GDP per capita (US$) (PPP[2])	3 342	1 590
Exports (% of GDP)	9.6	38.6
Investment (% of GDP)	10.3	29.0
Agriculture (% of GDP)	7.4	26.2
Industry (% of GDP)	35.2	31.3
Services (% of GDP)	57.4	42.5
Current account bal. (% of GDP)	−1.3	−7.5
Govern. budget bal. (% of GDP)	−2.9	−2.2
Inflation rate (%)	1.9	19.7
External debt (US$ thousands)	10 146	9 800
FDI (% of GDP)	2.3	7.2
FDI (% of GDCF[3])	22.6	24.8
Employment: state (%)	77.7	8.9
Employment: non-state (%)	22.3	91.1
of which private (%)	8.6	37.0
Unemployment	6.8	5.6
Telephone lines (per thous. inh.)	34	21
Life expectancy (years)	76	68
Literacy rate (%)	98	92.5
Infant mortality (per thous. inh.)	7	29
Medical doctors (per 10 000)	544	43
Nurses (per 10 000)	687	60
Hospital beds (per 10 000)	738	258
Human development index	0.729	0.560

[1] exchange rate;
[2] purchasing power parity;
[3] gross domestic capital formation.
Sources: *World Bank Atlas*, 1999; UNDP, *Human Development Report 1999*; EIU, *Cuba Country Report*, 2nd quarter, 1999; EIU, *Vietnam Country Report*, 2nd quarter, 1999; *The Sex and Age Distribution of the World Populations*, UN, New York, 1996; plus data drawn from the various book chapters in this volume.

so-called globalization are mixed. At the end of the century some of the negative aspects are obvious, as witnessed not least by the Asian financial crisis that began in 1997, followed by yet another collapse of the Russian economy, and the depression-inducing devaluation of the Brazilian real. The Washington Consensus itself is in crisis. George Soros (1998) belatedly expressed his *mea culpa*, warning against overbelief in the markets to solve development problems, and Joseph Stiglitz of the World Bank conceded the same point in early 1997 (Stiglitz, 1998).

The income and wealth gap between the rich and the poor, among and within countries, has probably never increased as fast as during the 1980s and 1990s. As a result, there is an increasing interest in models of development that offer an alternative to the predatory capitalism of the orthodox emphasis on unrelated markets. As a minimum, such alternatives would evaluate efficiency criteria in terms of equity concerns and environmental priorities. More fundamentally, fostering competitiveness would be reconciled with public demands for social justice and democracy. This is the basic challenge in a globalized world: to what extent are 'economies in transition' capable of strategies that produce equity with growth and efficiency, environmental sustainability, and political participation? The chapters in this book address this question for Cuba and Vietnam. In combination, they provide insights into the lessons provided by unorthodox transition strategies, and shed light on whether there is a future for socialist development in the Third World.

The globalization controversy

Since the word 'globalization' is one of the most used words in contemporary political and economic discourse, it might seem superfluous to discuss what it is, much less whether it is an objectively identifiable phenomenon. Nonetheless, there is an important debate on precisely this issue. Some writers claim that there is in principle nothing new in relation to earlier *internationalization* trends in the world economy; it is alleged that for the presently industrialized countries at the beginning of the twentieth century, foreign trade as a share of GDP was as big as, or bigger than, it is today (see, for instance, Hirst and Thompson, 1996). This proves to be so in some cases, if one uses *current* prices, but as Maddison (1995) and others (for instance, Brundenius, 1998, and van Bergeijk and Mensink, 1997) have demonstrated, the result is quite different if trade shares are calculated in *constant* prices (see Table 1.2). When measured in constant prices the trend is quite clear: the interdependency of the major economies significantly increased after 1950. For the world economy as a whole, the share of exports in the world global product increased from 7 per cent in 1950 to 16.4 per cent in 1998. This can be compared with the earlier internationalization trend at the beginning of the century, when the world export share peaked at 9 per cent in 1929. In some cases the increase has been dramatic, as in Germany (from 6.2 per cent in 1950 to 43.2 per cent in 1998) and in smaller industrialized countries (e.g., Denmark (from 12.5 to 44.0 per cent over the same period)).

Among Asian countries, Japan, the Republic of Korea and Taiwan experienced rapidly increasing export shares, with the last perhaps unprece-

Table 1.2 Exports as a percentage of GDP in selected countries and regions, 1870–1998 (exports and GDP at 1990 prices)

Country/region	1870	1913	1929	1950	1973	1992	1998
USA	2.5	3.7	3.6	3.0	5.0	8.2	11.0
England/UK	12.0	17.7	13.3	11.4	14.0	21.4	26.4
Germany	9.5	15.6	12.8	6.2	23.8	32.6	43.2
Denmark	8.6	13.3	15.7	12.5	24.6	41.8	44.0
USSR	n.a.	2.9*	1.6	1.3	3.8	3.0*	6.5*
Japan	0.2	2.4	3.5	2.3	7.9	12.4	13.5
China	0.7	1.4	1.7	1.9	1.1	2.3	3.4
Taiwan	n.a.	2.5	5.2	2.5	10.2	34.4	33.0
Rep. Korea	0.0	1.0	4.5	1.0	8.2	17.8	35.9
India	2.5	4.7	3.7	2.6	2.0	1.7	2.0
Latin America	9.0	9.5	9.7	6.2	4.6	6.2	8.4
World	5.0	8.7	9.0	7.0	11.2	13.5	16.4

*Russia
Source: Maddison (1995), calculated from table 2–4; the figures for Denmark are derived from tables C–16a and I–2 in the same source. 1998 figures updated by the authors, using Maddison's methodology, based on data in OECD, 1999 (Appendix tables 1 & 40); IMF, 1999 (table 1); ADB, 1999 (tables A1 and A11).

dented and subsequently unmatched in its increase. From a low level, China's trade also grew rapidly. Exceptions are India and Latin America (and no doubt also Africa although reliable comparable data are lacking), where the export shares have been virtually constant for almost the last 50 years of the twentieth century. An important conclusion is that there seems to be a clear correlation between economic growth (if we accept the GDP measure) and export growth in the postwar period. The economies that have advanced to the top of the growth league during the last 25 years, coinciding with a slow-down of the world economy, are those which showed increasing shares of world trade. Self-reliance and delinking that was so fashionable in the 1960s and 1970 would appear to no longer present viable development strategies.

However, even these clear and unambiguous trends do not have a straight-forward interpretation. The word globalization is not typically used to describe the long-term process by which trade has increased over a century or more; rather, it refers to a hypothesis about the last decade or two that the world economy has entered into a new 'globalized' era which is qualitatively different than before. In this new era, the old development paradigms of socially-regulated markets and welfare states in the developed countries, and import-substitution strategies in the underdeveloped countries, are no longer relevant or possible. And a key part of this fundamental change has been the dramatic increase in world trade. So powerful, goes the argument, is the force of international competition, that national development strategies based on industrial policy, labour market protection and protection of national cultural norms will, if continued, be swept away by the power of international markets. If this is the globalization hypothesis, the trade data do not support it. Statistical analysis reveals that not in the 1980s, nor in the 1990s, was the growth of world trade or trade by regions significantly different from its trend over the last few decades of the twentieth century (Weeks, 1998). A casual inspection of international statistics reveals that international trade in the 1990s was a higher proportion of world output than in previous decades. However, this in itself does not support the 'new era' argument, since trade has grown faster than output in every decade since the end of the Second World War. This increased trade has been associated with concrete national and international policies, including the various agreements within the framework of the General Agreement on Tariffs and Trade (GATT) and the progressive economic integration of the Western European countries. In support of the 'new era' hypothesis, it must be shown that in the 1980s and 1990s this long-term trend accelerated significantly.

To empirically test this hypothesis, we inspect the behaviour of the export – GDP ratio for five country groups and the world as a whole: the sub-Sahara, South Asia, East Asia, Latin America, and the OECD countries. The hypothesis was tested by regressing the share of exports in GDP (logarithmic form) against a time trend and dummy variables for five-year periods, with the first five-year period omitted. The results are presented in Table 1.3 with all non-significant coefficients omitted. Inspection of the last row of the table shows that for every country group there was a significant and positive trend in the export–GDP ratio over the 38 years, 1960–97. As to be expected, the highest trend is for the East Asian countries, for which the ratio increased at 7 per cent per annum. However, the tests for differences across periods prompts the rejection of the 'new era' hypothesis. For two country groups (South Asia and the OECD) and the 'world', there was a significant *upward* shift in this measure of 'openness' only in the pre-globalization period 1975–79. For the OECD countries, this was probably the result of the increase in intra-European trade. For the 'globalization' periods, none of the shift-coefficients are significant, with the exception of the *negative* shift for South Asia. Thus, the share of exports in total production, for groups of countries and the world as a whole, was no different in the 1990s than one would have expected on the basis of long-term trends. Further, if in 1985 one had calculated the trends for each group over the previous 25 years, then projected to 1997, the predicted value would not have been significantly different from the actual value.

To pursue this point further, in Table 1.4 the growth rate of constant-price exports is subjected to a similar statistical test. In this case no trend is included, so the test is for differences in export growth across periods. Again, the 'new era' hypothesis fails to gain support. Only for the countries

Table 1.3   Exports as a proportion of GDP and long-term trend, by period compared to 1970–74, and by region (OLS method)

Periods	sub–Sahara	South Asia	East Asia	Latin America	OECD members	World
1975–79	nsgn	+1.1	nsgn	nsgn	+1.2	+1.1
Debt Crisis						
1980–84	nsgn	nsgn	nsgn	nsgn	nsgn	nsgn
Globalization						
1985–89	nsgn	−1.3	nsgn	nsgn	nsgn	nsgn
1990–94	nsgn	nsgn	nsgn	nsgn	nsgn	nsgn
1995–97	nsgn	nsgn	nsgn	nsgn	nsgn	nsgn
Trend	+0.8	+3.0	+6.0	+1.3	+0.7	+1.2

Note: Only coefficients with a probability of .10 or less are considered significant; nsgn = notsignificant. The period shift coefficients and the trend have been converted from logarithms to percentages.
Source: World Bank, *World Bank Stars 1996* (1960–69), and World Bank, *World Development Indicators 1997* (1970–96), both on cd-rom; and United Nations (1997).

Table 1.4   Rate of growth of exports, compared to 1970–74, by region (OLS method)

Periods	sub-Sahara	South Asia	East Asia	Latin America	OECD members	World
1975–79	+2.3	nsgn	nsgn	nsgn	nsgn	nsgn
Debt Crisis						
1980–84	nsgn	nsgn	nsgn	nsgn	−1.9	−1.8
Globalization						
1985–89	+2.2	nsgn	nsgn	nsgn	nsgn	nsgn
1990–94	+3.6	+7.3	nsgn	nsgn	nsgn	nsgn
1995–97	+4.8	nsgn	nsgn	nsgn	nsgn	nsgn

Note: Only coefficients with a probability of .10 or less are considered significant; nsgn=notsignificant. The period shift coefficients have been converted from logarithms to percentages.
Source: World Bank, *World Bank Stars 1996* (1960–69), and World Bank, *World Development Indicators 1997* (1970–96, both on cd-rom; and United Nations (1997).

of the sub-Saharan region is export growth consistently and significantly higher in the 'globalization' periods, yet these countries, by general agreement among globalizationists, were the ones least integrated into the world economy. South Asia displays one significantly higher coefficient (for 1990–94), and all the others are non-significant.

Table 1.5 Foreign direct investment as a proportion of GDP and long-term trend, by period compared to 1970–74, and by region (OLS method)

Periods	Sub-Sahara	South Asia	East Asia	Latin America	China
1975–79	nsgn	nsgn	nsgn	nsgn	no data
Debt Crisis					
1980–84	nsgn	nsgn	nsgn	nsgn	(base period)
Globalization					
1985–89	nsgn	nsgn	nsgn	nsgn	nsgn
1990–94	nsgn	nsgn	nsgn	nsgn	nsgn
1995–97	nsgn	nsgn	nsgn	nsgn	nsgn
Trend	+0.2	+0.2	+0.6	+0.2	+0.8

Note: Only coefficients with a probability of .10 or less are considered significant; nsgn = not-significant. The period shift coefficients and the trend have been converted from logarithms to percentages.
Source: World Bank, *World Bank Stars 1996* (1960–69), and World Bank, *World Development Indicators 1997* (1970–96), both on cd-rom; and United Nations (1997).

For direct foreign investment (Table 1.5) the evidence is even stronger against the 'new era' hypothesis. When one accounts for the trend of direct foreign investment in GDP (positive for each group), for none are there significant globalization coefficients. Further, the level of foreign direct investment is less than 2 per cent of GDP for each region, or considerably less than a tenth of gross domestic investment. This small proportion implies that, except for unusual cases, it is not credible to assert that foreign direct investment could be the engine of growth or even technology transfer for most countries.

The established positive relationship between GDP growth and export growth over the last five decades does not establish causality. It may be that 'open economies do grow faster' (Dollar, 1992), but this may be because rapid growth fosters rapid productivity change and export competitiveness, not the reverse; or, that the two are derivative from some third variable, such as investment in physical plant or research and development. In other words, the trends of the last five decades do not, in themselves, establish the strong policy conclusion that initiating trade liberalization to open an economy fosters faster growth. Doubt about this conclusion is all the greater when one discovers that a number of countries with rapidly growing export shares experienced this while pursuing strongly interventionist industrial policies (see for example Amsden, 1989, on the Republic of Korea).

But the globalization process is not only, perhaps not even primarily, a question of expansion of world trade. International capital flows have accelerated far faster than trade. Since 1985 foreign direct investment flows have increased at a rate of 14.3 per cent, compared to 6.7 per cent for the export volume and 3.2 per cent for world output, both measured in constant prices (Rowthorn and Kozul-Wright, 1998). But, again, the growth of foreign direct investment, either for the world or regions in the 1980s or the 1990s was not significantly above its trend line during the postwar period (except for China, see Weeks, 1998).

Above all, it has been the phenomenal increase in the international movement of financial capital that has characterized the last two decades, and especially the 'trade' in currencies. This process was not the outcome of any inexorable technological development (though communications changes facilitated it), but was the result of the deregulation of international financial markets and the opening of national capital accounts to speculative money flows. It has been estimated that the *daily* transactions on global currency markets increased from about US$18 billion in the early 1980s to over US$1500 billion in the late 1990s, of which the lion's share was for speculative purposes. This speculation led to legitimate concerns that the nation-state would rapidly lose control over the most fundamental instruments of development policy; above all, over the *direction and character* of the development process. This deregulation of capital markets has clearly resulted in an anarchic process in which 'development issues' are increasingly being left to the 'invisible hand of the market'. For many developing countries the result has been disastrous. This makes it tempting to blame the national economic instability on globalization, and that, in turn, on the triumphant neo-liberal revival during the last twenty years, especially after the collapse of socialism.

In this context it is important to distinguish between globalization as a process and the measures to cope with it. For the majority of humankind there may be few blessings associated with globalization as it manifested itself in the 1990s. But globalization is not an invention by the neo-liberals; it has been appropriated by the neo-liberal ideology. The neo-liberal recipes have led to so-called winner-take-all societies, in which increasing numbers of people are forced to compete with less social restraint in a society that encourages waste, income inequality and impoverished cultural life (Frank and Cook, 1996). Critics of the excesses of neo-liberal globalization and its associated IMF-style liberalization of capital markets now include former champions such as George Soros and Jeffrey Sachs.

The neo-liberal project sustains itself in part because there appear to be no readily available alternatives. 'Socialist integration' is not viable anymore, or at least will not be in the foreseeable future. Is there room for any alternative development paths that would allow for development with a human face, or what has been known as Third World socialism? More specifically, is there an alternative for the former socialist countries, the 'transitional economies'?

The transition economies

The fall in output in the transition economies in Eastern Europe and the former Soviet Union (FSU) has been so deep and long-lasting that the phenomenon of *depression* easily comes to mind (see the statistics in Chapter 2). We might even talk about a new Great Depression (see e.g. Rostowski 1997) or worse, for the declines in many of these economies are unprecedented in modern times. For example, the falls in output in Russia and Ukraine are unique; not even during the Second World War did production drop as much (World Bank, 1996, Figure 2). With the 1930s as a point of reference, there was no case of such *deep* and *long-lasting declines* in output. In the United States, the hardest hit apart from Germany, output had fully recovered by 1937, from a drop of 30 per cent (1933 compared to 1929). In contrast, when Russian GDP in 1997 *apparently* reached the bottom of the trough, the economy had shrunk by more than half since 1989, with a *continuous* decline from 1990. In 1998 the Russian economy showed positive, although modest, growth for the first time since 1990, but a further collapse occurred in August in the aftermath of the Asian financial crisis. Predicting the future of the economy brings to mind a black Russian joke: the optimists in Russia believe that the economy is suffering a catastrophic disaster, the pessimists think the catastrophe is coming.

All East European and former Soviet republics (and especially the latter) lack *new* investments in the *productive* sphere. There have been some investments in the non-productive sphere as a result of privatization (and usually for speculative purposes), but long-term *industrial* investment is virtually non-existent and the overall investment rates have fallen even faster than GDP, implying negative net investment growth. The transition to capitalism in these countries, which advocates promised would bring efficiency and growth, has tended to flourish in speculation, commerce and finance.

As a result, living standards have fallen for a large portion of the populations of these countries, and a majority in some cases. The deterioration has been particularly severe in the former Soviet Union. According to a recent World Bank study (Milanovic, 1998), between 1987/88 and 1993/95 the share of people measured to be below the poverty line increased from *4 to 45 per cent* in all transition economies taken together (that is Eastern and Central Europe plus the former Soviet Union). That percentage increase implies that the poor increased from 13.6 million to 168 million people, *an addition of 154 million newly poor* in this region in less than a decade! In Russia, poverty incidence increased from *2 to 50 per cent*, for an increase from 2.2 million people to 74.2 million people (in this case 'achieved' in barely four years of 'transition', 1987/88 to 1993/95). Poverty generation was worse still in the Ukraine and the Central Asian republics. Apparently, the worst case was the Kyrgyz Republic, whose increase in the poverty share, from 12 to 88 per cent, must set a peace-time record (and challenge the worst war-time outcomes). Central and Eastern Europe have fared better, but would be judged as having good outcomes only on the basis of low expectations: in Poland, viewed as a transition success, the share of poor people increased from 6 to 20 per cent of the population. Hungary, the Czech Republic, Slovakia and Slovenia are the only countries in which poverty increased only marginally; in no country for which poverty was measured did it decrease (Milanovic, 1998, table 5.1). It was to these uniformly negative examples that the policy-makers in Cuba and Vietnam looked when they sought the solutions to the new international pressures constraining their economies.

What went wrong in the transitional economies

It is beyond the scope of this introduction to consider the political forces that prompted the policy choices that produced the disastrous outcomes in Russia and the former Soviet republics. However, one can identify the intellectual and theoretical mistake that prompted the orthodox transition strategies. These were based upon a naturalistic rather than a social view of the nature of markets, and almost without exception, the design of the transitional strategies was dominated by economists, Western neoclassical economists (most from the United States) or nationals trained in that school of thought. In this framework, markets are not social institutions but arise from the self-interested nature of human beings (Adam Smith referred to the human 'instinct' to 'truck, barter and exchange'). In this approach, markets exist everywhere and at all times; should they be absent, incomplete or ineffective, this is the result of their suppression by the state. Markets lie dormant, awaiting liberation, as suggested by the title of a World Bank working paper on Vietnam, 'Awakening the Market' (Leipziger, 1992). As part of this general approach, entrepreneurial skills are treated as an inherent aspect of the human character, which need not be learned and, therefore, are always in unlimited supply.

With this view of markets, it followed that price liberalization was the key to transition, since the natural self-interest of individuals would be liberated through 'market signals'. In response to these signals, *homo economicus* would marshall resources, organize production, and respond to the needs of consumers. The markets through which this would happen would arise spontaneously; indeed, the actions of buying and selling between individuals *would be* the markets. Unfortunately, disastrously for millions of people, markets do not arise spontaneously; they must be constructed through the creation of a social structure in which they can operate. For example, if a private farmer in Russia were to make an informed profit calculation, he or she would require a developed and active land market to value the land input; an effective credit market that allocates capital across producers of different commodities on the basis of relative returns; the mobility of labour, which itself depends on a flexible housing market; a commercially-oriented transport system; and a decentralized information system on prevailing prices, anticipated demand, weather conditions, and so on. This list includes only the more mundane prerequisites, almost none of which were fulfilled in the transitional economies. Relative success in Poland and Hungary was in great part explained by these countries having been the most market-oriented of the transitional economies prior to 1990.

Much more profound changes were required in most of the countries, which would convert the appearance of markets into a market system. Most obviously, the conversion requires clarification of property rights, which is considerably more complex than establishing clear titles (see Stiglitz, 1997, pp. 173–4). Clarification of property rights is related to the nature of the state, and capitalist societies have capitalist states. The capitalist state is the basis of the division between the public and private sectors, in which private producers are relieved of most welfare functions because these have become the responsibility of the public sector. This form of the state implies a range of new institutions, such as political interest groups, and radically altered roles for existing institutions such as trade unions.

The imposition of a capitalist pricing regime upon non-capitalist societies (in the faith that the former would sweep the latter away) goes far in explaining the transition disasters. Cuba and Vietnam have rejected the orthodox recipe precisely to avoid this ill-conceived and ill-fated strategy, in which a few people prospered fabulously, most suffered income declines, and a large minority fell into poverty.

Cuba and Vietnam: lessons for alternative strategies

If, at the beginning of the twenty-first century, socialism remains a practical alternative development strategy, it will assume a form in which markets play a major role. Through its focus on Cuba and Vietnam, this book addresses that issue and closely related ones: how far can a government introduce market regulation and still preside over a socialist economy? Can heterodox strategies combine reducing the pain of transition with necessary structural change and a satisfactory rate of growth? During the difficult process of transition, how do households cope with fundamental and socially destabilizing change?

The analysis begins with a comparison of the manner in which each country adjusted to a severe external-sector imbalance. It is well-known that Vietnam made this adjustment with extraordinary success, achieving one of the fastest growth rates in the world during the 1990s. Weeks argues that the large trade gap at the end of the decade should not be interpreted as a reversal of that success. Cuba and Vietnam provide useful comparisons, but no discussion of alternative strategies would be complete without reference to China. No chapter could do justice to the variety of experience that characterizes this huge country (with approximately 20 per cent of humanity within its borders). But Newfarmer and Liu (Chapter 3) provide a thorough synthesis of the necessary role of financial reform and enterprise restructuring for adaption to pressures from the world economy. These two issues are singularly relevant for Cuba and Vietnam, and are discussed in several subsequent chapters. The experience of China shows that the state productive sector must undertake basic changes to raise efficiency, or there will be a progressive decline in relation to a more dynamic non-state sector (which, the authors maintain, has occurred in China).

Part II of the book deals with Cuba, whose economy suffered a catastrophic decline in the early 1990s. However, in the context of most transitional economies, the Cuban decline was relatively modest. Further, it is argued that the Cuban recovery, when compared to recoveries in other Latin American countries after severe declines, proved relatively rapid. The major unresolved problem is whether the basis has been laid for the structural change which will allow for sustained long-term growth. Romero (Chapter 4) addresses the question of structural change, which is associated with a long-standing discussion in Cuba going back to the 'socialist transition' debate of the 1960s. After detailing the sharp contraction of the Cuban economy in the early 1990s, and the subsequent recovery, Romero concludes that the recovery is fragile because Cuban exports remained overwhelmingly concentrated in primary products; in his view 'not compatible' with the products whose demand is dynamic in world markets. Thus, at the end of the decade the primary challenge to policy-makers was the diversification of exports.

Figueras (Chapter 5) takes a different angle on 'insertion' by considering, first, the Multilateral Agreement on Investment, then its relationship to the US Helms–Burton Act (which seeks to restrict foreign investment in Cuba). The Act derived from an alleged illegal confiscation of US property in Cuba after the revolution. The story Figueras tells reveals some quite extraordinary facts about these 'confiscations'; in particular, that the US government of the day refused to negotiate over the issue of compensation. Among the more amusing revelations in his chapter is that the Helms–Burton Act was passed for the ostensible purpose of facilitating claims on assets in Cuba, and by March 1998 *only one valid claim had been received by the US government.*

First and foremost, the crisis of the early 1990s (the 'special period') had a profoundly unsettling effect on the Cuban population, generating a sudden and dramatic fall in living standards. Rosendahl (Chapter 6) analyses how households dealt with this potentially devastating blow. Central to household survival was the growth of a 'second economy', and complex barter relations within and among extended families. These survival strategies frequently came into conflict with the collectivist values which developed under the socialist system of state provision and community cooperation. Rosendahl questions whether socialist values will survive the period of scarcity and household-based survival strategies.

Closely related to people's perception of an uncertain future is the effect of the crisis and policy changes on the distribution of income and wealth. Key to the population's support for a socialist path was a high value placed on social and economic equality. Chapter 7 by Fabienke suggests that changes in distribution have been substantial. Prior to the overthrow of the *ancien regime* in 1959, the Gini coefficient for income was .55, far from the highest in Latin America but well above the level for developed countries. Over the next 25 years inequality fell impressively, to a Gini of .22 in the mid-1980s. In the context of a careful and detailed review of policy changes and their impact on various income sources, Fabienke concludes that income inequality in the late 1990s had returned to near its pre-revolution level. The implications of this finding for the dynamics of policy reform are profound.

With the profound changes that have occurred in Cuba in mind, Brundenius and Monreal (Chapter 8) set out to take a long-term view of the Cuban development process. On the one hand, they note the impressive recovery after 1993; on the other, they stress its limited basis. The recovery derived from activating unutilized capacity, with very little new investment (except in tourism and nickel mining). This leads to their basic conclusion that, 'Cuba's insertion into the world economic system has not yet provided an adequate...[basis] for Cuba's long term growth and economic development'. They argue that this problem will only be resolved through a substantial rise in the investment share (which had fallen to about 7 per cent of GDP in the 1990s) associated with a 'massive re-allocation of labour, particularly in [state-owned enterprises]'. By use of an open-economy model to simulate growth, they produce three 'scenarios', in which imports are the binding constraint. They conclude that the policy framework in the late 1990s was 'not conducive to [high] levels of investment', that 'neither [could] modest reforms...solve the problem'. However, they believe that there exists a reform programme for sustained and rapid growth which is consistent with a socialist development strategy.

Part III of the book considers Vietnam, a country which the 1990s implemented much more basic reforms than Cuba. Indeed, it could be argued that by the end of the decade, Vietnam had a managed market economy, in contrast to Cuba's socialized economy with limited markets. Mallon and Irvin (Chapter 9) endorse this perspective, and through a detailed analysis of sector growth dismiss the more apocalyptic predictions of pending crisis. In particular, they argue that the large trade deficit should not be interpreted as a disequilibrium, since it is entirely financed by foreign direct investment (also argued by Weeks in Chapter 2). They view policy reform as an ongoing process whose pace should be set pragmatically, and conclude that 'Vietnam appears to be facing up to the main problems of promoting sustainable, market-led growth'. Kokko (Chapter 11) has an opposite view in his contribution, seeing the trade gap as an unambiguous signal of fundamental structural rigidity in the economy. He does not deny that the state sector has performed flexibly, but feels that the overall thrust of policy, which he calls import substitution, has outlived its usefulness. In his opinion, the only viable policy scenario is one in which privatization of state enterprises is the centrepiece, supported by rapid trade liberalization.

One consequence of the East Asian meltdown is that Vietnam would potentially be more vulnerable to external economic instability than Cuba. Tønnesson (Chapter 10) addresses this possibility, analysing the impact of the Asian financial crisis, which began in 1997, on the Vietnamese economy. Because of the limited convertibility of the currency, the dong, Vietnam avoided instability transmitted through the capital account of the balance of payments. However, there remained two major growth-reducing impacts. First, the severe economic contractions in several countries of the region would reduce the demand for Vietnam's exports. Second, exchange rate devaluations (and collapse in Indonesia) might, after the initial inflationary and instability effects, leave the dong dangerously overvalued compared to the currencies of competitor countries. Tønnesson places these potential problems in the context of three contrasting 'stories' about the Vietnamese reform process: an orthodox story which attributes virtually all maladies to the inadequate pace of reforms, a heterodox story which interprets the measured pace of reform as the source of the economy's protection against external instability and a third more mixed and pragmatic story. Tønnesson concludes that the last story is the more credible.

Foreign direct investment has played a major role in Vietnam's transition to a market-regulated economy, and there is no doubt that this foreign investment served as a major stimulus to growth. Tran (Chapter 12) suggests that its social impact has, at least in some cases, been quite problematical. Her interviews confirm the poor working conditions in garment factories which have been widely-reported in the media. As in other countries, this sector in Vietnam has an overwhelmingly female labour force. Her chapter suggests the need for research on several issues: the comparison of working conditions before and during policy reform; a comparison of conditions in state and private factories, and in export and non-export oriented firms; and the role of workers' organizations as market forces play a larger role.

The social impact (social *cost*, many would write) of Vietnam's transition to market regulation, not withstanding rapid growth (or because of it) has been a subject of considerable controversy. McCarty (Chapter 13) concludes, however, that the social consequences of transition in Vietnam have been overwhelmingly favourable with incomes rising for most segments of the population, although relative income gaps have increased in the process. This process also saw deterioration in education and health services.

Taken together, these chapters seek to unravel the lessons that might be learned from an inspection of two countries reacting to the defining process of the 1990s: the political and economic collapse of the Socialist bloc. With minor exceptions, the authors treating the same or similar issues agree on the facts. However, the conclusions drawn from these facts are often different, indeed in some cases are diametrically opposed. This is hardly surprising since the issue of the transition from closed economy socialism to a viable integration into world markets is a continuation of the great ideological debate of the twentieth century: does unregulated capitalism serve the general welfare, and, if not, is it to be overthrown or reformed? And if the latter, what will be the nature and focus of the reform? The collapse of the Soviet Union did not end this debate (Fukuyama, 1992, not withstanding), but merely shifted it onto other terrain.

2
A Tale of Two Transitions: Cuba and Vietnam

John Weeks

Introduction

At the end of the 1980s, the collapse of the Soviet Union brought forth drastic economic adjustments in some thirty countries (over half of which had not previously been independent). For almost all of these, the adjustments would involve a fundamental change in economic, political and social organization, with a substantial minority combining this with debilitating civil wars, separatist conflicts or armed border disputes. In the short run, the governments faced an immediate balance of payments crisis. With a few exceptions, the trade of these countries had been concentrated within COMECON; in the cases of the former Soviet Republics trade had been largely internal to the USSR. Thus, all but a few of the countries (e.g., China) encountered a common problem, to convert from COMECON trade to trade in 'hard' currencies.

This chapter considers the process by which, in the short run, two countries, Cuba and Vietnam, adjusted their balance of payments in the aftermath of the collapse of the Soviet Union. Of the underdeveloped countries that were a part of the Soviet bloc, Cuba and Vietnam implemented the most extensive and comprehensive forms of central planning. This is in contrast to the nominal central planning in several African countries, which was largely form rather than essence. While planning may not have covered the entire economy in either country, the state controlled external trade in both cases. Therefore, the transition to a hard-currency trading regime represented a fundamental readjustment in both Cuba and Vietnam.

The analysis of the transition to new trading regimes in Cuba and Vietnam takes three parts. First, the balance of payments crisis suffered by each country is placed in context, in comparison to other countries of the relevant region and in comparison to other centrally-planned states. This is followed by sections that deal with Cuba's adjustment, then that of Vietnam. The conclusion is that both countries adjusted with relative success compared to other centrally-planned states, and compared to countries in their region.

The crisis in context

The collapse of the Soviet Union resulted in an economic crisis for the countries within the Soviet trading system, which took the immediate form of a balance of payments crisis. This balance of payments crisis can be distinguished analytically from the dismantling of mechanisms of central planning, especially since in almost every case, when the latter occurred, it worsened rather than eased the former. Whatever else transition to market regulation might have achieved, it did not, in the short run, contribute to closing trade gaps; on the contrary, trade liberalization tended to provoke an increased flow of imports, while the export response was at best sluggish.

Prior to considering the consequences for Cuba and Vietnam of the end of the Soviet trading system, the relevant differences between the two countries need be noted. On the eve of the collapse of the Soviet Union, Cuba was one of the more developed countries of Latin America in terms of social indicators. While calculations of per capita income are sensitive to the prices used, any reasonable measure implies that per capita income in Cuba was of the order of ten times that of Vietnam. While Cuba was perhaps 80 per cent urban and 20 per cent rural in 1990 (depending on the definition of an urban area),[1] the proportions for Vietnam were the reverse. Both countries suffered from economic and political sanctions by the United States, but after 1990 these were of minor importance for Vietnam. For Cuba, on the other hand, the negative impact of sanctions may well have increased in the 1990s, with the Helms–Burton law especially important.

Two countries so different are compared because each pursued an adjustment strategy substantially different from that promoted by the Western Powers and the international financial institutions. By contrast, in Central Europe[2] and Russia adjustment was based upon 'Washington Consensus' macroeconomic policies, including rapid trade liberalization, deregulation of capital markets, privatization and demand compression. For the Asian states of the former Soviet Union strategies were more mixed, from the highly liberalizing Kyrgyz Republic to relatively non-liberalizing Uzebeki- stan (Weeks, 1997).[3]

In order to assess the severity of the adjustment problem, Table 2.1 provides the basic indicators for Cuba and Vietnam (with GDP growth shown graphically in Figure 2.1). Here and below, the discussion will be in terms of two time periods, pre- and post-collapse of the Cold War trading regimes (1986–89 and 1990 onwards). The economic performance of the two countries was quite different before the collapse of the Soviet Union; while Cuba's growth was quite modest, averaging less than 2 per cent per annum, Vietnam grew at a relatively robust 5 per cent. Vietnam's economic performance

Table 2.1   Basic economic indicators for Cuba and Vietnam, 1986–98

(a) Cuba

	GDP				*Parallel exchange rate*
Years	*Growth (%)*	*Exports (US$ curr.)*	*Imports (US$ curr.)*	*TB/GDP*	
1986	1.8	5322	7596	−12.3	n.a.
1987	−1.6	5401	7612	−12.2	n.a.
1988	4.8	5518	7579	−10.8	n.a.
1989	1.5	5400	8140	−14.3	n.a.
1990	−3.1	5415	7417	−10.2	7.0
1991	−9.4	2980	4234	−7.7	20.0
1992	−11.6	1779	2315	−3.2	35.0
1993	−14.9	1137	2037	−6.0	78.0
1994	0.7	1381	2353	−6.3	95.0
1995	2.5	1507	2992	−9.2	32.1
1996	7.8	1866	3657	−10.1	19.2
1997	2.5	1815	3853	−10.8	23.0
1998	1.2	1661	4048	−12.3	21.0

Sources: CEPAL (1996); Banco Nacional de Cuba (1996, 1997); Ministry of Economy & Planning (1997, 1998); Morris (1997, 1998); Triana (1997); EIU (1999).

(b) Vietnam

	GDP			*PPP*	
Years	*Growth (%)*	*Exports (US$ curr.)*	*Imports (US$ curr.)*	*TB/GDP*	*exch. rate*
1986	2.0	494	1121	−5.2	21
1987	3.7	610	1184	−4.7	15
1988	5.9	733	1412	−5.4	23
1989	8.0	1320	1670	−2.6	100
1990	5.1	1731	1772	−0.3	80
1991	6.0	2042	2105	−0.4	83
1992	8.6	2475	2535	−0.4	79
1993	8.1	2985	3532	−3.2	65
1994	8.8	4054	5826	−9.5	59
1995	9.5	5198	8155	−14.5	53
1996	9.3	7337	11144	−17.1	50
1997	8.8	9269	11743	−10.2	51
1998	5.8	9356	11390	−4.5	n.a.

Notes: US$ curr. = current US dollars;
   PPP = purchasing power parity; TB = Trade balance.
Sources: Tran Hoang Kim (1996); Kokko and Sjöholm (1997). The data for calendar year 1997 were provided from the Bank of Vietnam, via the Institute for Economic and Development Research, National Economics University. For 1998, the Economist Intelligence Unit, *Report for Vietnam*, 2nd quarter 1999.

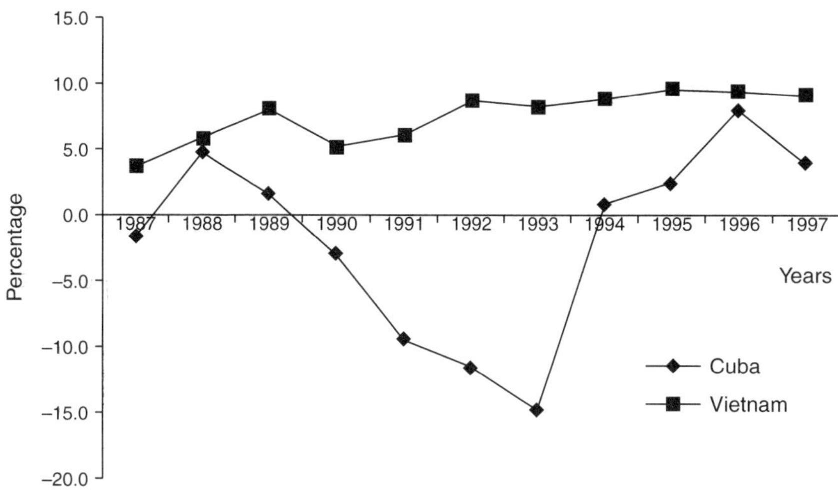

Figure 2.1 GDP growth for Cuba and Vietnam, 1987–97

cannot be explained by a putative reform process in the second half of the 1980s, since GDP growth during 1980–85 was slightly higher (Tran Hoang Kim, 1996, p. 209).

In the four years following the collapse of the Soviet Union (1990–93), the Cuban economy suffered a catastrophic contraction, towards 40 per cent, with each year's decline exceeding the previous. By striking contrast, Vietnam's growth rate increased to an average of 7 per cent annually, compared to 5 per cent for the previous four years. The proximate cause of the difference is obvious: during 1990–93 Vietnam's trade gap fell to near zero (about 1 per cent of GDP), while Cuba's, though lower than previously, averaged 7 per cent of GDP. The statistics in Table 2.1 tell a simple stylized story: Cuban policy-makers found themselves forced to narrow the trade gap through import compression via contraction of the economy; Vietnam closed the trade gap through export growth.

Several structural factors account for the different paths to balance of payments stability. The first is shown in Figure 2.2. Before the collapse of the Soviet trading system, Vietnam's economy was quite closed to international trade, with the average of exports and imports accounting for less than 10 per cent of GDP. From this low base it was possible to expand exports dramatically in the short run, as discussed below. On the other hand, trade accounted for over one-third of national output in Cuba prior to the crisis, a ratio disproportionately high even when one accounts for size and development of the economy. Thus, on a purely numerical basis, the possibility that Cuba could dramatically increase its exports was considerably less than for Vietnam. Second, while both countries formally suffered from a

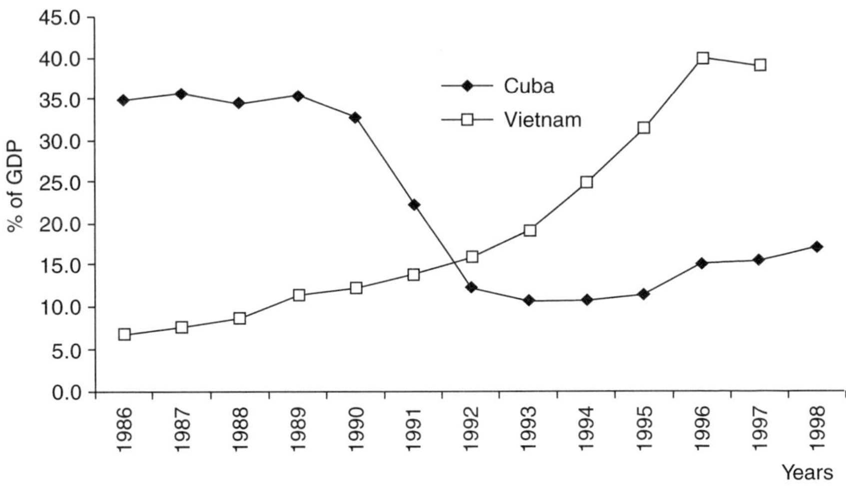

Figure 2.2   Cuba and Vietnam: trade ($[X+M]/2$) as a percentage of GDP, 1986–98

trade embargo with the United States, the associated sanctions were considerably less effective for Vietnam. By the early 1990s, Japan and several European Union countries were prepared to ignore US pressure and substantially increase their trade with Vietnam. Perhaps the single most important element in stimulating trade between these countries and Vietnam was the putative discovery of large reserves of natural gas off the southeast coast of the country. In addition, and unlike in Latin America, several of Vietnam's neighbours, especially Singapore,[4] increased bilateral trade as well as direct investment. At the same time, US sanctions against Cuba made expanding hard currency trade quite difficult.

The effect of these differences was an exponential growth of Vietnamese exports after 1990, while Cuban exports declined continuously during 1990–93. By 1996, trade as a share of GDP in Vietnam exceeded Cuba's at its 1989 peak, and during 1990–93 Cuba's trade had fallen almost to Vietnam's pre-1990 level. Figure 2.3 shows the trade deficits of the two countries, which move in a similar manner. The main difference was the very quick closure of the Vietnamese gap, to near zero during 1990–92, compared to a slower adjustment in Cuba. After 1994, the trade gaps for both increased, reflecting a more sustainable situation based on capital inflows in the case of Vietnam and earnings from 'invisibles' in the case of Cuba, primarily tourism.

To evaluate the adjustment to balance of payments pressure, it is useful to assess the severity of the economic crisis potentially faced by each country in 1990. Table 2.2 compares Cuba and Vietnam to the countries of Central and Eastern Europe (CEE) and the former Soviet Union (ex-SU). During the pre-crisis years, 1986–89, the average growth rate of the CEE countries was just

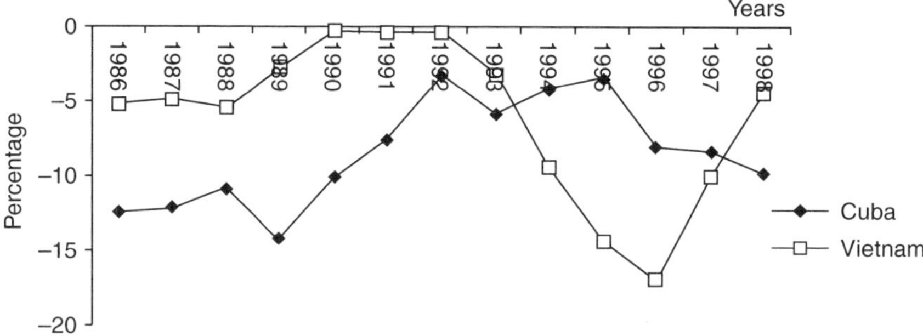

Figure 2.3 Cuba and Vietnam: trade balance as a percentage of GDP, 1986-98

over 2 per cent, and of the ex-SU countries 3.4 per cent (see Figure 2.4). By comparison, Cuba's growth was considerably inferior and Vietnam's substantially better. During the crisis years, 1990–93, the 21 CEE and ex-SU countries suffered severe declines, with the single exception of Albania (whose collapse would come in the late 1990s). Inspection of the table shows that the division of the countries is not merely geographical, for the average decline of the ex-SU states was almost three times that of the CEE countries. The greatest decline for the CEE countries was minus 8.5 per cent annually for Bulgaria, and only four of the 14 ex-SU countries had growth declines less than this. A statistical exercise that tests for the difference in growth rates shows that during 1990–95, the ex-SU states had growth rates over 8 per cent lower than for CEE countries, significant at less than 1 per cent (see Weeks, 1997, pp. 4–6).

There are at least two important structural factors explaining the substantial differences in growth declines between the CEE and ex-SU countries. First, the rates of GDP decline across the 21 countries are negatively related to per capita income (*ibid.*, Table 2). The ex-SU states had income per head considerably lower than for the CEE countries, with the exception of Russia itself and the Baltic states. This tendency, for the countries with higher per capita income to perform better over the period, might be explained by relative ineffectiveness of 'shock therapy' policies in relatively less-developed economies. Mosley (1991), among others, has argued that the liberalization and deregulation policies of structural adjustment programmes in market economies were more likely to improve economic growth the higher is the level of development of the adjusting country. He argues that the early stages of development tend to be characterized by policies of intervention, including import-substitution, which shifts to an outward, export-orientation as industrialization increases. The relative underdevelopment of markets in such countries limits the ability of those markets to transmit price incentives that follow from liberalization.

Table 2.2 GDP growth rates, formerly centrally-planned countries, Cuba and Vietnam, 1986–97

Region and country	1986–89	1990–93	1994–97
Central & Eastern Europe			
1 Albania	3.1	2.9	4.4
2 Bulgaria	4.7	−8.5	−3.4
3 Czech Republic	2.3	−5.7	3.3
4 Hungary	1.7	−3.3	2.3
5 Poland	2.5	−2.9	5.8
6 Romania	−2.4	−5.9	3.3
7 Slovak Republic	2.5	−7.1	6.2
Average	*2.1*	*−4.3*	*3.1*
Former USSR			
1 Armenia	2.9	−23.7	6.2
2 Azerbaijan	−3.0	−17.7	−5.4
3 Belarus	6.9	−5.5	−3.8
4 Estonia	2.7	−12.1	2.4
5 Georgia	−2.1	−27.3	3.9
6 Kazakstan	1.0	−8.5	−6.1
7 Kyrgyz Republic	6.4	−8.6	−4.4
8 Latvia	4.5	−14.6	1.2
9 Lithuania	7.4	−12.5	3.0
10 Tajikistan	2.6	−13.0	−13.7
11 Ukraine	3.2	−9.0	−12.6
12 Uzbekistan	6.1	−3.0	−0.1
13 Russian Federation	3.0	−7.9	−6.2
14 Mongolia	5.5	−6.5	n.a.
Average	*3.4*	*−12.1*	*−2.7*
Cuba	1.6	−9.7	3.4
(no. < Cuba)	(4)	(7)	(15)
Vietnam	4.9	6.9	9.2
(no. < Vietnam)	(15)	(21)	(20)
Other			
China	9.1	10.4	10.7
Laos*	3.9	5.9	7.7

Notes: Lagos, through 1995. Bosnia & Herzegovina, Croatia, Macedonia, Moldavia, Slovenia, Turkmenistan and Yugoslavia (Serbia & Montenegro) are omitted due to incomplete data.
Source: World Bank, *World Development Indicators 1997* (cd-rom); United Nations (1997).

Second, institutional characteristics of the ex-SU states provided major obstacles to adjustment to a market-regulated system. These countries were in most cases more closely integrated to the Soviet Union in trade than those in the CEE group. Perhaps more important, trade was organized as internal commerce without the institutions for managing trade (see discussion by Griffin, 1995, chapter 2). This rather obvious and apparently trivial

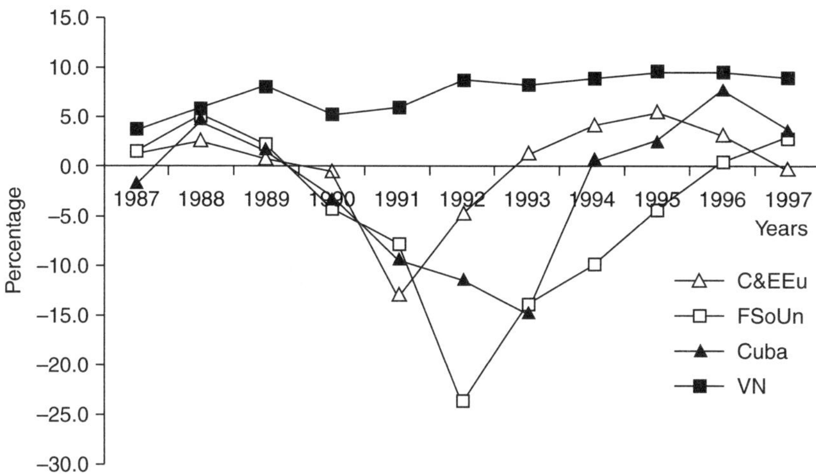

Figure 2.4   Growth rates for former centrally-planned countries, Cuba and Vietnam, 1987–97

point implies a second, more general one: after independence these countries had to create mechanisms of economic management for activities which had previously been carried out in Moscow or by local functionaries of the central government. Thus, in addition to the disruption associated with the shift to market regulation, the former states of the Soviet Union found themselves lacking key institutions of economic management.

The decline of the Cuban economy during 1990–93 was more than double that for the CEE group, but less than for the ex-SU states. The intermediate position of Cuba might be explained by the two points discussed above. In terms of per capita income, Cuba was closer to the ex-SU states, though markets were highly developed before the revolutionary seizure of power. Because of this underdevelopment and the small size of the economy, there was relatively little production of capital and intermediate products for industry. This greatly restricted the technical potential for substitution of domestic for imported inputs. More important, Cuba's trade had become more concentrated with the Soviet Union than for most of the seven CEE countries. As to be expected, the CEE countries with the smallest declines during 1990–93 tended to be those with the least Soviet trade (e.g., Albania and Poland).

In summary, Cuba's decline was substantially greater than for the CEE countries, and at about the median point for the ex-SU countries. In contrast, Vietnam seemed from another world: while the CEE countries declined at an average of more than 4 per cent and the ex-SU countries at 12 per cent, Vietnam *grew* at 7 per cent. This difference was despite the extremely low development of the economy and an overwhelming concentration of trade with the Soviet Union before 1990. An explanation of this phenomenal performance is deferred to a subsequent section. Returning to discussion of Cuba, Table 2.2 reveals a further important relationship. Though Cuba's comparative performance during 1990–93 was mediocre at best, and perhaps more accurately described as a collapse, the country's recovery during 1994–97 exceeded that of 13 of the 21 CEE and ex-SU countries. It had a growth rate above four of the seven CEE countries, even though those countries received considerable foreign direct investment (especially Hungary) and capital inflows from the International Monetary Fund, the European Development Bank, the World Bank, and bilateral lenders (e.g., Germany and the United States). One can only speculate about the counterfactual: what would have been Cuba's post-crisis recovery had it had access to international lending and the absence of sanctions that blocked foreign investment?

Cuba's crisis and adjustment

The adjustment process in Cuba occurred in the context of a severe crisis of the external sector. The severity of the crisis is suggested in Table 2.3, which provides growth comparisons between Cuba and other Latin American countries from 1986 through 1997. During 1986–89, Cuba's GDP growth rate was below the Latin American average by almost a percentage point. More relevant in terms of social welfare, *per capita growth in Cuba was above the average*, exceeding that of 12 countries. This highlights the severity of the decline during 1990–93, when Latin American per capita income was virtually constant but Cuba's fell by over 10 per cent annually. This catastrophic decline makes the performance in the subsequent period all the more striking: Cuban per capita income rose by almost 3 per cent per year, while for the other Latin American countries the increase was more than a percentage point less.

Tables 2.4–2.6 provide statistics to judge how impressed one should be by the Cuban recovery of 1994–97. The pressing short-term problem for the Cuban government was to close the trade gap, and the seriousness of the problem can be assessed by comparing the Cuban trade gap with that of other Latin American countries. During the pre-crisis period, Cuba's trade gap averaged over 12 per cent of GDP. If one excludes the Dominican Republic and Panama, both of which had large trade deficits for structural reasons, only the Nicaraguan and Salvadorean deficits approached Cuba's in size. This was partly the result of import-compression throughout Latin America during the mid-1980s, associated with the Washington Consensus approach to debt-servicing. Still, in the Latin American context the Cuban deficit was extremely large in the late 1980s, exceeded only by the deficits in two war-affected countries. The qualifier, 'in the Latin American context', is quite important. The Cuban deficit was not notably large by comparison to those in many sub-Saharan countries for which deficits in excess of 20 per cent of GDP were not uncommon (Weeks, 1998). The deficit was sustained in

Table 2.3 Latin America: annual average growth of GDP and GDP per capita by time periods, 1986–97 (%)

Countries	1986–89	1990–93	1994–97
GDP growth			
Argentina	**0.4**	5.9	3.6
Bolivia	**1.5**	4.2	4.0
Brazil	3.7	−0.2	3.8
Chile	7.3	6.9	6.6
Colombia	4.8	3.8	4.8
Costa Rica	4.9	5.0	**2.2**
Dominican Republic	6.0	1.7	5.2
Ecuador	1.9	3.4	**3.0**
El Salvador	**1.3**	5.7	4.8
Guatemala	2.9	3.9	3.5
Honduras	3.9	3.8	**2.5**
Mexico	**0.7**	2.9	**2.1**
Nicaragua	**−3.9**	0.0	4.4
Panama	**−2.6**	7.0	3.7
Paraguay	4.1	2.8	**2.8**
Peru	**−0.6**	1.3	7.4
Uruguay	4.5	3.5	3.9
Venezuela	1.8	5.7	**0.7**
Average	*2.4*	*3.7*	*3.8*
Cuba	1.6	−9.7	3.4
(no. < Cuba)	(7)	(0)	(6)
GDP per capita growth			
Latin America	0.0	0.2	1.9
Cuba	0.5	−10.5	2.8
(no. < Cuba)	(12)	(0)	(15)

Note: Countries with growth rates lower than Cuba's have their numbers in bold.
Sources: CEPAL (1991, 1997).

Table 2.4 Latin America: merchandise trade deficit as a proportion of GDP, 1986–96 (%)

Country	1986–89	1990–93	1994–96
Argentina	3.5	1.7	−0.4
Bolivia	0.4	−2.3	−0.3
Brazil	4.0	3.0	0.7
Chile	6.7	2.1	1.7
Colombia	2.9	2.2	−4.0
Costa Rica	−1.0	−5.3	−4.9
Dominican Republic	−15.0	−21.9	−38.2
Ecuador	4.1	6.3	2.2
El Salvador	−9.4	**−14.9**	**−15.1**
Guatemala	−3.0	**−6.9**	−7.0

Table 2.4   Cont.

Country	1986–89	1990–93	1994–96
Honduras	−1.9	−5.5	**−11.1**
Mexico	3.1	−2.8	−1.0
Nicaragua	**−16.3**	**−24.7**	**−20.4**
(Panama	−47.6	−75.5	−81.3)
Paraguay	3.5	**−9.8**	**−17.8**
Peru	0.2	−0.7	−2.8
Uruguay	3.9	0.1	−3.8
Venezuela	3.9	9.6	11.1
Average	*−3.2*	*−8.1*	*−10.7*
excluding Panama & Dominican Republic	*0.3*	*−3.0*	*−4.6*
Cuba	−12.4	−6.8	−8.5
(no. > Cuba)	(1)	(4)	(4)

Note: Country figures greater than Cuba in bold. Non-relevant comparisons, Dominican Republic and Panama are bracketed.
Source: World Bank, *World Development Indicators*, cd-rom (where there are errors), and CEPAL 1997.

Table 2.5   Latin America: IMF and World Bank (IBRD & IDA) loans as a proportion of GDP, 1986–95 (%)

Country	1986–89	1990–93	1994–95
Argentina	5.2	2.9	3.4
Bolivia	**15.0**	17.3	18.6
Brazil	3.8	2.1	1.0
Chile	**12.4**	7.5	3.2
Colombia	10.1	7.6	3.6
Costa Rica	11.7	7.1	4.1
Dominican Republic	8.5	4.5	4.3
Ecuador	10.9	**8.1**	6.8
El Salvador	5.0	3.6	3.7
Guatemala	4.7	3.1	1.2
Honduras	**17.4**	22.9	24.7
Mexico	7.4	5.9	**8.2**
Nicaragua	2.8	8.3	12.7
Panama	**16.5**	9.5	4.4
Paraguay	9.4	4.5	2.5
Peru	9.0	5.4	4.8
Uruguay	8.6	4.8	3.2
Venezuela	0.7	7.8	6.3
Average	*8.8*	*7.4*	*6.5*
(> Cuban td. def.)	(4)	(9)	(4)

Note: Countries with figures greater than Cuba's trade deficit (td. def.) marked bold.
Source: World Bank, *World Development Indicators 1997* (cd-rom), where there are errors in reporting of GDP in current US dollars.

Table 2.6   League table, negative growth rates of GDP in Latin America after 1980 (%)

		Year(s)	Cumulative	Following 3 years
One-year declines > 5.0				
1	Panama	1988	−16.0	
2	**Cuba**	**1993**	**−14.9**	
3	Chile	1982	−14.1	
4	Nicaragua	1988	−13.4	
5	**Cuba**	**1992**	**−11.6**	
6	Peru	1989	−11.5	
7	Peru	1983	−10.9	
8	Uruguay	1982	−9.4	
9	**Cuba**	**1991**	**−9.4**	
10	Bolivia	1983	−8.6	
11	Peru	1988	−8.4	
12	El Salvador	1981	−8.3	
13	Venezuela	1989	−7.9	
14	Ecuador	1987	−7.3	
15	Costa Rica	1982	−7.3	
16	Bolivia	1982	−6.6	
17	Mexico	1995	−6.6	
18	Argentina	1981	−6.2	
19	El Salvador	1982	−5.6	
20	Venezuela	1983	−5.6	
21	Mexico	1983	−5.3	
22	Dominican Republic	1990	−5.2	
23	Peru	1990	−5.1	
Two-year declines > 10.0				
1	**Cuba**	**1992–93**	**−26.5**	**3.8**
2	Nicaragua	1988–89	−17.5	0.2
3	Peru	1989–90	−16.6	2.6
4	Panama	1988–89	−16.3	7.9
5	Bolivia	1982–83	−15.2	−2.4
6	Chile	1982–83	14.8	4.7
7	Uruguay	1982–83	−14.4	2.7
8	El Salvador	1981–82	−13.9	0.9
9	Argentina	1981–82	−11.4	0.2
Three-year declines (all)				
1	**Cuba**	**1991–93**	**−35.9**	**3.8**
2	Peru	1988–90	−25.0	2.6
3	Nicaragua	1987–89	−18.2	0.2
4	Bolivia	1982–84	−18.9	−0.3
5	Uruguay	1982–84	−16.2	6.0
6	Nicaragua	1986–88	−15.1	−1.2
7	El Salvador	1981–83	−14.6	1.3
8	Bolivia	1983–85	−13.3	1.0
9	Venezuela	1983–85	−7.3	5.4
10	Argentina	1988–90	−7.6	8.4

Table 2.6   Cont.

		Year(s)	*Cumulative*	*Following 3 years*
11	Bolivia	1984–86	−7.2	2.8
12	Nicaragua	1984–86	−6.5	−6.1
13	Nicaragua	1985–87	−5.8	−5.9

Note: For two and three-year declines, growth must be negative in each year.
Sources: CEPAL (1985, 1991, 1997).

whole or part, before 1990, by concessionary trade with the Soviet Union. The implied level of assistance was quite high by Latin American standards, but not by African comparison. For example, during 1990–94 seven of the 20 Eastern, Central and Southern African countries received concessionary aid in excess of 20 per cent of GDP (Weeks, *ibid.*).

External finance for the balance of payments was quite important for several Latin American countries, as Table 2.5 shows. Without entering into the debate over the size of Soviet aid to the Cuban economy, we see from Table 2.5 that during 1986–89, four Latin American countries received IMF and World Bank loans as a proportion of GDP equal to or greater than Cuba's trade deficit. During the 1990s, when import compression was forced upon the Cuban government, other Latin American countries received on average IMF and World Bank support as a portion of GDP *greater* than Cuba's trade deficit. Had Cuba had access to foreign borrowing at the level of the average Latin American country (or even below), considerably less import compression would have been necessary.

As a consequence of the lack of external finance, the Cuban economy suffered a contraction during 1991–93 which was probably unprecedented in Latin America in this century. Table 2.6 provides a 'league table' of Latin American economic contractions since 1980, for one-year, two-year and three-year periods. The contraction of the Cuban economy in 1993 (−15 per cent) is second to that of Panama for 1988, but Cuba's two-year decline, 1992–93, is 9 percentage points above the next highest (Nicaragua, 1988–89). Only the Peruvian collapse of 1988–90 approaches Cuba's three-year decline of 36 per cent (1991–93). The table also provides growth rates for the three years following the two-and three-year declines, to allow inspection of relative performance in recovery.[5] Comparing across two-year declines, Panama had the fastest recovery rate, followed by Chile, with Cuba close behind. For comparisons across the 13 three-year declines, the Cuban recovery rate stands in fourth place.

Without external finance and export-constrained by US sanctions (in contrast to Vietnam), the Cuban government had no choice but to achieve external balance through output contraction. Table 2.7 shows that the burden of adjustment was placed on investment and, to a lesser extent, private consumption. In 1996, when recovery was in process, total GDP remained 27 percentage points below the 1989 level, with investment 74 percentage points down.[6] The fall in investment is further indicated by imports of capital goods, which declined from about a quarter of total imports during 1989–90, to less than 5 per cent in 1993 and 1994 (last row of Table 2.7). For consumption, the private component fell considerably more than the public sector (33 compared to 15 percentage points). These percentages reveal a conscious strategy of the government to sustain the supply of essential public goods during the adjustment process. Vietnam, facing more favourable external conditions, was able to pursue an adjustment through growth strategy. Unable to do this, the Cuban government opted for minimizing the social impact of adjustment.

As a result, the recovery of the Cuban economy was on the basis of excess capacity, with little new investment. In the medium term this strategy could not be sustained as capital equipment deteriorated and its obsoleteness resulted in lower competitiveness in key sectors (notably in sugar). By reducing output, especially investment, the trade deficit narrowed from almost $US3 billion in 1989, to US$800 million in 1994 (see Table 2.8). However, without Soviet aid or access to external borrowing, even this deficit level could not be sustained. As is well-known, the remaining deficit was covered by earnings from tourism, which rose from less than US$400 million during 1989–91, to well over one billion in the mid-1990s and to over two billion by the end of the decade. By 1994, tourist revenue almost matched the trade deficit, though not in the following years. During the latter years inflows of direct foreign investment have increasingly provided the foreign exchange cover for the increase in imports.

Because of the low level of investment during the crisis and recovery, it is doubtful that the Cuban economy was less import-dependent than it had been in the 1980s. On the contrary, the rapid increase in tourism implied that in the short and medium term, the economy became more import-using at the margin. It follows that that Cuba's recovery involved relatively little structural change in the medium term, and should not be considered sustainable. By the end of the 1990s, the government faced a challenge equal to that of overcoming the crisis of the first half of the 1990s: to restructure the economy to make it less import-using in tourism, while developing new export sectors to replace sugar. Extraction and export of nickel proved to be the most successful of the latter in the 1990s.

The analysis of the Cuban crisis and subsequent recovery can be summarized as follows. Following the collapse of the Soviet Union, the Cuban economy declined by considerably more than the economies of Central and Eastern Europe, but less than for the former members of the Soviet Union. One might explain these differences by the degree to which countries had their trade concentrated within the Soviet bloc. The severity of

Table 2.7   Annual growth rates of investment and consumption in Cuba, 1989–98 (%)

	1989	1990	1991	1992	1993	1994	1995	1996	1997	1998
Investment	10.1	−2.9	−45.9	−58.3	−39.7	1.9	35.3	22.9	17.9	7.0
Consumption	2.2	−3.7	−10.0	−10.8	−5.1	0.7	1.6	3.6	2.1	2.2
public	0.9	0.1	−10.4	−5.2	−1.1	−1.9	−0.6	4.0	1.3	2.0
private	2.9	−5.8	−9.8	−14.0	−7.9	2.5	3.0	3.3	2.6	2.3
GDP	1.5	−2.9	−9.5	−9.9	−13.6	0.6	2.5	7.6	2.5	1.3
Investment goods as % of total imports	24	26	22	8	4	3	7	10	11	13

Source: CEPAL, 1997, Table A1; Annario Estadístico de Cuba 1996, 1997, 1998 (ONE 1998, 1999, 2000)

Table 2.8   Merchandise exports and imports and tourist earnings, 1989–98 (current $US millions)

	1989	1990	1991	1992	1993	1994	1995	1996	1997	1998
Exports, goods	5400	5415	2980	1779	1137	1381	1507	1866	1823	1444
Imports, goods	8140	7417	4234	2315	1984	2353	2992	3657	4088	4230
Trade balance	−2740	−2002	−1254	−536	−847	−972	−1485	−1791	−2265	−2786
Tourist earnings	319	347	387	567	756	850	1100	1350	1500	2076
Trade balance + tourist earnings	−2421	−1655	−867	31	−91	−122	−385	−441	−765	−710

Source: CEPAL, 1997, pp. 34,37 Annario Estadístico de Cuba (ONE 1998, 1999, 2000)

Cuba's economic decline was the result of a trade deficit rendered unsustainable by the end of Soviet aid, and the contraction of exports to the Soviet bloc. Had Cuba enjoyed access to the Bretton Woods institutions (or international capital markets), the output contraction associated with the trade deficit would have been considerably less. Not withstanding this lack of access, recovery from the sharp output contraction was relatively rapid. However, this recovery involved little structural change, and could not be considered sustainable into the new century.

Adjustment in Vietnam

Compared to the Cuban story, the Vietnamese tale of transition is quite simple. As Table 2.9 shows, the country's growth rate prior to the collapse of the Soviet Union was about two-thirds that of the average for the so-called high-performing Asian economies (HPAEs, see World Bank, 1993a). Over the next four years, the Vietnamese growth rate exceeded that of the HPAEs, and

Table 2.9 East and Southeast Asia: growth of GDP and GDP per capita by time periods, 1986–97 (%)

Countries	1986–89	1990–93	1994–97
Hong Kong	8.2	**5.0**	4.9
Indonesia	5.8	**6.5**	7.6
Korea	9.8	7.1	7.9
Malaysia	5.9	8.3	9.1
Philippines	5.0	**1.2**	4.8
Singapore	7.6	7.6	8.4
Thailand	9.6	8.7	7.9
Average	*7.4*	*6.3*	*7.2*
Vietnam	4.9	6.9	9.2
(no. < Vietnam)	(0)	(3)	(7)

Note: Countries with lower growth rates than Vietnam's have their numbers in bold.
Sources: World Bank, *World Development Indicators 1997* (cd-rom) and United Nations (1997).

Table 2.10 Vietnam: official development assistance and direct foreign investment, 1990–95

Years	Bilateral aid/GDP	FDI/GDP	IBRD & IDA/GDP	IMF credits/GDP	Total
1990	n.a.	0.8	0.0	n.a.	n.a.
1991	2.5	1.5	0.6	0.0	4.6
1992	5.8	1.6	0.6	0.0	8.0
1993	2.0	1.7	0.4	0.0	4.1
1994	5.9	5.6	1.2	1.8	14.5
1995	4.1	8.7	1.1	1.9	15.8

Sources: World Bank, *World development Indicators 1997* (cd-rom) for aid, IBRD & IDA, and IMF; Trâ'n Hoâng Kim (1996) and Kokko and Sjöholm (1997) for foreign investment.

Vietnam had the fastest growing economy in East and Southeast Asia during 1994–97, with the exception of China. Vietnam achieved this growth performance, first, by closing the trade gap through export growth, then, by combining export growth with inflows of capital (see Table 2.10). In every year, 1991–95, capital inflows to Vietnam exceeded the trade gap, a notable contrast with the situation for Cuba.

In this context, the World Bank in its 1993 report on Vietnam commented that 'Vietnam has shown strong growth throughout its adjustment program'. It went on to write, 'Vietnam's recent economic success is attributable to an ambitious adjustment and reform program which it has undertaken without significant support from outside' (World Bank, 1993b). While both these statements are true, the case of Vietnam was distinguished from other adjusting countries by the central role played by the state, rather than leaving adjustment to the dictates of the market. The World Bank interpretation of the Vietnamese stabilization success was that policy-makers achieved price stability through implementation of tight monetary and fiscal policy. In the World Bank view, the reduction of bank financing of the government deficit was especially important. This interpretation is also suggested by Irvin: 'a problem [i.e., inflation] – it is argued – rectified mainly by the adoption of an IMF-style stabilization package in 1989' (Irvin, 1994, pp. 5–6).

A review of macroeconomic indicators suggests a different interpretation of what happened in Vietnam during 1989–92 (see Table 2.11). As discussed above, before the stabilization programme of 1989, Vietnam's GDP growth rate was quite high for countries in transition. At an average of 5 per cent per year during 1986–89, national income increased significantly faster than population growth. This statistic is important, because stabilization is considerably easier to achieve when growth performance is strong. Second, the stabilization period, 1989–92, did not see a large reduction in the fiscal deficit compared to the previous four years. During 1989–91 the fiscal deficit was a *higher* proportion of GDP than during 1986–88, yet the rate of inflation fell dramatically: for 1986–88 inflation averaged over 350 per cent a year, and for 1989–91 the average was less than 70 per cent. While it is true that a very low deficit in 1992 was associated with inflation of less than 40 per cent, a lower deficit the previous year coincided with inflation twice as high. One cannot construct a credible story that links the decline in inflation to the reduction of the deficit.

Table 2.11   Vietnam: indicators of external and internal balance, 1985–92

Year/item	T – G/GDP	X – M/Exports	Inflation	GDP/Growth
1985	−12.0	−82.7	192	5.7
1986	−4.7	−126.7	487	2.0
1987	−4.1	−94.1	317	3.7
1988	−7.7	−92.6	311	5.9
1989	−11.4	−26.5	76	8.0
1990	−8.0	−2.4	29	5.1
1991	−2.5	−3.1	83	6.0
1992	−3.8	−2.4	38	8.6
Annual averages				
1985–88	−7.1	−99.0	326	4.3
1989–92	−6.4	−8.6	57	6.9

Notes: (Taxes–Government expenditure)/GDP = ratio of the budget deficit to GDP; (Exports–Imports)/Exports = ratio of the trade deficit to exports.   X = Exports, M = Imports
Sources: Tran Hoang Kim (1992) and World Bank (1993).   T = Taxes, G = Government Expenditure

Changes in the trade deficit provide a more convincing explanation of the successful stabilization. Table 2.11 shows that during 1985–88, the trade deficit averaged almost 100 per cent of exports (i.e., imports were double exports). Then, for 1990–92, it fell to an average of less than 3 per cent of exports (and less than 1 per cent of GDP). Table 2.12 shows that the trade deficit was almost eliminated by the dramatic increases in exports of marine products, rice and petroleum, with the latter two products close to zero in 1985–86. The expansion of petroleum exports might be interpreted as the good luck of being endowed with this natural resource, but the phenomenal increase in rice exports from zero in 1988 to over US$400 million in 1992 occurred as a result of government policy.[7] While the increase in rice exports reflected a dramatic increase in production, the expansion of marine-product exports involved a diversion from domestic consumption.[8] These three products together accounted for 9 per cent of total exports in 1985, then rose to almost half in 1989.

Vietnam's success in transition can be explained as *a process of export-led stabilization*. Faced with an unsustainable balance of payments position in the mid-1980s, the government embarked upon a policy that had two aspects: institutional reform to make the economy responsive to standard macroeconomic instruments in the medium term (see Irvin and Mallon in this volume), and emergency measures to increase exports to stabilize the economy in the short term. Expansion of petroleum exports would not have been sufficient, in themselves, to achieve external balance; nor could rice or marine products alone have done this. The combination of the three, along with capital inflows, stabilized the exchange rate by 1992. In the subsequent

Table 2.12   Vietnam's foreign trade, 1985–92 (exports and imports in US$ millions)

				By product				
Years	Total export	Per cent convertible	Trade balance	*(1)* Rice	*(2)* Net oil	*(3)* Marine products	*(4)* Light manuf.	*(1)–(3)* as % of Total exports
1985	497	68	−406	0	0	45	22	9.1
1986	494	62	−627	0	0	95	65	19.2
1987	610	71	−574	0	30	113	30	23.4
1988	733	63	−679	0	79	124	18	27.7
1989	1320	74	−350	316	200	133	20	49.2
1990	1731	73	−41	272	34	220	20	30.4
1991	2042	98	−63	225	96	285	204	29.7
1992	2475	100	−60	420	141	302	321	30.0

Notes: Per cent convertible = percentage of exports in convertible currency.
Source: World Bank (1993), pp. 239–40.

two years the dong appreciated considerably, from a high of around 13 000 to the dollar to below 11 000 in 1993. The exchange rate movements made the task of controlling inflation a relatively easy one. Once the economy entered into an export-led stabilization process, it was possible for the authorities to maintain a relatively expansionary monetary and fiscal policy.

The standard stabilization package, implemented with little success in the transitional economies of Europe, calls for demand reduction through restrictive monetary and fiscal policy. This was not the policy implemented in Vietnam. On the contrary, economic management in Vietnam placed growth as the first priority. By maintaining, then increasing, export growth, the government was able to stabilize the exchange rate and bring inflation under control. The circumstances of each country in transition are different, so it is dangerous to attempt to draw general lessons from the experience of one country. However, the success of Vietnam can be placed in a wider context. First, considerable accumulated evidence from IMF programmes over several decades indicates that balance of payments adjustment and reduction of inflation are more easily achieved in a growing economy that through restriction of demand (Pastor, 1987). Second, it would seem obvious that institutional reforms aimed at creating markets and linking nominal to real variables should precede stabilization measures. The process of transition is not one of 'awakening markets',[9] but of constructing the institutional mechanisms by which producers can respond to policy measures. In this context it is a misinterpretation to refer to the pre-1989 reforms in Vietnam as a 'half-hearted attempt' (Leipziger, 1992, p. 1); on the contrary, the reforms of the mid-1980s initiated the process of transforming the economy from central planning to market regulation.

After 1992 the trade deficit began to rise, reaching close to 20 per cent of GDP in 1997. In the absence of permanent non-trade flows of foreign exchange, a deficit of this size is difficult, if not impossible, to sustain. Kokko and Sjöholm interpret the growth of the trade deficit to be an indicator of the much deeper problem of the failure of the government to pursue reform of the economy:

> [D]uring the past couple of years, it has become increasingly well understood that it may not be possible to sustain the gains of the *doi moi* program unless a second generation of structural reforms is introduced.
>
> Most of the structural weaknesses in the Vietnamese economy are related to a development strategy that is based on import substituting state-owned enterprises (SOEs). These weaknesses have recently been manifested in a trade deficit corresponding to some 15 per cent of GDP, weak profitability in SOEs, and the virtual absence of a modern, private industrial sector. (Kokko and Sjöholm, 1997, p. iv)

The quotation is confusing, with its allusion to an unspecified consensus ('increasingly well understood') and an undefined term ('second generation of structural reforms'). However, the implication is clear: that the trade deficit (along with other maladies) resulted from the Vietnamese government pursuing a development strategy at odds with the mainstream emphasis upon a relatively passive role for the state (see Kokko in this volume).[10] It may or may not be the case that the Vietnamese government would have been well-advised to vigorously pursue privatization and market liberalization; given the economy's performance in the 1980s and 1990s without these measures, some would hesitate to make such a generalization. Since the authors provide no quantitative evidence to relate it to the ownership structure of the economy, the specific link between state-led growth and the trade deficit can be considered an interesting but unsubstantiated hypothesis.

The speculative nature of this hypothesis is all the greater because macro data offer a much more obvious explanation of the growth of the trade deficit: movements in the real exchange rate and the growth of direct foreign investment. If one takes 1989 as an index of 100, and an increase represents a devaluation, a standard purchasing power parity measure of the real exchange rate was 21 in 1986.[11] By 1993 the exchange rate had appreciated to 65, falling to 50 in 1996 (see Figure 2.8). Given the decentralization of decision-making in state enterprises during the 1990s, an appreciating exchange rate would have encouraged imports and discouraged exports. In the household sector, the appreciation would have provided incentives for consumption of imported commodities. Also during the 1990s, foreign direct investment increased dramatically as a portion of GDP (see Table 2.10), and a large part of this increase financed imports, especially for construction.

Table 2.13 reports the results of two regression exercises, both derived from the simple formulation:

$$xn_t = xn_t \, (RER_t, \, FDI_t)$$

where xn_t is net exports, RER_t the real exchange rate, and FDI_t the share of foreign investment in GDP.

In the first estimation, FDI is treated as a binary variable assuming the value of unity when foreign direct investment rises above 1 per cent of GDP. In the second calculation, the numerical values are used. In both cases the estimation explains over 60 per cent of the variation in net exports, there is an absence of serial correlation, and the coefficients are of the predicted sign (and significant). While one should hesitate to draw conclusions from regressions with 9 degrees of freedom, Table 2.13 provides *prima facie* evidence for causal relationships well-known in economic theory: appreciating exchange rates tend to worsen a country's trade balance, and foreign direct investment tends to finance imports rather than domestic costs.

Table 2.13   Vietnam: the trade balance in GDP as a function of the PPP exchange rate, shift variable, (1992–97), and foreign direct investment, 1986–97

Variable	Coefficient	t-statistic	Sign. of t
Ln[Trade balance] (constant)	5.310	3.66	.005
Ln[real exch rate]	−1.296	−3.46	.007
Shift (after 1992)	2.223	4.52	.001
Adj *R*–square = .696			
F = 13.62			
Sign. of *F* = .002			
D–W = 1.666			
DF = 9			
[Trade balance] (constant)	−53.550	−4.76	.001
Ln[real exch rate]	11.750	4.21	.002
Ln[DFI/GDP]	−3.077	−4.65	.001
Adj *R*–square = .646			
F = 11.02			
Sign. of *F* = .004			
D–W = 1.806			
DF = 9			

Note: When the logarithmic form is used, the trade balance must be made a positive number, but is negative in the second formulation. This explains the reversal of signs of coefficients.

Vietnam's adjustment to the collapse of the Soviet trading system can be explained in terms of short-term measures of expediency taken within a longer-term strategy of state-led development. It remained to be seen if the latter can be sustained. However, it was clear that the short-term measures were successful. In the late 1980s and early 1990s the government used a range of interventions to force a higher ratio of exports to GDP, combining this with exchange rate devaluation. By the mid-1990s, tactics had shifted to fostering foreign direct investment and negotiating concessional capital flows from multilateral institutions (including the Asian Development Bank). This shift in policy resulted in a rapid increase in the trade deficit. Given the size of that deficit in 1997, it became likely that policy would shift back to devaluation and export-financed growth, rather than foreign-capital-financed, investment-led growth. This strategy shift would be in a less favourable context given the Asian financial crisis (see Tønnesson in this volume).

Conclusion

It was generally recognized that the 1980s and 1990s were characterized by considerable economic instability of the world economy. During these two decades underdeveloped countries, particularly the highly indebted, passed through processes of adjustment that involved severe social costs. For most of these countries, external assistance for the adjustment process required governments to accept the conditions of the so-called Washington Consensus. The key features of this 'Consensus' were sharp and rapid reductions in fiscal deficits, restrictive monetary policy, trade liberalization, reduction of state interventions in domestic markets, and privatization of public enterprises. By the late 1990s, even mainstream commentators accepted that this orthodox approach had been 'incomplete' and 'sometimes misguided'.[12]

Vietnam and Cuba had governments which did not endorse the Consensus policies, even when they were being pressed upon governments throughout the underdeveloped world. Explaining why they did not, when virtually all other governments did is beyond the scope of this chapter. However, it is clear that the economies of both countries did not suffer the extreme and prolonged collapses that occurred in Central and Eastern Europe and Russia. In Vietnam's case, performance was considerably better than even the most spectacular 'high performers'. While Cuba's adjustment and subsequent recovery could at best be described as modestly successful in terms of growth, by comparison to relevant alternative country strategies, it emerged from crisis less scarred and devastated. It remained problematical how recovery would become sustainable growth.

Neither country provided a clear alternative strategy of adjustment which could be generally followed in place of the Consensus orthodoxy. However, the relative failure of the latter in many countries, and the relative success of the former heterodoxies in two countries, suggested that there was a range of macroeconomic policies which governments could employ in face of severe balance of payments crises.

Note

1 For example, the communities in Cuba associated with sugar refineries should be considered urban in this context, though populations were small for many of them.
2 'Central Europe' refers to the independent states of the Soviet bloc: Albania, Bulgaria, Czechoslovakia (later the Czech Republic and Slovak Republic), Hungary, Poland and Romania. The German Democratic Republic disappeared into a greater Germany. 'Eastern' Europe is used to refer to the European countries formerly part of the Soviet Union (Armenia, Belarus, Estonia, Georgia, Latvia, Lithuania, Moldova and Ukraine). Falling into a category of their own are the European states formerly part of Yugoslavia: Croatia, Macedonia, Slovenia and Serbia/Bosnia.
3 For a useful, though highly subjective 'league table' of liberalizers, see World Bank (1996, p. 14).
4 Some of the trade with Singapore was via local subsidiaries of US corporations.
5 A simple regression test provides no support for the hypothesis that growth rates during recovery are correlated with rates during the decline, either positively or negatively (the test statistics are not significant).
6 At its nadir in 1993, investment fell in real terms to 15 per cent of the 1989 level.

7   The system of interventions is briefly described in World Bank (1993), p. 130. Rice production increased from an average of less than 16 million tons during 1985–87, to over 20 million during 1990–92 (Trâ'n Hoàng Kim, 1996, p. 302).

8   Rice production increased from an average of less than 16 million tons during 1985–87, to over 20 million during 1990–92, or 29 per cent. The increase for marine products was just over 4 per cent for the same years (Trâ'n Hoàng Kim, 1996, pp. 302, 322).

9   This is the title of World Bank working paper on Vietnam by Leipziger (1992).

10   For example, the authors write:

> We suggest that the alternative where development is built on *large centrally controlled SOEs* [state owned enterprises] would lead to the emergence of domestic oligopolies and monopolies, a concentration of resources to areas where Vietnamese comparative advantages are weak, a reduction of foreign capital inflows, and a significant fall in the growth rate. (Kokko and Sjoholm, 1997, p. iv, emphasis in the original)

11   The real exchange rate in this case is measured as the nominal exchange rate for the dong times the ratio of the US wholesale price index to the Vietnamese GDP deflator.

12   This judgement is from Joseph Stiglitz, former chief economist of the World Bank (Stiglitz, 1998, pp. 34, 1).

3
Adapting to Globalization: Lessons from China

Richard Newfarmer and Dana M. Liu

Introduction

China entered the new millennium confronting one of the most complex economic situations since the reform period began over two decades ago. At home, internal demand slackened as five years of austerity began to take their toll; and abroad, most of China's neighbours were still adjusting to the wrenching recession that gripped East Asia after the collapse of the Thai baht in July 1997. The Chinese economy initially escaped relatively unscathed, partially insulated by huge foreign exchange reserves, relatively low short-term debt, and a semi-closed capital account. However, as the momentum for growth from the domestic market declined, and export growth slowed with the collapse of its East Asia markets, authorities searched for new ways to rekindle both growth and exports.

The problem facing the government was that short-term policy measures to boost the economy's sagging internal demand tended to undermine medium-term reforms necessary to make growth sustainable. Stimulating the economy meant stimulating investment, and this in turn required expanding credit, a large portion of which went to state enterprises. However, for five years the government sought to discipline state enterprises by restraining their access to credit, to compel them to operate in a market-determined environment. Whether China could maintain its long-term growth path would depend critically on how it managed this dilemma.

The stakes were high. China must *reform to continue growing*. Reform was necessary to free new sources of productivity in the industrial and agricultural sectors. Unlike previous phases of reform, the next phase of state enterprise and banking sector reforms would create a large number of 'losers' in the process; state enterprise workers would be laid off and managers would lose the perquisites of their positions. Others who would lose would be party bureaucrats affiliated with the bureaucracy administering controls over enterprises, or participating in the governance of enterprises directly, and bank managers unable to collect on debts to state enterprises. To prevent discontent or social disruption from arising from the massive process, the government needed economic expansion to create jobs and to create business opportunities for potential business people and managers. In other words, China had to maintain the reform–growth–reform virtuous circle, or risk unleashing a potentially vicious circle of instability and slow growth.

One response to these intense internal and global pressures could have been to devalue the currency in an effort to generate export-led growth. The government eschewed this path in favour of a more complex, threefold strategy: (1) stimulate domestic demand to boost short-term growth; (2) maintain a modulated pace of domestic reform to ensure productivity gains to secure long-term growth; (3) press for WTO entrance to stimulate exports and reinforce domestic reforms. This chapter reviews the complex interplay among these three strategies.

Stimulating domestic demand

China's economy during the transition from plan to market became notoriously unstable. Price liberalization in the early 1980s outpaced the development of monetary instruments to control inflation, which resulted in everlarger cycles of expansion and inflation, followed by demand contraction to control inflation. The process peaked in 1993 when the economy recovered from the 1989–90 recession, and inflation again threatened to rise out of control. The policies fostered[1] by Zhu Rongji successfully brought down inflation over the next five years, and accomplished this without subjecting the economy to abrupt contractions of aggregate demand that precipitated the slow growth at the end of the 1980s.[2]

Zhu accomplished this task through a combination of steady progress on structural improvements of macroeconomic policy and command-economy instruments. On the one hand, the government undertook what in retrospect can be seen as a profound reform of the financial sector; a new law that gave powers of monetary management to the central bank. This culminated in 1996 with the introduction of open market operations. Added to this was a commercial bank law that converted the large state banks to commercial entities. The reforms resulted in a widening scope for market-oriented interest rates, and unification of the foreign exchange regime. On the other hand, the 16 point programme of July 1993 included the first of several administrative measures that helped to reduce inflation. This combination of instruments steadily reigned in credit, reduced the power of the provincial and municipal authorities to authorize credit (usually for state enterprises), and helped shift reliance of the economy onto the emerging non-state sector, including private enterprises. This had the twin benefits of bringing down inflation and restraining credit to state enterprises to promote reforms.

The results were impressive. Inflation declined from a high of 24 per cent on an annualized basis in the fourth quarter of 1994, to virtually zero in

1998. Growth came down progressively, but not abruptly, from over 13 per cent to 7.8 per cent in 1998, and rural incomes recouped some of the ground lost compared to urban incomes, so that the poorest began to participate more in the economy. The steady falls of absolute poverty, temporarily in abeyance during the 1988–92 contractionary phase, resumed. By the time the East Asia crisis hit in mid-1997, China was already showing tendencies towards deflation.

But by early 1998, it became obvious that China was confronted, for the first time since 1949, by anaemic internal demand. Deflation threatened to push growth well below the target of 8 per cent. Three forces were responsible for this. Export growth, robust in 1997, sagged in 1998 under the weight of Japanese and Korean stagnation and contraction. Second, the government's five-year campaign to establish a more modern monetary authority finally reigned in the power of so-called franchise central banking, in the People's Bank network of subsidiaries, and, as a consequence, restrained credit growth. Provincial and municipal authorities could no longer create credit for favoured activities and enterprises. One consequence of this credit restraint was to prompt reform of state enterprises. Third, the reform of the commercial banks laid down strict guidelines for lending, made banks responsible for their financial performance, and even threatened managers with personal accountability for non-performing loans. The absence of managerial capacity to evaluate credit risk accurately made bank mangers extraordinarily cautious about providing loans for which they might be held personally responsible. Since banks were for the most part prevented from lending to the dynamic non-state sector, credit growth declined.

This left the government to confront a dilemma. For years it had sought to restrain credit growth to inefficiency and money-losing state enterprises, and to force banks to make creditworthy loans. However, it could expand credit only with the risk of making finance available to the same state enterprises that it sought to reform through its tight credit policy. In mid-1998, the government acted by loosening both monetary and fiscal policy. Interest rates were cut, and credit growth increased. Because inflation fell so dramatically, real interest rates remained high and the burden of stimulus fell on fiscal policy. To avoid providing massive credit to inefficient state enterprises and adding to the non-performing loans in the banking system, the government sought to invest in infrastructure, primarily in rural areas, as opposed to a wholesale stimulus approach.

The success of these aggregate demand strategies would depend in the near term upon the recovery of consumption and investment in the non-state sector, as well as the continued growth of the world economy. In the medium term, it would depend on the quality of investment affecting productivity growth of the economy. If government investments created poor quality infrastructure or if credit were channelled to inefficient enterprises (state and non-state), the economy would not sustain its high-growth momentum. For these reasons, policy initiatives had the goal of ensuring that short-term stimulus did not obstruct reform, but rather complemented ongoing efforts at reforming state enterprises and banks.

Reforming the state enterprise and banking sectors

The growth slowdown came at a critical moment in the government's phasing of reform, which involved the most intractable and potentially volatile state-owned enterprises (SOEs) and banks. Reforms of both entered a new phase. State enterprises had no choice but to lay off workers to achieve productivity improvements necessary to become viable, and it seemed that many might close or leave the state sector altogether. Only by reforming the state enterprises could the government make progress in the next phase of banking reforms, and only by carrying through both sets of reforms would the productive system produce the productivity gains necessary to establish the conditions for long-run growth.

Once the key drivers of China's industrial sector, SOEs increasingly became a drag on the Chinese economy. The state enterprise, a legacy of the command economy, traditionally provided for all the needs of employees and their families: access to housing, health care, education and pensions, and constituted the only, albeit frayed in the late 1990s, safety net for urban workers. Many of these welfare responsibilities gradually shifted to municipal governments. At the end of the century, state enterprises employed about 75 million workers, of which 40.4 million worked in industrial enterprises. These enterprises dominated the urban labour market, employing two-thirds of the workers in cities, which made them an important urban political constituency.

Other SOE characteristics that shaped reform included concentrated ownership, sub-optimal scale, local government ownership, and highly-leveraged companies. The largest 5 per cent of industrial companies in the mid-1990s accounted for 57 per cent of output, 43 per cent of employment and 62 per cent of net fixed assets. This concentration is not strikingly high by Western standards, but it highlights the importance of the government's decision to focus reform efforts on the largest 1000 companies. For the most part these industrial companies operate at considerably smaller scales of production than international norms. Most operate primarily in one province and, therefore, do not benefit from economies of scale or multi-plant economies. Many have had only partial access to international technologies, and are far from the frontier of modern technology. Integrating the domestic market further, and integrating with the global economy coupled with more flexible ownership, would create the potential to increase productivity growth for the next decade. However, exposing industry to the shock of international trade competition could create significant labour dislocation, and this possibility explains why the government insisted on phasing the reduction of trade protection.

Tax-sharing arrangements introduced in 1994 shifted some of the fiscal burden of loss-making enterprises from central to local governments, providing the latter with a greater incentive to carry out enterprise reforms. About 75 per cent of state enterprises, mainly the smaller ones, were under the ownership or control of major municipalities. Thus, the implementation of much of China's reform effort occurred and would continue to occur at the provincial and municipal levels. Yet, local governments remained resistant to reforms that might generate unemployment and simultaneously remove social welfare provisions to protect the unemployed before creation of new institutions to serve the welfare function. Beginning in the mid-1980s, the central government policy sought to reduce transfers from the budget by encouraging state enterprises to borrow from banks. This had adverse consequences for the banks, and left companies with high debt-to-registered-capital ratios, close to three to one. Much like the problem encountered by corporations in South Korea, this situation exposed SOEs to rises in interest rates.

Lower productivity and deteriorating performance

From the beginning of China's economic reform initiatives in 1978, state-owned industrial enterprises were caught between competition in the marketplace and government mandates to provide security for employees and undertake specific investments. A bureaucratized system of management and production also resulted in poor internal incentives. Management lacked full autonomy in wage-setting, hiring, pricing, input purchasing and investment. Wage increases often did not reflect productivity gains, and non-cash benefits in housing, education and other social welfare services nearly equalled the value of monetary wages. At the same time, managers have had no accountability to state owners.

Similarly, the lack of a bankruptcy threat and easy access to finance through the directed credit system provided weak external incentives to improve profitability. The investment and credit plan, the weak financial system and pricing distortions combined to channel state-enterprise investment into activities with lower productivity. Studies by Jefferson, Rawski and Zheng (1996, pp. 146–80) show that state enterprises had total factor productivity growth of only 50–75 per cent of that of the non-state sector. At the same time, the government facilitated the rapid growth of non-state enterprises, at first in the rural sector to create off-farm employment, and subsequently in the rapidly growing private sector. In the 1980s, rural township and village enterprises transformed the economy, with reported annual growth rates of nearly 22 per cent during 1980–95, and claiming a 25 per cent share of industrial output by 1995. With the 1990s came the rise of a semi-private sector, comprised of individual enterprises, joint-stock companies, domestic joint ventures and foreign-invested enterprises. With superior quality products and lower costs, these non-state firms steadily expanded their market share at the expense of SOEs. The state share of industrial output fell from 78 per cent in 1978 to 26 per cent in 1997 (see Figure 3.1).

As market share fell, so did state-enterprise profits.[3] The rate of return on fixed assets dropped from over 20 per cent in the 1980s to about 5 per cent in

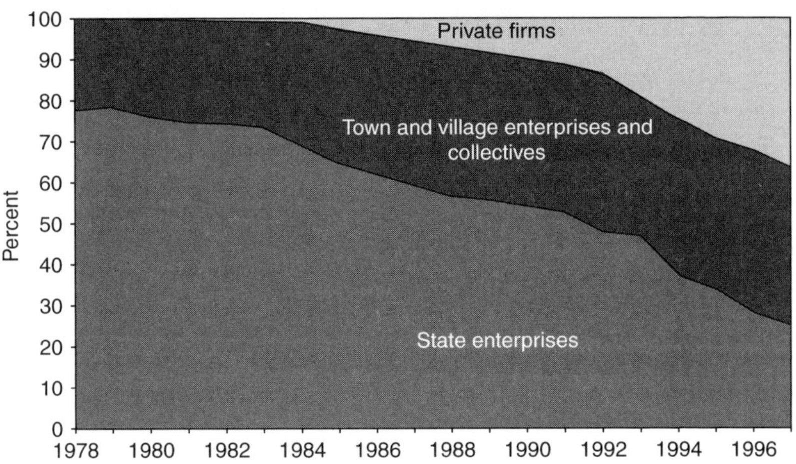

Figure 3.1a   State enterprise statistics
Source: 1998 *China Statistical Yearbook*

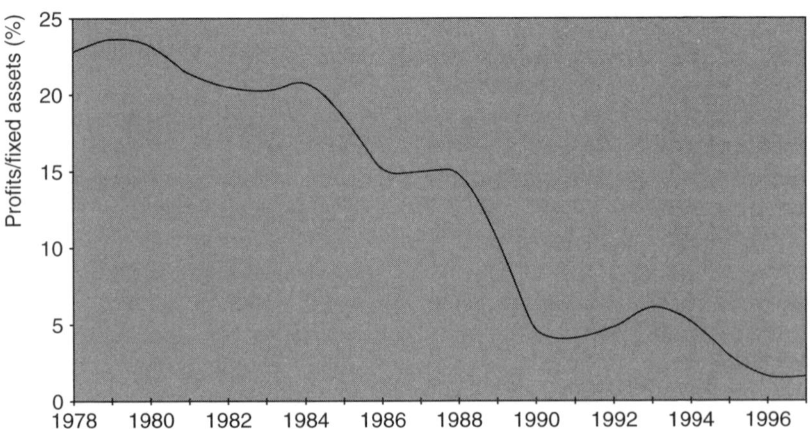

Figure 3.1b   State enterprise profitability
Source: 1998 *China Statistical Yearbook*.

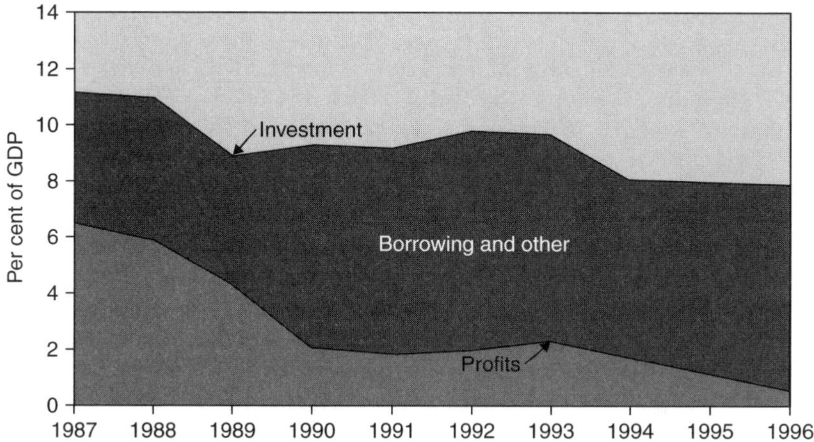

Figure 3.1c   State enterprise statistics for China, 1978–96
Source: World Bank staff estimates. See World Bank (1996) *China: Reform of State-Owned Enterprises*, Annex 4, for methodology.

1994. This fall was well below the 8.4 per cent for collectives and the 9.9 per cent for joint ventures, and further declined to 1.7 per cent in 1997. As profits declined and the state share of output has contracted, SOE profits in industry as a share of GDP have fallen by more than 70 per cent. In 1998, the combined profits of SOEs was about yuan 40 billion (US$4.8 billion), down from yuan 45.1 billion a year earlier. Losses of SOEs increased 21.9 per cent year-on-year in 1998 to yuan102.3 billion. The loss in earnings was partly the result of weaker domestic and external demand due to the Asian financial crisis. Profits of industrial firms fell 17 per cent to yuan147 billion (US$17.8 billion) in 1998 compared to 1997 (National Bureau of Statistics, 1999).

However, the reasons for the declines include some important changes that would benefit the economy in the long run. For example, the government increased depreciation allowances to more economically reasonable rates, reduced subsidies on energy, cotton and other inputs, and improved social security accounting methods. Aggregate profits dipped below 1 per cent of GDP in 1996–97, the lowest in the reform period. The percentage of SOEs suffering losses rose from about 25 per cent in 1992 to nearly 40 per cent in 1996 (Cao, Qian and Weingast, 1997, p. 24). By 1996, profits of the state-enterprise sector were only two-thirds of their level the previous year; factory capacity utilization rates had dipped to below 60 per cent for half of all state plants; and at the end of the 1990s, loss-making state-enterprises numbered some 2346, or 31 per cent of the 7680 large-and medium-sized enterprises. About 43 000 managers or leaders at state-owned enterprises were demoted or removed in 1998 as a result of inadequate job performance.

Policy efforts to reform

In his opening speech on 5 March 1999 of the National People's Congress (NPC), Premier Zhu indicated that 1999 would be a crucial year in the government's reform programme. There would be a deepening of the reorganization, restructuring and management reforms of state-owned enterprises proposed by the Central Committee in 1997. His emphasis followed the policies presented in 1998 at the Ninth National People's Congress, which ratified ambitious objectives to complete state-enterprise reforms within the next three years by 'keeping the large and letting go the small firms' (*zhuada fangxiao*). The government set the following ambitious objectives for itself: to make one-third of loss-making state enterprises profitable in 1999, and another third in 2000, leaving only 15 per cent of the operating state enterprises unprofitable. Policies would boost investment by non-state enterprises to ease the growing pressure of unemployment; seen by the government as necessary to facilitate the transition from a planned to a market economy. Perhaps to stimulate private investment, constitutional amendments at the National People's Congress formally recognized private enterprise as an 'important part of the socialist, market economy', and granted their owners legal protections for the first time.

These announcements came against a backdrop of earlier reform efforts. Most important was the gradual diminution of preferential access to subsidized finance for state enterprises, applying to them the so-called hard budget constraint. Subsidies through the budget, and implicit subsidies through the financial system, fell from more than 7 per cent of GDP in 1987 to less than 2 per cent in 1995, and perhaps half that in 1999 (see Figure 3.2). This, together with tighter regulatory control over banks, provided the single greatest impetus to restructuring since 1993. Nevertheless, the increase in losses of loss-making SOEs in 1998 resulted in domestic banks writing off yuan40 billion of bad debts for the state sector in 1998, compared to 30 billion of non-performing debts in 1997, mainly for large and medium-sized SOEs.

The reduction of subsidies reflected improvements in the legal basis for administering and receiving public financing from the central bank. Local governments had to balance their budgets, and the law strictly regulated local borrowing. District branches of the central bank and commercial banks were no longer allowed to follow the dictates of mayors and governors to finance favoured SOEs, and central bank branches had their authority to extend loans to state bank branches revoked. Net credit to the financial system fell drastically after 1994,[4] and the reorganization and reduction of the size of the central government in 1997–98 further diminished the state's role in the enterprises. The number of ministries was reduced, and several line ministries whose sole function was to regulate SOEs were eliminated. As the reductions in subsidies had their effect, the government offset the

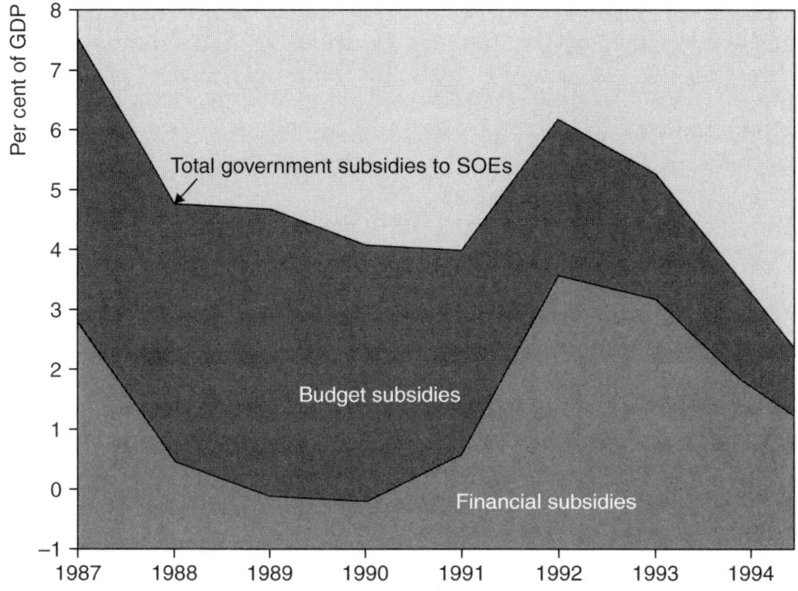

Figure 3.2   Subsidies to SOEs as a share of GDP, China, 1987–95
Source: See World Bank (1996) *The Chinese Economy: Fighting Inflation, Deepening Reforms*, table 2.1, vol. I and annex 3, vol. II, for methodology.

negative impact somewhat by granting tax exemptions and preferential tax rates on income, value-added taxes and even customs duties. However, these exemptions were unlikely to continue, because the hard budget constraints applied to the national and sub-national governments alike, and tax revenues remained low. Thus, the programme had three important elements: first, the state-enterprise sector would shrink further, including through *ownership* reforms; second, *layoffs* of state enterprise employees would occur; and third, *financial reforms* would move in tandem with SOE reforms.

New forms of ownership[5]

Ownership reforms began in November 1993 with the passing of the Company Law, when the government issued its pilot blueprint for reform in the so-called 10/100/1000/10 000 Programme, and later reaffirmed in the 'grasping the large and letting go the small' programme. As of 1997, of the 100 large enterprises chosen in 1994 for incorporation, 93 were incorporated and 84 had boards of directors. Incorporation, which involved the development of a clear corporate governance structure and transparent accounting procedures, was a prerequisite for more independent firm behaviour, discipline in investment and pricing strategies, and at least some asset divestitures. Meanwhile, the original list of 100 has expanded to 512. These 512 firms accounted for 55 per cent of all SOE assets, most of the gross profits of the industrial sector, and 85 per cent of taxes collected. To these should be added the 2500 large municipally-controlled enterprises that underwent similar incorporation. By June 1997, 1989 of these firms had been similarly converted, and 63 per cent had boards of directors.

Also in 1993 the government began to encourage the mergers of SOEs to increase the average size of firms, achieve some scale and multi-plant economies, and provide an alternative to bankruptcy for loss-making companies. A main tool to deal with financially distressed larger SOEs continued to be merger, acquisition or group integration by other SOEs. Formal bankruptcies happened increasingly in the non-state sector, but were discouraged and infrequent in the state-enterprise sector. Political leaders, and the State Economic and Trade Commission (SETC), cautioned against hasty SOE reform in view of unemployment and social and political risks. Municipalities were asked to favour distress-motivated mergers over bankruptcies, and to be careful with SME privatization.

Progress on reforming small state enterprises was probably one of China's best-kept secrets. Local governments began taking the initiative for reform in 1994, and the pace subsequently intensified. As the banking system reduced lending to some non-viable SOEs, many local governments sought ways to phase down their fiscal responsibility for the enterprises. The programme of 'grasping the large and letting go the small' allowed local governments to convert companies into worker cooperatives, set up management contracts with outside firms, divest whole or part of the equity of an SOE to new investors, or sell companies outright to foreign firms. Three forms accounted for more than half of ownership changes by 1997: sales to domestic or foreign investors (11 per cent); corporatization into limited liability or joint-stock companies (8 per cent); and stock cooperatives (35 per cent). By 1999 in Shandong Province alone, 50 per cent of small SOEs became stock cooperatives; in Jiangsu Province, more than 80 per cent converted to such an organizational form; in Henan Province, 33 per cent; and in Jilin Province, 40 per cent. Low capitalization made it both easy and attractive to convert small state enterprises into employee-owned companies. Employees could afford to purchase the enterprises with their savings. In some cases, governments ceded ownership at no cost provided that the new owners serviced enterprise debt.

Labour reform

A second major policy initiative dating back to the 1998 NPC was the official recognition that worker layoffs were necessary. Labour Minister Li Boyong announced that SOEs were expected to make 8–10 million workers redundant in the subsequent three years, not including job losses in other sectors (People's Republic of China, 1998). With as much as 30 per cent of the SOE workforce unproductively employed, the release into the labour force of large numbers of workers during restructuring must occur. Though rapid layoffs could cause social unrest, the process was set in motion. Net employment in the SOE sector fell by 8.8 per cent from 1995 to 1997, with the bulk occurring in 1996 and 1997. By the end of 1998, more than 17 million workers were 'furloughed' (*xiagang*), an increasingly common vehicle for releasing labour, and over six million redundant workers were reemployed.[6]

For many workers, the impact of layoffs was cushioned somewhat by retaining their housing. In addition, the government established income-maintenance programmes in 300 cities, which guaranteed jobless urban workers a minimum income, and subsequently expanded the programme to other cities. In Beijing, support amounted to yuan 200 (US$24) per month. The new Unemployment Insurance Regulation issued in January 1999 would have workers contribute to their insurance, and was funded mainly from fiscal budget and fees collected from firms. China planned to have 140 million workers covered by unemployment insurance by the first half of 1999, compared with 80 million in 1998 (National Bureau of Statistics, 1999). Former Minister of Finance Liu Zhongli announced at the National People's Congress that the central budget had allocated yuan 9.4 billion (US$1.1 billion) in 1998 to subsidize losses incurred by SOEs. This amount represented a slight increase over the 1997 figure. Government-organized projects would assist laid-off workers in finding employment and ensure a minimum standard of living through funds from enterprises, the government and social security. Financial departments would increase expenditures to relocate employees to jobs in other cities and provide loans to enterprises experiencing difficulty meeting payrolls.

Nonetheless, labour unrest was a major concern for senior policy-makers. Officially recognized, the registered urban unemployment rate was 3.1 per cent at the end of 1998, the same as at the end of 1997, and was expected to rise to 3.5 per cent in 1999 (National Bureau of Statistic, 1999). These numbers understate unemployment, because the official rate omitted the unregistered unemployed that are idle but still on the books at work units. In many cities, actual rates surpassed 8 per cent, especially in the so-called rust-belt cities of the northeast. With reforms, the erosion of the labour rules tying workers to a particular work unit (*danwei*) augmented the problem of an urban 'floating' population. Enterprise reform underscored the crucial need to create a new social safety net to replace the *danwei* system.

Reports of worker demonstrations surfaced sporadically in Chinese newspapers. In the spring of 1997, workers in Nanchong, Sichuan Province, took over the city centre for more than a day to demand payment of salary arrears. Eventually, special bank credits were arranged. Street demonstrations occurred in Wuhan, Hubei Province, in 1998 to protest at enterprise closings, and on 18 January 1999 laid-off cotton-mill workers staged a sit-down strike on a highway bridge to demand three months' back pay, before police peacefully cleared the protestors away (Saywell, 1999). An expanding economy would be crucial to maintaining stability.

Pressures on banks

Poor enterprise performance has immediate impacts on banks. For much of the early part of the 1990s, the government had reduced transfers to enterprises with the result that SOEs had borrowed heavily from banks. Total loans grew faster than GDP, and the government used credit to channel resources to the SOEs. As competition and other factors drove profitability down, the number of enterprises that could not service their loans rose; and because banks loans to state enterprises represented the bulk of the banks' portfolios, the failure to service these loans put enormous pressure on banks' cash flows. Only the steady rise in deposits relieved this pressure, but this could not serve as a permanent solution.

The government put in place a new financial system intended to relieve these mounting pressures. The commercial bank law, that revamped the structure of the financial system, was the first step in transforming the four huge state banks into commercial banks. Later, the government progressively abolished the practice of directing credit. It has attempted to enforce financial responsibility for loans down to bank managers, but, laden with the heavy burden of non-performing loans and narrow spreads dictated in part by remaining controls on interest rates, the capital of banks slowly eroded. Non-performing loans were estimated to be from 20 to 40 per cent of the total portfolio (World Bank, 1998). In 1998, two of the four state commercial banks reported losses, and Standard and Poor lowered the credit rating of these banks: the Agricultural Bank of China, the Bank of China, the China Construction Bank, and the Industrial and Commercial Bank of China.

Other warning signs appeared in 1998. Many of the investment and trust companies, mainly investment arms of municipal governments, began to experience difficulties after the bankruptcy of the Guangdong Investment and Trust Corporation in October 1998. The central government refused to compensate foreign creditors, so worried foreign creditors began to withdraw credit from other foreign debt-issuing international trust and investment companies (ITICs). Soon, ITICs in Dalian and other cities also began to experience difficulties as it became apparent that their portfolios performed poorly and creditors might not be paid. This segment of the financial market was small, less than 5 per cent of assets, and the government moved aggressively to monitor and reform the more than 200 ITICs across the country.

Reforming the banking system proved difficult because the non-performing portfolio was so large. However, of perhaps greater importance to the banks' long-term health was the adoption of a new loan classification system which would allow the central bank to classify bank loans by risk. The new system divided loans into five categories: normal, special-mentioned, substandard, doubtful and loss-to-be-written-off. Proper loan classification and provisioning would help create a modern system of prudential regulation. The formal abandonment of the credit plan on 1 January 1999, and the current development of a capacity to supervise banks, were the final pieces in the mosaic of bank supervision.

The government also took steps to recapitalize banks and collect the non-performing portfolios. It allocated yuan 40 billion (US$4.8 billion) to reduce SOE liabilities, in addition to the yuan 9.4 billion (US$1.1 billion) previously assigned for SOE losses. While this took various forms, financing bankruptcies, allowing mergers and worker redundancies, or reducing interest charges, the majority of the funds were used to convert bank debt to equity. At the same time, the government announced a programme to recapitalize banks. In 1998, a special issue of Treasury bonds of yuan 270 billion (US$33 billion) strengthened the capital base of the four state-owned commercial banks, and special domestic bonds were expected to be issued in 1999. The proceeds would be used to increase the banks' capital adequacy ratios. In early 1999, the government announced the formation of the Xinda Asset Management Company, to purchase the non-performing portfolio of the China Construction Bank. In theory, Xinda would purchase the loans at par, and subsequently collect them. In practice, questions remain: would the asset management company be able to convert debt to equity, restructure the operations of the defaulting debtor company, fire poor management, and take other actions that would restore value to past loans.

Time for reforms is limited

Two inexorable trends constrained the time the government could take to implement these profound reforms. First, despite the closed capital account, domestic financial agents were spontaneously integrating with foreign markets, and as trade expanded into foreign markets it would become increasingly difficult for the government to control cross-border financial transactions. Financial agents would become sensitive to changes in risk-weighted returns, and if the returns in Chinese banks fell too low, or if risks rose, financial agents would increasingly shift funds abroad. The steady rise in deposits that provided the large state commercial banks with liquidity might stop increasing, or begin to decline. If these banks did not strengthen their portfolios, this would undermine the cash flow of banks. At the end of the 1990s, unrecorded outflows in the balance of payments averaged US$15–20 billion annually. Thus, China's reforms ran a race with globalization.

Second, China's cities continued to grow at about 4 per cent annually as labour migrated from the countryside. Maintaining rapid job-creation in the long run would be essential to keep labour markets from severe over-supply. Further, growth was directly related to the pace of reform in the state enterprises and banks. Of course, no one could foresee precisely when these two trends would begin to constrain policy options, but policy had to stay well ahead of them to maintain stable growth.

The third key element in the Chinese strategy emerged in early 1999: to press boldly for entrance into the World Trade Organization. Although exports played a leading role in China's astounding growth after 1978, the country began integrating into world markets after decades of near-autarchy from an extremely small base, allowing growth to be rapid and with little consequence for international trading partners. However, by 1994, exports had climbed to more than 20 per cent of GDP, and China claimed a share of world export trade of more than 2 per cent (World Bank, 1997a).[7] Net exports contributed more than 30 per cent of aggregate growth during the 1994–96 period. Nonetheless, after 1997 export growth slowed in late 1998 and early 1999.

The international financial press speculated that the pressures of anaemic internal demand and falling exports would lead the government to depreciate the renminbi (yuan) against the dollar. By making its exports cheaper and imports more expensive, depreciation would rekindle export growth and boost employment. Others argued that the pegged exchange rate was rigid and, as Thailand demonstrated before its devaluation of July 1997, potentially dangerous, and an early depreciation would provide flexibility to the economy.

As of late 1999 the government had not chosen this course for several reasons. First, the rise of the yen to about 120 to the US dollar, and the renewed stability of the other currencies against the dollar, effectively devalued the renminbi in real terms by 13 per cent in 1998. While not yet sufficient to rekindle strong export growth, these cross currency movements appear to have stabilized reserves, which showed no sign of falling in the first quarter of 1999. Second, in the short term the government was able to use other instruments to cope with declining exports, notably the VAT rebate. The government increased the share of value added tax payments to exporting enterprises, effectively offering a greater incentive to export. These rebates in principle were for taxes already paid on imports and domestic processing. The rebate removed a competitive disadvantage facing China's exporters. In practice, the system was poorly administered and many firms exported products for which no taxes had been collected. This failure to collect taxes led the government to reduce the rebates below the amounts that should have been paid. Second, it is important to note that around 50 per cent of China's exports was processing trade, with a large component of import content. This structure of trade sharply reduced the net export responsiveness to a devaluation. The net effect of the rebates and the effective devaluation was to reestablish Chinese competitiveness.

Third, the service on foreign debt of the government would rise in renminbi as a consequence of devaluation, and place an additional burden on China's already weak administration to collect the taxes to make the greater payments. Fourth, the government was concerned that depreciation might have adverse effects on the Hong Kong dollar peg. Though the economic arguments for this link are weak, investors in Hong Kong might panic and withdraw funds, putting pressure on the Hong Kong dollar. Finally, the government was aware that a Chinese depreciation could trigger another round of deterioration in currency values through the region. Thus, a nominal depreciation might not produce gains in real terms, only create more financial instability for fragile trading partners in the region.

Instead, the government chose faster world market access through joining the World Trade Organization, thus buying time for reformers within the senior political leadership. The agreement would consolidate enactment of productivity-increasing reforms through a gradual, if accelerated, pre-announced timetable that would commit the country to the reform process and send a signal to domestic and foreign investors alike. Second, it would offer a measure of protection for China's exports from the protectionist political alliance forming in the United States.

Zhu Rongji went to Washington in April 1999 with a bold offer to break the stalled WTO accession talks. The WTO offer included a reduction of tariffs for industrial products from an average of about 24.6 to 9.4 per cent by 2005 (with two-thirds by 2003). Tariffs on some high-technology products of special interest to the USA and other East Asian exports would be eliminated. For agricultural products, tariffs would fall to an average of 17 per cent, half the prevailing level. For all products, quotas would be eliminated by 2005 with most removed by 2003. Services such as telecommunications, banking, securities, professional services, audio-visual and travel and tourism would be opened for the first time in post-1949 history to foreign direct investment and trade competition (United States Trade Representative, 1999).

This proposal was an unprecedented offer that marked a major shift in the Chinese position. The US administration, divided internally, at first signalled that the offer fell short of the conditions for WTO entry, and despite signing an accord on agricultural trade with the United States, Zhu left Washington disappointed. On a trip along the East Coast of the United States he met with business leaders in major cities; realizing the degree of movement on the Chinese side, these business people, joined by influential US senators, issued strong calls for an early WTO deal. In Washington, further analysis led the administration to a more positive conclusion, and new negotiations, that were originally slated to begin at the year-end were quickly rescheduled for late April 1999 (Sanger, 1999).

The Chinese offer increased the pressure in the WTO negotiations that was already high for the political leadership on both sides of the Pacific. Politicians in Washington and European capitals confronted strong constituencies at both ends of the political spectrum that would have preferred a slower integration of China into the world economy. The Chinese reformist leadership was also taking risks, as trade would add to the pressures already evident on state enterprises. Allowing foreign entry into banking would certainly produce new competitive stresses on an already weak banking system, and, finally, agriculture, the heart of the labour-intensive part of the Chinese economy, would come under new import competition. If it could respond, these pressures would spur increased rural–urban migration.

Winning the reform race with globalization

China has placed a considerable political capital on accelerating integration with the global economy. The results of this-three pronged approach will be revealed in the medium term at the earliest, and success cannot be guaranteed: the short-term demand stimulus might produce ephemeral growth and subsequent fiscal retrenchment as debt levels became onerous, resulting in slow growth. Similarly, ownership reform, especially of the large enterprises, involves difficult economic problems of reconciling conflicting mandates and conflicting stakeholder interests (government organizations, state-enterprise managers, banks and labour). Labour reform is also difficult. Banks might not respond with sufficient speed to provide adequate credit flows to the dynamic, highly-productive sectors, especially to the non-state companies. Finally, the international community has not been very supportive of China's bid to join the WTO.

Nonetheless, the government has some advantages as it pursues this bold strategy. Low inflation and low initial public debt provide flexibility for macroeconomic policies; and, second, public confidence in the banks, the implicit government guarantee of deposits, and lack of immediate financial investments because of the closed capital account combine to give China time to undertake financial reforms. But the clock is ticking as financial integration occurs spontaneously, and financial sector weaknesses, if ignored, could eventually lead to the spread of the East Asian financial fragility to East Asia's largest country. Finally, the international community has as much to gain from China's accession to the WTO as China. Not only will the agreement provide new market access for imports into China, it will also institutionalize reforms that will increase productivity in the Chinese economy. How the government will manage these problems in the first years of the new millennium might well shape the first decades to come, not only for China but for the world economy as well.

Notes

1 At the time Vice-President of the State Council and governor of the People's Bank of China.

2 It could be argued that this decline in growth contributed to the Tiananmen Square upheaval in 1989.

3 As is the convention, we use profits to measure state-owned enterprise (SOE) performance. Up to a point this is useful, in particular to show the trend; but profits are an incomplete measure of SOE performance, with several limitations. First, many SOEs performed social functions and some were in effect fiscal agencies; for them, profits were not a relevant measure of performance. Profits were probably more meaningful for competitive SOEs, which were only a subset of all SOEs. Second, many SOEs hid their profits to avoid irregular fees and levies. This suggests that the measured profits were probably an underestimate of true amounts. Third, it should be noted that foreign-funded enterprises also suffered losses. Some estimates suggest that up to 60 per cent were unprofitable. Foreign enterprises also underreported profits to avoid regular taxes.

4 Article 48 of the central bank law prohibited a local government, government departments at all levels, social organizations and individuals from forcing the People's Bank to make a loan. See, 'People's Bank of China Law', *China Law and Practice*, June 3, 1995, pp. 23–31. Article 41 of the commercial bank law prohibited units or individuals from compelling a commercial bank to extend a loan or provide guarantees for a loan (*New China News Agency*, 'Commercial Bank Law of the People's Republic of China', 11 May 1995, reprinted in *FBIS*, China, 95–094, 16 May 1995, pp. 27–35).

5 This section, and the next section on Labour Reform, draw heavily on Keidel (1998).

6 The official number of urban unemployed was about 11 million, but this did not include the 3–4 million workers laid off each year from the state-enterprise sector. The Chinese Academy of Sciences estimated that the true urban unemployment figure was closer to 15.4 to 16.4 million at the end of 1998, or 8 to 8.5 per cent of the total workforce.

7 According to the 1998 *Statistical Yearbook*, China's total annual exports from 1994 to 1997 averaged 20 per cent of GDP.

Part II
The Case of Cuba

4
Crisis, Economic Restructuring and International Reinsertion

Antonio F. Romero Gómez

Introduction

To understand the process of transformation in Cuba and the problems of reinsertion into the world market, it is, above all, important to specify the structural character of the deep economic crisis which emerged at the beginning of the 1990s. The changes in the world scenario in the late 1980s also disrupted the basis of Cuban external economic relations for the previous 30 years; that is, the special relations of economic integration with the Soviet Union. Therefore, it became obvious that the crisis could only be overcome by Cuba's reinsertion into the world market. I will in this chapter give a background to the crisis, describe the economic measures taken by the Cuban government, briefly discuss their results and, finally, consider the problems facing Cuba with respect to reinsertion into the global market.

The Cuban economic crisis

The economic crisis of the 1990s resulted from the accumulation of a series of imbalances and contradictions over several years, which manifested themselves in the process of Cuban economic development. These problems represented structural bottlenecks that were not overcome in spite of the significant socioeconomic progress in the country. It is necessary to recognize the many positive developments that took place after 1959: GDP grew by 4.3 per cent on average during 1959–89, implying a per capita growth rate of 2.8 per cent. To achieve this result the country invested the equivalent of 63 billion dollars and labour productivity grew at an annual average rate of 2 per cent during the same period.[1]

More significant, this economic growth was obtained simultaneously with a progressive redistribution of income, due to profound changes in the social structure. However, these positive developments were partially offset by the lack of appropriate internal backward and forward linkages in the productive structure, the lack of a diversified trade sector in spite of an impressive industrialization effort, and significant dependence on imports of intermediate goods and capital equipment. In addition, there was a high degree of technological obsolescence in many productive sectors. This resulted in a decline in economic efficiency and the yield of capital, which reduced the effect of the enormous investments made and the growing technical skills of the workforce.

Some analysts claim that it is clear that the so-called extensive development model[2] showed growing symptoms of exhaustion by the mid-1980s. As a result, from 1986 the Cuban authorities implemented the 'rectification of errors and negative tendencies' programme, an attempt to gradually modify the system of planning and economic administration. This modification of economic policy did not yield the expected results, and for that reason 1986–90 was characterized by a perceptible deterioration in several of the principal indicators of economic activity.[3]

In 1990 the changes in the former socialist countries began to have a serious impact on the Cuban economy. It should be recalled that the former Soviet Union with the former socialist countries of Eastern Europe since the beginning of the 1970s accounted for approximately 85 per cent of Cuba's external trade under preferential treatment. The collapse of this trade led to the emergence of the deepest crisis experienced by the country in more than 60 years. Initially, the government and society at large viewed the serious problems of the national economy to be the result, almost exclusively, of the abrupt interruption to trade and aid from the COMECON countries.

In spite of the large number of studies that have been published illustrating the graveness of the crisis of the Cuban economy, it is worthwhile to point to some basic characteristics of this process. Between 1990 and 1993, Cuban GDP declined by more than 40 per cent, a per capita reduction of 43 per cent. Consumption and investment were significantly reduced; total consumption falling by 28.2 per cent during the period, with private consumption declining considerably more than public consumption. The government tried by all available means to maintain an equitable distribution of consumption. Gross investment was reduced by more than 85 per cent in the four years, and few sectors of the economy managed to maintain minimum investment levels to keep output stable. By 1993 the level of investment had fallen to 5.4 per cent of GDP, compared to 28 per cent in 1989.

During this period there were also unprecedented reductions in capacity utilization, which in some cases involved the total paralysis of production with an associated decline in labour productivity of more than 39 per cent between 1990 and 1993. Exports of goods and services fell from almost US$6 billion in 1990 to less than US$2 billion in 1993, or by one-third in relation to 1990. Imports of goods and services fell from 8 billion to 2.4 pesos in the same period (with an official exchange rate of one peso to the US dollar). These declines implied a major external constraint on the Cuban economy,

Table 4.1   Evolution of the exchange rate on the parallel market, Cuba (pesos/US$)

Year	Mid-year	End of year	Year average
1990	n.a.	7.0	7.0
1991	n.a.	20.0	20.0
1992	35.0	45.0	35.0
1993	55.0	100.0	78.0
1994	130.0	60.0	95.0
1995	35.0	25.0	32.1
1996	22.0	19.0	19.2
1997	23.0	23.0	23.0
1998	20.0	21.0	21.0
1999	20.1	20.2	20.0

Source: ECLAC (2000, table 27).

with the purchasing power of Cuban exports in 1993 just 30 per cent of what it had been in 1989.

Although economic policy, as such, was not at the root of the crisis, there is no doubt that some economic measures worsened the crisis, or perhaps the slowness by the government to initiate the necessary reforms did so. Perhaps the most conspicuous evidence of problematic policy was the sharp increase of liquidity in the hands of the population. This resulted partly from the government's attempt to guarantee full employment and stable nominal wages even under conditions of paralysis or drastic reductions in the levels of production. This policy implied an automatic monetization of the growing budget deficit, which to a large extent was determined by the large, and increasing, subsidies to state enterprises, which accounted for all industrial activity. As a result of monetizing the deficit, an inflationary spiral developed expressed in the rapid expansion of black or underground markets, with prices that were out of reach of most Cuban consumers. The peso depreciated rapidly against the US dollar on the parallel market, rising from seven at the end of 1990 to 100 pesos per dollar at the end of 1993 (see Table 4.1). During this period the official exchange maintained a fixed parity rate to the dollar of one-to-one. This enormous imbalance, coupled with other negative impacts of the crisis, generated apathy among many Cubans towards work, whose real wages fell sharply, and many questioned the very system of social values that had been at the heart of the Cuban development project.

Economic policy under crisis and recovery

The external shocks and the deep crisis implied, by necessity, a gradual shift in economic policy in order to cope with the grave situation. Obviously, the subsequent changes in policies provoked diverging reactions and interpretations of the events unfolding as the crisis deepened. In the first stage of the crisis, from 1990 until mid-1993, the prevailing interpretation was that the crisis was essentially the result of negative changes in the external environment, and the major economic measures were directed to the external sector. Major measures implemented in this period were the development of the National Food Programme which tried to increase the domestic production of foods, an important component in total imports. This was to be achieved through the introduction and diffusion of indigenous innovations, and through an investment programme for the agricultural sector, along with new systems of labour organization on farms. The government also sought to increase export incentives for both traditional and non-traditional commodities. Related to this was an attempt to concentrate investment in productive areas which could increase foreign exchange through import substitution. One important aspect of export incentives was a process to decentralize foreign trade, which eventually eliminated the state trading monopoly and which required amendment to the Constitution. Scientific research was given top priority and the quick incorporation of the results into production played a decisive role in managing economic problems. The promotion of different forms of collaboration with foreign capital played an important role in generating and saving foreign exchange; this was the case not only in tourism, but also in power production. Industrial sectors which would otherwise have been paralysed by a lack of imported spare parts were given priority for attracting foreign investment.

Domestically, almost all goods and services were rationed, while the government tried to guarantee full employment through public employment, irrespective of production and profit levels. This employment policy reflected the objective that the costs of the crisis should be shared by all Cubans in accordance with the egalitarian ethics that had given political legitimacy to the revolutionary process after 1959. The economic measures in this first stage had certain positive effects, but were rapidly offset by the imbalances and contradictions they generated: enormous monetary overhang, drastic declines in labour productivity, decline of real wages, expansion of the black market, and emergence and consolidation of a dual economic structure.[4]

By the middle of 1993 it became clear that fundamental restructuring of the economy was necessary, a restructuring that would affect not only consumption and the external sector, but also fundamental social and economic aspects of the Revolution. Starting in mid-1993, Cuba entered a process of transformation and economic restructuring that was complex, contradictory and unfinished at the end of the century, as expressed in various measures of economic policy implemented in this period. Among the most important measures were the following. The government decriminalized the holding of foreign currencies, a crucial measure, but also one of the more contradictory since it implied simultaneous circulation of dollars and pesos in the country. In this way, Cuba became one of the few economies in the world that had internal convertibility of its currency. Along with this, the government implemented a restructuring of management of the agricultural sector, a measure which implied radical changes in land ownership. The changes are illustrated by the following figures: in December 1989, the agricultural area under state property represented 78 per cent of the total cultivated surface, cooperatives 10.2 per cent, with only 11.8 per cent in private hands. This changed radically with the reform, and by December 1995 the state's share had decreased to 25.7 per cent, while the cooperative sector increased its share to 58.7 per cent and the private sector to 15.6 per cent of total cultivated land.

In both rural and urban areas policies increased the possibilities for self-employment. These measures, together with the significant co-operativization of large parts of agriculture, especially in sugar with a greater role for foreign capital companies, implied the loss by the state of its quasi-monopsonistic position as employer. As a consequence, major changes took place in the employment structure. While in 1989, 95 per cent of the labour force worked in the state sector with only 3.3 per cent in the non-state sector, by the end of 1996 non-state employment increased to 24 per cent of the total labour force (see Chapter 7 in this volume). The change in employment patterns was accompanied by the creation of relatively unregulated markets for agricultural, industrial and handicraft products. In these markets, prices are determined by competition, and producers could sell in these markets after meeting their commitments to the state. The condition that state demand be met first guaranteed that a minimum basket of products would be supplied through a rationed and equitable system to the population. The opening of competitive markets was an explicit recognition of the necessity of using price signals in the process of economic restructuring, in order to stimulate production.

These economic reforms were supported by changes in legislation in relation to the treatment of foreign investment. In September 1995 a new law on foreign investment was promulgated, which in spite of certain limitations went beyond Decree-Law 50 of 1982 which had previously served as the legal basis for attracting foreign capital. The new code was notably more transparent and flexible, creating the possibility of free trade zones and industrial parks.

Another series of important economic measures after 1993 were directed towards macro-stabilization, in an attempt to reduce the government budget deficit which by 1993 had reached unsustainable levels (see Table 4.2). Prices of non-essential goods such as tobacco and liquor were increased, some employee gratuities eliminated, telephone and electric tariffs increased, and a clear line drawn between the finances of state enterprises and the state administration. As a result, subsidies to state enterprises were gradually

Table 4.2   Some economic indicators, Cuba (Annual rates of change, constant prices of 1981)

Indicator	1993	1994	1995	1996	1997	1998	1999
GDP	−13.6	0.6	2.5	7.6	2.5	1.3	6.2
GDP/capita	−14.2	0.2	2.2	7.2	2.1	0.9	5.7
Consumption	−5.1	0.7	1.6	3.6	2.1	2.2	2.7
public	−1.1	−1.9	−0.6	4.0	1.3	2.0	0.7
personal	−7.7	2.5	3.0	3.3	2.6	2.3	4.0
Gross domestic investment	−39.7	1.9	3.5	22.9	1.4	7.3	9.4
Exports of goods & services	−24.9	9.1	4.3	24.6	5.8	2.1	1.1
Imports	−5.4	19.2	11.5	24.2	11.1	8.0	3.0
Labour productivity	−12.6	2.9	1.8	7.9	0.5	0.4	5.4
Fiscal deficit[a]	−33.5	−7.4	−3.3	−2.3	−1.9	−2.2	−2.2
Monetary liquidity[a]	73.2	48.8	40.2	38.9	38.3	37.5	35.4

[a]   As percentage of GDP; at nominal prices.
Sources: (CEPAL) (2000) tables 1,3, 26); CEPAL (1997) tables A.26, A.28).

eliminated or drastically reduced. These cuts were instrumental in bringing the budget deficit down from a record high of −33.5 per cent of GDP in 1993 to −1.9 per cent in 1997. At the same time, a tax system was gradually put in operation, the first since 1964, to replace revenues from the operating surpluses of state enterprises. Deficit reduction also resulted from the restructuring of the central government, making it more flexible and efficient; and at the end of 1996 the banking system was reformed. These economic changes, together with the creation of the important preconditions for stimulating growth, at last opened the way to economic recovery that had begun in 1994 (see Table 4.2).

In spite of the recovery that continued during the rest of the decade, several years would be required to achieve the income level of 1989. More significant is that the macroeconomic adjustment programme that began in 1993, supported mainly by fiscal instruments, managed to decrease the fiscal deficit as well as considerably reduce the monetary overhang in the economy. This has resulted in a much more stable macroeconomic environment. The reduction of the fiscal gap and the decrease of the rate of inflation led to a gradual appreciation of the peso on the parallel exchange market. Notwithstanding the recovery, economic growth would depend on the country's capacity to solve some important problems. First, the future effects of the policies taken to reduce the public deficit became rapidly exhausted. Thus, it would be necessary to apply new economic policies, including improved tax collection and additional measures to reduce excess monetary liquidity. Second, as part of the transformation of the economy, income inequalities began increasing at an alarming rate, thus jeopardizing one of the priority areas of the Revolution (see further Chapters 6 and 7 in this volume). This problem, although a logical result of the many necessary economic measures, needed urgent attention, not only for the implications it had for growth, but above all for possible implications for a national political consensus. Related to the above, the growth of a 'dual economy' leading to a significant fragmentation of the economic structure of the country could result in a perverse allocation of resources.

With regard to the external sector, the chronic deficit in the balance of trade maintained a severe current account imbalance. As a result, Cuba by the end of the 1990s was facing a huge external financial constraint; outstanding foreign debt was around US$10.7 billion at the end of 1996. This degree of external indebtedness, together with a tightening of the economic blockade by the United States with the approval of the Helms–Burton Act, considerably restricted the policy options of the government. The solution to this and the other problems would no doubt lie in deepening the reform process in some areas. In other areas, reforms already in place would have to be adjusted, replaced or intensified.

There has been an important reform process in Cuba since 1993. Paradoxically, however, many analysts still consider these reforms as marginal when compared with the reforms in many so-called transition economies. Although it is beyond the scope of this article to discuss the international comparability of the recent Cuban experience, it should be stressed that, by whatever measure, it is clear that Cuba underwent substantial changes in its socioeconomic strategy during the 1990s. These substantial modifications of the Cuban development model are as follows. First, there has been a gradual process of diversification of property rights in the country, along with which the economic planning and administration system was modified. Although the process remained unfinished, the economy passed from being highly centralized to being substantially decentralized, and from a system focused on material balances to one based on financial balances, switching from direct to indirect economic regulation. As a result, perceptible changes occurred in the structure of employment through the reduction in the number of people employed in the state sector. Workers were moved towards better-remunerated sectors of the economy such as the cooperative enterprises and mixed property with the presence of foreign capital, as well as the private sector.

Changes in the external sector

With the demise of the Soviet Union and the disintegration of the socialist camp, the basis of the international specialization of the Cuban economy within COMECON disappeared. Hence, the opening of Cuba towards the international market was an irreversible process. This process was led by the state, and included important changes in the institutional mechanisms of external economic relations. In terms of trade, Cuba maintained its traditional export structure, concentrated on primary commodities. But in addition to a continued effort to raise sugar exports after the dramatic decline at the beginning of the 1990s there has also been an effort to diversify exports through the promotion of exports of other commodities (e.g. nickel and tobacco) as well as the promotion of cement and construction materials. Biotech, chemical and pharmaceutical products and software are all science-intensive with a high value-added component, and Cuba in the last two decades has invested considerable amounts into these sectors. These products constituted a high potential for the Cuban export industry although at the end of the 1990s they did not match, neither in volume nor value, the hard currency generated by the traditional export sector. This structure of Cuban exports was not optimal with respect to the dynamics of world markets, and was inconsistent with the investment effort of the previous decades. Cuba's weakness was its reduced capacity to benefit from the windows of opportunity offered by dynamic world markets.

With respect to imports, in the 1990s Cuba maintained a great concentration of imports of intermediate goods, primarily fuels and food products, and these items became priorities during the extreme shortage of foreign currency. On average in 1990–95, 71 per cent of all imports were intermediates, 17.3 per cent were consumption goods, and only 12 per cent capital goods. Simultaneously, there was an increase in the openness ratio of the Cuban economy. At market prices, exports of good and services rose from 13 per cent in 1993 to 22 percent in 1997. For imports, the ratio rose from 16 per cent to 26 per cent in the same period.[5] Geographically, Cuban trade also changed in character. The number of trading partners increased, and this diversification benefited Cuba as it made the country less vulnerable to sudden and unexpected changes on the international market. After 1990, international transactions in goods and services were carried out in a completely different way compared to those applied in Cuba in the context of the COMECON cooperation.

The services share in the Cuban external trade increased dramatically in the 1990s. This trend was closely linked to the promotion of international tourism, although tourism was not the only explanatory factor. The rise in tourism fitted with the general trend in international trade in goods and services. It is possible that Cuba had certain competitive advantages in terms of exports of some professional services, which together with tourism revenues would generate a surplus in the services account in the balance of payments.

The most outstanding features of the institutional changes can be summarized as follows. Significant changes were made to the Constitution, including changes in property rights, recognizing new forms of property and demonopolizing external transactions. Linked to the above-mentioned was a process of decentralization, and a restructuring of the Cuban economic administration and managerial system (including state companies) such that the number of companies with direct external links increased. The tariff and trade legislation regime was fundamentally revised. Due to the type of economic relationships that the country maintained in COMECON, the Cuban tariff code did not, in practice, carry out a meaningful economic function. With the promulgation of the Ordinance Law 124 in October 1990, the use of tariffs as an economic policy tool was reactivated as a control of transborder transactions, a devise to stimulate foreign investment, an instrument to protect domestic producers, and as a framework for the external commercial relations of the country.

Cuba also carried out a comprehensive process of adjustments in its commercial policy to achieve a gradual concordance with the rules approved in the last round of multilateral commercial negotiations (Uruguay Round), and subsequently to assume the commitments implied as a full member of the World Trade Organization (WTO). Without doubt, when one tries to make a general evaluation of the tendencies in the foreign trade policy of Cuba, one could conclude that in spite of the enormous difficulties the country gradually adapted to the new conditions. By the end of the 1990s, 100 per cent of Cuban external commercial relationships were carried out on market principles, arrangements completely different to those that characterized the external transactions with the countries of Eastern Europe and the Soviet Union.

Lack of access to financial markets remained the most serious external constraint. In spite of favourable Cuban conditions for inflows of foreign direct investment, the structural conditions of the economy, the 'impasse' situation in connection with the huge foreign debt, together with the North American blockade, implied that Cuban access to external commercial and banking finance was under very hard conditions, with high interest rates (14–16 per cent on average) and short-term repayment. Total hard-currency foreign debt at the end of 1997 was estimated at US$12 billion, around US$4.5 billion of which was principal contracted before 1986 and US$2.2 billion was interest arrears. All debt servicing on both commercial bank and bilateral official debt with Western governments was suspended in 1986 when it proved impossible to reach a rescheduling agreement with bank creditors. In 1997, approximately 64 per cent of the total foreign debt stock was short-term, and total debt amounted to 64 per cent of GDP. Efforts to renegotiate the debt produced an important result in March 1998, when an agreement was reached to reschedule yen100 billion (US$69 million) of commercial debt to Japan.[6] The reinsertion of the Cuban economy into the world economy had to develop simultaneously with the continuing process of economic restructuring which was needed for the productive transformation of the country. The challenge to Cuban society in the new decade will be to continue the restructuring process.

Notes

1 José L. Rodríguez, 'La economía cubana', in *Estado, nuevo orden democracia en América Latina*. Nueva Socieded, Caracas, December 1992, pp. 217–23.
2 Extensive development refers to the tendency in Soviet-type economies to rely on capital investment for expansion, rather than increasing efficiency and labour productivity.
3 In the second part of the 1980s there were already many important problems in the socialist economic integration scheme (Council of Mutual Economic Assistance – CMEA, better known as Comecon in the West), of which Cuba was a member since 1972. These problems, together with the changes in international economic relations which negatively affected the Third World economies and the initial transformation in the Soviet Union as part of perestroika, had adverse consequences for the Cuban economy. Obviously, adverse consequences could be considered as marginal if compared with the Cuban economy's external shock during the 1990s.
4 In the Cuban case, 'dual economy' refers to the division of the national economy into two different sectors with differentiated economic and currency rules.
5 EIU Country Risk Service, 2nd quarter 1998, Cuba, p. 12.
6 EIU Country Risk Service, Cuba, 2nd quarter 1998.

5
Globalization, the Multilateral Agreement on Investment and Nationalization in Cuba

Miguel Alejandro Figueras

Introduction

After the collapse of socialism in the socialist camp and the subsequent dissolution of COMECON, it was evident that Cuba had to adapt to a new reality. It became essential for the island to enter into the global market economy, with all its advantages and disadvantages. But this has not been an easy task. One problem, often forgotten in the debate about the Cuban crisis and the urgent need of transformation, concerns the obstacles encountered by countries that seek to take advantage of these new opportunities arising in a globalized world economy, but to do so with continued self-respect, national dignity and sovereignty. In the case of Cuba, the major obstacle was hostility from the United States government, which from the beginning of the Revolution in 1959 did all in its power to destroy that Revolution and its values. In this chapter I discuss the implications of a specific act of US aggression, the Helms–Burton Act. First I will present facts that shed some light on the unsolved nationalization issue; that is, the nationalization of foreign-owned property in Cuba in the early 1960s. This is important because it has served as the pretext for successive US governments not to normalize relations with Cuba.

Myth and reality about Cuban nationalizations

United States negotiators have not been reputed for deep knowledge of history. The Cuban nationalization of US property in the 1960s was in no way unique in recent world history. The new privatization wave that swept over the world in the 1980s and 1990s included many enterprises that were previously nationalized. The question then arises, why target Cuba? The United States used the issue of nationalization of American property without compensation by Cuba's Revolutionary Government in the 1960s as a pretext of carrying out economic warfare against Cuba. It is, however, a myth that the Cuban government in the 1960s nationalized US property without offer of compensation. Thus, we can ask further questions: what was the nationalization issue about, and what was its connection with the ill-fated Multilateral Agreement on Investment (MAI) and the Helms–Burton Law. I address these issues below, but first consider the facts about the Cuban nationalizations.

When the US occupation army managed the Japanese economy, it undertook an agrarian reform whereby it distributed land and paid compensation to the former landowners over 30 years, at bonds bearing an interest rate of 2.5 per cent. The agrarian reform supervised by the same US army in South Korea was even more drastic. Japanese landowners, in control of virtually all the land in South Korea, were expropriated *without compensation.*

On 17 May 1959, an agrarian reform law was enacted in Cuba. This law was applied to Cuban nationals and foreigners alike, and recognized the constitutionally-guaranteed compensation rights of the affected proprietors. So-called Bonds of the Republic were issued, yielding a maximum annual interest rate of 4.5 per cent, to be paid off over 20 years. *Thus, had this offer been accepted, owners would have been fully compensated by the end of the 1970s.* The bond owners were granted a ten-year tax exemption and other benefits. If compared to the reforms undertaken in Japan and South Korea, the Cuban agrarian reform was considerably more favourable to the former landowners. However, in the Cuban case the US government claimed cash compensation without delay for the expropriated US companies that owned 40 per cent of the arable land in the country. In a diplomatic note dated 12 June 1959, the US government said that

> [T]he United States recognises that, according to International law, a State is entitled to expropriate within its jurisdiction for public purposes in the absence of contract provisions or any other agreement to the contrary. However, this right must be accompanied by the relevant obligation a State may have entered into, in the sense that such expropriation shall entail the payment of prompt, adequate and effective compensation.
>
> (Cronologías 1987:220)

In another note, dated 22 February 1960, addressed to the US government, the Cuban Foreign Ministry stated that

> [T]he Revolutionary Government, following its willingness to resume, through diplomatic channels, the already started negotiations on pending issues between Cuba and the United States, has decided to appoint a commission for such purposes, which can start its negotiations in Washington on the date agreed by both parties. Cuba's Revolutionary Government would like to make it clear, however, that the renewal and further development of such negotiations will not be subject to any

unilateral measure adopted by your country's Government which prejudges the outcome of the aforementioned discussions, or may cause damage to the economy of the Cuban people. It seems obvious to add that the adherence of Your Excellency's Government to this point of view, will also reaffirm the spirit of fraternal friendship that has tied and ties our peoples.

(Cronologías 1987:220)

The US government, however, had no interest in finding a solution to the compensation issue and to the differences it had with the Cuban government. This was quite clear from its response to the above note:

The US Government cannot accept the negotiation terms expressed in Your Excellency's *note*. There [are] unilateral measures [which] will be adopted by the US Government which may affect Cuba's economy and its people, either by the Legislative or the Executive branches.

(Cronologías 1987:231–2)

In April 1960, a month after sending the reply, two CIA officials met with President Ydígoras of Guatemala, obtaining his authorization to train a military force that would invade Cuba. In May that same year the Trax Training Base became operational in Guatemala, and a few days later the New York-based Thompson & Cornwall Inc. Company, under a CIA contract, started building a modern airport from which, nine months later in April 1961, B-26 airplanes would take off to bomb Cuban towns, and C-54s filled with paratroopers would fly towards the Bay of Pigs.

Law No. 851 of 6 July 1960, issued by the Revolutionary Government, authorized the nationalization of US property, but guaranteed the payment of compensation to the former owners and defined the ways to create a Compensation Fund. The United States responded by eliminating the sugar quota for Cuba in the US market. Confronted with an increasingly hostile situation threatening vital points of the Cuban economy, the Revolutionary Government nationalized yet more American companies considered to be strengthening the Cuban economy. These companies were: (1) the Cuban Electric Company, generating 95 per cent of the country's electricity; (2) International Telephone and Telegraph, operating 100 per cent of the telephone system and 80 per cent of the telegraph network; (3) two oil refineries – Esso Standard and Texaco – processing 80 per cent of the oil consumed; (4) eight sugar corporations, controlling a third of Cuba's sugar output; (5) two nickel plants, producing 100 per cent of Cuba's second-largest export production; (6) three banks, granting 25 per cent of all loans in the country; and (7) four tyre plants, covering 100 per cent of the Cuban market.

From the second half of 1959, most of these companies had suspended their investment and operation plans; they could receive orders from

Washington at any time to paralyse Cuba's economy. But in spite of US hostility, culminating with the attempt to invade Cuba with a mercenary force, the Cuban government continued to offer a negotiated settlement of the differences with Washington. Nine months after the Bay of Pigs invasion, the Cuban President stated,

> Cuba, from the initial deterioration of Cuba–U.S. relations up to now, has always been willing to negotiate through diplomatic channels, or any other appropriate means, the ongoing differences between the United States and Cuba. Furthermore, as stated by our Council of Ministers: Cuba would have paid compensation to US citizens and property affected by the laws of the Revolution, if economic act of aggression had not stood in the way and if that country's Government had been willing to negotiate on the basis of respect for the will, dignity and sovereignty of our people.

However, the US administrations that followed were not interested in settling the compensation issue. The pressures that US corporations could exert with the aim of reaching an understanding with the Cuban government on this issue became an encumbrance to US administrations. Since its main objective remained to destroy the Cuban economic and social system, the following administrations focused on other measures aimed at mitigating this pressure from the corporations. This was, for instance, done by the Treasury Department allowing US natural and legal persons to deduct from their taxes the total or partial value of lost property in Cuba.

This meant that the compensation claim on Cuba through Title III of the Helms–Burton Act would not come from corporations or natural persons, since they already received compensation through the deduction from their taxes. Therefore, the only claimant would be the Treasury Department if a Global Compensation Agreement were eventually to be discussed. But there is also another aspect to be considered. Seventy per cent of the value of the claims originally, and unilaterally, accepted by the Claims Commission of the US Congress, were concentrated in 26 large corporations. In the huge ocean of takeovers, mergers and liquidations that characterized the business world, not least in the United States, many of these corporations disappeared.

At the beginning of the 1990s until the enactment of the Helms–Burton Law, a growing number of representatives from large US corporations went to Cuba on fact-finding missions to prepare for the day when the embargo would be lifted. Many of these business people were concerned that the Treasury Department could claim the return of the amounts deducted from taxes (with a compound rate of 6 per cent per annum) should the corporations obtain any direct compensation from Cuba. Therefore, it was unlikely that many US companies would make claims on the Cuban government. In any case, such claims should come from the Treasury Department.

In the midst of the 1992 presidential election campaign, the US Congress passed the Torricelli Amendment, aimed at tightening the economic embargo against Cuba, keeping subsidiaries of US corporations based in third countries from trading with Cuba, and adopting measures which unilaterally interfered with the freedom of maritime transportation. The Act was widely criticized by the international community. In February 1996, Congress and another president passed the Helms–Burton Act, that focused directly on the Cuban economy and was intended to prevent foreign investment flows to Cuba. To understand the full importance of the Act it must be placed in the context of the Multilateral Agreement on Investment (MAI).

Birth and death of the MAI

In 1994, and after seven years of negotiations, the Uruguay Round came to a conclusion. The World Trade Organization (WTO) came into being with the signing of the General Agreement on Trade in Goods and the General Agreement on Commercial Services, two main pillars of the executive board of the world economy. But that board lacked an important support: a general agreement which would regulate the treatment of foreign investment. The aspiration for such an agreement was more than 50 years old, first appearing in the Charter of Havana of 1947. But the initial proposal failed to make progress, because of the projected International Trade Organization (ITO) collapse when the US Congress refused to ratify the relevant treaty. The investment issue was not negotiated within the GATT (the weak replacement of the ITO) during the decades that followed.

A Multilateral Agreement on Investments (MAI) had been discussed since 1995 within the Organization for Economic Co-operation and Development (OECD). As discussions proceeded, it became clear that everything was being done in the wrong place, with the wrong methods, and with the wrong participants (only the developed countries were full participants). Those supporting the MAI heralded success as early as 1995, but in 1998 the trumpets fell silent and the draft Agreement, virtually complete, collapsed through lack of support. Therein lies a story of birth and subsequent collapse, with strange links to the attempts by the US government to destablize and sabotage the Cuban Revolution.

Background and sequence of events

During the 1990s, foreign direct investment (FDI) flows grew at a faster rate than world trade in goods and services. Between 1991 and 1996, investment flows increased at an annual rate of 10 per cent (from US\$198 billion to US\$345 billion), and global FDI stocks rose to US\$3.2 trillion in that year. Thus, FDI quadrupled in less than ten years (UNCTAD, 1997).

The leading transnational corporations sought an international comprehensive legislation on investment that would enforce the new multilateral system and 'level the ground' for their investments in all countries. Their concern was that a world with many bilateral investment agreements would complicate the carrying-out of business. While there were 435 bilateral treaties registered in 1989, the number by 1998 had increased to 1600, and it was predicted to rise to more than 2000 by the end of 1999. To make matters worse, several regional integration agreements were in place, whose by-laws and regulations provided for different treatments and rules of foreign investment flows (e.g., NAFTA, MERCOSUR, Andean Pact, European Union). Others were being negotiated, or about to begin the negotiation process. For example, of the 11 NAFTA working groups, the most advanced was that which considered foreign investment, and which after September 1997 was ready to start negotiating a Regional Investment Agreement following a summit meeting held in Santiago de Chile.

Up until the First WTO Ministerial Meeting (Singapore, December 1996), the European Union and Canada found it convenient to draft a MAI in the context of that organization, rather than within the OECD. However, a large number of Third World nations were initially hesitant to add this issue to the Singapore agenda. Some countries from Asia and North Africa strongly opposed the inclusion of the issue, arguing that it should have been carefully examined by UNCTAD, which would have taken years, and later drafted within the WTO. Without a preconceived position, the posture adopted by this group of countries in practice strengthened the US position. The US government did not want the MAI drafted in the WTO, but in the narrow forum of the OECD, where the requirements of large investors would take priority.

At the Singapore Meeting it was agreed that a working group would be established within the WTO where the 132 member countries could accumulate and study data relating to foreign investment. From 1999 onwards, a new ministerial meeting would decide whether or not the MAI negotiations would start in WTO.

MAI negotiations in the OECD

On the basis of the experience gathered during the long negotiations creating and drafting the General Agreement on Commercial Services, the US government anticipated the difficulties of achieving a MAI. Thus, it started to exert pressure on its main allies to locate the negotiation of a Multilateral Agreement on Investment at the OECD. Locating the negotiations within the OECD would facilitate an agreement emphasizing international deregulation and highly protective of foreign investment. The intent was to create an 'open' treaty that would be adopted by non-member countries of the OECD willing to accept its obligations. For OECD non-member countries, the conditions of adherence to the MAI would simply be on a take-it-or-leave-it basis.

In May 1995, the Ministerial Council of the OECD set up a Negotiating Group, which for two years should have been involved in drafting the MAI, the deadline being May 1997. When that date expired and the draft MAI was not ready, the term was extended to April 1998. The MAI Negotiating Group was composed of some 250 officials, many of whom travelled from their capitals to Paris on a monthly basis. Most of the representatives came from ministries of economy or finance; there was little involvement of foreign ministry officials and politicians. A draft MAI was published every two months with the label 'Confidential', incorporating changes arising from negotiations. In Latin America, the OECD Negotiating Group hosted three regional seminars during 1996 and 1997, two in Brazil and one in Mexico. Cuba was excluded from all three seminars.

Between September 1995 and April 1997, the MAI Negotiating Group at the OECD worked intensively, meeting for a week every month, and many issues were clarified, with the following objective:

> [T]he agreement shall be based on the experience gathered through the investment instruments in place at OECD, shall reinforce the results obtained, and shall create new disciplines aimed at providing international investments with a general framework. It shall also set forth high-level standards for the liberalisation and protection of investments and shall comprise procedures for the settlement of disputes.
>
> (Figueras, 1998)

During the first twenty months of the drafting of the MAI, no reference whatsoever was made to expropriations of foreign property *in the past*. This was reflected in the OECD Informative Note dated March 1997, and entitled 'On the Progress made in relation to the MAI':

> Quick progress has been made in drafting the MAI terms concerning the measures relating to investment protection. This should be attributed to the vast experience gathered by OECD member countries in negotiating Bilateral Investment Protection Treaties. The MAI provisions are mainly based on the principles included in those Treaties.
>
> (Figueras, 1998)

That same Note explained how the issue of nationalization or expropriation would be treated:

> Expropriation, or any other measure having similar effects, both directly and indirectly, shall only be permitted if for a purpose which is in the public interest, on a non-discriminatory basis, and in accordance

with due process of law against prompt, adequate and effective compensation.

The MAI and the Helms–Burton Act

In March 1996, the US Congress and government enacted the Helms–Burton Act with the objective of deterring and reversing Cuba's foreign investment flows. The text of the Act made no reference to the MAI. After six months of fruitless appeals by the world community to the US administration to come to reason and repeal the Helms–Burton Act, the EU on 3 October 1996, requested the WTO to appoint a Panel of Experts to examine and pass judgement on the contravention of that organization's regulations arising from the Act. Canada, Mexico, Japan, Malaysia and Thailand joined the EU as third parties to the Panel.

The US administration threatened to use reasons of national security to impose the extraterritorial measures contained in the Helms–Burton Act. If it had done so and challenged the Panel's eventual decision, that action would have wreaked havoc in the WTO, which had only been created three years before; the WTO would have been seriously and irresponsibly undermined in its leading functions of regulating world trade.

To avoid such a crisis, the United States and the European Union, on 11 April 1997, reached an 'Understanding'. The US Administration undertook to continue waiving all claims-related lawsuits under Title III of the Helms–Burton Act,[1] and negotiate with Congress the possibility of modifying that Act with a view to including waivers on its Title IV.[2] Furthermore, commitments were made to reach an agreement concerning the Iran–Libya Sanctions Act (ILSA). The EU, for its part, pursuing the objective of not undermining the WTO, temporarily cancelled the Panel's proceedings.

From the Understanding itself, the negotiation process relating to the Helms–Burton Act was transferred from the WTO to the OECD, where the MAI was being prepared. The United States, in negotiating an Understanding with the European Union governments on an individual basis, excluded the other OECD member countries from discussing a decisive aspect of the MAI. The United States attempted to leave the defendant's seat it had occupied at the WTO and then dictate, in the context of the OECD, new disciplines in international law with a view to treating as illegal the nationalization of property that had taken place over 40 years previously. The main purpose of this manoeuvre was to deem illegal the Cuban nationalization of US-owned property. In practice, it would have turned Title III of the Helms–Burton Act into an international rule, under the umbrella of a multilateral treaty at OECD. A second possible objective would have been to apply these disciplines to other countries, as deemed convenient by the US government and Congress.

Until September 1997, the international press ran few articles on the Group's progress; it was practically excluded from all publicity. This technical and partially secret environment, with compartmentalized information for political circles, was convenient to US negotiators. It facilitated reorienting the MAI against Cuba. On 17 September 1997, the OECD called an Informative Meeting on the Progress of the MAI for the Representatives of Non-Member Countries. Cuba was among the first to request an invitation. In light of the opposition coming from the US State Department, the OECD excluded Cuba (the only country whose participation was denied). Anticipating a possible negative answer, Cuba had prepared a document titled 'Report to the Participants in the Informative Meeting', denouncing the US manoeuvre to use the MAI to internationalize the Helms–Burton Act. This document was distributed in French, English and Spanish to all Paris-based embassies on 17 September, just before the Meeting began.

That same day, the document became public knowledge on the Internet. The document was also handed out at the UN General Assembly on two occasions, in October and November 1997. Now political and social groups in many countries, including the United States, complained about the lack of information in relation to what was developing in Paris, and the international press became increasingly critical of MAI.[3] At this point, a non-governmental organization (NGO) obtained a confidential copy of the draft MAI and placed it on the Internet. It was through the Internet that many groups, including trade unions, discovered the state of MAI negotiations, triggering a socio-political movement which rejected the MAI even in the OECD member countries. Several NGOs published web pages denouncing the MAI. In February 1998 a coalition of 600 NGOs from 67 countries, including 150 from the United States, launched a joint campaign against the MAI, opposing it on the grounds that it would undermine consumer protection measures, employees rights and the environment, while legalizing unprecedented powers for transnational corporations.

On 11 March 1998, the European Parliament agreed – with 437 votes in favour, 8 against and 62 abstentions – to urge EU governments and parliaments not to sign the MAI without carefully examining its impact on the Union's social, environmental, economic and cultural policies. Many Euro-deputies denounced the MAI for unacceptable interference in national sovereignties, even suggesting that it should be taken to the European Court of Law. Neither the EU Parliament nor civil society at large were given any information whatsoever, even though the MAI would have undesirable social and environmental effects, as well as undermining relations with the countries of the Lomé Convention. This would be a new vehicle of colonization of OECD non-member countries.

If the drafting of the MAI in Paris had not become entangled after the Understanding dated 11 April 1997, the Negotiating Group would probably have concluded its task and the MAI would have been approved by all governments with maximum discretion. This would probably have occurred even though many parliaments and social groups would have been excluded from the decision process, and, as a consequence, failed to fully understand its real implications.

Within the OECD, France and Canada are the strongest opponents of the MAI because of extra-territorial laws and the lack of a clause to exclude cultural activities. Many other countries also share this position. There was a strong movement in cultural and union groups against the MAI in order to keep transnationals from controlling television networks, radio stations, movie-making and the press, and to defend workers' rights. It was a movement against what was called 'the Hollywood invasion'.

Never so much at stake to win so little

The steps taken by the US government have affected two institutions of the utmost importance to transnational corporations: the WTO and the MAI. They jeopardized the authority of the WTO to impose economic and commercial disciplines, and threatened to use the argument of national security if the EU Panel's decision clearly stated the extra-territoriality of the Helms–Burton Act. The steps also prevented the MAI from being agreed at the OECD.

If the MAI at the OECD 'was fighting for life', in a stage of 'clinical death' or 'sinking like Titanic', as claimed by many periodicals, then it would be fitting to ask who was culpable? Leaving aside the inadequacy and lack of ethics of the MAI, the US government must carry the blame after the MAI failed to be successfully concluded and approved. The United States had consistently exerted silent pressure and favoured large transnationals in its design, but when the MAI and the extra-territorial laws overlapped, the fate of the MAI was sealed at the OECD.

Only three months from the MAI deadline, May 1997, the Deputy Secretary General of the OECD stated, at the opening ceremony of the MAI Seminar in Brasilia, that the timetable of agreement would be adequately fulfilled. But a string of actions conspired against that outcome. The Helms–Burton Act had been enacted the year before, and President Clinton had appointed Stuart Eizenstat, Under-secretary of Commerce and later on Under-secretary of State, to coordinate with the EU and mitigate the protests triggered by the extra-territorial character of the Helms–Burton Act and the D'Amato–Kennedy Act.[4] However, it proved impossible to mitigate anything. The EU requested that a Panel be established in the WTO, and following the Understanding of April 1997, negotiations started.

The major mistake of the US government lay in its obsessive policy to overthrow the Cuban Revolution. In the early 1960s, the United States had imposed its economic blockade on Cuba, which was still in force at the end of the century, setting a record as the longest blockade in history. With the collapse of socialism in Eastern Europe in 1989–90 and the subsequent disappearance of the Soviet Union in 1991, it seemed the time to annihilate Cuba through economic measures. In October 1992, the US Congress passed the so-called Torricelli Amendment which further tightened the blockade, contained extraterritorial clauses, kept US subsidiaries and branches of transnational corporations from doing business with Cuba, and imposed sanctions on other countries (e.g. ships calling on Cuban ports). But that Amendment made no reference to foreign investments.

Even though in 1982 a Cuban decree-law had been approved to allow the creation of partnerships between Cuban enterprises and foreign capital companies, ten years later the number of major joint ventures in the country was low, less than 50, many of which were actually quite small. Ironically, it was precisely after the enactment of the Torricelli Amendment that foreign investment in Cuba began to increase, with large-scale joint ventures in oil exploration and extraction, the telephone network, the nickel industry, and tourism. The flow of European, Canadian and Latin American investors to Cuba and the concern expressed by US enterprises which were not allowed to invest in Cuba, caused panic in rightist lobbying organizations and other anti-Cuban groups. Business pressure could have resulted in the partial or total suspension of the economic blockade, as was the case in Vietnam in 1993.

Representatives of 400 US enterprises visited Cuba in 1994, and that figure increased to 1000 the following year. For the anti-Cuban groups, something had to be done to stop that trend, so the old skeleton was removed from the wardrobe – claims on US-owned property nationalized at the beginning of the Revolution. That was why the Helms–Burton Act came into being, passed only 40 months after the Torricelli Amendment. Washington had apparently not anticipated the interest that investors from other countries would have in Cuba. The Helms–Burton Act caused some damage, by increasing the cost of credit and insurance policies as well as the country's risk rating, but it failed to achieve its main goal. During 1996 through 1999, the number of joint ventures operating in the country increased by more than 50 per cent (from 220 in March 1996 to 370 by March 1999). None of the 220 ventures existing when the law was passed was terminated, and none of the investors withdrew in spite of attempts at intimidation.

The governments of other countries strongly reacted to the new intervention. The bilateral investment treaties signed by the Cuban government increased from 15 when the Helms–Burton Act was enacted, to 32 by the end of 1998. These treaties involve seven EU member countries, Italy, Spain, the United Kingdom, Germany, Greece, France and Luxembourg.

A 'new understanding'

On 18 May 1998, the European Union and the United States reached a new Understanding, whereby Title IV of Helms–Burton would not apply to European enterprises, and all sanctions would be suspended for European enterprises that had made investments in Cuba before the date of the Understanding. In the future, EU governments would undertake to discourage investment from EU member states in Cuba, if made in former US-owned property. There would be a registry of claims on property nationalized in contravention of international law, and according to the information provided by the claimants it would be decided if the European investments in such property should be discouraged. If so, this would be implemented by refusing credit guarantees and insurance and commercial assistance by the EU member states. Both parties undertook to convince the other OECD nations to include the essence of this Understanding in the MAI once the Negotiating Group went back to negotiations in October 1998. During his stay in Geneva, two days prior to the Understanding, Cuba's President Fidel Castro warned:

> The question that Cuba asks itself is if the differences between the US and the EU over an extraterritorial law is going to be worked out at Cuba's expense, for that infamous law essentially maintains the ruthless blockade imposed on Cuba for almost 40 years now, and precisely on the eve of the Fiftieth Anniversary of WTO.
>
> (Granma 1998)

Three days later, on 19 May during his presentation at the WTO Plenary Session, Castro referred to the Understanding that had already been approved:

> The world has plenty of reason to feel humiliated and concerned, and the WTO must stop the economic genocide. Any differences between the US and the EU on account of the Helms–Burton Act should not be worked out at Cuba's expense. It would be an unthinkable dishonour to Europe. The agreements announced yesterday in London are confusing, contradictory, threatening to many countries and not at all ethical.
>
> (Granma 1998)

The new Understanding was confusing and its terms too weak to be implemented; and it could be used by the US government to give the impression of legality in actions against Cuba. The Administration spokespersons would tell the press that they had won the battle and that the Europeans had to accept their terms. The spokespersons of the Commission, on the other hand, could argue that they had come out with flying colours, and that now the enterprises of Europe could invest in both Cuba and Libya without sanctions. But in the Understanding, the EU had accepted the basic US position, although they reiterated many times that it was unacceptable. The European Commission also accepted the extra-territorial nature.

European negotiators were well-aware that the Understanding would be difficult to implement from the economic point of view, and impossible to enforce legally, for it no longer opposed the extra-territoriality of the Helms–Burton Act and the D' Amato–Kennedy Act. The commitments made by the US government in the Understanding of April 1997 to change extra-territorial laws went completely unfulfilled. What is more, while negotiating the April Understanding, during summer 1998, Congress approved new amendments aimed at further tightening the Helms–Burton Act.

On 4 June 1998, the head of the US negotiators, Stuart Eizenstat, appealed to the House of Representatives International Relations Committee to adjust the Helms–Burton Act to US foreign policy. The Committee's president anticipated that it would be very difficult to design the modification requested, and pointed out that the 18 May Agreement had several serious shortcomings and that therefore there was not a feasible replacement for the sanctions. Even though the Committee members undertook to review the request, the prevailing mood was to reject the modifications to the Helms–Burton Act.

Two days after the Understanding was approved, the German daily *Handelsblatt* wrote:

> If one takes a second look, it is clear that the EU has given up. It shall never again be able to enjoy credibility when insulting Washington's sanctions laws. It has stopped being an accuser. Two weeks ago, it withdrew its accusation from the WTO Lawsuit Settlement Tribunal in order to give Washington a sign of goodwill on the eve of the EU–U.S. Summit. The fact was that the Iran–Libya Sanctions Acts, as well as the law against Cuba, were still there.

The daily *El País* from Madrid wrote in the same vein on 28 May 1998 that the Understanding was contradictory to the European viewpoint because several EU countries had signed investment agreements with Cuba, but now an agreement was reached with the United States to discourage investments on the island. On the other hand, Cuba had already signed several Agreements of Compensation with many European countries with enterprises that had been nationalized, for example, with France, the United Kingdom and Spain. These agreements had led to compensation for losses. These were major EU member states whose governments now embraced the absurd idea of acting against their own enterprises on the basis of dubious US claims for compensation.

Even more absurd was that the original US claimants were not interested in compensation. On 12 March 1998, Michael Ranneberger, Co-ordinator for Cuban Affairs at the State Department, made a statement saying that:

> We have publicised our efforts with US claimants, including in the Cuban-American community, through radio, newspapers, US mail and the Internet, and vigorously sought information about foreign business involvement in US claimed properties in Cuba. However, in the past two years (since March 1996) we have received only one inquiry from a certified claimant. We have received more than 150 inquiries from potential non-certified claimants, but when asked only two provided documentation to support their claims, and these involved the same case of possible trafficking.
>
> (Ranneberger 1998)

Nonetheless, the US–EU Understanding was confusing and created uncertainty and fears for potential investors in Cuba. Therefore, it might have discouraged some short-term investments even though it could not be fully implemented.

Epilogue

The work of the MAI–OECD Negotiating Group came to a halt in April 1998 because of the unsolved negotiations between the United States and the European Union. In addition, there were a large number of reservations raised by several countries. For example, both Canada and Australia generated numerous requests for clarification or changes. By comparison, the EU submitted only a few requests for exceptions.

The disagreements between the MAI negotiators regarding the US government's actions were evident. To many it was not clear whether the United States really wanted a MAI; the position adopted by the US government was ambiguous in that it, too, submitted a lengthy list of requests for exceptions to the draft MAI. On 14 March 1998, *The Economist* of London, a former supporter of the MAI, ran an in-depth article on it and an editorial opposing it. In both, one could sense a pessimistic cloud looming over the OECD. *The Economist* explained why the MAI should never have been drafted within the OECD:

> [I]t only has 29 members and excluded Third World countries from the negotiation process, which, in turn, are the most sought after by TNCs. That's why the MAI should have been prepared at WTO from the outset, which has 132 members; unlike WTO, OECD has no sanctions mechanisms in place to force its members into fulfilling agreements.

The OECD was experienced in studies and recommendations, but inexperienced in complex negotiations. In contrast, the WTO was far more skilled in complicated negotiations. According to *The Economist*, Third World countries have seen this attempt as a new neo-colonial gimmick; the magazine looked forward to closing this chapter, protecting the prestige of the OECD, and transferring negotiations to the WTO.

The Ministerial Council of the OECD met on 27 April 1998, and the released press communiqué ratified the ministers' interest in achieving a multilateral comprehensive investment scheme with high levels of liberalization and protection of enterprises. They recognized all existing difficulties and concerns, and decided to have a period of reflection and consultation with all the parties involved. To that end, the work of the Negotiating Group was suspended until October 1998. If not dead, the MAI lay dormant.

Notes

1 Title III provides for legal action in US courts against foreign companies that are 'trafficking' in property nationalized by Cuba in the early 1960s.
2 Title IV provides for the negation of entry into the United States of corporate managers and major shareholders who have been 'trafficking' with nationalized US property in Cuba.
3 See, 'la Vie et la Mort', *La Tribune*, Paris, 27 March 1998; 'El AMI, avance hacía el Totalitarismo del Capital', *PROCESO*, Mexico, 29 March 1998; and 'Ceder Soberanía. El AMI nueva amenaza', *SIEMPRE*, Mexico, 15 April 1998. 'Maybe moving too quickly was one of the problems', statement made by Donald Johnston, Secretary-General of OECD, for Reuters, Paris, 27 April 1998.
4 The D'Amato Kennedy Act refers to an act adopted by the US Congress in May 1996, that puts constraints on foreign investment in countries which support terrorism in the Middle East, Libya and Iran.

6
Household Economy and Morality during the Special Period

*Mona Rosendahl**

Introduction

In 1990, economic crisis struck Cuba. The Soviet Union and the East European countries, which were Cuba's main trading partners, were shifting to a market economy and stopped deliveries to their Cuban counterparts or demanded dollars for exports. This, together with the US trade embargo pushed the country into a severe crisis, which the Cuban leaders named 'the special period'. During 1993–97, when the field visits for this study occurred (Havana, Pinar del Rio, Santiago, and small towns in the countryside of Cuba), the issue uppermost in people's mind was the scarcity and a feeling of uncertainty in the wake of economic decline. *No es facil* (it isn't easy), people said, when they talked about their survival responses to the crisis. During this time the second economy developed explosively. On the streets in the spring and summer of 1997 there were clear signs of the second economy, of which every Cuban had a thorough knowledge but which was seldom mentioned officially. People appeared well-nourished and most were well-dressed and wore shoes. At the same time most people had a job with a salary, the peso equivalent of US\$7–10 per month. Their inexpensive

---

* The empirical material in this chapter emanates from social anthropological fieldwork carried out in 1988–90 in the south-eastern part of Cuba, in a rural municipality which I call Palmera (see Rosendahl, 1997a). Between 1993 and 1997 I made various visits to Havana, Santiago de Cuba and Palmera, spending a total of seven months there. In 1995 I started a new project on cultural and social changes following the economic crisis, funded by the Swedish Humanistisk Samhällsvetenskapliga Forskningsrådet (The Research Council for the Humanities and Social Sciences). As I did not receive a research permit from the Cuban authorities I did not do any formal fieldwork, but have collected material through informal conversations, participation in family life among friends and acquaintances and through secondary sources. Data on household economy was relatively easy to come by, because the difficulties to obtain goods and the scarcity were a constant source of preaccupation and conversation.

monthly food ration lasted only a fortnight. For most of the seven years that the economic crisis had lasted, cloth, clothes, shoes and many other articles had only been available for dollars or very expensively on the black market.

In this chapter I consider the second economy from the point of view of the household. I argue that the change of emphasis for many Cuban families from the planned to the second economy meant an adaptation to a more multifaceted household economy resembling that of poor sectors in market economies. During the special period households could not rely on their salaries alone and buy what they needed in state-owned shops. It was necessary to engage in many different economic activities, among them transactions that were illegal or semi-legal. This change of emphasis brought with it a moral dilemma. People who felt that after 1959 they had more opportunities and a better life were proud to have taken part in the building of this new, more just society. They were reluctant to engage in the illegal and semi-legal transactions, but considered it necessary to do so. This moral dilemma was accentuated by the invisibility of the second economy in official discourse. Earlier, economic aspects of people's lives were publicly discussed to show the success of the revolution. The new situation was seldom mentioned in political speeches and the media, thereby increasing the secrecy and shame that many people felt in regard to the economic transactions that they undertook.

The second economy as a concept is problematic. It includes so many different transactions and activities that it can become meaningless. Following Sik (1992, 1994) and Pérez-López (1995) I define the second economy as related to a socialist political system including both legal transactions in the market sector and semi-legal or illegal transactions carried out on the black market.[1] I use the term second economy here to stress that in the 1990s, from the point of view of the Cuban state, there was definitely a difference between economic activities outside the planned economy and within it. For the Cuban leaders this was mainly an ideological question, as the political leadership regarded the planned economy as the norm. Market aspects of the economy and black-market transactions in particular were seen as deviations forced on the country by external forces. This view of the division between the planned and the second economy spilled over to the perceptions of ordinary people, whether they regarded the planned economy as something desirable or not. From the point of view of the household, on the other hand, the concept second economy is less relevant.[2] Households engage in economic transactions they feel necessary and their principal interest is the reproduction of the social unit. For most people, the concrete difference is between legal and illegal economic activities, since illegal transactions are more risky and can be considered morally questionable. And there was a considerable difference between people's perceptions and actions regarding economic matters before and after the special period. In the most thorough account of the second economy in Cuba, Pérez-López (1995) claims that even before 1989, corruption and transactions in the black market were widespread. There is little evidence to support this view.

The second economy existed before 1989, but its legal and illegal aspects were much less prevalent. One reason for Pérez-López's view might be his use of aggregated data in which information from large cities, principally Havana, dominate. In the countryside corruption and the black market were much less widespread (Rosendahl, 1997a). Another reason for his conclusion might be that he has used secondary sources and, among these, interviews carried out by others, with recent émigrés to the United States. He was aware that this might lead to bias. Émigrés, Pérez-López wrote, 'may exaggerate the severity of the conditions of the first economy and the breadth and depth of the second economy' (1995, p. 79). This is a substantial bias, which cannot be ignored. Judging from what I learned during my fieldwork in 1988–90,[3] people who wanted to leave Cuba were more involved in the second economy than those who continued to live in the country. This could have many reasons. Émigrés were usually more dissatisfied and less loyal to the government and 'the revolution', and, therefore, had no moral qualms about doing business in the black market. They might also have lost their jobs when applying for emigration visas and been forced to enter into the second economy. It is probable that all this gave the émigrés a very different view of the second economy.

In addition, journalists and scholars who visited Cuba before the special period, and who were Pérez-López's sources, usually stayed in Havana where they would be exposed to the black market, and which would lead to a tendency to exaggerate its importance. The difference between before and during the special period is a difference in degree and in kind. There were people working as self-employed and private farmers before 1990, but these were few. The black market existed but it was not very extensive. During the economic crisis many more engaged in activities in the second economy as it expanded in scope. But there is also a difference in kind. Before the special period what could be obtained from the second economy was an addition to what was received from the state. During the special period the predominant part of what many people needed came from the second economy.

The crisis in Cuba

During the late 1980s the planned economy gave Cuban households a rather high standard of living, and most households could live on the salaries that their members earned, which averaged between 150 and 250 pesos a month per person. The *canasta básica*, the food rations given to each individual, cost around 9 pesos and lasted for about two weeks. When their rations were consumed, people could afford to buy additional goods in the state-owned parallel markets which sold food, clothes and household equipment at prices which fluctuated but which were generally much higher than for the rationed goods. Though people complained of scarcity, many felt that they participated in the construction of a new and better society. There was comparatively little corruption on the lower levels of political organizations. The greatest problems prior to the special period lay in the shortage of non-necessary articles, and the poor organization of production and distribution which made obtaining goods the most time-consuming activity of the household economy. Reciprocity was important both socially and economically; for example, the swapping of information about the location of available goods was intense. Mainly due to the US embargo, imported articles like clothes, underwear, make-up and shoes were scarce, and people had to search for them, sometimes even to enter into the black market to get hold of them.

Most people were at some time or other involved in the black market or in the grey zones of the economy. They re-sold *libreta* (ration card) items or bought clothing that a *bisnero* (black marketer) obtained from dollar shops for foreigners, which at that time were off-limits for Cubans. Before the special period, economic crimes existed but in the countryside they were few and not very serious; they included changing pesos illegally, stealing from workplaces, and peasants selling produce outside state channels. According to Pérez-López (1995, p. 110), in 1989 only 4.3 per cent of all workers were engaged in private activities; for example manicurists, carpenters, barbers, hairdressers, seamstresses or farmers. Thus, in the second half of the 1980s the planned economy functioned and gave rather equal opportunities to all, and the state could provide for the people. This to a large extent depended on the aid from and trade with the Soviet Union and other socialist countries, but to the ordinary citizen it seemed as though 'the revolution' was an adequate provider.

When the economic crisis struck, the standard of living fell drastically. During the special period, from 1990 onwards, the political leaders in Cuba stressed that although market-oriented reforms had been introduced, the planned economy was the backbone of the country and socialism was still the only possible political system. Yet the second economy grew extensively during these years, and both its legal and illegal aspects became more and more important for the everyday survival of people (Malinowitz, 1997).

During 1992–94, scarcity was severe, people starved at times and often went hungry, there was very little to buy, and especially the shortage of cooking fat and proteins became critical.[4] The earlier rather heavy Cubans became thin, and a feeling of shock was visible in many people. The distribution of electricity was cut to such an extent that workplaces shut down and households had access to electricity only a few hours a day. People were laid off from work, transportation broke down, and people were desperately looking for food. This meant that many only attended work sporadically and production decreased, thefts and robbery increased, and people fled the country in *balsas* (rafts).

As the economic crisis worsened, the Cuban government took measures to improve the situation. One measure allowed some jobs to be carried out *por cuenta propia*, in self-employment, which meant that people could have a business but could not hire non-family members. They could buy goods in the free markets, and keep the profit made from their enterprises. People sold trinkets, light food, drinks and old books on the street, they repaired cars and made shoes, clothes and adornments. Larger enterprises, notably restaurants (paladares) opened, and people let rooms to foreigners. The possession of dollars was legalized in 1993, after which Cubans could shop in the dollar shops, which grew in number. Tourism expanded through joint ventures and those who worked in that sector received tips in dollars. This was the legal side of the second economy, which was regulated by laws, taxes and fees and supervised by the state (cf. Pastor Jr. and Zimbalist, 1997). But there was also another part of the second economy, which grew rapidly, namely the illegal side – stealing, pilfering, prostitution and black-market activities.

The household economy

At the household level, salaries stayed at almost the same level as before the crisis, while prices rose. During the first years of the crisis many people could live quite well because of their savings, which they used to buy goods on the black market, and they also held reserves of household articles such as sheets, clothes and cloth which lasted for some time. Once these assets were consumed, and there was little to buy in the state markets, household members, principally women, found that considerable time was required to find basic necessities such that shopping became a stressful and tiring activity.

Many items on the market could be obtained but only by paying in dollars, which made it important to have income in this currency. The state opened exchange booths in some of the bigger cities where pesos could be exchanged for dollars, and in the summer of 1997 the rate was 20 to one. Another consequence of the opening of the dollar market to Cubans was that prices for goods, which could be bought in pesos on the legal 'free' market, were also calculated in dollars. At an open market in Havana, for example, hand-made leather sandals were sold for US$12 in 1997. This was inexpensive for a tourist, but for a Cuban buying with pesos the price of 240 pesos was equivalent to a rather high monthly salary. Each person still received a ration card for food, and each household also had one for additional items. The food *libreta* included rice, beans, peas, fat and a small amount of fish or minced soy 'meat'. The rice, beans and peas were said to last 10–15 days, while the fish or meat was sufficient for one meal. As a consequence, a family had to find other means of nourishment for at least half the month.

During the special period, many items on the food *libreta* were not available. The opening of the *agros* (farmers markets) in 1994 was a relief for many households, although the prices were high, because then, at least, there was something to buy (Abbassi, 1997). Families pooled resources and could overcome some of the worst scarcity by buying tubers, meat or vegetables.[5] The *agros* functioned well in the bigger cities, but in the countryside the markets often had little on offer. This could have been partly because people in rural areas had greater access to cultivating and raising animals, and partly because farmers preferred to go to the bigger cities to sell their products for higher prices.

A household economy consists of the incomes and expenditures as well as the activities in which the members engage. In Cuba this could involve cultivation, raising animals, creating alternatives to unaffordable goods, and sharing, gift-giving, bartering and swapping of goods and information. Cuban households were often extended families, comprised of mother, father or the mother's partner, children and some other relatives. Due to the lack of housing, it was common for one or more of the children to live at home as adults, with her or his spouse and children.

My fieldwork focused on an extended family[6] comprised of three households[7] which could serve as an example of how a joint household economy was arranged.[8] This family lived in the outskirts of Havana and was composed of the mother, Alina, her daughter, Edita, and Edita's husband, Pito, who lived in an old house where Alina and her late husband had lived for many decades. A block away Alina's son, Miguel, lived in a house of his own with his wife, Lola, and their three children. Not far away Alina's sister, Agniesa, shared a house with her son, Pedro. In this extended family, Alina and her children and their families were at the core and Alina's sister and nephew in the periphery (Table 6.1).

Table 6.1 The extended household and incomes, Cuba

Household member & income source	*Income per month (pesos)*
Alina, pension from municipality	80
Edita, university teacher	300
Pito, cadre in mass organization	180
Miguel, engineer, foreign company	300
Lola, teacher	250
Agniesa, pension	70
Pedro, nurse	200
Total income	1380

The salaries in this family were equal to or higher than the average in the country. Each member had a *libreta*, which determined the amount of food they could buy each month at the state-owned shops. As for many other families, this household could not live adequately without additional income and by sharing, reciprocating and bartering with other households. In the spring and summer of 1997 the family joined in several different activities to increase their household income. Miguel and his family had a rather big garden with trees that gave fruits during most of year, and at harvest-times Miguel gave fruit to his mother and sister and sometimes to his aunt. The women made sweets from guava and mangoes, and the limes were used to season dishes. In the spring of 1997 Miguel also raised a pig in his garden; the rest of the family brought any leftovers they had to feed the pig. When he finally slaughtered the pig, Miguel gave meat to his mother, sister and his aunt. His mother and sister received a big part, because they had contributed quite a lot of food to it and looked after it when Miguel, his wife and children could not.

In July, Alina's and Agniesa's brother, who had lived in the United States after the revolution, visited the family. The brother and his wife brought gifts for everyone, mainly clothes and shoes. While visiting they bought food, liquor and hygienic articles for everyone, both at the dollar shops and the *agro* (farmers' market). To reciprocate, the different members of the family invited the relatives to their houses for dinner or lunch and took them to visit old friends. Miguel, who worked for a foreign company, received from the company every month a collection of goods which included shampoo, soap, detergent and sometimes clothes. He would share these with the family, principally with his mother's household. In May, Edita was chosen to go abroad for a job for three weeks. When she returned, she brought three suitcases bursting with items she had bought – clothes, shoes, hygienic articles, underwear, some household equipment and, to the great joy of her teen-age children, a stereo. She distributed gifts to everyone in her husband's family and also to her own family, some of her friends and workmates. She had used most of the money she earned, but she had lived very inexpensively while abroad and still had some cash left that the family would save for a rainy day. She complained, however, that she had to pay 25 per cent of her earnings to the University as a fee.[9]

In this manner, sharing incomes, the family lived quite well. The members who earned dollars contributed more, as dollars were the most important vehicle to living well. Every member made a contribution. Pito, for example, who worked in a mass organization, had access to a car, which he sometimes used to transport his relatives. Pedro, who worked in a hospital, helped people jump the queue to see a doctor. He then received presents from grateful patients, which he shared with his family. The two old women had few goods to contribute, but did necessary chores such as collecting rationed goods, and cooking and mending for the extended family. Below I will discuss these and some other ways that households have of coping in times of economic crisis.

The invisible second economy

In 1997 the second economy was the crucial source for Cuban households. Two concepts, *inventar* and *resolver*, illuminate people's increasingly difficult struggle to cope with the crisis. *Inventar* literally means to invent, and refers to all activities and transactions in which people used their imagination to find solutions to the lack of food, clothing and other necessities. During the special period there was a peak in people's inventiveness. They crocheted new shoes onto old soles, made detergent from twigs, created new dishes with the meagre ingredients that were available, and cultivated food on small plots between highrise houses. They also raised animals in yards and on balconies, and remade clothes. *Resolver* has a starker meaning of 'taking care of' or 'solving', and was often a euphemism for illegal or semi-illegal activities, patron–client relationships and corruption. People used their positions, their relations with people having access to scarce goods and services. They stepped outside the legal boundaries to obtain advantages. Most people were proud of their ability to *inventar*, but more ambiguous about their efforts to *resolver*. The two concepts stressed culturally appreciated abilities of flexibility and adaptation to any situation, always seeking to 'making the best' of it.

Reciprocity and sharing had been an important part of the household economy for some time (see Rosendahl,1997a). Prior to the crisis reciprocity was upheld partly for economic reasons, to alleviate scarcity, but also for social reasons, to maintain relationships with neighbours, friends and relatives. In 1997, reciprocity and sharing was a necessity and had changed its forms. Most families immediately consumed the foodstuffs they obtained, both because they had only a small freezer in their refrigerator and because most Cubans like fresh food. Few families could afford to buy meat, fish or other fresh food every day. Thus, supplies depended on constant reciprocity and sharing among families. The extended family became even more important than before the crisis, and sharing occurred primarily among relatives. Trust (*confianza*) was a vital part of reciprocity because of the importance of illegal and semi-legal activities.

Anita and Papito lived in a small town in the south of Cuba. He was retired and she worked as a teacher. They lived in a highrise building, and for years they had cultivated tubers and vegetables and raised chickens and pigs on a small plot outside the building. In the summer of 1997 when their pig was going to be slaughtered, Anita invited her sister and brother-in-law to visit. Papito invited two of his adult sons, a neighbour and a friend. Early in the morning the men killed the pig and began to cut up the meat. They started a fire and fried the rind in a large cauldron to extract the fat (*manteca*) and to make *chicharrones* (crackling), a favourite snack. One of Papito's brothers came around with some food bananas. Anita's sister took care of the blood and rinsed the intestines, then she and Anita stuffed the intestines with a paste of blood and spices to make *morcilla* (blood sausage) while the men were working out in the lot with the meat and drinking rum. The women made lunch and all the men who were helping were invited to eat pork fricassee, rice and beans and tubers. During their work in the lot several men and women visited the men to ask Papito if he was selling some of the meat, but received a negative answer. After the slaughtering, however, all the men who had participated received a part of the meat. In the following days Anita and Papito also gave gifts of meat to others relatives and friends. At times Anita sighed and seemed reluctant to give away especially the *manteca* (fat), but both she and her husband seemed to feel that it was necessary and out of the question that they should refuse. A few times, friends and neighbours also came to the family and went away with a full *jaba* (shopping bag) after a hushed conversation in the kitchen. Whether they received meat as a gift or were sold some meat I do not know, since I was not invited to take part in these transactions. However, the distribution of pork was a way for the family to keep up a reciprocal relationship with relatives and friends, and to ascertain that they would in turn receive help or goods when a relative or friend had something to spare. These kind of transactions between households on a daily basis – barter, gift-giving and selling of surplus – had the most impact on ordinary people during the economic crisis.

Remittances from abroad were legalized at various times after 1959, and were an important addition to household economies for those with relatives abroad. During the special period, money and gifts sent from relatives, mainly in the United States, often became the key to whether a family lived well. These gifts of money also became a means of earning money for the messengers. People received 20–30 dollars to carry a package from Florida to Havana, and it was said that those who did so paid for their trips with these fees. Some émigrés sent regular money gifts which resulted in a stable addition to the standard of living of their relatives in Cuba, but the occasional gifts from relatives who visited, or which were brought by messengers, were more common.

Tania and her mother, Rita, received a telephone call from Rita's sister in the United States, who asked for the shoe-sizes of family members so that she could send them shoes. Tania was ecstatic as she waited for the shoes. 'I'm sure they will send the modern kind, I want one of those pairs that look like slippers with high square heels', she said many times. When the shoes arrived they were a great disappointment to Tania – they were modern but not the kind that Tania wanted, those were sent to her sister. Tania cried out of disappointment and refused to use the shoes. Her mother found this ridiculous in a grown woman and scolded her for being ungrateful. When she understood that Tania would indeed not use the shoes, she phoned one of her distant friends and offered her the shoes for a price which was set according to the prices for the same sort of shoes in the dollar shop US$17. The friend bought the shoes and Tania received the money to buy a pair that she liked. Naturally, Rita's sister in the United States was never told of this altercation. This is one example of how goods that reached a household were converted into a useful resource.

Sociolismo[10] is a concept alluding to informal relations, a type of corruption, which existed within the political arena in Cuba. It could be seen as a type of patron–client relationship, in which a person with access to scarce resources such as jobs, education and goods enters into a relationship with a person who needs those items. Before 1990, in countryside Palmera where I carried out fieldwork, these transactions existed and were done quite openly on a rather small scale. It was often difficult to know when these were politically sanctioned dealings between politicians and their constituents, or more illicit transactions. Political leaders commonly helped arrange for goods and services which were not accessible to the ordinary citizen through other channels. Gifts were seldom given in direct reciprocity, but were passed to a politician from people when they had something to give, as an insurance for crises to come. Most political leaders in Palmera had a standard of living similar to that of their constituents, which made it improbable that they had any considerable income from these dealings. Furthermore, people trusted many of their political leaders and did not consider them corrupt. During the special period, the demand for this type of transaction increased (cf. Pérez López, 1995, pp. 101–2; Font, 1997, pp. 43–4). Earlier, those with access to coveted resources were mainly men in the political hierarchy and workers in state enterprises. During the economic crisis this changed, and the most attractive partners in *sociolismo* were not primarily people in the political system, but those who had access to hard currency or other goods and services which had become scarce. Medical care, which functioned very well before 1990, deteriorated during the special period principally because of lack of medicine and hospital equipment. Quite a few doctors and nurses left their jobs to work in the tourist sector where they could earn dollars. Also, it seemed as if scarcity and stress in the wake of the crisis made people fall ill more frequently, such that the pressure on hospitals and doctors was great. Medical personnel, like others, had greater need for additional income, so access to a doctor or special treatment through personal relations or by giving 'presents' to medical staff increased.

In the summer of 1997 in Havana I heard many stories of doctors and nurses who had helped friends and friends of friends to gain access to medicine and hospital visits receiving presents and promises of help in return. Those who did not have contacts in the right places had problems in obtaining medical care. I met a woman who came with her son to Havana from a small village in the west of Cuba; the son was ill and needed to see a specialist at a hospital in the capital. He had a remittance to this hospital but had waited for a very long time without being called. His mother then used a contact she had to pass the queue, but this contact was a guard at the hospital who did not really have any access to the doctors. The woman brought with her presents of food for the guard and even gave him some money, and he promised to talk to a doctor he knew. The woman and her son stayed with relatives and waited each day for the guard to call them with news about the meeting with the doctor, but he did not succeed in getting an appointment with the doctor and never called. After a week the mother and her son had to return to their village, without their gifts and without an appointment with the doctor.

Pilfering or stealing from workplaces was another way of alleviating the scarcity of everyday life. This was done before the special period, and the articles were sold on the black market, though on a relatively small scale compared to the years after 1990. My informants told me that during the special period it was quite common for those who worked in shops where the rationed goods were sold to put aside a part of the product and sell it literally behind the counter to trusted customers, at a higher price. If they themselves did not steal or pilfer, people usually experienced these illegal activities through door-to-door selling. People came to sell eggs, toilet paper, carpets, ham and many other products. Some of these were agricultural products, which farmers themselves produced and sometimes sold, or sold to middlemen who went door-to-door re-selling. This was not legal, though those who sold the items did not pay the fees that other self-employed tradesmen had to do. Often, however, items had been stolen from workplaces.

Late one evening Iliana met a neighbour in the staircase of their building. He worked at a cafeteria and asked her to come to his apartment because he had something to show her. Iliana accompanied him to his home, where he offered to sell her a large sausage. She said that she was interested, and would go home for her wallet. She immediately went to her sister, who lived nearby, to ask if she wanted to share the sausage which would cost 70 pesos. Her sister agreed, Iliana bought the sausage, which they divided. *Está acabando con aquella cafeteria!* (He sure is finishing off that coffee shop!), she joked. Iliana said that she did not like buying stolen goods, but it was a unique opportunity to obtain a virtually non-existent item. Though quite high, the price was lower than in the *agro*. When items were sold which were not available on the market to ordinary people, the price was higher because there was no competition, and because of the risk of selling those items. To spread the risk, the illegal items were often divided and resold many times, so that the item when it reached the buyer could not be traced. Together with different kinds of reciprocity this was probably[11] the most common manner of engaging in the second economy. Pérez-López (1995, pp. 100–1) maintained that diversion (*desvío*) and short-changing customers were common behaviour in the black market before 1990, but my research suggested that this increased enormously during the special period. Due to the sensitive character of these transactions, 'trust' was of great importance. People who were not trusted, for example those seen as too close to the government, were not allowed to enter into these transactions.

That many of these transactions were illegal was recognized by the participants, but in some instances it was difficult for people to judge whether transactions were legal or not. The authorities turned a blind eye to much of the illegal economy because it served as part of household survival strategies. Therefore, illegal transactions could go on for many years, until one day the authorities might decide to enforce an existing but dormant law, or introduce new legislation. *Jineterismo*, tourist hustling, occurred on a grand scale during the special period. (*Jineteros* were the people who made transactions with tourists, guiding, selling cigars, paintings, and even their bodies.) At an early stage in the special period government officials publicly acknowledged that prostitution and hustling took place, but initially they claimed that prostitution was a luxury activity engaged in by young women who sought adventure. In 1996 the government carried out raids to drive prostitutes off the streets, but not until 1997 was there a law passed prohibiting the activity. This did not stop prostitution, but removed some of its more blatant forms from public places.

When legislation was introduced or enforced, the laws often made those engaged in the transaction go 'underground' to continue illegally (cf. Pérez-López, 1995, pp. 10–11). For example, a man who had a *paladar* decided to close it when he felt that the fees and taxes that he had to pay were too high. He claimed that he paid 2100 pesos, plus US$600 each month in taxes and fees. He worked with his wife and children in the *paladar* and bought raw materials at a dollar shop or *agro*, the receipts for which had to be submitted to a tax controller. With all this he felt that his profits had become too small compared to the work he put into his restaurant, so he decided to close it and start doing 'catering' instead. Because he had friends within the foreign business community in Havana he could obtain orders for meals that he would serve in his home, without having an open restaurant. Thus he could go on with his business, now 'underground', without paying the fees and taxes that he did before. In 1996 and 1997 several *paladares* were closed by the authorities because of illegal activities or by the owners themselves.

The economic activities mentioned above were crucial to all households, yet the state seldom officially acknowledged these economic transactions, making it an invisible economy.[12] A large part of these transactions, like reciprocity, bartering and black-market transactions, were carried out within and between households. Because they were particularly associated with women and their domestic unpaid household labour, some authors have stressed its invisible character, including activities which are usually not enumerated in the national accounts (Bryson, 1996). Large-scale legal activities in the second economy, such as joint ventures and tourist enterprises, were explicitly recognized by the political leaders in speeches and the media; but other, illegal, second economy activities were only implicitly highlighted when sanctions were applied. There were often reports on television of big thefts from factories and other workplaces, with the authorities using these broadcasts as warnings to show that the perpetrators were being caught. Never discussed publicly, however, was the core issue: that the second economy had become the most important part of the household economy, the very means of survival, bringing with it economic, social and moral problems.[13]

Moral aspects

For many Cubans who had experienced poverty and oppression before 1959, participation in the collective building of a new, revolutionary society was more than a response to the country's leaders. It was a real opportunity for integration into society, to live with dignity, and help develop a better life. Therefore, they were reluctant to take part in illegal transactions. They might buy on the black market or take some small items from work, but strongly condemned more substantial pilfering and stealing. However, as the economic crisis deepened, most people were forced to take part in these illegal or semi-illegal transactions, and this led to a change in opinions.

Maribel and her mother, who lived together, struggled constantly to obtain the goods that they needed. Maribel, who had a demanding job, was critical of the Cuban government and socialism, saying that she did not have time to search for food for hours each day, when the rationed food was finished. Maribel's mother was old and ill, and thus could not go to the market herself. Maribel made contacts with people who sold 'black-market' milk, eggs, chicken and other items door-to-door. Her mother objected to this, often sending the salespeople away. This made Maribel furious, so that she quarrelled with her mother who refused to eat the food that Maribel bought 'on the black market'. 'She does not like counter-revolutionary cows', Maribel joked, when her mother often refused the fresh milk and, instead, used milk powder bought in the state shop. Maribel could understand why her mother objected, but she said that she did not have time to follow that morality. Maribel's brother, a party member, also quarrelled with his mother about this issue. He argued that although he knew black-market transactions were not correct, he would continue to buy black-market food if this was his only way of feeding his children.

This was a very common outlook in Cuba in the summer of 1997. People's feelings of alienation towards their own society had increased. When the crisis began, they did what they felt was necessary to support themselves and their families, even if they did not approve of what they did. With this new practice, their view of what was acceptable slowly changed. The more they engaged in the illegal and semi-illegal transactions, the more they convinced themselves that what they were doing was necessary and right. At the same time corruption increased, and leaders were judged as less and less credible. This led to apathy, and offered an excuse to do what earlier had been judged as wrong.

The attitude of many people can be described as a 'suspension of the ethical',[14] analysed by Scheper-Hughes (1992) in her book on the attitude to death in a poor area in Brazil. Many Cubans suspended the ethical. They did not change their moral outlook completely; many still condemned the illegal transactions, and many more found it difficult and disturbing to take part in these activities. However, they found excuses for doing so because it was extremely difficult to survive by using legal channels only. This generated stress and anxiety in people about their own actions. At the beginning of the special period there were people who felt shame that their country and the revolution might move backwards (see Rosendahl, 1997b), and these people attempted not to use the illegal second economy, but most of them had to succumb.

Conclusion

The situation of Cuban households during the special period could be interpreted as an example of the 'the formal economy creates its own informality' (Adler Lomnitz, 1988, p. 54). In a planned economy, the state should provide for the citizens by redistributing resources through salaries, medical care and schooling. But in Cuba the provision by the state was insufficient, and even before the special period the scarcity and disorganization of the planned system created a second economy with reciprocity, patron–client relationships and illegal and semi-illegal transactions (Pérez-López, 1995; Rosendahl, 1997a). Searching for goods, buying and selling on the black market, attempting to obtain information about where goods could be bought, and inventing food and other necessities, was earlier done to improve the economic situation. During the special period, when the state could no longer provide for its citizens, economic activities in the second economy increased and became crucial for the survival of families. A major difference compared to the time before 1990 was that in 1997 most families did not have sufficient money to buy what they needed, so that they spent considerable time and effort to find economic solutions.

The extended family, relatives and close friends became increasingly an important means of survival, in which all members contributed to the household and shared their assets. Not all households engaged in all of the above-mentioned activities, but all found it necessary to do many things to support themselves. The women spent many hours a day shopping, often going to markets far away (especially in the bigger cities) and returning empty-handed. They tried to cook inexpensive food, sew, mend and make inventions to save money. The men of the household looked for food wherever they were, cultivated, raised animals and bartered goods when that was possible. Everyone in the family used her or his networks to enter into reciprocal relationships.

During the special period the household economy for many Cubans became similar to what one would associate with the economy of the poor in capitalist countries, where people usually take on various jobs and complementary incomes to survive. In Cuba people did not hold many jobs, but they entered into a 'wheeling-and-dealing' which most people had not done in previous decades. This wheeling and dealing often took place in illegal or semi-illegal arenas, which made people worried about being discovered and denounced to the police. The element of trust was more important than before in these relationships, and people were more careful with whom they entered into transactions.

The moral dilemmas turned the economic crisis into a crisis of confidence in the political leadership. Before the special period the state, often called simply the Party or Fidel, could claim that its rhetoric was manifest in everyday life. 'The revolution' was, as the leaders said, continuously developing into higher stages (Rosendahl, 1992). The state could provide for the people by guaranteeing them work or social security, by redistributing rationed food and household items, through low rents and access to free medical care and schooling. In this context, the legitimacy of the leadership was high. During the special period, most Cubans found that the state could not provide for the people; that in their rhetoric the leaders never spoke of what people felt as the most vital aspect of their life, the struggle for survival. People felt uncertain about what was right and wrong as they perceived a difference between the rhetoric of the leaders and their actions. They began to question the legitimacy of the system. The shift from a planned to a more market-oriented economy led to a more unequal society in which some Cubans, especially in the bigger cities, became prosperous and led very different lifestyles compared to the majority of the population. Those who had been most loyal to the government felt that they lost the most, because they refused as far as possible to enter into activities that would have given them advantages.

As Adler Lomnitz (1998) emphasized, informal economic activities are culturally embedded. In Cuba, external circumstances have been important factors in triggering the economic activities of the special period, but these activities often reactivated or strengthened already existing relationships, norms and networks. The informal activities became less important during a time when the standard of living was high and the state could provide; the second economy was a way of supplementing what was received from the planned economy. During the special period, however, when scarcity became 'normal', people turned to the cultural values of reciprocity, patronage, inventing (*inventar*), resolving (*resolver*) and trust (*confianza*). As the state could no longer provide enough, the household, relatives, friends and acquaintances became much more important.[15] Flexibility and the skill of seizing the moment, which has always been important in times of scarcity, became a necessity for many Cubans. Combining all the opportunities that were given from day to day, buying something inexpensive in the market, receiving a gift of tubers from a relative, selling something valuable or letting a room to a tourist, people could live rather well but also very precariously, never being sure of how they would meet their daily needs.

Notes

1 According to this definition the same activities in a market economy are called an 'informal economy'.
2 For a similar discussion of the concept 'informal economy', see Morales (1997).
3 I did not explicitly study this aspect of Cuban society, though.
4 This led to an epidemic which affected the eyes and legs of many Cubans.
5 In May 1997 a pound of pork cost 45 pesos, a pound of ham 50 pesos, cucumber three pesos each, mango 2–4 pesos each, plantains 50 centavos each, and avocado 7 pesos per pound (in July).
6 I define the whole group as an extended family, as they have close emotional and economic consanguine and affinal kinship relations.
7 Here I define the household as those who live together in the same dwelling.
8 For the sake of anonymity this is a family which does not exist as such. I have put together various families into one, although every person exists and every event described has happened.
9 Each person working at the University who earns money abroad has to pay a percentage (25–50 per cent) of the earnings to the University.
10 This satirical concept alludes both to socialism and *socio*, a word for partner, buddy and 'chum'.
11 Because of the nature of the transactions, it is impossible to know about their exact extent in the second economy.
12 Galasi and Sik (1988) talk about invisible incomes in the Hungarian context but do not include 'non-monetary corruption' and 'intra- and inter-household activities'.
13 At the seminar where this paper was discussed, some of the Cuban participants argued that the second economy is indeed discussed officially. They were not able to convince me, however, that the point that I think is most important, namely the role that the second economy plays in most households, has been officially discussed.
14 This expression was coined by Martin Buber (1977, chapter 7).
15 This also happens in a market economy in recessions where family and informal economic activities become more important.

7
Labour Markets and Income Distribution during Crisis and Reform

Rikke Fabienke

Introduction

After decades of continuous reduction of income inequality, Cuba at the end of the 1990s seemed to be back at its pre-revolutionary stage of high inequality. Due to the economic crisis of the 1990s, the government was no longer able to provide the population with the same amount of social transfers as before. As a result, the importance of personal income increased. Parallel to this development the Cuban labour market structure underwent a considerable diversification, and different parts of the economy began to offer highly unequal opportunities for income generation. Complementary sources of income deriving from shadow economic activities and remittances, essential for the well-being of large part of the population, further began to distort the transparency of income distribution. Official household surveys on the topic have been classified, and in general only very little has been known about the correlation between the changing labour market structures and the rising income inequality. Nevertheless, in this chapter I will try to shed some light on the recent changes within the two fields. Towards the end I will try to give an estimate of what segments of the Cuban population have been winners and losers from the structural changes.

Social achievements of the revolution

Reforms within a number of fields since the first days of the Revolutionary Government have led to diminishing inequalities among the Cuban population. Among these are free and universal access to health care and education, a rationing system which has ensured the coverage of basic needs for everybody, life-time employment guaranteed by the state, and agrarian and other reforms which have equalized the levels of income between different groups of the population (e.g. between rural and urban workers).

The effect of these initiatives is reflected in a number of indicators. The reduction of income inequality is, among other things, illustrated by the lowering of the Gini coefficient which dropped from 0.55 in pre-revolutionary Cuba in 1953, to a level of 0.22 in 1986.[1] Also, the concentration of income among the top 5 per cent of the population has dropped significantly during the same period of time (see Table 7.1 below). Universal health care has indirectly contributed to the rise in life expectancy from 65 years at the beginning of the 1960s to 75.5 years in 1995, and the drop in infant mortality from 42 per 1000 live births in 1962 to 9.4 in 1995 (UNDP, 1997b, p. 54). Cuba's public education system is often mentioned as one of the best in Latin America (LACCAR, 1999, p. 8), and human resources have for many years been a valuable asset for the country. For many years it has been relatively easy for the Cuban government to prioritize social spending since the country, due to its relations with the Soviet Union and the COMECON countries, has received assistance and has been enjoying very favourable terms of trade. However, by the 1990s the external conditions changed abruptly.

With the collapse of the socialist camp in 1989–91, the Cuban economy was thrown into one of its worst crises ever. The economy experienced severe drops within almost all fields. From 1989 to 1993 (which was the year the crisis peaked), foreign currency income and soft financing were reduced by some US$700 million. Old trade channels broke down and new markets only slowly developed. As a consequence, in 1993 the volume of exports was no more than 52.6 per cent of 1989 levels, and the 1993 volume of imports had dropped to some 35.9 per cent of 1989 volumes. By 1992, the terms of trade were no more than 50.6 per cent of the 1989 level, and between 1989 and 1993 GDP decreased by more than 30 per cent (CEPAL, 1997, pp. 5, 366).

During the years of crisis, income inequality has increased considerably. Though the government has admitted that disparities have grown, there are no official figures available on the current income distribution which, indeed, is also very difficult to estimate. Mesa-Lago (1998, p. 871) gives a few illustrating examples of income inequalities, but a Cuban economist from the *Instituto Nacional de Investigaciones Económicas*, INIE (Havana), Quintana, has made a more systematic attempt to estimate income distribution in the mid-1990s. Quintana (1995a) estimates two variants of income

Table 7.1 Gini coefficients for income and percentage of income generated by the top 5 per cent of the population, Cuba (selected years)

	1953	*1962*	*1978*	*1986*
Gini coefficient	0.55	0.35	0.27	0.22
Top 5 per cent	26.5	12.7	9.5	10.1

Source: 1953, 1962 and 1978 figures from Brundenius (1984, pp. 113–16); 1986 figures from Zimbalist and Brundenius (1989, pp. 161–2).

distributions (based on monthly average incomes of 240 pesos and 290 pesos, as shown in Table 7.2 below).

If these estimates reflect reality they imply tremendous income gaps. Based on Quintana's figures, I have calculated the Gini coefficient for 1995 which shows a shocking increase by 33 Gini points to 0.55 from 1986 to December 1995. In the same period, the share of income earned by the top 5 per cent of the population shows an increase by some 20 percentage points to 31 per cent of total income. The tendency towards rising inequality in Cuba, illustrated by the rise in the Gini coefficient, is supported by a growing concentration of wealth reflected in the pattern of deposits in personal savings accounts. In June 1995, 13.6 per cent of the people with savings accounts held 82.4 per cent of deposits.[2] Since deposits in ordinary savings accounts represented 64 per cent of all accumulated liquidity in June 1995 (Carranza et.al., 1996:97), the above distribution of deposits quite unambiguously reflects a skewed distribution of wealth.

The Gini coefficient is one of the most frequently used ways of illustrating distribution (Meier, 1995, p. 17). It is an easy way to get a first impression of the degree of inequality, but one should, however, be cautious comparing Gini coefficients from different studies. Firstly, the definition of income may vary from one estimate to the other, and, secondly, the Gini coefficient in itself does not explain why income distribution has developed the way it has. In his article, Quintana does not present the method he has used to calculate the estimates, and they therefore merely illustrate the general trend towards increased inequality rather than pretending to show exact figures.

The development within a number of social fields seems to have continued in a positive direction despite the crisis. However, there are also fields

Table 7.2   Estimated monthly income distribution, Cuba, 1995

Groups	Average monthly income (pesos)	Variant I 240 pesos/ month (1000 people)	Variant 2 290 pesos/ month (1000 people)
0–50	40	2144	1689
51–100	75	2522	2291
101–200	150	2778	2806
201–300	250	1392	1517
301–400	400	1221	1442
501–800	650	621	778
801–1200	1000	263	351
1201–1500	1350	77	108
1501–2000	1750	56	82
2000–	6000	49	77
Total		11123	11123

Source: Quintana (1995a), p. 48.

where the development seems to mirror the increasing complexities of the new labour market structures, and others whose development during the crisis partly explains why personal income has become more important for Cubans.

While trying to integrate the economy into a highly globalized world, the Cuban government has sought to distribute the negative effects of the crisis as equally as possible. In 1996, the share of social expenditures[3] in GDP amounted to almost as much as before the crisis, namely 22.4 per cent (compared to 23 per cent in 1989). During some of the toughest years of the crisis, social expenditures reached as much as 30 per cent of GDP (29.1 and 30.1 per cent in 1992 and 1993, respectively) (ONE, 1998, p. 99). However, since GDP, with respect to 1989, dropped significantly during the years of crisis, social spending in real terms could not avoid decreasing. Furthermore, some fields have had higher priority than others, and the effect of the budgetary changes has therefore varied.

Throughout the period 1990–96, budgets for health, in nominal terms as well as in per cent of GDP, have been higher than they were in 1989. The high priority of health has meant that life expectancy, despite the harshness of the economic crisis, continued to rise, and in 1995 it reached 75.5 years (UNDP, 1998, p. 129). The infant mortality rate also continued to improve during the crisis, and was as low as 9.4 per 1000 live births in 1995 (UNDP, 1997b, p. 54).[4] Also in comparison with other transition economies Cuba has performed quite well within these fields. In 1995 life expectancy was, on average, not more than 70.3 years for Eastern Europe and 68.6 years for the former Soviet republics (dropping from 70.8 and 69.9 years in 1990, respectively). The lowest figure is found in Russia where life expectancy in 1995 was only 65.5 years, and no more than 59.2 for men (compared to 73.9 in Cuba).[5] In 1994, the infant mortality rate per 1000 live births was, on average, 14.8 for Eastern Europe and 21.1 for the Soviet republics (dropping from 20.2 and 27.5 in 1990, respectively).[6]

Though budgets for education in per cent of GDP have risen during some of the years of crisis, budgets in nominal terms have dropped throughout all of the 1990s, and were in 1996 14 per cent lower than in 1989. The number of students enrolled at high-school and university level dropped remarkably from 1990–91 to 1996–97; in 1996–97 the number of high-school students was only 71 per cent of the 1990–91 level. Of this figure, the number of students enrolled in the pre-university in 1996–97 was only 39 per cent of the 1990–91 level. In 1996–97 enrollment of university students was 54 per cent lower than in 1990–91 (ONE, 1998, p. 298). One explanation of this development could be that the government has decided to take in fewer students at these levels of education; but another explanation could be that young Cubans during the last few years have seen too many examples of professionals not being able to make ends meet with the income from a job within their profession, and too many examples of people making huge sums performing unskilled work within the 'right' economies. This imbalance is one of the many aspects of the new labour market structures, and it will be further examined later on in the chapter.

The state's universal provision of basic foodstuffs and goods through the rationing system, *la libreta*, has traditionally been sufficient for Cubans to satisfy their most basic needs. However, during the years of crisis the rationing system has been weakened remarkably. Whereas expenses on food (except meals outside the home) only accounted for 23 to 59 per cent of income (dependent on the kind of household) in 1980 (Brundenius, 1984, p. 112), most households have had severe difficulties in making ends meet during the years of crisis. According to the Cuban economist Togores from the *Centro de Estudios de la Economía Cubana*, CEEC (Havana), a basket of 12 products calculated to last for a month, in the mid-1990s only lasted for approximately ten days. In order to cover the daily needs for the last 20 days of the month, Cubans were forced to turn to alternative markets where goods are sold at market prices in either pesos (as in the agricultural markets) or hard currency (as in the various foreign currency recovery outlets, the so-called *Tiendas de Recaudación de Divisas*, TRDs) (interview, 1998). Products sold in the TRDs have had a 240 per cent VAT imposed on them by the government,[7] and in general prices in the alternative markets are 10–100 times higher than at the market for rationed goods (see Tables 7.3 and 7.4 below).

Considering that a Cuban average family consists of four persons (ONE, 1995, table V-2), and in many cases has a monthly income of around

Table 7.3 Prices of selected products in different markets (in pesos), Cuba, 1996

Product	Unit	Subsidized price (*la libreta*)	Free market price	Ratio market/subsidized
Milk	Litre	0.25	5.00	20.0
Rice	pound	0.24	4.30	17.9
Bread	one	0.05	1.00	20.0
Egg	one	0.15	1.50	10.0
Beans	pound	0.30	8.10	27.0
Butter	pound	0.30	30.00	100.0
Meat	pound	6.00	20.00	3.3
Sugar (brown)	pound	0.08	2.50	31.3
Sugar (white)	pound	0.14	4.00	28.6
Salt	pound	0.10	3.00	30.0
Soap (washing)	one	0.20	10.00	50.0
Soap (bathing)	one	0.25	8.00	32.0
Fish	pound	0.50	5.00	10.0

Source: Cuban public ration book, test sample of the free market (Oficina Nacional de Estadísticas); estimates by Togores (1997).

Table 7.4   Selected[9] monthly basket per capita, 1996 (in pesos)

Products	Expenses, subsidized prices (mercado normado)	Expenses market prices
Rice	1.44	25.80
Bread	1.50	30.00
Egg	2.10	21.00
Beans	0.45	12.15
Oil	0.20	30.00
Meat	3.00	20.00
Sugar (brown)	0.24	7.50
Sugar (white)	0.42	12.00
Salt	0.10	3.00
Soap (washing)	0.20	10.00
Soap (bathing)	0.25	8.00
Fish	1.00	10.00
Total	10.90	189.45

Source: Test sample of the free market, Oficina Nacional de Estadísticas, Cuban public ration book; estimates by Togores (1997).

400 pesos (more or less a traditional average wage of two adults, as will be shown below), it becomes clear that around another 400 pesos/month are needed to provide a family with the basic necessities. It is clear that many Cubans, at least when the crisis peaked, were unable to provide for a nutritious diet. Statistics show that the daily calorie intake had dropped to some 1863 calories, covering only 78 per cent of daily needs, in 1993 (UNDP, 1997b, pp. 56–7). Cubans have to an increasing degree been obliged to supplement the universally distributed but insufficient amount of rationed goods by monetary means.[8] Cuban wage differentials have traditionally been quite small, but the immense changes which the country has undergone during the 1990s have implied that different economies today offer highly unequal opportunities for generation of the now more important personal income.

Cuba's new labour market structure

From 1989 to 1996, non-state employment has grown from around 6 to 28 per cent of total employment (dependent on the estimate), and a range of new economies/sources of income have gained importance. Table 7.5 shows an overall division of the Cuban labour market into four economies. Since especially the number of people within the private non-agricultural economy (the self-employed) is discussed, I have chosen to put forward two variants of an employment structure: variant 1 where the number of self-employed is equal to the number of licences issued as at 31 December 1996, and variant 2 where each of the licenceholders have been allotted two assistants. Some authors use the term 'second economy' about non-state (and illegal) activities (e.g. Pérez-López, 1995), but I find the term too all-embracing to give a balanced picture of reality and therefore have chosen not to use it. In order to better understand the relationship between labour market structure and income distribution it is necessary to break some of the above categories into smaller, more homogeneous entities which reflect opportunities for income generation. In Table 7.6 I try to give a more complete picture of the present labour market structures and of the most important sources of complementary income, as I perceive it.[10] Income from complementary sources in most cases 'overlaps' that from employment in terms of recipients, and to a higher or lower extent adds to people's employment-based income.

The state economy may be divided into two sectors which function according to different rules and thus also remunerate differently, namely the 'traditional economy'[11] and the 'emerging economy'. The traditional economy comprises traditional public services (non-tradeables) and large part of state industry, for example public administration, education, health, defence, transportation, utilities, state agriculture, the sugar industry, food processing industries and most other industry. By far the largest part of transactions are in pesos.[12]

The term emerging economy (*economía emergente*) was developed by a group of researchers at the INIE in 1992–93.[13] The term appeared with the creation of a group of financially and managerially autonomous para-statal enterprises, mainly operating (in hard currency) in the internationalized part of the Cuban economy. The companies usually take the legal shape of different kinds of para-statal limited companies, with the most well-known being the so-called *sociedades anónimas*. In broad terms, the emerging economy may be said to comprise high-priority state activities which either reduce the state's hard currency costs or generate hard currency (like tourism, dollar-store retailing (*exportaciones en frontera*), export–import trade, and servicing of diplomatic corps and international organizations) (Ritter, 1995, p. 118).

There are no offical figures from which to deduce the relative share of the two parts of the overall state economy. However, on the basis of information from the Minister of Economy and Planning, José Luis Rodriguez (CIEM, 1998, p. 7), I have made a rough estimate showing that the traditional economy makes up some 45–49 per cent of total employment, whereas the emerging economy makes up around 26–29 per cent of total employment (see Table 7.6).

The joint ventures between the Cuban state and foreign companies also often take the form of *sociedades anónimas*. Partnerships with foreign companies have been allowed in Cuba since 1982, but foreign investment was quite limited during the first years. Not until there was a serious need for

Table 7.5 Changes in overall employment structure, Cuba (per cent of total civilian employment)

	1989	*1996 Variant 1*	*1996 Variant 2*
State	94.1	77.8	71.3
Mixed	–	3.1	2.8
Private	4.3	9.4	17.1
Cooperative	1.6	9.6	8.9

Sources: By the author. 1989 data from Comité Estatal de Estadísticas (1989, p. 111). 1996, data from ONE (1998, pp. 109, 194), Ministerio de Trabajo y Seguridad Social, and CEPAL (1997, p. 378).

Table 7.6 Employment-based and complementary sources of income in Cuba, end-1990s (figures and percentages relate to 1996)

		Variant 1		*Variant 2*	
	Economy/ ownership form	*Number employed*	*% of employment*	*Number employed*	*% of employment*
Employment-based income	Stae				
	traditional	1 775 025	49.0%	1 775 025	45.0%
	emerging[a]	1 042 475	28.8%	1 042 475	26.3%
	Joint ventures[b]	110 300	3.1%	110 300	2.8%
	Private				
	non-agricultural	166 959	4.6%	500 877	12.7%
	private farmers	175 000	4.8%	175 000	4.4%
	Cooperative	348,800	9.6%	348 800	8.9%
Complementary income	Shadow	n.a.		n.a.	
	Remittances[c]	49.5% of Cubans		49.5% of Cubans	

Sources: By the author. Number of employees in the state economy, joint ventures and cooperatives from ONE (1998, pp. 109,194). Number of self-employed in variant 1 from licenses issued as at 31 December 1996, Ministerio de Trabajo y Seguridad Social; variant 2 from licenses issued as at 31 December 1996 added two assistants per license (166 959 × 3). Number of private farmers from CEPAL (1997), p. 378. a   The size of the emerging economy does not appear in any statistics. The percentage found is therefore an approximation which has been found by deducing the 37% of people employed within the state economy who receive incentive payments either in-kind or in hard currency (CIEM, 1998, p. 4) from the total number of state employed, since incentive payments are mainly given to employees within high priority activities (= the emerging economy). b   The figure comprised by the heading '*Empresas mixtas y sociedades mercantiles*' without specifying whether these last-mentioned were also joint ventures. c   In mid-1997, 49.5% of Cubans had, one way or the other, access to hard currency (CIEM, 1998, p. 4).

foreign capital had the government to redefine its role in a new foreign investment law in 1995; joint ventures became more apparent and rose from 2 in 1989 to 317 in 1997 (Everleny, 1998, annex 1) with investments from around 50 countries (CEPAL, 1997, p. 27). Joint ventures have so far been most numerous within mining, oil-extraction, tourism, manufacturing industry, and construction/production of construction materials (CONAS, 1995–96, p. 19). By mid-1995 foreign contributions to joint ventures had reached more than US$1 billion, with commitments of more than twice that amount (CEPAL, 1997, p. 28). Joint ventures account for approximately 3 per cent of total employment.

The private economy may be divided into a non-agricultural economy and a group of private farmers. The non-agricultural private economy is made up by different sorts of self-employment activities, including small private restaurants (*paladares*),[14] and rental of private property. Since September 1993, private activities have been gradually legalized in order to offer alternative occupations to the increasing number of people who were made redundant with the rationalization of the state economy, and to increase supplies of goods and services. The number of self-employment licences rose from some 41 400[15] before the crisis to 166 959 in December 1996, spread over 157 activities.[16] Only producers and vendors of foodstuffs are allowed to hire assistance, and only family members. Despite this regulative limitation of the field of self-employment, it is, however, widely believed that each licence-holder is backed up by a number of assistants ranging from two (Quintana, 1997, p. 114) to three or four (EIU, 1996/3, p. 12). A conservative estimate of the real number of people occupied within self-employment in 1996 would therefore be some 500 877 people. The five most common self-employment activities are the preparation and sale of food and drinks, domestic services, small-scale trade, taxi-driving and being a *mensajero* (person who picks up the rationed goods at the various state outlets) (CEPAL, 1997, p. 384). The non-agricultural private economy operates in both pesos and dollars, and makes up some 5–13 per cent of employment.

The private peasantry has existed throughout the time of the revolution, but in 1993, in response to the pronounced lack of foodstuffs and in order to increase the production of inputs for the export-oriented agricultural industry, a considerable amount of state land was handed over to families. As a consequence, private farmers grew almost 17 per cent of cultivated agricultural land in 1996 (ONE, 1998, p. 192). The economy comprises different kinds of producers: (a) full-time small-scale farmers, the majority organized in so-called *Cooperativas de Crédito y Servicio* (CCSs), typically producing mixed cropping, or coffee, tobacco and cocoa; (b) a broad group of people (rural and urban) growing self-sufficiency plots on a part-time basis, the so-called *parceleros* (Deere, 1997, p. 656 and Figueroa, 1997, pp. 43, 61). The private farmers make up around 4–5 per cent of total employment.

The cooperative economy, which also covers agricultural production, gained importance in 1993. Before the outbreak of the economic crisis, around 70 per cent of Cuba's agricultural land was grown by state farms, but during the first years of the crisis it became evident that the then existing production cooperatives, the so-called *Cooperativas de Producción Agropecuario* (CPAs), were by far outperforming state farms in terms of efficiency (Deere, 1997, p. 652). Therefore, in September 1993 when the lack of foodstuffs was as its height and efficiency needed to be increased and subsidies had to be cut, 64 per cent of state land was cooperatized and turned into so-called *Unidades Básicas de Producción Cooperativa* (UBPCs). By 1996, only around 26 per cent of cultivated agricultural land was grown by state farms, whereas some 58 per cent was grown by the two kinds of cooperatives: 48 per cent by the newly-created UBPCs, and 10 per cent by the 'older' CPAs. In 1996, the UBPCs had 286, 645 members, whereas the CPAs had some 62 155, and the cooperative economy amounted to some 9–10 per cent of total employment (ONE, 1998, pp. 109, 192, 194).

When looking at income distribution in Cuba, aside from the employment-based sources of income I believe that two sources of complementary income are so important that they also have to be taken into account.[17] These are the illegal activities (the 'shadow economy') and remittances from relatives abroad. By 'illegal' is meant activities which do not comply with existing laws/regulations as well as activities which are directly against the law (criminal). The term 'shadow economy' is the term traditionally linked to illegality in centrally-planned economies (Welfens, 1992, p. 115). Since these activities are illegal, it is of course difficult to know the character of the activities with certainty, or to estimate the size of the economy. However, few deny the existence of a shadow economy in Cuba, and some (for example Rosendahl, Chapter 6) even believe that the amount of illegal activities has grown during the years of crisis.

About one million Cubans are living abroad (Mesa-Lago, 1995, p. 61) with the majority being settled in the USA. Furthermore, a number of Cubans regularly go abroad to work for shorter periods of time. Remittances from these migrants make up an important source of complementary income for many Cuban families and are, in terms of net injection of hard currency, today a more important source for the Cuban state than industries such as sugar and tourism (Monreal, 1998, p. 2).

The Cuban economist Monreal (1999) supports Poirine (1994) who believes that migrants should be perceived as an *overseas modern sector*, which offers workers considerably higher income than the home country due to higher levels of productivity (Poirine, 1994, 1997). Monreal argues that export of labour is one of Cuba's strongest comparative advantages at the moment, and that remittances have replaced the resources historically transferred from the socialist camp and today are one of the country's primary ways of insertion into the world economy (together with sugar and tourism). Current transfers (donations and remittances) have on average showed an annual growth of 242 per cent in the period 1992-96, more than ten times the growth of tourism, and in 1996 the flow of remittances represented 27 per cent of the value of Cuban exports of goods (Monreal, 1999, pp. 2, 18).

Migration has usually contained a political element, but during the 1990s the economic incentives seem to have grown. Remittances have been decisive for the economic well-being of many Cubans during the economic crisis, and an important mechanism to reach higher social mobility in an economy where only a limited number of economically attractive jobs are available. Every family seeks to maximize its use of family members' capacities, but to most families the short-term effect of remittances is not as important as establishing a transnational family strategy to secure an improved standard of living for the family in the long run (op. cit. pp. 19–20).

The traditional economy

Nominal wages within the traditional economy have stayed more or less unchanged since the last national wage reform in 1981. Before the crisis, when 94 per cent of Cubans were employed within this economy, the ratio between the highest and the lowest paid was no more than 5:1 (Mesa-Lago, 1998, p. 871). In 1997, the average monthly salary was 214 pesos (compared to 188 pesos in 1989) with some small sectoral differences (CIEM, 1998, p. 7). In order to exemplify wage differences, the minimum wage (in 1995) was 105 pesos (Rodríguez, 1995, in Deere, 1997, p. 664), and towards the end of 1996, secretaries and labourers in government and state enterprises were paid 150–200 pesos, while engineers and professionals received some 300–425 pesos (Peters, 1998, p. 3). Though nominal wages have risen slightly, the crisis has, however, implied almost a halving of real wages (see Table 7.7 below).

The traditional economy has so far not had sufficient resources to offer its employees extra payment in order to increase motivation and efficiency.[18] However, faced with competition for skilled labour from other economies, and the necessity of raising efficiency, the government in August 1998 launched a plan titled *Bases generales de perfecionamiento empresarial* (LAC-CAR, 1998b, p. 5). Apart from seeking to raise managerial standards in state enterprises, the plan will put in place an incentive scheme which links pay

Table 7.7   Average wage in nominal and real terms, Cuba (1990 = 100.0)

	1989	1990	1991	1992	1993	1994	1995	1996[a]
Average wage, nominal terms	99.8	100.0	98.0	96.6	96.3	98.4	103.9	107.6
Average wage, real terms	103.8	100.0	96.4	86.2	77.2	59.5	56.1	58.6

[a]   Estimates.
Source: CEPAL in CIEM (1998), p. 23.

with results, dividing the pay scale into 18 categories from 130 pesos to 700 pesos a month. The plan covers state enterprises within a range of sectors,[19] and by late December 1998, 95 enterprises had been included in the new programme.[20] (EIU, 1999/1 pp. 16–17; LACCAR, 1998, p. 5). The emerging economy is, however, able to offer higher levels of income.

The emerging economy

People employed within the emerging economy are, as a point of departure, receiving the same fixed wage as employees within the traditional economy. What makes the important difference between remuneration in the two economies is the incentive payment which is put on top of the monthly wage. In order to motivate and raise efficiency, schemes of direct and indirect incentives have been put in place during the years of crisis. Within the emerging economy, two kinds of incentives are used: (1) hard currency bonuses linked to results; and (2) in-kind motivation (interview with Monreal, 1998).

In 1997, 902 875 workers received some kind of direct or indirect hard currency motivation payment on top of their normal peso wage (some 74 864 more than in 1996). Adding to this the number of workers who receive in-kind bonuses in the form of clothes, shoes and personal hygiene items, the total number of people receiving motivation payment (*estimulación*) rises to 1.4 million or around 37 per cent of the people employed by the state and the cooperatives (CIEM, 1998, p. 7). Among the people who receive such incentive payments are employees within high-priority sectors such as oil extraction, fishery, tourism, the steel and nickel industry, shipyards, and in cement, sugar and tobacco production (Ferriol Muruaga, 1998, p. 93). There are no official figures on how much each employee receive on top of the normal pesowage, but a few examples may help giving an idea of why it has become so much more attractive to work, for example, in a gas station or in a supermarket (one of the TRDs) rather than as a teacher or a doctor. (Where no other source is mentioned, the following two paragraphs are based on information from an anonymous Cuban researcher).

Annual hard currency bonuses (*estimulación en divisas*) are, among other things, given to employees within the pharmaceutical and biotechnological industries, amounting to US$25–100 (500–2000 pesos) dependent on results. Within the nickel industry, which is an important export sector, employees receive between US$50 and US$70 (1000–1400 pesos) a month, dependent on their result, besides their normal wage. Workers within the sugar industry are given hard currency bonus coupons for use in special shops, very similar to the TRDs.

The so-called *jaba* – a basket of basic products – is one of the most common forms of in-kind motivation in Cuba. A large number of employees within the emerging economy receives a *jaba* on the top of their peso wage each

Table 7.8   Example of a monthly basket within the emerging economy, Cuba (for a woman)

Products	US$	Value Pesos ($1 = Ps20)
1 tube of tooth paste	1.50	30.00
1 packet of sanitary towels	2.30	46.00
1 bottle of cleanser	3.40	68.00
1 soap	0.40	8.00
1 roll of toilet paper	0.40	8.00
1 shampoo	2.00	40.00
1 deodorant	1.00	20.00
1 bottle of cooking oil	2.40	48.00
Total	13.40	268.00

Source: Anonymous Cuban researcher.

month, and a calculation of the basket's value reveals that it may increase their real wage by some US$13.40, or around 268 pesos – more than the monthly average wage (see Table 7.8). Besides the monthly *jaba*, many employees within the emerging economy also receive a pair of shoes, some underwear, perfume and so on once a year. Furthermore, employees are usually offered the chance to buy a certain amount of high-quality clothing at very low prices, a so-called *módulo de ropa*. To illustrate the value of such a *módulo*, an emerging-economy employee would only pay some 40 pesos (around US$2) for an item which would typically cost around US$30 (equivalent to 600 pesos) in the shops.

Apart from this, it is worth keeping in mind that chances to increase a person's income through such fringe benefits as tips etc. are far greater within businesses in the dollar economy, like the emerging economy, than within the traditional peso economy, since in general it has a closer contact with tourists. Finally, outlets for hard currency products like the various kinds of TRDs (supermarkets, gas stations, fast-food restaurants and so forth) offer far better opportunities for fraud than most other parts of the economy.

The joint ventures

An investment report worked out by the Economist Intelligence Unit argues that wages in joint ventures are usually 15–30 per cent higher than the traditional wage level (EIU, 1997, p. 143). However, according to the Cuban economist Monreal from the *Centro de Investigaciones de la Economía Internacional* (CIEI) in Havana, some employees in joint ventures have considerably higher incomes. Many employees in commercial and service companies receive part of their wage directly in dollars, and though this is not legal it is a tolerated and common practice, and a system which includes all levels from secretaries to executives. Secretaries will typically receive between US$50 and $100 (1000–2000 pesos) a month, whereas executives, as a minimum, receive some US$400 (8000 pesos) a month (interview with Monreal, 1999). Another group of employees in joint ventures who receive higher payment are production workers within, for example, the nickel industry or working at shipyards. These workers receive direct bonuses in dollars and *jabas* of a much higher value than the one described above. As a result, their monthly average income may very well amount to some 1500–2000 pesos (anonymous Cuban researcher).

The private non-agricultural economy

Traditionally, people undertaking private activities in Cuba have been accused of making huge profits, which was also one of the reasons for introducing the so-called Rectification Process in 1986 when most private activities and the free agricultural markets were closed down. During the 1990s, the fear that people within the private economy would gain unacceptably high incomes has been reflected in the government's reluctant stance on liberalizing private activities,[21] and was the main reason for introducing income tax on self-employment in April 1996.

According to the Cuban annual statistical yearbook, the income of the private non-agricultural economy was 243.3 million pesos in 1996 (ONE, 1998, p. 7). Divided among the number of licence-holders, the monthly income of self-employed, according to this source, amounted to no more than 121 pesos. However, the self-employed interviewed by Peters (1998) in December 1996, seemed to have profits ranging between 300 and 1200 pesos a month (Peters, 1998, p. 3). Referring to 1995, Mesa-Lago (1998) gives examples of private entrepreneurs earning 3000–160 000 pesos a month (1998, p. 871). A hairdresser is said to earn 3000–4000 pesos, a taxi driver with tourists 3000–15 000 pesos, and a small restaurant owner 80 000– 160 000 pesos (Mesa-Lago, 1998, p. 871). The table in which the figures appear, is titled 'Income Inequalities by Occupation', which, however, may be a bit misleading. Though the estimate of 121 pesos seems to be very low, it is my experience that far from all (rather, only very few) owners of private restaurants are able to generate such high incomes. For example, not many owners of peso-restaurants in non-tourist areas would be able to do so. According to Togores (1997) most self-employed are not better off than other Cubans, something which has to do with the characteristics of the people within the economy. In 1996, 26.3 per cent of the self-employed were women, and around 70 per cent of these were women who during the worst years of the crisis had given up their jobs within the state economy and had become housewifes (*amas de casa*),[22] or women who had never been incorporated into the labour market (Togores, 1997, p. 5).[23] During the same period, the number of Cubans registered as unemployed (*sin vínculo laboral*) increased by more than 60 per cent, and according to Togores around 30 per cent of the self-employed is constituted by these *desvinculados*. The fact that these two groups of people, at least in 1996, made up almost 50 per cent of all self-employed indicates that self-employment is not necessarily a mechanism for obtaining large incomes, but simply an alternative source of income for those left without a job (*Ibid.*). This has especially been the case in the Eastern part of the country where more than 40 per cent of the self-employed are *desvinculados*.[24]

As mentioned above, the income level of the self-employed also depends on the geographical location of the licence-holder. In general, tourist areas offer far greater opportunities for income generation for private entrepreneurs, and the largest profits are often generated when operating in dollars. This is also reflected in the taxation scheme which, for example, distinguishes between rental of private property in tourist and non-tourist areas, and where self-employed are charged taxes in the same currency as they undertake their business. The fact that the self-employed have no legal access to a wholesale supply system makes it difficult for them to predict prices and profits, and together with the last few years' tightening of regulations and control of self-employment, it has become still more difficult for many entrepreneurs to stay in business. Personal income taxes are meant to equalize income generation among Cubans and to encourage unlicensed workers to move into the legal economy, since the consequences of not complying with the regulations are quite severe. For example, taxi-drivers without a licence risk fines of 500–1500 pesos, 2–7 times a monthly average wage within the traditional economy (Ministerio de Justicia, 1997, p. 337).

As a result of the increased regulation and control, private non-agricultural activities now pose less of a threat to key state enterprises, and chances of making huge profits have been considerably limited. Since some self-employed have difficulties paying the licence fee, and because of increased competition, the number of licences has dropped slightly since it peaked in 1995. However, as always when regulation is implemented, new loopholes are discovered. For example, pizza vendors who before would have had their business shut down because they could not produce sales tickets for their flour etc., now just buy such tickets at a new 'market' for their sale. Incentives to be 'creative' are too big to stop the cheating (anonymous Cuban economist).

Private and cooperative agriculture

Prior to the revolution in 1959, rural households were among the poorest in Cuba. A survey from 1956–57 shows that households of agricultural wage-earners earned only 25 per cent of the national average. However, the 1959 and 1963 agrarian reforms secured a lot of people year-round employment on the new nationalized farms at increased wages, and in many cases also turned over property rights to the people who farmed the land. Since then, wages of agricultural workers have improved substantially. In 1975, state agricultural workers earned 80 per cent of the average annual wage, and after the 1981 wage reform the figure had risen to 94.5 per cent (Deere, 1995, pp. 215–16). However, in 1991, according to a household survey carried out by the University of Havana, the average household net income of private peasants was still 19 per cent higher than that of members of production cooperatives (which at that time only counted CPAs), and 61 per cent greater than the average income of households at state farms (Deere, 1995, pp. 216–17).

It is widely believed that private farmers continue to be the wealthiest group within agriculture, and even one of the wealthiest social groups in Cuba (Deere, 1997, p. 665). It is argued that the rising inequalities in the distribution of income and wealth (illustrated by the Gini coefficient and the pattern of savings accounts above), may to a large extent be explained by the concentration of wealth among the private farmers (Carranza *et al.*, 1996, p. 98). According to the Cuban annual statistical yearbook, the income of private farmers, calculated on a monthly basis, amounts to no more than some 230 pesos (ONE, 1998, p. 97 – see Table 7.9). However, other sources confirm the notion that private farmers have far higher incomes; for example, Mesa-Lago (1998, p. 871) estimates the monthly income of private farmers in 1995 to between 6000 and 10 000 pesos. Though prices in the agricultural markets have dropped considerably since then, this example still indicates levels of income many times higher than those claimed by official sources.

During the 1990s, there seem to have been two major sources generating huge profits within agriculture: the black market for foodstuffs (in the period up to October 1994), and the agricultural markets for above-plan production (since their opening in October 1994). As argued above, the severe shortages of foodstuffs (and other consumer goods) led to an excess money supply, and prices within the black market skyrocketed.[25] Tremendous sums were generated within the black market due to the desperate shortages during 1992–94. The opening of the agricultural markets lowered prices on foodstuffs considerably (see Deere, 1997, p. 663) but since the markets were opened in an environment of highly distorted prices, vendors were in a monopoly-like situation and were able to make huge profits which bore no relation to the cost of production or the value of labour employed. Enormous amounts of the excess liquidity in circulation at the beginning of the 1990s is believed to have ended up in the hands of a small number of people within the agricultural economy. The agricultural markets have, so to speak, worked as a 'vacuum cleaner' draining the population of liquidity and

Table 7.9 Approximate monthly employment-based income within different economic sectors, Cuba

Sector	Variant 1		Variant 2		Approximate monthly income span (pesos)[*]	Ratio to traditional average wage (214 pesos)	Comments on variation within economies
	Number of employees	*% of total employment*	*Number of employees*	*% of total employment*			
State							
traditional	1 775 025	49.0	1 775 025	45.0	105–425	0.5–2.0	No great variation
emerging	1 042 475	28.8	1 042 475	26.3	482–2000	2.3–9.3	Moderate variation. Occupations which allow employees to gain tips may, however, increase monthly income by at least 600 pesos ($1/day – conservative estimate)
Joint ventures	110 300	3.1	110 300	2.8	530–8000	2.5–37.4	More pronounced internal disparities. Employees in key positions/with special skills may receive commissions in foreign exchange which increase their real income considerably
Private non-agricultural	166 959	4.6	500 877	12.7	121–15 000	0.6–70.1	Brutal disparities. Some may earn less than 121 pesos and others more than 15 000 pesos (there are examples of private incomes up to 160 000 pesos/ month). The main source of extremely high incomes is tourism
Private farmers	175 000	4.8	175 000	4.4	230–10 000	1.1–46.7	Great disparities. Poor farmers may earn less than 230 pesos though much indicates that private farmers often have had some of the highest incomes (Mesa-Lago, 1998, p. 871, estimates incomes of 6000–10 000 pesos)

Cooperatives							
CPAs	62 155	1.7	62 155	1.6	267	1.2	The two figures are average incomes of cooperatives derived from official figures. No other figures have been available, but they correspond quite well with statements from Cuban researchers. UBPC-members working for private farmers may have earned more
UBPCs	286 645	7.9	286 645	7.3	222	1.0	
Total	3 618 559	100	3 952 177	100			

Sources: Developed by the author. Number of employees in state economy, joint-ventures and cooperatives from ONE (1998), pp. 109, 194. Number of self-employed, variant 1: number of licenses as at 31 December 1996, Ministerio de Trabajo y Seguridad Social; variant 2: number of licenses as at 31 December 1996 plus two non-registered assistants per license. Number of private farmers from CEPAL (1997), p. 378.

* a   In the case of the emerging economy, the lowest of the two figures in the income span is arrived at by adding the value of an average *jaba* (268 pesos) to the monthly minimum wage of the traditional economy (105 pesos).

b   In case of the joint ventures, the 397 pesos have been arrived at by multiplying the monthly minimum wage of the traditional economy (105 pesos) by the 15% and 30% wages in joint ventures are said to be higher (EIU, 1997:134), and taking an average of the two. On the top of this is added the value of an average *jaba* (268 pesos).

c   In the case of the private non-agricultural sector, the private farmers, and the cooperatives, the lowest of the two figures in the income span has been generated by dividing the annual income of the respective sectors with the number of people working within the sector. Figures are derived from *Anuario Estadístico de Cuba* (ONE, 1998:97).

savings. According to Carranza Valdés *et al.* (1996) the money which has been taken out of circulation has not been the 'excess' liquidity, but rather what may be termed 'necessary' liquidity, since, as we have seen above, it has been primarily those accounts with the smallest deposits that have been reduced (Carranza Valdés *et al.*, 1996:97, 99).

The reason for private farmers' high incomes should hence, besides their participation in black market activities, be found in their participation in the agricultural markets. Apart from the cane-producing UBPCs (which are bound to turn in all of their produce to the state), all sorts of agricultural producers are allowed to participate in the agricultural markets. Nevertheless, private farmers have clearly dominated sales. From the opening of the markets in October 1994 until September 1996, private peasants accounted for around 78 per cent of total sales value, whereas the UBPCs and the CPAs accounted for only 2–3 per cent of the sales each (with the figure dropping from 1995 to 1996) (Deere, 1997, pp. 662–3). Hence, a group of agricultural producers growing only 17 per cent of cultivated land accounts for more than three-fourths of profits within agricultural markets.[26] Apparently this trend seems to have continued in 1997. According to the Cuban central bank, the income of private farmers increased by 20.4 per cent in 1997, compared to an increase of only 4.7 per cent of the population in general (Banco Central de Cuba, 1997, p. 21).[27]

However, according to Figueroa (1997), not all private farmers generate huge profits; they are stratified in layers of rich, medium and poor farmers (Figueroa, 1997, p. 47). The stratification is, above all, explained by the size of the land and the quality of the soil to which they have access, the profile of specialization, the degree of technical expertise, knowledge, and the position and linkage to the market (*op cit.*, p. 48). In the above-mentioned household income survey from 1991, farmers who were perceived to be well-off were those with access to more than 12 hectares of land, growing either sugar cane, mixed cropping or holding livestock (Deere, 1995, pp. 227, 231). Though landholdings within tobacco, coffee and cocoa cultivation tend to be smaller, the survey did not examine incomes within these kinds of private agriculture, and it is therefore not known how they perform.[28] Therefore, if this pattern has not changed significantly since then, the private agricultural economy may very well cover pure survival as well as immense wealth. Furthermore, according to Deere, an overwhelming number of vendors in the agricultural markets (at least in Havana City) are either *parceleros* or representatives of farmers (*intermediarios*) from the province of Havana (Deere, 1995, p. 661).

According to the annual Cuban statistical yearbook, total incomes for the CPAs and the UBPCs were 198.9 million pesos and 765.1 million pesos, respectively, in 1996 (ONE, 1998, p. 97). Divided among the number of cooperativists, this indicates a monthly average income of some 267 pesos in the case of CPA cooperativists, and 222 pesos for the UBPC members.

Whether the value of self-sufficiency production or profits from their sale in the agricultural markets are included in the income is not specified. Neither do the figures reveal any difference in income between the cane and non-cane UBPCs though it is believed that the UBPCs which produce sugar cane generally have lower levels of income than the non-cane UBPCs (anonymous Cuban economist). All in all, incomes within cooperative agriculture do not seem to be very high, however.

In 1996, around 47 per cent of UBPCs were dedicated to growing sugar cane, and for that reason could not participate in the agricultural markets. As we saw above, this is where the high incomes are made within agriculture. The reason why sales from non-cane UBPCs do not make up a larger share of total sales at the agricultural markets is that production arrangements with state enterprises do not leave much of the production remaining. Non-cane UBPCs are obliged to turn in around 80 per cent of their produce to state enterprises at fixed, and relatively low, prices. In order to give an idea of the difference in profits, the 80 per cent of the produce which is sold to the state brings in only 20 per cent of the profits of the UBPCs, whereas the 20 per cent which is sold at the markets generates around 80 per cent of their total profits (anonymous Cuban economist). The notion that there are severe distortions between administered prices and agricultural free market prices is backed up by CEPAL (1997, p. 179). This relationship discourages those who are forced to turn in large amounts of their produce at low fixed prices.

The government is well aware of the disadvantageous position of the UBPCs, and of the ones producing cane in particular. In 1997, 37 per cent of the members of UBPCs were therefore given incentive payments (either in kind or in hard currency) (CIEM, 1998, p. 7). There is no information available on how much each member receives, but apparently members of non-cane UBPCs still have a little higher incomes than those of cane-producing cooperatives (anonymous Cuban researcher). Deere (1997, p. 658) furthermore argues that members of UBPCs are often able to earn much more by working for private peasants, and that it is not unusual that they do so, a notion which is supported by the fact that UBPCs are still suffering from labour instabilities. This once again emphasizes the strong position of private farmers within the agricultural economy.

Whereas private farmers' incomes are made up by the profits of their sales, cooperativists' income are (primarily) made up by a monthly advance payment (a so-called *anticipo*) and a share of the annual distribution of profits/losses. Despite the low share of CPAs in agricultural market sales, these 'older' cooperatives, are in general performing considerably better than the UBPCs. In 1997, 80 per cent of CPAs were profitable compared to only 40 per cent of the UBPCs. Besides the different background and design of the two kinds of cooperatives,[29] one of the important reasons for the large difference in profitability is the extent to which incomes of the cooperativists are based on advance payments or on the actual year-end profits. In the case of the CPAs, only around 60 per cent of members' incomes derives from advance payments, while for UBPCs around 90 per cent of income is based on advance payments (Granma International, 1998). The UBPCs therefore operate with a much lower margin of risk, and in case the year-end results are lower than planned, the money has already been spent.

The shadow economy

The shadow economy is probably one of the 'sub-economies' with the largest internal disparities, including some of the poorest and some of the wealthiest Cubans. At one end of the scale we find those people to whom illegal activities are just a means of survival; often people who are unable to find a job within one of the legal economies or retirees trying to supplement their modest pension (which may be as low as 70 pesos a month, see Rosendahl in Chapter 6), and whose symbolic income would vanish if they complied with regulations. As we have seen above, there has been a serious drop in the number of self-employment licences during the last few years, and it is commonly believed that a considerable part of these people are still performing their activities, but doing so without paying taxes (though the increased controls have made people more careful in undertaking self-employment without a licence).

At the opposite extreme we find people who, due to their distinct skills or key positions within a company, are making huge sums illegally. As already described, these people are usually employed within the foreign currency economies. A distinct group of employees within the mixed economy are given considerable hard currency commissions as a reward for their good efforts and in order to motivate them. Commissions are fully legal in most countries, but in Cuba employees are not allowed to receive them, and they therefore break Cuban law by doing so. The extra money, of course, does not figure on the pay slip, but is usually put aside in a bank account abroad (anonymous Cuban researcher).

Another well-known feature linked to the emerging economy and to joint ventures is bribery. People who due to their central position in the decision-making process are able to demand bribes, for example to give a contract to one supplier (of e.g. furniture/equipment for a hotel) instead of another are also able to become very wealthy.

Aside from these sorts of illegal activities, the old vicious circle of theft and resale of items and raw materials from state enterprises has increased the economy. According to one Cuban economist, most cases of theft do not make people rich, but usually just help people who are really badly off to get along. Due to the self-employed's lack of access to wholesale markets, products stolen from state enterprises often end up as 'inputs' in self-employment activities. It is not unusual that flour, milk and so on is extracted from large institutions like hospitals and schools, to which no specific amounts have to be delivered, or that papers/orders and so on in the supermarkets are falsified. 'Unforeseen accidents' in construction sites, where quick solutions in the form of new deliveries of building materials are often needed, also provide private entrepreneurs with a range of necessary inputs (anonymous Cuban economist).

Remittances – the great unknown

Traditionally, migration as well as remittances have been subject to severe restrictions, and though legislation has been loosened, according to Monreal (1999) the actual number of migrants does not reflect the real demand for Cuban labour abroad (which is much higher), just as a significant potential of remittances remains unexploited (Monreal, 1999, pp. 17–18). In connection with legalizing the possession of dollars by Cubans in August 1993, the regulation on remittances and visits by exile-Cubans was also made more flexible. It was promised that it would be made easier to obtain visas, and that visitors would be allowed to bring an unlimited amount of dollars and would not be forced to change their money to Cuban pesos (Mesa-Lago, 1995, p. 61). As part of the embargo, the United States has put a limit on the amount of dollars which Cuban-Americans are allowed to remit to relatives in Cuba. At present, Cubans abroad may transfer a maximum amount of US$1200/year, and spend a maximum of US$700/week when visiting the island (EIU, 1998/2, p. 10). Such regulation is, of course, difficult to enforce, and though some exile-Cubans may not remit the maximum amount, others may very well exceed it, since money easily passes through informal channels (e.g. a third country).

There is some disagreement on the actual amount of remittances pouring into Cuba, but whatever the exact figure, the amount is large and seems to have grown during the 1990s. Mesa-Lago (1995) estimates that in the years prior to legalizing the possession of dollars in August 1993, about 90 per cent of Cuba's total foreign exchange, some US$100–300 million derived from remittances. Mesa-Lago estimates the 1994 revenue from remittances (dependent on the scenario) to have been between US$160 and 600 million, arguing that US$300 million is probably the most realistic (Mesa-Lago, 1995, pp. 61–3). The official Cuban figure for net current transfers (remittances and donations) in 1996 is US$743.7 million (ONE, 1998, p. 289) of which Monreal (1999, p. 2) estimates some US$500 million to be remittances.

The largest part of remittances originates from permanent migrants (mainly in the USA), while money from temporary migrants plays only a minor role. Remittances may be the repayment of an informal loan (explaining the most stable part of remittances) or just a 'helping hand', and the money is usually used for consumption or for investment (e.g. in a small business) (Monreal, 1999, p. 20). By taking a look at statistics on

Cuban-Americans (the largest group of Cubans living abroad[30]) published by the US Bureau of the Census in April 1997, one gets an impression of the socioeconomic state of those who send remittances, and also a vague idea of who the recipients may be. Recent figures confirm the notions of Díaz-Briquets (1994) who in an earlier study divided the Cuban migrants into two main groups according to their propensity to remit. He argued that the financial situation of the migrants arriving before 1980 is in general better than that of those arriving after 1980 (around 40 per cent of all Cuban-Americans), while at the same time stating that the first group of migrants has fewer close relatives left in Cuba, and therefore has less interest in remitting than the last arrived who, in turn, are less able to do so (Díaz-Briquets, 1994, pp. 8–9). Almost 38 per cent of the the Cubans who entered the United States after 1980 live below the poverty line, making up 62 per cent of the total number of Cuban-Americans living below that level. Around 89 per cent of the latest arrived Cubans have incomes below US$19 999 a year, compared to around 60 per cent of the first group of immigrants which, of course, might lead to a tapering off of remittances in the longer run. Since the relative percentage of employed and unemployed (including 'people not in labour force') is more or less the same for two groups, the difference in income seems to be explained by the varying educational background of the two groups, and the related possibilities of getting a well-paid job. The number of migrants without a high-school degree is significantly higher in the group arriving after 1980 than in the first group of migrants (43.3 per cent vs 31.4 per cent), and, furthermore, only around 28 per cent of the lastly arrived Cubans had a high school degree or some college experience (against more than 46 per cent of the first immigrants). Finally, only 8 per cent of the second group of immigrants had obtained either a bachelor or professional degree (against almost 22 per cent of the firstly arrived) (US Bureau of the Census, 1997, table 6).

In 1997 it was estimated that, on average, 49.5 per cent of the Cuban population had access to dollars.[31] In 11 provinces between 30 and 65 per cent of the population had access to dollars, and in three provinces less than 30 per cent held foreign currency. CEPAL (1997) argues that 68.1 per cent of the population's hard currency income derived from remittances, services, tourists and others (CEPAL, 1997, p. 418). Though more Cubans had access to dollars in 1997 than in 1995 (44 per cent), and though we are dealing with a foreign currency in which no Cuban wage is paid, there is still 50 per cent of the population which has no access to this important parallel currency which gives access to, for example, the TRDs (CIEM, 1998, p. 4). Since it is supposed that remittances are sent to family members, black Cubans are apparently less likely to receive extra income in the form of remittances than white Cubans, since only 2.6 per cent of all Cuban-Americans are black. Furthermore, almost all of the black Cuban migrants have arrived during the second 'round' (1980–96), and therefore belong to the poorest of the two groups of Cuban-Americans. Since the racial background of Cubans is only registered by the general census once every 10 years it is difficult to say anything about the number of Cubans with less probability of receiving supplementary income in this way. Furthermore, not much attention is generally paid to the census figures, since the definition of 'race' is very subjective, and because there is a general tendency towards 'whitening' in the census (blacks who say they are mulattos, and mulattos who say they are white). However, 'mixed' black and white couples and families are not at all unusual in Cuba, and part of the black Cubans, without migrated relatives of their own, may therefore be receiving remittances anyway. Finally, though it cannot be deduced from any figures, the most loyal revolutionaries may, all else being equal, have fewer relatives abroad, and therefore be less likely to receive supplementary income in the form of remittances.

Summary

In Table 7.9 I gave an estimate of the approximate income span of monthly employment-based income within each of the sectors of the Cuban economy. As mentioned above, since income distribution in Cuba after 1990 is quite a new field of research, the estimates are primarily aimed at giving an idea of the recent pattern of income distribution. In short, there seem to be three main explanations to the increased income inequalities illustrated by the rising Gini coefficient: (1) inequalities among sectors; (2) inequalities within sectors; and (3) the unequal distribution of complementary sources of income.

Firstly, there are wide disparities between monthly incomes within the traditional and the cooperative economies, and the remaining economies. The ratio between the average wage in the traditional economy and maximum incomes within the other economies is up to 70 times (compared to a ratio of only 5:1 between highest and lowest paid workers at the end of the 1980s). Employees within the two first-mentioned economies, constituting more than half of Cuba's labour force, have employment-based incomes which on average are too small to make ends meet, at least if these employees are to provide for a family. The well-being of these people is therefore highly dependent on their access to complementary sources of income, either those focused upon in this chapter, or part-time private activities, self-consumption plots or non-monetary means (see Rosendahl in Chapter 6). Secondly, the great internal disparities within joint ventures and the private economies, and to a minor degree within the emerging economy, have pushed inequalities upwards. Monthly incomes within these economies range from being pure survival mechanisms to being immense fortunes. Finally, the distribution of complementary income (deriving from the shadow economy and from remittances) is highly unequal. These sorts of income could help to equalize income distribution among Cubans since they cross the lines of the various economies. If remittances (set at US$500 million in 1996) were equally dispersed among the 49.5 per cent of Cubans claimed to have access to dollars (in 1997), each of these persons would receive some US$91.7 a year (equivalent to around 155 pesos a month). However, this is not very likely, nor is there any guarantee that it is the people with the lowest employment-based income who would receive the money.

The rising inequality in income-generating opportunities in Cuba during the last decade poses a severe threat to one of the core pillars of the Cuban development model: social equity. From the outset of the Revolution securing equality has been a deliberate goal for the Cuban government, which during the years of crisis has several times emphasized that the social costs would be distributed as equally as possible. The government has often argued that the reforms introducing new kinds of employment as alternative occupations to the people made redundant by the downsizing of the state economy were only 'necessary evils' implemented to preserve the goals of the Revolution.

Though it is out of the scope of the present discussion, one could ask whether the rise in inequality could have been avoided, or at least limited. However, what is perhaps more important in the long run is to consider the future viability of the Cuban development model keeping in mind the present situation of the Cuban economy. The transition has implied a substantial contraction of the overall economy, and the size of the 'cake' which is to be distributed among Cubans has shrunk considerably. As a consequence, it may therefore not be sufficient to talk about 'distribution', but also necessary to talk about future 'growth'. In order for Cubans not to end up in equally shared poverty, it is important that growth be spurred, even if this may lead to a certain degree of inequality in the short term. If Cuban entrepreneurs to a larger extent were allowed to establish small and medium-sized enterprises this might imply a growth potential and create employment, just as it might also secure a more productive use of the foreign exchange deriving from remittances (as will be discussed in Chapter 8 by Brundenius and Monreal). However, even if there is a rapid growth in the next 5–10 years, that alone will not solve the problem. Drastical additional measures will be needed in order to get social equity back to the level it was.

Another important matter for discussion in relation to the survival of the Cuban development model is the future shape of social transfers. As shown, the government is no longer able to provide the population with the same amount of services as before, and several authors, among them Deere (1997, p. 667), Ritter (1995, p. 130) and Mesa-Lago (1999, p. 105), suggest a redesign of parts of the social security system. One of the traits of the future provision of social transfers might be that assistance, to a higher degree, is targeted towards those groups who really need it.

Notes

1 The closer the coefficient gets to one, the more unequal the distribution – the closer it gets to zero, the more equal the distribution.

2 Only half a year earlier, in December 1994, the relation was 14.1 per cent to 77.8 percent (Banco Nacional de Cuba, 1995, p. 15). Since 1995, figures on the structure of private savings accounts have not appeared in the *Informe Economico* by Cuba's national bank.

3 Education, health, social security and social assistance, housing, culture and art, and sports.

4 In 1998 the infant mortality rate had dropped to 7.1 per 1000 live births (UNESCO in LACCAR, 1999, p. 8).

5 1990 figures from World Bank (1993), p. 41; 1995 figures from UNDP (1998), pp. 128–9, 132.

6 1990 figures from World Bank (1993), p. 41; 1994 figures from World Bank, (1996), pp. 198–9.

7 The VAT is thought of as a redistributive mechanism (a method which has been used throughout the revolution).

8 Though non-monetary incomes/activities are also important supplements to most households (as shown by Rosendahl in Chapter 6).

9 Only the rationed goods that regularly are offered for sale in the public outlets are comprised in the table. Some products (e.g. oil for cooking) actually do appear in the ration book, but are hardly ever available, and are therefore not include here.

10 Though the sources of complementary income are not directly linked to the labour market structures, it could be argued that they in a way support them since the monthly income generated within several of the economies is insufficient to make ends meet if it was not supplemented by these sources of income.

11 Carranza Valdés *et al.* (1996, p. 20) and Ritter (1995, p. 115) use the term 'traditional sector'/'traditional socialist sector' about those state enterprises which, among other things, do not have transactions in dollars, which to a higher extent are controlled by central planning, and which usually are characterized by lower levels of efficiency. In this discussion the concept of the 'traditional economy' refers to this use of the term 'traditional.'

12 A limited number of traditional state enterprises sell part of their production to hard currency outlets, the so-called 'export within the borders' (*exportaciones en frontera* – see also Chapter 8 by Brundenius and Monreal).

13 The first time the term appeared was in the work by Nieves Pico and Amelia Mendoza: *Caracterización de las formas legales y organizativas que operan en la economía emergente*, published by INIE in May 1993.

14 The *paladares* are not allowed to have more than 12 seats, and may not serve dishes which include beef or shellfish.

15 *Anuario Estadístico de Cuba* 1988 in Núñez Moreno (1998), p. 45.

16 The number of self-employment licences peaked by the end of 1995 when 208, 786 people were registered. Tighter regulation and probably increased competition caused the figure to drop to some 155 174 by March 1998 (Ministerio de Finanzas y Precios).

17 In some cases, some of the employment-based sources of income (e.g. self-employment and private agriculture in the form of self-sufficiency plots) may also have the role of complementary sources of income.

18   For example, such extra payment in the Ministry of Higher Education has been limited to giving each employee a pair of shoes once every two years (anonymous Cuban economist).

19   Among other things within basic industry, mining, farming, construction, fishing, transport, communications, finance and civil aviation (LACCAR, 1998, p. 5).

20   Twenty of these are said to be export-oriented (nickel enterprises), which implies that they form part of the emerging economy. However, since the total number of employees said to be affected by the plan is 115 000, that should still secure some improvement of wages within the traditional economy (LACCAR, 1998, p. 5).

21   Self-employment activities were first really permitted from September 1993, private restuarants (*paladares*) from June 1995, and rental of private property from May 1997. Self-employment is not allowed for professionals within their original profession.

22   In order to take on the time-consuming task of providing the family with foodstuffs and other daily necessities, often including hours of queueing.

23   This tendency is supported by the fact that the number of women formally registered as housewives increased by almost 65 per cent between December 1994 and December 1995 (Togores, 1977, p. 5).

24   *Ministerio de Trabajo y Seguridad Social* in Núñez Moreno (1998), p. 46.

25   In order to illustrate the tremendous rise in prices, the black market price of a pound of rice in June 1994 was 50 pesos (compared to 0.24 pesos in the market for rationed foodstuffs and 4 pesos in the agricultural markets in January 1997). In the same way, the price of a pound of black beans in June 1994 was 30 pesos (compared to 0.30 pesos in the state markets and 9 pesos in January 1997) (Deere, 1997, p. 663; Togores, 1997).

26   In 1994 (October–December), *sales* in the agricultural markets amounted to 420 million pesos. In 1995 and 1996 sales amounted to 1574 million pesos and 1229 million pesos, respectively (ONE, 1998, p. 90).

27   The fact that participating in the agricultural markets enables producers to make high profits only repeats the pattern from the free farmers' markets of the 1980s, the so-called *Mercados Libres Campesinos*. From 1982, only private farmers, *parceleros*, and intermediaries were allowed to participate in the markets, and towards the end of the 1980s the contrasts in profits between private and cooperative farmers (CPAs) were evident (Figueroa, 1997, pp. 40–41).

28   In 1987, almost 43 per cent of private farmers had access to less than 5 hectares of land; only 14 per cent of private farmers grew more than 20 hectares (Figueroa, 1997, p. 48).

29   Unlike the CPAs, the UBPCs have only a few years of experience with being cooperative, and in terms of management most of them are still affected by the 'mentality' which dominated when they were state-owned. In terms of members, they are, on average, almost twice as large as the CPAs and have inherited a highly mechanized, large-scale production system which is very dependent on fuel, spareparts etc., inputs that have been difficult to acquire since 1989. Finally, the UBPCs are directly linked to state agricultural enterprises, which are accused of intervening too much and of increasing bureaucracy (Deere, 1997, pp. 658–60).

30   In 1997, 772 000 *foreign born* Cuban-Americans were living in the USA, 72 per cent of them being 16–64 years of age (US Bureau of the Census, 1997, table 6).

31   In 1998 this figure had risen to 56.3 per cent (Negocios en Cuba, 1992, p. 2).

8
The Future of the Cuban Model: A Longer View

Claes Brundenius and Pedro Monreal González

Introduction

The disintegration of the 'socialist camp', and especially the collapse of the Soviet political and socioeconomic system, sent shock waves to the Cuban economy. Cuba had by the end of 1980s become almost entirely dependent on trade with CMEA (Comecom) partners, and particularly with the Soviet Union which supplied Cuba with its fuel needs and also accounted for the lion's share of Cuba's sugar export markets, at preferential prices. These arrangements went down the drain practically overnight. The first reaction in Havana was a wait and see attitude (probably in the hope that the process in the Comecon countries might be reversible, at least in the former Soviet Union. Therefore, it was only in 1993, when import capacity had drastically declined by almost 70 per cent (in relation to 1989), that the government started serious reforms. The decline in import capacity was both the result of a decrease in export volume and terms of trade. By 1993 it was clear to the Cuban leadership that the process in the former ally countries was irreversible and that thus something had to be done in Havana.

A series of measures were undertaken in order to get the macro balances in order, especially to do something about the huge government budget deficit (-30.4 per cent in 1993) by decreasing the expenditure side primarily through cuts in subsidies to state-owned enterpises (SOEs). Other reforms were, *inter alia*, cooperativization of state farms and legalization for citizens to keep, and trade with, dollars. Cuba fared relatively well with respect to macroeconomic stabilization within a short-term perspective, also in comparison with other 'transition economies' (especially the republics of the former USSR). However, the reforms have had a social cost (see chapters by Fabienke and Rosendahl in this volume) that could be justified on many grounds ('a necessary evil' or 'a painful but necessary medicine'), and Cubans have been used to belt-tightening in the past and could probably also swallow this medicine provided that there would soon be some light at the end of the tunnel. And this still remains the key issue. After recovery what? What are the prospects for Cubans in the longer run (by year 2005 and beyond)? What are the requirements for growth in a longer perspective and what are the consequences for the celebrated Cuban model? These are some of the issues addressed in this chapter.

Economic recovery

In 1999 the Cuban economy entered its sixth year of economic recovery after having experienced its most severe contraction in recent history. Recovery has been slowly underway but it is far from clear how long it will take to reach the levels of total output that existed a decade ago. At the end of 1998, total output was still only 74.4 per cent of its previous peak in 1989. More important, the prospects for long-term growth and development are still controversial isssues. Even with official projected rates of growth of around 4 per cent per year, the Cuban economy would be back to its pre-crisis levels only by the year 2005. Thus, the economic impasse of the 1990s would represent 15 years of lost economic growth for the country. The post-1993 recovery has to a large extent been based on increases in private consumption and to a lesser extent on the expansion of the exports of goods and services (see Tables 8.1 and 8.2). Investment has played a minor role and it has been unable to offset the contraction in government consumption. In fact, the low rate of investment reflects a process of decapitalization of the Cuban economy even in the midst of recovery. At 6.7 per cent of gross domestic product (GDP) in 1996, gross investment was approximately just one-quarter of the average rate of investment of the 1980s (CEPAL, 1997, table A.2)

Economic growth in Cuba has traditionally been import-dependent, associated with progressively increasing imports. This is a structural problem that partially reflects the lack of a well-developed and up-to-date capital goods sector, the import substitution nature of a large share of Cuba's output (which is only viable thanks to imports of intermediate goods), and the extensive growth pattern of accumulation. The stagnation in the exports of goods has been partially offset by net exports of services (particularly tourism) and net transfer payments (remittances), and the resulting current account deficit has been financed by external financing (loans and foreign direct investment). However, given the relatively low level of inflows of foreign direct investment and the limits and high cost of available foreign loans, several administrative measures (import quotas and resticted allocation of hard currency) were adopted in 1996 to contain the deficit in the current account, contributing to the slowdown of the recovery. Since 1997, the short-term dynamics of economic growth has been increasingly dependent on export growth and remittances. Export growth has been moderate on commodities but remarkable in services, while remittances (mainly from families abroad) have been growing at a very fast pace although under current policies it could soon be reaching a point of saturation.

Table 8.1 Gross domestic product, sector breakdown and gross investment in the 1990s, Cuba (million pesos, 1981 prices)

	1989	*1993*	*1994*	*1995*	*1996*	*1997*	*1998*	*1998/89*
GDP	19 586	12 779	12 868	13 184	14 218	14 572	14 755	0.75
Index (1993 = 100)	153.3	100.0	100.7	103.2	111.3	114.0	115.5	–
Gross investment (GI)	5 279	692	705	954	1 172	1 382	1 479	0.28
GI as % of GDP	27.6	5.4	5.5	7.2	8.2	9.5	10.0	0.36
GDP breakdown by economic sector								
Agriculture[a]	1 925	925	879	915	1 075	1 074	1 108	0.53
Mining[b]	123	96	98	152	177	182	184	1.50
Manufacturing	4 886	3 104	3 341	3 555	3 835	4 154	4 291	0.88
Electricity, gas & water	452	335	350	384	398	422	427	0.94
Construction	1 350	386	384	412	539	556	588	0.44
Commerce & tourism	5 151	2 936	2 935	2 985	3 251	3 176	3 090	0.60
Transport & communications	1 353	733	709	748	813	845	855	0.63
Finance & banking	585	513	492	484	519	545	599	1.02
Services	3 762	3 748	3 681	3 548	3 616	3 618	3 703	0.98

[a] Includes fishing and forestry; [b] includes quarrying and petroleum extraction.
Sources: Anuario Estadístico de Cuba (1996, 1997, 1998); Banco Central de Cuba (1997).

By increasing the disposable household income, net transfer payments have been an important factor behind the relative strength of private consumption and for the reactivation of domestic supply chains structured to meet that demand. The direct dollar sales to consumers of products and services by state entities have been, together with net tourism earnings, a key factor in the revenue performance of the state sector, improving to some degree the government capacity to save and invest, but at levels still far removed from real needs. The reform of the banking system and the new guidelines for financing state-owned enterprises have also been conducive to a more efficient system of savings concentration and state investment under the existing limited availability of funds. However, this does not directly address two key issues: the expansion of savings and the most efficient allocation of investment.[1]

The first six years of recovery were based on the reactivation of existing productive capacities, but mid-to long-term growth requires investment at levels that cannot be supported by current levels of domestic savings and

Table 8.2   Balance of payments statistics, Cuba, 1993–98 (million current pesos/dollars*)

	1993	1994	1995	1996	1997	1998
Exports of goods & services	1 969	2 541	2 926	3 707	3 785	3 932
goods (f.o.b)	1 137	1 381	1 507	1 866	1 823	1 444
services	832	1 160	1 419	1 841	1 962	2 488
of which tourism	756	850	1 100	1 350	1 500	2 076
Imports of goods & services	2 339	2 850	3 566	4 126	4 531	4 550
goods (f.o.b)	1 984	2 353	2 992	3 657	4 088	4 230
services	355	497	574	469	443	320
Trade balance	−847	−972	−1 485	−1 791	−2 265	−2 786
Service balance	+477	+663	+845	+1 372	+1 519	+2 168
Income balance*	−264	−423	−525	−493	−483	−599
Net transfer payments	+263	+470	+646	+744	+ 792	+ 820
Current account	−371	−262	−519	−168	−437	−397
Capital account	+356	+262	+596	+174	+457	+413
Long-term capital (net)	+118	+817	+24	+308	+787	+ 633
of which FDI flows	+54	+563	+5	+82	+442	+207
Other capital (net)	+238	−555	+572	−134	−330	−219
Variation of reserves	+16	−2	−79	−8	−21	−17

* In Cuban national accounts of the external sector, one $US = Cuban peso.
Sources: ONE (1996, 1997, 1998) *Anuario Estadístico de Cuba*; Banco Central de Cuba (1996, 1997, 1998) *Informe Económico*.

external financing. Investment would be needed, but at rates that will require a high savings environment. The possibility of the expansion of domestic savings would be a function of growing personal income and increased state revenues, while access to external financing will depend on the availability of increased remittances, international loans and inflows of foreign investment. To begin with, the modest economic growth expected in Cuba (around 4 per cent per year) is not exactly the most favourable context for increased domestic savings and additional availability of external financing, but the problem is more complex than this.

Finally, Cuba's insertion into the world economic system has not yet provided an adequate matrix for Cuba's long-term growth and economic development. Beyond any doubt, there has been an evident and rapid transition from delinking to reinsertion into the world economy, but by the end of the 1990s Cuba was still far from being successfully relinked to the global system. To be more precise, a survival status has been reached but much more volume and upgrading is needed for long-term viability.

The current modern and traditional sectors cannot by themselves sustain long-term economic development in Cuba, even under the assumption of more volume and some upgrading of current export activities. A profound restructuring, implying increased competitiveness and utilization of the country's potential, is needed. The current structure of output and employment is not viable in the long run; there is considerable waste and unproductive use of resources (particularly of the skilled labour force), and a vast segment of the Cuban workforce has been *de facto* sidetracked from worldwide trajectories of technological change and skill absorption. Cuba's development prospects are to a large extent conditioned by how additional segments of the country's output, not currently traded in world markets, are incorporated into those markets. The solution to the problem basically depends on several key factors, primarily efficiency, innovation and investment.

The challenges for future transformations

The recent process of reinsertion of Cuba into the world economy clearly shows the limits for upgrading within the system under current and announced policies. Second, a successful reinsertion of Cuba into the world economic system, a key condition for its viability as an open economy, needs a major transformation in the structure and qualitative nature of its tradable output.

Simple logic suggests that the magnitude of this task is only compatible with a high growth environment; any effort to find a rationale for low economic growth could not be conducive to development in Cuba. This is a key issue since high rates of growth are not simply the result of investment but also a crucial factor conductive to accelerated investment (domestic and foreign). The most dynamic sectors of the international economy are structured as global industries and therefore insertion into those activities is vital for the absorption of new knowledge and technologies by the Cuban workforce. Foreign investment could play a central role in that process but the conditions of the domestic economy would also be a powerful factor. First, because global insertion would be most effective if its associated learning potential could find diffusion in the domestic economy; and second, because the localization of foreign investment is dependent on productive density (clusters) and entrepreneurship; and finally because a high-growth economy will generate domestic savings that will support general economic growth which, in addition, is an important factor in attracting foreign direct investment.[2]

We will now focus on some problems that have to be tackled if obstacles to the trajectory of high growth and economic transformation are to be removed. Those problems are (a) efficiency; (b) innovation; and (c) sources of investment. The problem of efficiency is ubiquitous since it involves labour productivity, the quality of production and services, investment processes, energy and material consumption patterns, and social efficiency criteria. The Cuban economy has undoubtedly shown poor results in most of those areas. Current economic policy has identified efficiency as one of the main targets and therefore increased labour productivity has been given top priority in official economic strategy. However, the first issue that needs further elaboration is the nature of the required solution to the problem. Is it sufficient with an incremental approach or is it rather a solution of 'discontinuity' that is needed? This is a highly controversial issue but the bottom line is that the past framework for accumulation in Cuba has been one of extensive growth (rather than intensive growth) where efficiency has played only a negligible role. A change in the model of accumulation is something that does not appear clearly formulated in the plans for current and prospective Cuban economic policy.

A second aspect related to the nature of the solution of the problem is the 'cultural' determination of efficiency. The organizational culture could be important to achieve efficiency, but a caveat is necessary in order to avoid a techno-deterministic conception of efficiency. The broad socioeconomic context is decisive for efficiency (including ownership, markets, structure of incentives and other economic relations), and therefore a focus on the cultural aspect of efficiency (i.e. management techniques or the 'consciousness' of cadres) is only part of the problem.

The most predictable impact of any meaningful increase in efficiency in Cuba would be a process of massive reallocation of labour, particularly in SOEs. But the problem is more complex given its qualitative dimension. The first challenge is the absorption of the displaced labour force, and the second is an absorption that is compatible with the productive utilization of existing skills and knowledge and with future trajectories of learning. The evolution of the Cuban manufacturing industry in the past is revealing.

Manufacturing has only slightly increased its share of total output in the last ten years (by approximately 25 per cent), and although industrial output in 1996 was only 75 per cent of the 1989 level, this sector is still the largest employer in the Cuban economy (CEPAL, 1997, table A28) with a large number of its employees now being part of the redundant labour force. There has already been a contraction in the industrial labour force but much greater displacement would take place because there is no other alternative as a consequence of two related processes: the decapitalization of industry and the shifting pattern of investment. Most industrial branches, including some export-oriented ones, are receiving very low levels of investment and therefore undercapitalization is transforming into vast obsolete areas of industry. On the other hand investment has been increasingly oriented outside industry, towards 'competitive advantages' (i.e. tourism and associated infrastructure). Even within the industrial sector there has been a radical restructuring in terms of the allocation of investment. Approximately 70 per cent of industrial investment is concentrated in just four activities – sugar, mining, power generation and the oil industry, and around 50 per cent is concentrated in sugar and mining alone.

Clearly, current investment is being directed towards resource-based exports and energy import substitution, which is necessary but not sufficient.[3] The future of most industrial activities is therefore at stake; they could vanish and Cuba would have lost valuable growth potential and possibilities for technological learning. After years of decapitalization, any sensible increase in efficiency in industrial enterprises could result in the massive reallocation of the labour force out of industry. The industrial activities currently receiving investment have no potential growth to employ displaced workers. As a matter of fact, the largest industrial recipient of investment – the sugar industry – would have to undergo substantial downsizing in order to be competitive. Any low-growth economic environment would make the absorption of displaced industrial workers very difficult even when the labour intensiveness of some growing sectors (e.g. tourism) could facilitate the process. The other problem is that although employment opportunities could exist in other sectors (such as construction and agriculture), the existing mismatch between those job opportunities and the skills of the displaced or redundant industrial labour force (from the sugar industry or light industries) highlights the downward side of labour reallocation under current trends. The so called 'self-employment' activities have contributed to labour absorption but this area is very restricted, full of negative incentives and entry barriers and with limited possibilities for upgrading under current policies.

The emphasis on the 'exogenous' dimension of the economic crisis of the 1990s tends to obscure a central feature of Cuba's economic system: its shortcomings for innovation. The problems in efficiency, observed before the recent crisis, reveal a wasteful use not only of material and human resources, but also of knowledge. Any economic system must deal with the problems of calculation, motivation and innovation, but the centralized planning system adopted in Cuba in the mid-1970s failed on those three counts and in fact the crisis rendered the whole planning model obsolete. The modified system of centralized planning currently being introduced (more decentralized and market-disciplined) could have an impact on calculation and motivation, although success in those areas cannot be taken for granted in advance.[4] However, the reformed system does not deal with the issue of innovation. To be precise, its approach to the problem is administrative-oriented and therefore not very relevant.

Innovation is not an administrative matter; it is not merely a problem of policy and implementation of policy. Neither could it be conceived from a techno-deterministic perspective, as growing directly from the forces of production. Innovation is a highly complex issue, subject to intense debate and closely related to the socioeconomic structure. The social mobilization of tacit, fragmented and dispersed knowledge is an essential part of economic processes, and in theoretical terms that function is performed by entrepreneurs. The issue of entrepreneurship must be clearly addressed given its role as a precondition for a mode of insertion into the global economy. This needs particular clarification in the case of Cuba. Entrepreneurship is a highly contentious issue, in part as a consequence of the centrality of the concept in the debates on the economics of socialism since the 1930s. Classical entrepreneurial skills are defined as the ability to seize new opportunities and take advantage of disequilibrium market situations. This dynamic function is played in the capitalist system by private entrepreneurs. Critics of socialism, like von Mises (1935), long ago considered that the socialist economy was doomed because it lacked agents capable of performing that function. The revival in the 1980s of the 'socialist economic calculation' debate and the failure of market socialism economic reforms in Hungary reactivated the debate on the issue of entrepreneurship in socialist economies. New models of market socialism were developed in the 1980s to focus on the need for discovery through entrepreneurial activity. However, those theoretical models have not been implemented anywhere. It is only fair to say that the old argument of von Mises is still largely uncontested on empirical grounds. The socialist entrepreneur is a normative concept but so far not the representation of reality.

Some authors, however, consider that the experience of the so-called township and village enterprises (TVEs) in China provides a clear, if uniquely Chinese form, of socialist entrepreneurship, although the issue is open to debate.[5] According to one current of thought (the so-called Austrian school), this function can only be successfully performed through entrepreneurship competition in the market, considered as the best mechanism to optimize the use of knowledge. The market plays, in this sense, a discovery and learning role. Knowledge is not only fragmented and dispersed but it is also tacit, and therefore it has to be discovered in a creative process of interplay. Thus, the most commonly accepted notion that knowledge is objectively given and readily codified and transmitted has been challenged.[6]

The issue is particularly relevant for socialist models, given previous failures in this area. Different alternatives have been advanced from a socialist perspective to deal with that problem, although this is a highly controversial issue among socialist scholars. Options include different versions of market socialism, participatory planning and hybrid approaches.[7] What could be important for the case of Cuba is that from a conceptual standpoint, the administrative framework has been largely discarded by most contemporary socialist models, and there has also been an increasing recognition of innovation as the result of a process of intense social discovery. The challenge for Cuba is precisely to fill the gap that exists today in this area of the economic system. Fostering entrepreneurship – not merely management skills – is part of the answer.

With regard to *sources of investment*, the prevailing view in Cuba today is that the keystone of current economic strategy is self-reliance on domestically-generated resources. It includes both efficiency gains and domestic economic surplus. In other words, domestic savings are considered the key to growth while external financing is supposed to play a secondary, auxiliary role. The explicit rationale is the lack of control on exogenous factors – that is, the US embargo, international trends of financial flows, and increased competition for foreign investment. Therefore, restrictions on the availability of external financing are assumed to be a limiting factor for growth that cannot be overcome by means of domestic policy-making.[8]

At first glance this appears to reflect an accurate description of the broad political and international context in which the Cuban economy must evolve. In fact, those are key issues to be considered in any strategy for economic growth in Cuba. However, a closer look reveals a more controversial aspect of that position. While it is true that the US embargo is a factor well-beyond the control of the Cuban government, or that its possible resolution would be dependent on unacceptable political conditions imposed by the US government, the other two factors – international trends of financial flows and increased competition for foreign investment – could be influenced by domestic policy-making. To a great extent this is the crux of contemporary policy-making in many countries. The problem is obviously one of considering what could be conceived as endogenous and exogeneous.[9]

Within the context of an increasingly interdependent world economy, the geographic location of economic activities, its organization and associated distribution of value are profoundly influenced by decisions taken at the transnational level, but countries and governments are not powerless and can influence the localization and characteristics of economic activity. One of the current paradoxes is that 'economic globalization actually strengthens, rather that weakens, the forces of localization in the world economy'.[10]

In the contemporary world economy, transnational corporations are not the sole controllers of the global economy nor are governments irrelevant. Global restructuring has eroded the discretionary power of states to define economic policies but they retain the ability to define the local context of global production. The possibility of endogenous control, as it was conceived in the past, is not relevant today. Economic strategy today could not be based on traditional considerations but on the notion of strategic insertion into the world economy, that is, integration up to the point that it is compatible with national interests and the country's economic growth.[11]

The first implication for the case of Cuba from the above mentioned dimension of contemporary policy-making is that economic policies could have a greater influence on the attraction of external financing than is currently perceived. The second possible implication is that domestic economic policy cannot be artificially separated from the general dynamic of the world economy. The corollary is that external financing could play a more important role in Cuba's economic growth and strategic insertion into the world economy, even under the conditions of the US embargo. This could make the difference between a path of low growth and a different scenario of higher growth. The problem to tackle, then, is the introduction of the necessary changes in economic policy-making. Let us examine very briefly current policies to attract foreign investment for industry.

As already mentioned, foreign investment has not been, with few exceptions (i.e. resource-based exports), an important factor in the reactivation or transformation of the Cuban economy. Policies designed to attract foreign capital, but biased against domestic entrepreneurship, are limited in this area. From the perspective of development, the 'right' local context for global production does not consist in the availability of low-wage workers or tax holidays and generous profit-remittance schemes. The interest of foreign capital in local industries should be encouraged on the basis of the existence of skilled and motivated people as well as reliable, flexible and high-quality domestic suppliers where entrepreneurship plays a critical role. Investment laws and foreign trade regulations are less effective in inducing in such cases global upgraded insertion than microeconomic factors such as strong incentive structures, entrepreneurship and a dense and flexible network of enterprises. A point has been reached where the creation of conditions for the local context of global activity has to be moved further, but that appears to be more a function of encompassing reforms than foreign investment or trade regulations.[12]

Comprehensive economic reform is also important given its possible impact on the domestic sources of investment. Increased efficiency as a result of reforms could be part of the answer as it could open the way for a less investment-intensive model of economic growth. However, by being concentrated in the state sector, efficiency-oriented reform could actually increase rather than reduce the need for investment (and resources) in the short to mid-term. The absorption of laid-off workers would need massive investment if they are to be reassimilated into the state sector. Most, if not all, of the efficiency gains would then have to be devoted to new investment replacing obsolete capacity but, beyond that, additional investment would be needed. Increased foreign investment could certainly smooth the process but the need to generate and mobilize additional domestic savings is very important for successful restructuring.

The existing potential for domestic savings beyond the state sector should not be underestimated; idle capacity in Cuba, including future idle capacity as a result of efficiency-oriented policies, should be allocated efficiently. As the recent experiment with agriculture has shown in Cuba, other forms of property and economic organization could be the answer to that problem. The capacity to create a vibrant domestic private sector in Cuba with a high potential for domestic savings is not disputed, although not openly recognized. In addition, the establishment of a private sector could attract new foreign investment and net transfers (remittances). The arguments against such a private sector are not based – as far as we know – on economic grounds, but on political considerations which certainly deserve proper attention. However, the possible impact of a private sector on economic growth in Cuba could be significant and thus it has to be factored into any equation of broad development of the country.

To summarize, some of the most important requirements in Cuba in order to sustain high economic growth and development are the following:

1   the adoption a model of intensive growth and the generation of adequate jobs (in quantity and quality) for a large share of Cuba's workforce;
2   fostering a process of economic innovation;
3   the creation of an adequate local context to attract substantially higher levels of foreign investment; and
4   the need to generate domestic savings and investment beyond the state sector.

Growth scenarios

To place the economic growth potential into a longer-term perspective, we have constructed a few scenarios to illustrate the possibilities and limits resulting from the external constraints of the Cuban economy. The objective is not to generate precise projections but only to evaluate the general logic of growth under different plausible circumstances in Cuba. The scenarios presented here deal with the possible impact of domestic policies on three key areas of the external sector – exports, net transfers and foreign savings – which could play a critical role in achieving higher rates of economic growth via increased demand and investment. A caveat is necessary, however, in the sense that these scenarios do not explore the possible impact of economic policies on other areas equally crucial for growth, such as investment and demand in non-foreign trade activities. The relatively limited perspective of alternative growth trajectories is justified considering the focus of this chapter on analysing the implications of Cuba's insertion into the world economy. A more comprehensive assessment of Cuba's paths of growth would have to include the analysis of the impact of possible reforms in the domestic sector of the economy.

The most important result of the scenarios is the level of goods imports since it is assumed that, according to previous experience, imports show a strong positive correlation with growth, particularly given their role in the supply of capital goods for investment. Historically, high rates of investment of 25 per cent of GDP in Cuba have been associated with import coefficients of 30 per cent of GDP, while rates of investment of 15 per cent of GDP have been related to import coefficients of around 20 per cent of GDP. Import coefficients below 15 per cent have been associated with very low rates of investment.[13] Therefore, in order to again achieve rates of investment of 25 per cent, and assuming moderate inflation, nominal levels of imports would have to be between 11 200 and 15 000 million pesos by 2005.[14]

Three scenarios have been formulated for two periods: short-term growth (1998–2000) and mid- to longer-term growth (2000–05). Since the emphasis of the projections is on processes that could be influenced by Cuba's economic policy, one key common assumption is adopted for both periods under the three scenarios: no substantial changes would take place in the state of US–Cuban relations. Another key assumption is that no major economic reforms would be adopted during the period. Given the centrality of reforms in future trajectories of the Cuban economy, that assumption needs further elaboration. We do consider that any estimate of the impact of economic reforms could be a tricky intellectual exercise since it would depend very much on the deepness, breadth, timing and sequencing of reforms, as well as their possible interaction with other factors (i.e. foreign investment). Therefore, if the issue at stake is the evaluation of possible reforms *vis-à-vis* other scenarios of no reform, then it appears to be more convenient to test a minimalist scenario of reform for which more plausible outcomes could be deduced. The point is that in doing this we are not predicting, in any way, that fundamental reforms would not be adopted in the period, our focus here is on scenario comparison, not on policy-making forecasts.

Among the possible scenarios, we are just interested in two basic alternatives: non-reform and reform, but we have accommodated a no-reform situation for two different possibilities: a sober estimate (more plausible) outcome, and an optimist (less plausible) outcome. Therefore, the three scenarios are:

- Scenario 1   low growth – stagnating reform process
- Scenario 2   moderate growth – stagnating reform process
- Scenario 3   accelerated growth – with modest continuing reform

To be more precise: scenario 1 is conceived as the logical continuation of current policies and trends; scenario 2 represents that continuation but under more optimistic assumptions (i.e. notable increases in efficiency, major oil discoveries and improved access to external financing); while scenario 3 represents modest economic reforms, particularly the expansion of private and cooperative activities (under the modalities of small and medium-sized firms) in addition to the existing state sector. In other words, the reforms assumed for scenario 3 are considered modest because they would create a non-state productive sector but with no privatization of state-owned enterprises.

We have addressed those scenarios in two different ways. First, from the viewpoint of the growth requirements of a Harrod–Domar type of perspective; that is, taking investment requirements as the starting point for warranted growth. And, second, we have checked the reasonableness of the scenarios looking at different alternatives in the dynamics of the external sector.

The following assumptions were made for each scenario (see Table 8.3 for the simulation results):

Scenario 1   low growth – non reform

- GDP growth from 1997 through 2005 – 4%;
- Investment increases from 8% in 1997 to 10% in 2000, and to 15% in 2005;
- Imported investment goods (capital goods) share of total investment increases from 49% in 1997 to 50% in 2000, and then stabilizes around that figure;
- The investment goods component of imports increases from 19% in 1997 to 20% in 2000, and then stabilizes;
- These assumptions determine the import volume requirements for the economy.

- *Scenario 2*   moderate growth – non reform

- GDP growth of 4% between 1997 and 2000, and then acceleration to 6% between 2000 and 2005;
- Investment rate increases to 20% already in the years after 2000 as a result of the expected speeding up of the growth to 6% of the economy after 2000;
- imported investment goods share of total investments has the same assumption as under scenario 1;
- The investment goods share of imports increases to 25% between 2000 and 2005 as a result of the increasing investment rate.

Table 8.3   Growth scenarios from a Harrod–Domar perspective, Cuba (figures in constant 1997 US$)

	1997	2000	Scenario 1 2005	Scenario 2 2005	Scenario 3 2005
GDP	19 767	22 139	26 883	29 650	35 581
Gross investment (GI)	1 522	2 214	4 032	5 930	8 895
GI/GDP (%)	7.7	10	15	20	25
Imp. inv. goods/GI (%)	49	50	50	50	50
Imp. inv. goods (IIG)	746	1 107	2 016	2 965	4 447
IIG/imports (%)	18.7	20	20	25	30
Imports	3 987	5 535	10 080	11 860	14 823

Note: Estimate of GDP in US$ for 1997 from EIU (2000).

- *Scenario 3*   The accelerated growth – modest reform
- GDP growth of 4% until 2000, then high sustained growth of 10% under the assumption that economic reforms will have a more positive effect on growth than the two previous scenarios;
- The investment rate increases to 25% in 2000 as a result of the investment requirements induced by the warranted economic growth of 10% after 2000;
- The imported investment goods share has the same assumption as under scenarios 1 and 2;
- The investment goods share of imports increases to 30% between 2000 and 2005.

These scenarios show that high import requirements, particularly imports of capital goods, will play a central role in any possible high economic growth trajectory. In other words, available financing to pay for imports will determine the rate of growth.

The dynamics of the external sector

In order to check the reasonableness of the growth requirements derived from the previous exercise, different key variables of the external sector are tested for each scenario. For scenario 1, rather benign assumptions have been adopted since the focus is not so much in identifying precise figures but in highlighting limits; for scenario 2, assumptions are somewhat 'wildly' optimistic; and for scenario 3, very modest (minimal) assumptions have been adopted. The purpose is to deduce alternative levels of imports, taking into account different possible configurations of the main factors that could influence imports. Assumptions are made for the following indicators: exports, service balance, income balance, net transfers and current account (see Table 8.4). Trade balance (goods) and imports (goods) are then calculated from the previous factors.

As can be seen in Table 8.5 the optimistic assumptions for scenario 2 have been adopted only from the year 2000 (i.e. no short term 'miracles' are expected), while in scenario 3 the short-term impact of reform is basically considered as a moderate increase in the availability of external funds as the consequence of a positive reaction from external actors to reform. For the mid- to longer-term period, under scenario 3, the impact is assumed to be greater availability of remittances, additional current account financing, and an increase (rather modest) in exports, originating in the emerging private and cooperative sectors.

What do these scenarios mean in terms of possible trajectories of growth? If the level of imports is the key indicator (given its correlation with growth), it is clear that the relevant period for the analysis is the mid to longer term since there are no significative differences in imports among scenarios for the period 1998–2000. In the short term, the assumed increase of imports appears to be compatible with modest economic growth (around 4%) fuelled by export growth, increased private consumption (partially supported by increased remittances) and moderate additional availability of external financing. Figures could be upwardly biased as a result of the adoption of benign assumptions (particularly sugar exports and current account financing), but the key point is that in the short-term economic growth would be possible with relatively low investment and therefore it could be compatible with a low savings and low investment context.

However, the mid- to longer-term scenario reveals the limits that could be met for growth under current policies, and differences among scenarios are revealing. The sober non-reform scenario appears to be a losing proposition in the sense that it projects a path of low economic growth ill-suited to solve the problems of the Cuban economy. In the other two scenarios imports are closer to the estimated level of imports that would be needed to have investment rates of 25% of GDP, although there are important differences between scenarios 2 and 3 that could be relevant for policy-making.

The optimistic non-reform scenario is highly dependent on the occurrence of an economic miracle. Some of its assumptions are largely out of the control of policy-makers and are also highly unpredictable (i.e. major oil discoveries), while other assumptions may be very hard to materialize (e.g. new export commodities) or relatively unrealistic (i.e. a 'jump' in efficiency and ample availability of current account financing). Trends in current economic policy seem in fact to have a low impact potential on the eventual unfolding of this miracle scenario.

Table 8.4 The external account in the scenarios, Cuba

	Scenario 1 sober – non-reform		Scenario 2 optimist – non-reform		Scenario 3 modest reform	
	1998–2000	2000–05	1998–2000[a]	2000–05	1998–2000[b]	2000–05
Exports (goods)[c]	10% annual growth, full potential by the year 2000	Stagnated at the levels of the year 2000	—	4% annual growth	10% annual growth, full potential by the year 2000	7% annual growth
Exports of services (tourism)[d]	13% annual growth	15% annual growth	—	15% annual growth	13% annual growth	15% annual growth
Net transfer payments (remittances)	10% annual growth, full potential by the year 2000	Stagnated at the levels of the year 2000	—	10% annual growth	20% annual growth	15% annual growth
Current Account[e]	Moderate expansion in the deficit, reflecting modest availability of financing	Moderate expansion in the deficit, reflecting additional availability of financing	—	Annual growth over 20% in the deficit, reflecting ample availability of financing	25% annual growth, reflecting positive reaction of foreign actors to reform	Stagnated at the level of the year 2000[g]
Imports	18% annual growth	8% annual growth	—	12% annual growth, plus import substitution of oil by 2 billion US dollars[f]	Annual growth over 20%	12% annual growth

[a] Scenario 1 and scenario 2 share the same assumptions for the short term. The optimist scenario (2) rests on factors that have low probabilities of occurrence in the short term (substantial increases in efficiency, relatively ample availability of external financing, sustained increases in new exports of goods, and major oil discoveries).

[b] In the short term, scenario 3 assumes strong, rapid and positive reaction to reforms by foreign actors.

[c] For the short term, under the scenarios, are adopted rather benign assumptions of rapid increases in the exports of traditional goods for the period 1998–2000 (75% for sugar, 20% for nickel and 100% for tobacco).

[d] For the three scenarios the growth of tourism is considered 'exogenous' with respect to domestic policies. All three scenarios share the same assumptions for the level of the service balance. Import of services are of US$600 million in the year 2000 and US$1200 million by the year 2005. The increase reflects higher levels of economic activity.

[e] All three scenarios share the same assumptions for the income balance deficit (factor services). Non-radical modifications are assumed for the short term with respect to the year 1997. Increases by the year 2005 reflect larger interest payments resulting from more ample availability of financing for the current account deficit.

[f] Import substitution of oil will mean additional availability of other inputs, therefore the real impact of increased imports on growth would be higher than the total level suggested by the import figures.

[g] That stagnated level is not probable but a minimalist approach has been adopted. For the period 2000–05 this scenario basically highlights the impact of reforms on new exports of goods and increased remittances.

Table 8.5   Scenarios until 2005: the dynamics of the external sector, Cuba (constant prices)

	1997	2000	2005 Scenario 1	2005 Scenario 2	2005 Scenario 3
Exports of goods	1 823	2 500	2 500	3 000	3 500
Exports of services	1 962	3 000	6 000	6 000	6 000
Total exports	3 785	5 500	8 500	9 000	9 000
Service balance	1 519	2 400	4 800	4 800	4 800
Income balance	−483	−600	−800	−800	−800
Net transfer payments	792	1 200	1 200	1 900	3 000
Current account	−437	−700	−1 000	−2 000	−1 000
Trade balance goods[a]	−2 265	−3 700	−6 200	−7 900	−8 000
Imports of goods[b]	−4 088	−6 200	−8 700	−10 900	−11 500

Notes: All figures for 1997 are taken from ONE (2000) *Annario Estadístico de Cuba 1998*.
[a] Calculated as the current account figure less the total sum of the service balance, income balance (factor services) and net transfer; [b] calculated as the trade balance (goods) less exports (goods).

The modest reform scenario, on the other hand, provides similar results to scenario 2 but it is based on processes under the control of policy-makers (i.e. economic reform). Scenario 3 reveals that even modest economic reforms could have the same impact on external constraints as the materialization of wild bets on economic miracles. The main difference is of course the degree of control and relative predictability of the process when it is dependent on tested economic policy (i.e. the expansion of non-state economic activities) and not on questionable expectations, as it is in the case of scenario 2.

The assumptions in scenario 3 are rather conservative and precisely for that reason the results of that scenario are significant. Economic reform is limited to the fostering of small and medium-sized enterprises (private and cooperative) but with no major restructuring of state-owned enterprises. To be more precise, no privatization of state assets is considered. In addition, the assumed growth of exports from non-state enterprises is relatively low relative to the actual potential in Cuba and relative to other experiences (e.g. China and Vietnam). The eventual response of foreign actors in providing current account financing has been underplayed while the assumption that is made in terms of increased remittances is rather conservative, taking into account that this is, beyond any doubt, the area with the greatest responsiveness (and lower economic costs) in terms of the mobilization of foreign savings. It should be expected that the creation of a non-state sector in Cuba would be conducive not only to increasing flows of remittances, but to a modification in the utilization of those flows as well. A large share of remittances would be directed towards investment.

The lessons from the scenarios are the following. First, current policies are conducive either to unsatisfactory economic inertia or high dependence on unrealistic economic miracles, while modest reforms could work better than current policies, or at least as well as expected miracles (in the absence of reform). Second, economic reform should be the most realistic approach to high growth although more fundamental reforms than the one assumed in this discussion would be needed since a modest approach to reform could not provide a relaxed environment to deal with external constraints, given that estimated imports under modest reforms would be too close to the minimum level of imports that are required for an adequate rate of invest- ment. Third, economic reforms, particularly actions directed towards the development of a private sector, have a tested potential in terms of stimulat- ing higher growth rates (via its impact on domestic sectors) and therefore they complement the effect of reform on the solution of external con- straints.

To summarize, the solution of the economic problems of Cuba needs high rates of economic growth which are dependent on adequate levels of invest- ment. Current policies are not conducive to those levels of investment via the solution of external constraints, nor could modest reforms solve the problem. More fundamental reforms are needed in order to clearly overcome external constraints and for the creation of a high-growth domestic sector.

Conclusions

The solution of Cuba's long-term economic problems is dependent on a path of high sustained economic growth. The recovery of the levels of total output that existed before the crisis (in 1989) could be reached by 2005 under the official assumption of an average rate of growth of 4 per cent per year, but that would mean that 15 years of economic growth would have been lost for the country.

More rapid economic growth is not, however, only a matter of accelerating the process of recovery and minimizing the duration of long-term stagna- tion. It is, above all, a necessary condition for the vast structural transforma- tion that the Cuban economy requires. If autarky is discarded as a realistic option, then the long-term viability of the Cuban economy within the contemporary world system would be dependent on its successful interna- tional insertion, which means that a relatively large share of the country's total output would have to find its way into world markets. That possibility rests on a substantial transformation of the current structure of output and will need a process of massive investment which would be determined by the availability of funds. There is no plausible reason to assume that this trans- formation is compatible with a low-growth trajectory of the economy. Sim- ply put, low growth is not conducive to a domestic high-savings environment, neither is it particularly attractive for external funding.

In addition, the success of that transformation will require much higher levels of efficiency, the intensive use of the factors of production where there is comparative advantage, adequate levels and quality of employment opportunities, and a sustained capacity for the absorption of technological learning. Economic transformation of this magnitude is not free of problems, particularly those of a social nature, but the fact is that designing and implementing social policies could be less of a problem in a growing economy than otherwise.

There are different theoretical alternatives to deal with these issues as well as diverse means at the disposal of policy-makers, but before reaching the point of implementation a clear decision has to be made as to which sector(s) will be prioritized for high economic growth. If that priority is adopted, then other factors should be considered instrumental to it and not as alternatives to high growth. In this sense, the deepness of economic reform is crucial. This chapter suggests that in the absence of economic reforms directed towards the development of a sizeable *domestic* non-state productive sector, sustained high economic growth should not be expected in Cuba.

This is not to say that economic reform should focus on downsizing the state sector, but only to make the point that a mixed economy is needed. Economic reform should include many other actions, including the revitalization of state-owned enterprises which could play an important role in the economy. There is no reason to discard the possibility of the existence of a productive and efficient state sector. Nonetheless, it is evident that the Cuban state has no means of its own to successfully implement the required economic transformations, and therefore private funds are necessary to achieve high rates of growth. In addition to funds, private capital could be the source of technological learning and more efficiency.

Foreign capital has played (under different modalities) a role in recent transformations of the Cuban economy, but by policy design the role of foreign capital has been relatively limited until now, although that could be changed to accommodate larger potential flows. However, even under the possible introduction of more flexible foreign investment regulations it would continue to be a limited process due to other factors that could only be overcome by economic reform. Private domestic capital has a very limited presence in Cuba (basically confined to agricultural production) although the cooperative sector is relatively large. Under current policies, the potential role of the non-state sector can only play a limited role in investment and economic growth. The so-called self-employment sector is the result of the formalization of the informal economy and in practice plays no important role in economic strategy, other than providing a survival mechanism for a sector of the population.

The issue to be considered is that high growth will require the mobilization and effective utilization of existing resources in the country, something that under current policies would be difficult to achieve, particularly given the almost exclusive emphasis on the state sector. The role of a domestic private sector could make the entire difference between a path of low economic growth and a high-growth trajectory. First, the idea that a domestic private sector could not make any sensible contribution given that it would be limited by its lack of hard currency to import critical inputs should be put into a better perspective. There are many labour-intensive and knowledge-intensive activities where this is definitely not the case. The potential of a developed private sector to attract remittances, and to allocate them to investment, could be the most cost-effective mechanism to attract foreign savings, and, in addition, it should be expected that foreign capital would also flow into the domestic private sector. Second, profits from domestic private enterprises could become an important source of savings and capital accumulation; and, third, the transfer to the private sector of assets inefficiently utilized by the state would improve the state's potential for accumulation.

Although we have not attempted in this chapter to outline a proposal, some policy-oriented considerations are suggested:

- a high growth strategy should be adopted as a priority in economic strategy; and
- economic reform should be directed towards the creation of a mixed economy with a sizeable presence for a domestic private sector.

The minimum course of action to be implemented could be the relatively limited approach of a 'private sector on the side', that is, a private sector in addition to the state sector but with no transfer of assets from the latter. This approach might not be sufficient in the longer run, however, to overcome the limits imposed on growth by external constraints.

Notes

1 Partido Comunista de Cuba, 'Resolución Económica del V Congreso del Partido Comunista de Cuba, *Granma*, 7 November 1997.
2 Domestic savings could contribute to investment in the absence, or near absence, of imported inputs, particularly in certain areas of agriculture and many other labour-intensive activities.
3 CEPAL, *op. cit.*, table A46.
4 It has been claimed that market socialism could be theoretically at least as efficient as neoclassical corporate capitalism in terms of calculation and motivation. Adaman and Devine (1997).
5 See, e.g., Bowles and Xiao-yuan Dong (1994) and Adaman and Devine 1997.
6 *Ibid.*
7 *Ibid.*
8 Partido Comunista de Cuba (1997).
9 There is a broader issue that will not be addressed in this chapter although it is very important: does it make sense – from a leftist perspective – to limit policy-

making to a process of adaptation to globalization? The answer to that question will depend very much on the understanding of globalization. Is globalization a technologically-driven process, and thus irreversible and inevitable, or is it politically-driven and thus a potentially contestable process? See, Panitch and Bienefeld in Miliband and Panitch (eds) (1994).

10   Gereffi (1997).

11   'Strategic' in the sense of being different from 'close' integration; Singh (1994).

12   The recent establishment of Export Processing Zones is not the answer to Cuban needs for foreign investment in industry. The current approach is not only very limited but also self-defeating in terms of attracting substantial upgraded activities.

13   CEPAL, *op. cit.*, table A2.

14   Assuming increases in the unit value of imports of 4% and 6% per year respectively.

Part III
The Case of Vietnam

9
Systemic Change and Economic Reform in Vietnam

Raymond Mallon and George Irvin

Introduction

A 1999 World Bank report on Vietnam's economy argued that 'Eighteen months ago, Vietnam's economy was "coasting downwind", spurred by 25 per cent annual growth in its exports, and plentiful foreign savings looking for investment opportunities. The situation today could hardly be more different' (World Bank, 1998).[1] It further argued that the business environment 'is seen by investors as increasingly hostile'. A 1999 Reuters report maintained that Vietnam 'has gone from being an E1 Dorado to an investment backwater in less than a decade...' (Reuters, 19 February 1999). This scepticism was despite Vietnam experiencing an average annual GNP growth rate of around 8.5 per cent from 1991 to 1998, and average annual export growth of more than 26 per cent over the same period. Inflation remained under 10 per cent in the late 1990s. As a ratio of GDP, foreign investment inflows were amongst the highest in Southeast Asia during the mid-1990s.

There is no doubt that the Asian financial crisis contributed to an economic slowdown, prompting official estimates of 5.8 per cent growth during 1998, with the prospects for growth in later years more uncertain. Trade growth and FDI approvals and inflows fell sharply, but by less than elsewhere in the region. The nominal exchange rate depreciated by about 17 per cent in the 18 months after the crisis, compared with nominal depreciations of between 30 and 80 per cent elsewhere in the region. This had major implications for the competitiveness of Vietnamese exports. The World Bank argued that the Asian financial crisis provided a 'kick in the stomach to the momentum of growth... equivalent to around US\$ 3 billion, or 12 per cent of GDP' (World Bank, 1998). If this were true, then Vietnam's 5.8 per cent growth in 1998 was particularly impressive.

The basic purpose of this chapter is to ask whether the increasingly frequent doom and gloom predictions about a turnaround in prospects for the Vietnamese economy in the 1990s and the beginning of the new century were not somewhat overdone. There is no doubt that levels of foreign investment approvals declined substantially, but whether there was evidence that the business environment had become hostile was quite another matter. This issue is related to whether it was ever the case that the Vietnamese economy was coasting downwind. This characterization must be considered in light of the performance of other countries in the region. Our basic approach in looking at these issues is to describe key indicators of change in the economic and institutional environment over the 1990s, and to provide indicators of economic performance relative to that of the 'tiger economies'.

In the next section are summarized Vietnam's main economic indicators, showing how these evolved between the Sixth Congress, when agreement was reached on the need to substantially change the system of economic management, and the Eighth in 1996. We then examine some of the main questions raised by the sceptics: for example, 'is the party really as committed to reform as it claims?'; 'what is happening in terms of poverty?' and 'is growth sustainable in the long term?' Vietnam's performance is then compared with that of other countries of the region, and future macroeconomic prospects are considered. Finally we conclude that despite important lacunae in the reform process, the impetus to increasing living standards and national income via a market-based allocation of resources was maintained into the new century.

Changes in the economic environment: 1986–96

The magnitude of change in Vietnam since the introduction of *doi moi* can be seen in key socioeconomic indicators at the time of the Sixth, Seventh and Eighth Party Congresses, set out in Table 9.1. At the time of the Sixth Party Congress at the end of 1986, the country faced a major economic crisis; despite price controls on most goods and services, the annual rate of inflation was over 700 per cent. The value of exports amounted to US$500 million, considerably less than half the total value of imports (US$1221 million). Although the government could claim notable achievements in health and education, the central government generated a large deficit by maintaining a large standing army and civil service, and supporting loss-making state enterprises. Inflation was fuelled by the monetization of the resulting deficit, people had to queue for food and sections of the population faced regular periods of famine. There was virtually no foreign investment; the technology gap between Vietnam and its neighbours grew; visits by Vietnamese nationals to market economies were rare; and, apart from a limited number of diplomats and aid workers, very few foreigners from market economies worked in Vietnam.

When the Seventh Congress met in 1991, previous reforms had provided greatly improved incentives for investments to increase the level and quality of production. Farmers had been given medium-term rights to the use of

Table 9.1   Key indicators of economic transformation, Vietnam

	Party Congress		
	6th	*7th*	*8th*
Indicator	*(1986)*	*(1991)*	*(1996)*
Economic growth (%)	3.4	6.0	9.3
Income/capital (US$)	n.a.	228	290
Consumer Price Index (%, year to Dec.)	775	67	4.5
Food grain production (kg of paddy/person)	301	323	385
Budget surplus	−6.2	−3.8	−0.7
Budget revenue	14.0	13.5	23.6
Capital investment	6.3	2.8	6.0
Government social service expenditure	3.2	4.4	7.6
Domestic savings	n.a.	13.2	16.7
government	n.a.	1.3	6.0
non-government	n.a.	11.9	10.7
Foreign savings	n.a.	1.9	11.3
National investment	n.a.	15.1	27.9
FDI (US$ millions)	–	220	1838
Official Development Assistance (US$ millions)	–	110	764
Exports (US$ millions)	494	2042	7330
Imports (US$ millions)	1121	2105	10480

land; prices and the exchange rate were largely market-determined; and laws on foreign investment, private enterprises and companies had been enacted. Economic growth accelerated to 6 per cent, but part of this growth, in the oil and electricity sectors, resulted from previous large investments financed by the USSR. The value of exports, at just over US$2 billion, was about four times that recorded in 1986, but was dominated by three commodities – oil, rice and sea products. Thus, there were doubts as to whether growth was sustainable.

At the beginning of the 1990s, the government intervened in a range of micro aspects of economic and personal decisions. The number of Vietnamese permitted to travel and study in market economies was beginning to increase, but few policy and decision-makers had experience outside the country. The number of foreigners working in Vietnam increased, but they required official permission for internal travel, which was limited to those provinces specified in the permit. Foreign businesses, embassies and international agencies had limited flexibility in the recruitment of local staff, and the 1980 Constitution provided little protection for the private sector and foreign investors. However, the economy suffered from the major external shock resulting from the collapse of economic cooperation with the former CMEA countries; major macroeconomic imbalances persisted, and prospects for sustained economic development were still very uncertain. 1991 inflation measured on a December-to-December basis was 67 per cent, after having being brought down to single-digit levels in 1989 (World Bank, 1996, table 6.1b). External assistance from the Eastern Bloc had effectively stopped; and access to financing from the IMF, World Bank and the Asian Development Bank continued to be blocked by the US government. As state enterprises were restructured and government finances reorganized during the period 1989–93, they laid off roughly a million employees and the central government another 160 000; most were absorbed by the emerging private sector, including rapidly increasing household business activity. Redundancies in state enterprises and government agencies (including the military) were politically sensitive issues.

Moreover, at the time of the Seventh Congress, the fiscal current deficit was 3.8 per cent of GDP with the share of government revenue a meagre 13.5 per cent.[2] Public investment was constrained both financially and by implementation capacity; total investment, at 15 per cent of GDP, was less than half that of most East Asian economies (ADB, 1996). Foreign investment approvals were increasing, but disbursements remained low. There remained considerable domestic and international scepticism about whether initial economic improvements could be sustained. In short, in 1991 it seemed far from certain that Vietnam could meet its goal of sustaining an 8 per cent annual growth rate, still less meet it without raising inflation and rekindling serious inflationary expectations which would have curtailed domestic savings still further.

When the Eighth Congress arrived in 1996, the situation had changed markedly. GNP growth for 1996 was over 9 per cent, and the average during the previous five-year period was 8.2 per cent. Inflation had been brought down to an annual rate under 3 per cent by October 1996. Inflation in the 12 months to December 1998 had increased to about 9 per cent partly as a result of the Asian financial crisis. Despite a 9 per cent appreciation in the real effective exchange rate from 1993–96,[3] convertible currency exports had trebled from US$2.1 billion in 1991 to US$6.8 billion for 1996. Equally important, exports were becoming more diversified, with strong growth in non-traditional exports including garments, footwear and processed agriculture commodities (coffee, tea, cashews and rubber). The share of government revenue almost doubled to reach 25 per cent of GNP in 1996. Importantly, in terms of sustaining economic growth, total investment doubled to 28 per cent of GDP, there was very rapid growth in FDI inflows and an acceleration in disbursements. Gross national savings increased to 17 per cent of GDP in 1996 (see Table 9.1 and Irvin, 1996).

While there were frequent complaints from foreign businesses about the problems of doing business in Vietnam, FDI inflows increased spectacularly in the mid-1990s. As a ratio of GDP, inflows have been high, even by East Asia standards. The ODA (official development assistance) disbursement ratio, previously constrained by the country's limited administrative experience with Western aid, increased sharply after 1996. Private property rights, recognized under the 1992 Constitution, were strengthened by the 9 November 1995 Civil Code and the 23 May 1997 Commercial Code. The number of registered private enterprises increased rapidly, albeit from a small base. Permission was no longer required for internal travel, and the number of Vietnamese visiting and studying in market economies grew.

In an apparent paradox, between 1991 and 1996 the reported share of the state increased from 33 per cent to 37 per cent of GDP (Table 9.2), despite growing legal protection for the private sector and a declining share of state-sector employment. Four factors explained this rise. First, the share of state revenue rose substantially after 1990, contributing to macrostability. Second, some major state enterprises modernized rapidly by obtaining new technology through foreign investment that they were favourably positioned to attract. Third, the state enterprise figures reflect two data problems: the treatment of joint venture output, discussed below, and the continued underrecording of private informal sector activity. With respect to the latter, considerable mistrust of the state bureaucracy by the small and medium-sized entrepreneurs continued, along with incentives to avoid taxes and reporting requirements associated with the formal sector. Given the continued low level of public sector salaries, 'rent-seeking behaviour' was unlikely to disappear, however much foreign businesses complained or the authorities sought to reduce corruption.

Table 9.2 Sector shares of GDP from the 6th to the 8th party congresses, Vietnam, 1986–96 (%)

	6th (1986)	*7th (1991)*	*8th (1996)*
Agriculture	43.8	39.2	26.3
Industry	25.7	23.1	31.9
Services	30.5	37.7	41.9
Total	100.0	100.0	100.0
State	33.1	33.2	37.3
Non-state	66.9	66.8	62.7

Note: Figures for 1986 and 1991 are at constant 1989 prices while constant 1994 prices are used for 1996. The dramatic shift from agriculture to industry (and to a lesser extent services) in the five years to 1996 thus reflects both relative price shifts and structural change.
Sources: General Statistics Office. 1998. *Statistical Yearbook 1997* and earlier editions.

State enterprises benefited greatly from foreign investment in the form of joint ventures. For example, foreign investment played an important role in improving technology and transferring skills in telecommunication services and oil production. However, official statistics recorded output from these sectors as 100 per cent in the public sector. There continued to be discrimination in favour of state enterprises, in access to decision-makers, import quotas and land, as well as preferential access to credit. These advantages contributed to the strong performance of state enterprises, and partly explain the continued interest shown by foreign investors' joint ventures with them.[4] Despite the 'level playing field' objection, the number of registered private enterprises and companies increased rapidly during the 1990s, from 770 in 1990 to about 30 000 by 1996 and more than 33 000 in 1997, compared with about 6000 state enterprises (Mallon, 1998b). Private enterprises were very small-scale in most cases, with the numbers rising. Most former industrial and service sector cooperatives were disbanded, but some were reorganized as private enterprises. The number of individual or household business operations was estimated to have increased from 568 000 in 1986 to 835 800 in 1990, and 2 215 000 by 1996 (Mallon, 1998b).

More generally, *doi moi* appeared to impact on the lives of the majority of the population by increasing the supply of basic commodities, in particular food, clothing and shelter. Strong economic growth contributed to marked improvements in per capita income in the 1990s, which appears to have increased in all parts of the country with the strongest growth in urban areas. The UNDP (1996) reported a fall in absolute poverty from 70 to 50 per cent since the beginning of *doi moi*, a quite cautious estimate.[5] The World Bank estimated that the proportion of people living in absolute poverty fell from 70 per cent to 30–35 per cent in 1998. On the political side, rapid growth and higher incomes, particularly in the countryside, mobilized sustained support for the party and the reform process.

These reforms took place despite the limited substantive changes in policy directions outlined in the Political Reports of the Party Congresses over the ten-year period. These reports stressed the leading role of the state in economic development, but were reluctant to explain what that meant for the future structure of the Vietnamese economy. The Eighth Party Congress documents recognized a long-term role for the private sector, whereas prior reports only suggested a role during a transition period. However, given the range of possible interpretations of these documents, it is difficult to draw any strong conclusions about future policy directions from the Report of the Eighth Congress.

Major policy issues

International observers expressed increasing concern in the 1990s about the degree of commitment of the government to reform. The political debates and delays in decision-making during the lead-up to and aftermath of the Eighth Party Congress contributed to such concerns, which were reinforced by the measures aimed at reducing 'unhealthy' foreign influences, including actions against advertisers and the press, and corruption, an issue which increased in importance in the 1990s. Inconsistencies in policy-making, such as those relating to land use, the property market and bank operations, and frequent changes in policies directly affecting the potential profitability of investments did not help. There were also a number of tensions between foreign investors and local partners which raised concerns about mechanisms for dispute resolution.

Despite these concerns, the increasing levels of actual inflows of foreign investment up until the East Asian crisis (Table 9.1) suggested that the major foreign investors, mainly from East Asia, were convinced of Vietnam's economic potential, demonstrating this with substantial annual inflows. The number of limited liability companies and shareholding companies continued to increase.

A second concern was the distributional implications of the reforms. After the introduction of *doi moi*, economic growth was broadly-based with strong expansion for most commodities.[6] While agriculture growth has been impressive by regional standards, much faster growth has been recorded in industry and services. Given that 70 per cent of the workforce is employed in agriculture, the more rapid growth of non-agriculture sectors implied a growing inequality in incomes between agricultural and non-agricultural workers, unless the former could find non-agricultural employment. Employment growth in industry and services, particularly in rural areas, would be important in the future for mitigating growing income inequality. However, in the 1990s, growth in formal employment has been much lower than economic growth and only marginally higher than population growth.

Government policy statements indicated that the reduction of poverty and economic inequalities were important objectives. The key to achieving this would be the creation of non-agricultural employment in rural areas, implying increased investment in small and medium-sized enterprises that would be most likely to have low capital–labour ratios. There were, however, contradictions between stated poverty alleviation objectives and a public investment plan that included substantial allocations to heavy industries, such as cement, steel and oil refining, that required large capital investments and would generate relatively little employment.

There was also concern about government attempts to protect capital-intensive industries through continued use of import quotas and taxes. These restrictions were in effect a tax on unprotected sectors, including many light industries, which were likely to generate the greatest employment. Equally, concern arose about the lobbying efforts of some foreign investors together with their state enterprise partners to secure protection from competition. Unlike South Korea, Vietnam made no effort to link old-style import substitution to export growth by making protection to domestic enterprise conditional upon their meeting export targets.[7] Clearly, the problem of inefficient commercial policy would need resolving if Vietnam were to implement the goals of tariff reduction quota elimination envisaged in ASEAN's commitment to completing the Asean Free Trade Area (AFTA) by the middle of the first decade of the twenty-first century.[8]

As noted earlier, foreign direct investment was a major factor in growth, and national investment doubled to almost 30 per cent of GDP by 1996 and 1997. Most of this growth was financed by rapid increases in foreign savings with sharply increased inflows of FDI and, to a lesser extent, official development assistance. However, there was some concern about the level of commercial foreign borrowings involving implicit or explicit government guarantees. While its share of total domestic investment might decline substantially, foreign investment would be likely to continue to play an important role in economic development even with the current Asian downturn.

Government savings and investment also increased as a result of improved revenue performance. However, while private domestic savings increased in absolute terms, the share of private domestic savings[9] in GDP was only about 13 per cent in 1996, and does not appear to have increased subsequently. Reported private domestic savings (and investment) remained low compared with most other East Asian economies. This partly reflected underdeveloped marked institutions, continuing suspicions about official institutions and continuing preferential treatment to state enterprises and foreign investment. If recent high growth would be sustained, greater emphasis would need to be given to these issues and increasing private domestic savings. Domestic private investment would be more likely to be directed to small and medium-sized enterprises that would generate a higher incremental output and employment for a given capital investment.

Vietnam recorded a growth rate just above the average for all Southeast Asian countries during the five-year period 1991–95. In 1995–98, the record has been even better. During the 1991–95 period Vietnam's economy, as measured by the country's gross domestic product (GDP), grew at a similar rate to that achieved by Thailand and Malaysia, and well above the Philippines and Burma (Table 9.3). Vietnam moved rapidly from a closed economy to an increasingly open economy. External trade and foreign investment flows as a percentage of gross domestic product compared favourably with that of Vietnam's rapidly developing neighbours (Table 9.4). Annual export growth averaged 25 per cent from 1991 to 1995, compared with 20 per cent in Thailand and 16 per cent in Philippines.[10] However, this was initially from a low base. Exports from Vietnam amounted to US$3.6 billion in 1994, compared with exports of almost US$13.4 billion from the Philippines and US$45 billion from Thailand. In contrast, exports from Burma were less than

Table 9.3   Economic growth in selected countries (per cent per annum)

Country	1991	1992	1993	1994	1995	1996	1997	*Average* *(1991–97)*	*GDP/pop* *1996 US$*
Vietnam	6.0	8.7	8.1	8.8	9.5	9.3	8.8	8.5	290
Thailand	8.5	8.1	8.7	8.6	8.8	5.5	−0.4	6.8	2 960
S. Korea	9.1	5.1	5.8	8.6	8.9	7.1	5.5	7.2	10 610
Philippines	−0.6	0.3	2.1	4.4	4.8	5.7	5.1	3.1	1 160
Malaysia	8.6	7.8	8.3	9.2	9.5	8.6	7.5	8.5	4 370
Laos	4.0	7.0	5.9	8.1	7.0	6.9	7.2	6.6	400
Indonesia	8.9	7.2	7.3	7.5	8.2	8.0	4.6	7.4	1 080
Myanmar	−0.6	9.7	6.0	7.5	6.9	5.8	5.0	5.8	n.a.

Source: ADB, *Asian Development Outlook, 1998.*

Table 9.4   Growth rate of trade in selected countries (per cent per annum)

	1991	1992	1993	1994	1995	1996	1997	*Average* *(1991–97)*
Exports								
Vietnam	18.0	21.2	20.6	35.8	28.2	41.0	22.2	26.7
Thailand	23.8	13.7	13.4	22.7	24.8	−1.9	3.2	14.2
Philippines	8.0	11.1	15.8	18.5	29.4	17.7	22.8	17.6
Malaysia	17.0	18.1	16.1	23.1	26.6	7.3	6.0	16.3
Indonesia	10.5	14.0	8.3	9.9	18.0	5.8	11.2	11.1
Burma	11.1	37.2	17.8	31.8	−2.8	4.6	7.5	15.3
Imports								
Vietnam	18.8	20.4	39.3	48.5	43.8	39.0	−1.6	29.7
Thailand	15.8	6.0	12.1	18.1	31.9	0.6	−9.3	10.7
Philippines	−1.3	20.5	21.2	21.2	23.7	20.8	14.0	17.2
Malaysia	26.8	10.1	17.8	28.1	30.4	1.7	7.0	17.4
Indonesia	15.7	7.8	6.0	13.9	26.6	8.1	4.8	11.8
Myanmar	−42.5	19.9	28.9	14.3	2.3	8.2	7.0	5.4

Source: ADB, *Asian Development Outlook, 1998.*

US$400 million in the same year. Vietnam's exports growth remained strong, reaching US$7.3 billion in 1996 and an estimated US$9.3 billion in 1998 (World Bank, 1998, p. 81).

As previously noted, inflows of foreign direct investment to Vietnam increased sharply in the first half of the 1990s,[11] with other East Asian economies the dominant source of investment. Foreign investment inflows to Vietnam during 1995 were high, even relative to other Southeast Asian countries, and further increased to US$2.2 billion during 1996 (Table 9.5)

Table 9.5   Foreign direct investment, Vietnam (FDI in US$ millions)

	1989	1990	1991	1992	1993	1994	1995	1996
Vietnam								
Total value FDI projects								
Approved	539	600	1223	1937	2800	4071	6616	8600
ADB estimates of FDI								
inflows	100	120	229	385	523	742	2000	2156
Other SE Asia FDI inflows								
Indonesia	682	1093	1482	1777	2004	2109	4348	7960
Malaysia	1668	2332	3998	5183	5006	4342	4132	5300
Philippines	563	530	544	228	763	1126	1478	1408
Thailand	1775	2444	2014	2114	1730	1322	2003	2426

Source: ADB, *Asian Development Outlook 1998.*

These inflows declined marginally in 1997, then sharply in 1998 with the curtailment of a number of large East Asian financed projects.[12] While foreign investors faced many difficulties operating in Vietnam, especially during the initial stage, major investors subsequently expanded operations beyond the levels initially planned and approved. FDI inflows are unlikely to exceed US$1 billion a year in the immediate future, but would be likely to remain high as a percentage of GDP compared with other East Asian economies.

The key question was whether Vietnam's capital inflows were sustainable. They would be unsustainable if, for example, they were used to finance consumption or led to growing foreign indebtedness and unserviceable levels of debt service. The ratio of interest and amortization payments to exports fell after 1990, and by 1997 was about 6 per cent. The World Bank did not expect this to increase beyond 8 per cent up to 2001 (World Bank, 1998, p. 85) and thus the growth of indebtedness did not seem to be a major constraining factor. However, private savings remained relatively low. Until 1997 it appeared that a high investment to GDP ratio could be maintained by relying on foreign savings to bridge the gap. Capital inflows then declined, leading to a fall in the investment ratio and growth in 1998. It was a reasonable expectation that between 1998 and 2000 average growth would be of the order of 5 per cent.

An equally vexed question concerns the sustainability of the trade deficit. In 1996 this was equal to about 10 per cent of GDP, although the 1998 estimate was less than 5 per cent. In fact, the trade deficit was largely accommodating large inflows of ODA and FDI; that is, the trade gap merely reflects the foreign savings 'wedge' between total investment and domestic savings. It is 'unsustainable' only to the extent that its composition shifts from intermediate inputs to consumption goods imports in excess of export earnings. While there is some concern that this might be happening, the government has reacted by tightening fiscal policy such that the overall budget deficit amounted to only 1.0 per cent of GDP in 1998 (World Bank, 1998, p. 11). The current account deficit fell sharply from 11.2 per cent of GDP in 1996 to an estimated 4.6 per cent in 1998. The greater challenges seemed to be increasing the firm-level efficiency in the state enterprise sector, improving the country's 'absorptive capacity' for foreign investment, and accelerating the modernization of financial and related institutions responsible for private domestic savings mobilization.

It has been estimated that GDP in Vietnam grew at a rate of 4.4 per cent in both 1998 and in 1999, a marked decline on recent years but impressive given the turmoil elsewhere in the region (Table 9.6). Most of industry still did well, although the very high rates of growth in garments and footwear slowed. Electronics, cement and petroleum remained strong; and most foreign investment ventures continued to be dynamic, though the growth in construction and services (except tourism) seemed likely to slow. The large oversupply of luxury hotel rooms would probably lead to promoting increasing travel to Vietnam. However, no substantive new foreign investments could be expected in some important areas which previously absorbed large levels of foreign investment, including property development, cement production, automobile production and oil exploration. New investments were more likely to be concentrated in smaller-scale manufacturing industries and possibly in a number of larger projects in the energy sector.

What view one took of Vietnam's prospects in the longer term depended partly on how one assessed the East Asian crisis; that is, as merely transitory or as provoking a far wider recession. It also depended on an assessment of the scope for further rapid improvements in productivity. Vietnam was able to adjust remarkably well to what was perhaps an even larger external shock in the late 1980s. Provided appropriate reform efforts continued, it was not unreasonable to expect Vietnam to emerge from the shock of the Asian

Table 9.6   GDP growth rates, 1997–99 (%)

	1997	*1998*	*1999*
Vietnam	8.2	4.4	4.4
Thailand	−1.8	−10.4	4.1
South Korea	5.0	−6.7	10.7
PR China	8.8	7.8	7.1
Philippines	5.2	−0.5	3.2
Malaysia	7.5	−7.5	5.4
Indonesia	4.7	−13.2	0.2
Singapore	8.0	1.5	5.4

Source: ADB, *Asian Development Outlook 2000* (Table A1).

financial crisis in a more competitive position. The need for further strong growth in productivity was all the more critical, because of the reforms adopted elsewhere in the region in response to the crisis. Dapice (1998) identified various policy areas of key importance if Vietnam were to minimize damage from the crisis, notably: exchange rate management, accelerating disbursement of ODA, pursuing sensible policies towards FDI, strengthening the Vietnamese financial sector, and crucially, 'levelling' further the private–public playing field.

The government demonstrated a pragmatic approach to exchange rate policy, including the adoption in February 1999 of a system of regular adjustments in response to market exchange rate movements. In April 1988, the Prime Minister, Phan Van Khai, issued a series of directives to ministry officials to accelerate their dealings with foreign firms, to lower land rents, and to give external investors further tax benefits. In the state enterprise sector, there was considerable scope for both advancing the 'equitization' of medium-sized state firms, and selling smaller firms to the private sector, a move that might pay handsome rewards in terms of savings mobilization and employment generation.[13] Decrees were issued during 1998 simplifying procedures to establish and register private companies, and making it much easier for private enterprises to obtain export licences. Adoption of a more 'private investor friendly' enterprise law was expected by the May 1999 session of the National Assembly. In the financial sector, the picture was far more uncertain. The overall ratio of overdue loans was reported to be 14 per cent of total loans outstanding in 1998, with two state-owned commercial banks and several joint-stock banks reporting overdue ratios of more than 20 per cent. Given weaknesses in loan classification, these figures may understate the problem (World Bank, 1998, p. 22). Given that state enterprises accounted for more that half the total loans outstanding, further progress in state enterprise reform remained an important issue.

Concluding remarks

While some aspects of the reforms in Vietnam moved ahead at a slower rate than some observers expected, or that might be considered desirable, a review of the 1990s should leave little doubt that the market-oriented reforms that had been implemented were substantive. Reforms contributed to considerable improvements in macroeconomic stability and growth in output, trade and inflows of foreign direct investment. Economic growth over the 1990s compared favourably with that of the best performers in East Asia. Nevertheless, Vietnam had a long way to go to catch up with the other ASEAN economies in terms of per capita economic output, trade and capital stock.

The country moved from a situation in which reforms tended to be crisis-driven to one in which the authorities began to develop a longer-term vision of the country's development. While the risk of an economic downturn remained, the possibility of economic collapse that existed at the time of the Seventh Congress appeared to have been averted, and this provided scope for greater consistency and predictability in policy-making. It also created opportunities for various interest groups to be better organized. In some cases this might imply the need for greater efforts to 'sell' reforms, including an improved capacity to undertake more sophisticated analysis of the distribution of the costs and benefits of proposed reform measures.

The nature of Vietnam's requirements was also changing. In order to sustain medium to long-term growth, there was need for a greater focus on institutional reforms and development. Some key medium-term challenges included: financial sector development to improve domestic resource mobilization and allocation; further progress towards a more consistent regulatory framework for all economic sectors to achieve increased and more efficient commercial investment; further reduction of institutional constraints to small and medium-sized enterprise development with the aim of ensuring more equitable distribution of the benefits of growth; improvement of corporate governance of state enterprises; increasing competition among remaining monopolies; further liberalization of trade (especially to reduce barriers to entry to external trade); accelerated implementation of programmes and projects to improve education, training and other social services; and accelerated development of the physical infrastructure. There remained much to be done to develop the institutions to support a market economy, including capital market institutions, and the strengthening of the legal framework and enforcement mechanisms for protection of property rights and commercial activity.

More generally, further public administration reform was required to streamline decision-making authority and to enforce established lines of authority and accountability. Regulations needed to be simplified to reduce the administrative discretion exercised by some government agencies in order to reduce incentives and opportunities for corruption, and generally to reduce the transaction costs of undertaking business activities in Vietnam.

In the late 1990s party and government documents included commitments to reforms in many of these areas. Previous experience suggests that progress in addressing the issues will be gradual, but the probability of maintaining strong growth (5–7 per cent per annum) in the new century remains a reasonable expectation. Given commitments to aid-financed investment projects and stated intentions by major donors to maintain current levels of aid,[14] continuing growth can be expected in ODA disbursements. Provided that accelerated progress in removing barriers to private domestic investments continues, the share of domestic private investment should increase. The share of foreign investment in GDP is unlikely to recover to earlier peaks, but could remain substantive if the government takes decisive action on a number of well-advanced projects in the energy sector. Also, the sharp reductions in foreign investment approvals were less pronounced in the manufacturing sector, and industrial output from foreign invested projects continued to record rapid growth. Importantly, a number of established foreign investors in the industrial sector are expanding their operations in Vietnam. Over the longer term, prospects for sustained strong growth will depend on continuing progress in developing market institutions. Many analysts of transition economies have substantially underestimated the time required to build the foundations of a competitive market economy. Indeed, the Asian financial crisis showed that the importance of institutional development had also been overlooked in many East Asian developing economies.

Notes

1   While the 1996 and 1997 World Bank economic reports noted Vietnam's successes in macroeconomic management, it is not readily apparent from these reports that Vietnam's economy was 'coasting downwind'.
2   See Irvin (1996) for a more detailed discussion of the government's fiscal weakness.
3   See World Bank (1996), figure 1.4, p. 13. This fell after nominal depreciation of the dong.
4   This is of course part of the 'level playing field' argument on which see Fforde (1995), particularly regarding the rural sector. The World Bank argues that state enterprises had an unfair advantage in attracting FDI and that privatization has been minimal. As Fforde argues, had state enterprises been privatized more rapidly, it is doubtful that as much foreign investment would have been forthcoming. Vietnam's policy in this respect can be seen as a variant of the Korean strategy of attracting FDI to key industries privileged by government. See Mallon (1997a).
5   The UNDP/UNICEF data was limited in two respects. First, the figure of 70 per cent refers to 1986; lack of accurate data at that time makes this little more than a guesstimate. Second, UNDP/UNICEF uses the same poverty line of 2100 calories per day used by the World Bank (1994) based on VLSS data and adopts a 'headcount approach' to measuring poverty. Moreover, the VLSS data-set was five years old, and it was most unlikely that the percentage of the total population in poverty had not fallen since then. See Irvin (1995) for projections that are more consistent with the more recent estimates of 35–40 per cent.
6   These included coffee, tea, rubber, cashews, other industrial crops, horticulture, marine products and livestock in the agriculture sector; energy, construction materials, garments, footwear, foodstuffs, chemicals and electronic assembly in the industry sector; and in the service sector there has been strong growth in trade, tourism, finance and public services.
7   The best account of South Korean industrialization strategy remains Amsden (1989); also see Akyüz *et al.* (1988) for a survey of Southeast Asian development.
8   The AFTA agreement was signed by ASEAN countries in 1992. For a study of the impact of trade liberalization on Vietnam, see Vu Quoc Huy *et al.* (1996).
9   GDS (Gross Domestic Savings) is defined as GNS (Gross National Savings) minus the sum of net factor payments and transfers, government current savings and foreign savings.

10 Major exports included crude oil, garments, marine products, rice, footwear, coffee, cashew nuts and coal. Major imports are petroleum products, machinery, vehicles, fertilizers, construction materials and consumer goods. East Asian countries, including Japan, Singapore, South Korea and Hong Kong are Vietnam's major trading partners.
11 Major sources of foreign direct investment approvals from 1987 to mid-February 1998 were Singapore (US$6.2 billion), Taiwan (4.3), Japan (3.5), South Korea (3.2) and Hong Kong (3.1).
12 The World Bank estimated US$600 million for 1998, but the actual figure was probably a little over US$1 billion (World Bank, 1998, p. 92).
13 A decree providing for the divestiture of small-scale state enterprises was expected during the first half of 1999.
14 Donors made this commitment at the December 1998 Consultative Group meeting in Paris, and also indicated that commitments might be increased if reforms were accelerated.

10
Vietnam in the Asian Crisis

Stein Tønnesson[*]

Three stories

Because of the legacy from Vietnam's epic struggles against Chinese, French and American domination, and the country's close alliance with the Soviet Union in the years 1976–91, its remarkable transition from central planning to a more market-oriented economy in the years 1986–97 drew much attention from scholars and commentators all over the world.[1] During the Asian crisis of 1997–99, the Vietnamese experience became strongly contested. Virtually every commentator claimed Vietnam as support for his or her ideological position, and three highly different stories were told about 'Vietnam in the Asian crisis'.

One went as follows. The main cause of the crisis in East and Southeast Asia was the cosy relationships which had developed between business leaders and governments, with cronyism and corruption, red tape and lack of transparency, privileged access to credit and incomplete markets. These features were even more prevalent in Vietnam than in other East Asian countries since Vietnam had mixed socialist institutions with a market economy. For this same reason, however, the effects of the crisis were artificially delayed. The country had strict currency controls, no stockmarket, and enjoyed a growing inflow of donor money propping up its balance of payments. Thus, economic growth continued through 1997 and the first months of 1998, and macroeconomic adjustments were limited to modest devaluations of the currency.

There was an illusion among the country's leaders that they could continue to enjoy high economic growth without further reform. The Communist Party increased its emphasis on socialist orthodoxy, with party leaders insisting on maintaining the state's leading role in the economy. The Viet-

* I would like to thank Glen Casanova, Rolf Hernø, Nguyen Vu Tu, Kristen Nordhaug, Tore Sund, Benoît de Tréglodé and Thaveeporn Vasavakul for their helpful and critical comments to earlier versions of this chapter.

namese government ignored warnings from the International Monetary Fund (IMF), and the market-oriented reforms which had been proceeding since the *doi moi* policy was introduced in 1986 ground almost to a halt. Only several months into 1998 did the government start to realize that the crisis was also having an impact in Vietnam. Markets elsewhere in the region contracted, which led to a reduction in the growth of Vietnamese exports. Low oil prices and drought further diminished the country's foreign currency earnings. Soon there was a serious drop in foreign investments, something that might stifle growth for several years. The government did not confront these problems, but instead decided to emphasize agriculture and the mobilization of internal resources.

In the summer of 1998, Vietnam renewed its talks with the IMF, but when the Central Committee met in October 1998, and again in January–February 1999, it was unable to resolve the country's problems. Instead, in January 1999 the party leadership expelled its most outspoken critic, Lt General Tran Do, who had demanded further market-oriented reforms and democratization of the regime. The party leadership reaffirmed ideological orthodoxy, notably the principle of the state's leading role in the economy. Since Vietnam was hesitant to undertake structural reforms while other countries in the region dramatically improved their business climate, the country was bound to lag further behind when growth resumed in the region. By the end of the twentieth century, as a disappointed commentator expressed it, 'Viet Nam became closer to Cuba than China',[2] and there was little chance the country could get out of its trouble unless the country's reformers were able to impose their views on the Vietnamese Communist Party (VCP) in the process leading up to the 9th Party Congress in May 2001. This story will be recognizable to readers of *Financial Times*, *Wall Street Journal*, *Time Magazine*, *Far Eastern Economic Review*, *South China Morning Post*, *The Economist* and other periodicals with a similarly liberal view.

The second story accounted for the same facts, but interpreted them in almost the opposite fashion, mixing jealousy with admiration for the Vietnamese experience. From this second perspective, 'Vietnam in the Asian crisis' was a success story. And success was explained by the same slow, or 'cautious' approach to reform that the liberal story deplored. Vietnam was given credit for not having shown the same haste as other countries to carry out US-inspired liberalization. Hanoi's leaders resisted the pressure and retained basic protective mechanisms which made it possible to ward off attacks from speculators, and to stay in control of the commanding heights in the economy. Thus, the government could ensure a minimum of stability and emphasize sectors of fundamental national importance: agriculture, energy and heavy industry. Some factors, of course, were uncontrollable. There was an inevitable drop in foreign investments and in exports of some items, but these costs were small and necessary in order to shield the country against the disruptive impact of unfettered global capitalism.

Official Vietnam-watchers in Cuba no doubt believed this story. The clearest expressions of it, however, came from commentators in Thailand and Russia. A January 1999 report from the Thai Farmers Research Centre took note that the Vietnamese economy had done better than that of any other ASEAN country in 1998. The report expected Vietnam and the Philippines to emerge winners in 1999, with growth rates of 3–3.5 per cent, while Thailand would not achieve more than 1 per cent, and Indonesia would remain in depression. Vietnam's shielded currency market had given it 'the perfect immunity'.[3] A more pronounced admiration was expressed in an article circulated by the Russian news agency *Inter Press Service* on 1 March 1999. It contrasted Russia's gloom with the enviable situation of its former Cold War ally and claimed the differing fates of the two countries had 'fuelled debate on which brand of transition to a market economy might be more sustainable in the long run'. IPS had interviewed a former chief energy expert in Vietnam, Pavel Bochenko, who praised the Vietnamese leaders for 'a clear economic vision and strategy'. Their slow approach to reform had kept Vietnam's economy relatively isolated, with no stockmarket, a non-tradable currency, and only a snail-pace 'equitization' of state-owned enterprises. This had helped Vietnam avoid the fallout from East Asia's crisis. Russia's hasty privatization, by contrast, had brought few, if any, positive results.[4] Russia had 120 000 private companies, but the economy shrank 5 per cent in 1998 and was expected to drop another 3–9 per cent in 1999. The gradual approach of the Vietnamese 'is no coincidence, but a well-calculated policy to shield themselves from external economic pressures,' said Vladimir Mazyrin, assistant professor of economics and Vietnam expert at Moscow University. Viktor Shevelukha, a communist deputy in the State Duma, added: 'Russia should learn from the Vietnamese experience of cautious reforms.'

The third story was more mixed. It acknowledged that the countries of East and Southeast Asia had structural weaknesses which needed rectifying, but this had been the case for many years and still there was rapid growth. The main cause behind the depth of the crisis in East and Southeast Asia during 1997–98 was a financial panic that spread across the region in the wake of speculators' successful attack on the Thai baht in the summer of 1997. Vietnam was saved from the panic because, like China and Taiwan, it did not have a fully convertible currency. In Vietnam there was also no stock exchange, and the country relied on foreign direct investments and official development assistance from the World Bank, the Asian Development Bank and donor countries, rather than foreign bank loans and portfolio investment. Since Vietnam was not vulnerable to the fluctuations of the international capitalist system, the government did not have to panic, let its reform programme be disrupted, nor listen to the dictates of foreign advisers. It refused to adopt radical and socially disruptive market-oriented reforms at a time when regional markets tended to decline, and even temporarily broke off relations with the IMF. Meanwhile, the new government of Prime Minister Phan Van Khai implemented laws and regulations which had been adopted since the reform period began in 1986. By the Spring of 1998, however, it was clear that Vietnam could not escape the regional crisis, and this placed the government in a difficult situation. It was forced to a second devaluation of its currency, and the National Assembly had to lower its growth target for 1998 from 9 to 6 per cent.

The government was obliged to reorient its economic policies, and there were drawn-out debates in the leading organs of the party concerning the proper course to follow. In order to avoid large-scale unemployment the leadership was reluctant to force state-owned enterprises into bankruptcy, so it took considerable time before any substantial number were equitized. In order to prevent further unrest of the kind that had happened in Thai Binh and Dong Ngai provinces in 1997–98,[5] and also because rice exports had become a major dollar earner, it chose to emphasize agriculture. Growth in agricultural production, mainly of rice, and also increased industrial exports to Europe, contributed to ensuring Vietnam an overall GDP growth at almost 6 per cent in 1998 and well over 4 per cent in 1999. To achieve such positive growth amidst the Asian crisis was in itself no small achievement, but the government was unable to attract much new foreign investment, and this became a serious concern. The government was united in its determination to continue the reform process, but also adamant that it would not give up the state's leading role in the economy or rapidly dismantle the system which had protected it against the financial panic. Vietnam, which followed a policy closely resembling that of China, seemed by the summer of 1999 to have got through the worst of the Asian crisis with only limited damage. Despite heated internal discussions among the party leaders over the proper course to follow, it looked as if the country was poised to benefit from renewed growth in the region while avoiding major threats to its social and political stability. This third, more detached, story will be familiar to people who remember the news bulletins from the *Vietnam News Agency*, the Chinese agency *Xinhua*, or who read *Vietnam News* and *Vietnam Investment Review*.

The three stories were obviously in conflict, although not necessarily in their account of the facts. The main difference was in interpretation, and in their implied prescriptions for future action. I do not attempt to test here which story that best accounted for the facts; instead I provide an alternative narrative of macroeconomic developments and decision-making in Vietnam during 1997–99, based on the presumption that national success or failure in the international context derive from each state's capacity to utilize its advantages, or assets, in the global marketplace. To do this, I point out Vietnam's main advantages. In the conclusion I return to the three stories and ask which is most likely to stand the test of time.

Reforms and 'reform'

The term 'reform' is crucial to each of the stories. The liberals criticized Vietnam for an inability or unwillingness to carry out reform. Non-liberals praised Vietnam for its slow approach to reform. However, one might perhaps place less emphasis on pace of reforms and more on their content. Reform can be defined broadly as *intentional change carried out by a government*. Intentional change can go in many directions, but in the 1990s the term 'reform' was generally associated with change in a liberal direction: liberalizing national and international markets, opening capital accounts, privatizing state-owned and collective enterprises, allowing foreign-owned companies to invest and compete freely, trimming down state bureaucracies, establishing a rule of law, respecting basic liberties, instituting political pluralism, and practising electoral democracy. 'Reform' became a liberal package. Other types of reform, such as policies to boost certain industries or target certain markets, channel investments to certain locations, institute cooperative schemes in agriculture, employ the unemployed or promote grassroots democracy, were not normally included under the term. Governments that concentrated on policies of the latter type were often considered retrogressive. In the global discourse on reform there was a tendency to knit economic liberalism, political freedom and multiparty democracy together. No consideration was given to the possibility that political democracy and state interventionism might well walk hand in hand, even in a globalized world.

The starting point for the liberal reform period in Vietnam was the central-planning system which had been instituted in the North from 1960 and in the South after national unification in 1975. The history of the Socialist Republic of Vietnam since its inauguration in 1976 was that of an unsuccessful attempt to apply the Soviet model, amended for a first time in 1979 and a second in 1986, each time by policies relying on the market. During the first phase of softening the central-planning system (1979–82) the market-oriented reforms were seen as temporary concessions to necessity, but in 1986 they were given a slogan, *doi moi*, and soon became irreversible. The party leaders remained careful, however, not to put the socialist regime in danger. The most radical changes were forced upon them, first by economic crisis in the mid-1980s and then by cancellation of Soviet aid at the end of that decade. Only in times of deep crisis did the Vietnamese Communist Party (VCP) institute drastic change.[6] In the years 1989–91, while proceeding with market-oriented reforms, the party leaders were frightened by the breakdown of socialism in the Soviet Union and Eastern Europe, and clamped down on the few dissidents calling for political pluralism. The party struck a difficult balance between a perceived need to maintain political stability and an urge to catch up with the Asian tigers through integration into the global market. Through the 1990s the VCP sailed between the

Scylla of economic stagnation and the Charybdis of subversive change. The Asian crisis made it increasingly difficult to steer the course.

Still the VCP managed to stay united and avoid much public exposure of internal disagreements. For more than fifty years the VCP was characterized by its capacity for suppressing disagreements in the name of unity; in comparison with other communist parties it had few purges. A practice of bargaining and compromise was cultivated under the leadership of Ho Chi Minh, the national father figure, or 'Uncle', who was born in 1890 and died in 1969. Subsequently, Secretary General Le Duan was the leading figure during the period of central planning, and Nguyen Van Linh was the first among equals in the early years of *doi moi*. But in the 1990s no single individual achieved a position comparable to that of Deng Xiao-ping or Jiang Zemin in China, Lee Kuan Yew in Singapore or Lee Deng-hui in Taiwan. The situation in the VCP rather resembled that of the Liberal Democratic Party (LDP) in Japan, a system of bargaining which was so time-consuming that decision-making became inflexible. Once a decision was made, however, there might be a powerful consensus. From 1991, the party in Vietnam was led by a triumvirate, first Do Muoi, Vo Van Kiet and Le Duc Anh, then from 1996 Le Kha Phieu, Phan Van Khai and Tran Duc Luong, secretary general of the party, prime minister and president, respectively. One came from the north, one from the south, and the third from the central region. One played the role of ideological watchdog, the second of wooing donors and investors, and the third of guaranteeing national security against foreign and domestic subversion. The system worked slowly, but gave a unity of purpose. As from 1996 the VCP was actually run by a double triumvirate, for Do Muoi, Vo Van Kiet and Le Duc Anh remained influential. They allowed the Army, as a guarantor of stability, to increase its political power.

Vietnamese political culture was characterized by patient stamina, but also a reluctance by leaders to take major, independent initiatives. The Vietnamese leaders would study how others did things and apply foreign models selectively.[7] Often they would try out one model in one place, another in another, to assess what worked best before they made their choice. The Vietnamese were accustomed to jealously guarding their independence, but were not inclined to pose as a model for others.

Growth targets and results

In 1999 the World Bank ranked Vietnam second in the world after China in terms of average annual growth during 1990–99.[8] According to the General Statistics Office of Vietnam, the overall growth in GDP was 8.2 per cent in 1997, the first year of the Asian crisis. This was slightly less than 1 percentage point lower than the official target for the year. Growth continued at a reduced pace in 1998, and ended as mentioned, officially, at 5.8 per cent, which was 3.2 percentage points under the official target.[9] The target for

1999 was set at 5 to 6 per cent, but actual growth was only 4.8 per cent (in the IMF's estimate 4.25). In the first half of 2000 the economy grew 6.2 per cent.[10] These growth rates can be compared to the average of almost 9 per cent for 1993 to 1998. Exports of coffee, tea, footwear and electronics rose rapidly, and cement production grew sufficiently to obviate the need for imports.[11] The main export earners were textiles, garments and footwear (23.2 per cent of the total in 1996), crude oil (18.5), rice (11.8) and marine products (9.0). The output of rice in the Mekong Delta, which accounted for 90 per cent of the rice exports, rose steadily after 1988. In the second half of the 1990s, Vietnam was the second-largest rice exporter in the world. The regional crisis, notably in Indonesia, increased demand for Vietnamese rice, which contributed to keeping prices high. In the first months of 1999, however, Vietnamese agriculture was affected by drought, and while rice exports continued from the Mekong Delta, there were reports of hunger in the central region. This was a familiar occurrence in Vietnamese history. However, the floods in the Mekong Delta in 2000 were the worst in 40 years.

In the second half of 1997 and the first months of 1998, the government was relatively unconcerned by the regional crisis. At a cabinet meeting in late February 1998, more than half a year after the crisis had struck in Thailand, ministers could enjoy reports that industrial production had increased by 13 per cent and exports by 20.4 per cent compared with the first two months of 1997.[12] In April 1998 the *Vietnam News Agency* proudly reported that Vietnam was expected to achieve the highest growth in the Asia Pacific region in 1998, at 8.7 per cent, and that forecasts from the United Nations' Economic and Social Committee of Asia-Pacific (ESCAP) for 1999 and 2000 gave Vietnam the highest GDP growth after China.[13] Export growth continued to be robust through April 1998, 19.8 per cent relative to the first four months of 1997. This growth occurred despite a prolonged drought in the highland areas of southern Vietnam with major reductions in the export of coffee, vegetables and nuts. The greatest increase was in rice exports, but garment exports also rose by 12 per cent and footwear by 13.7 per cent.[14] Businesses with participation by foreign investors maintained their impressive growth rates as far as exports were concerned, reaching US$ 590 million in the first four months of the year, which was 41.1 per cent more than the same period in 1997.[15]

In early May 1998, Secretary General Le Kha Phieu held a press conference for foreign journalists where he insisted that there was no reason for the government to alter the 9 per cent growth target for 1998.[16] Only two months later the target had to be adjusted downwards, but in his opening speech to the National Assembly in late October 1998, Prime Minister Phan Van Khai remained optimistic. The Communist Party's vigilance, he said, had protected the country from international speculators through a non-convertible currency, and capital controls had insulated Vietnam from the turmoil afflicting its neighbours: 'Political stability has enabled the country to continue to grow steadfastly.'[17]

The first clear indications of economic slowdown were falls in aircraft traffic, tourist arrivals and office rents in the major cities. Reports of significant reductions accumulated during the first months of 1998. Soon there was also a drop in exports to other Asian countries, notably those most badly hit by the crisis (Thailand and South Korea). However, these effects were not dramatic since Vietnam's main trading partners were countries in the region which were less affected by the crisis: Singapore, Taiwan and Japan (at that point not yet in recession).[18] During the second half of 1998, Vietnamese exports grew only marginally relative to 1997, and the overall growth in exports during 1998 was only slightly less than 1 per cent (a figure that cast doubt on the official GDP growth rate of 5.8 per cent).[19] In the first months of 1999, exports continued to grow very slowly. On 1 March 1999, when VCP General Secretary Le Kha Phieu was ending a week-long visit to China, the normally benevolent Chinese news agency *Xinhua* reported from Hanoi: 'Vietnam's Export Performance in First Two Months Is Not Ideal.' In the second quarter, however, the situation improved in Vietnam, as elsewhere in the region. Exports grew considerably in 1999, and at an accelerated pace in 2000, despite low prices for rice and coffee.[20]

To an extent Vietnam could compensate for reduced exports to Asian countries by utilizing extended export quotas in the European Union,[21] but the country did not have normal trade relations with the United States (formerly called 'most favoured nation' status) or Japan. Negotiations with the United States started when diplomatic relations were established in 1995, but stalled when the US government presented Vietnam with a draft agreement in April 1997 which included demands for Vietnam to open up its economy to foreign competition. Normal trade relations with Japan were established in May 1999. Negotiations with the USA moved slowly, but had a breakthrough in the summer of 1999. However, when a treaty was ready to be signed in September 1999, the politburo of the VCP balked. Party elders seem to have blocked it, arguing that it represented a sell-out of the nation. In May 2000 during the run up to the US Congress decision to grant China normal trade relations on a permanent basis, Deputy Prime Minister Nguyen Tan Dung called for renewed negotiations towards signing the stalled agreement: 'We must strive to actively accelerate the process of integration into the world economy, particularly negotiations to join the World Trade Organization and to sign the bilateral trade agreement with the United States and other countries.'[22] This led to renewed talks, and the trade agreement was signed on 13 July 2000. It gives Vietnam the same normal trade relations, subject to annual renewal by the US Congress, as China had until it secured permanent normal trade relations in the spring of 2000. Although the agreement will not be ratified by the US Senate till after the presidential elections, it has already spurred high expectations for increased Vietnamese exports. On the other hand it obliges Vietnam to carry out a range of changes in the direction of an economy that is open to foreign competition. It is one of the most detailed and comprehensive trade agreements ever signed.

In the first fifteen years of market-oriented reforms in Vietnam, the lack of normal trade relations with the United States and Japan clearly contributed to preventing the country from keeping up with the pace of growth in China.[23] Now that Vietnam will enjoy normal trade relations with the world's two biggest economies, it will be able to boost its exports considerably, but then of course Vietnamese companies will also be exposed to much more fierce foreign competition on the home market and Vietnam will be obliged to dismantle or privatize a range of state-owned enterprises.

Critics of Vietnam's slow response to the regional crisis argued in 1998 that Vietnam would lose competitiveness to Asian rivals (notably Thailand) because the dong was overvalued. In mid-1998, Vietnam devalued the dong, but by less than 15 per cent.[24] The IMF urged a more radical devaluation to impress international markets; with such a small devaluation, Vietnamese labour costs would not be low enough to attract foreign investors, the IMF argued. According to critics there had been a dramatic increase in Thai, Indonesian and Malaysian competitiveness after their currencies had depreciated so radically. However, the devaluations did not at first seem to have the expected results in those countries.[25] Companies in the crisis-ridden countries were too severely affected by debts and interest payments, rising costs of imports and declining domestic markets to boost their exports. The crisis may also have been so serious in some of the other Southeast Asian countries that investors withdrew. Some transnational companies may have preferred to maintain production in the relatively stable Vietnam, but on this point the situation would change in 1999–2000 when some countries (notably Thailand and Malaysia) returned to a rapid pace of growth.

At the height of the Asian crisis there was no capital flight from Vietnam, but many investment projects were delayed and there was a drop both in investment pledges and in the actual inflow of investment capital. Substantial pledges of foreign investment had begun in the early 1990s, and from then onwards the Vietnamese government had been proud to publish annual figures showing increases in pledged investment. When asked in May 1998 about the effectiveness of foreign investment during the past ten years, the Vietnamese Minister of Planning and Investment, Tran Xuan Gia, replied that foreign direct investment accounted for 27–30 per cent of the country's total development investment and had created 250 000 jobs.[26] Investment figures increased significantly through 1996, but in 1997 the pledges dropped by about 40 per cent, to US$5.1 billion, down from 8.7 billion in 1996. The actual inflow of capital continued to grow from US$1.8 billion in 1996 to 2.4 billion in 1997, but in 1998 both the pledges and the actual disbursements dropped significantly.[27] They decreased further in 1999, and in the first half of 2000 new foreign investments were at an alarmingly low level.[28] An example of how Thailand's recovery affected Vietnam was that the shoe company Nike chose to expand in Thailand rather than continue its investments in Vietnam.[29] Vietnam now faced competition as a low-cost manufacturer from countries which had used to be on a higher cost level. One comforting aspect, however, of the downturn in investments in 1998–99 is that it mainly concerned real estate (hotels and office buildings); a greater share of the decreasing foreign investments went into industry which allowed Vietnam to have a steady growth in exports. In the first half of 2000 exports rose significantly despite the lack of new investments.

For some time it was feared that the drop in foreign investment would threaten the balance of payments. This was probably why the Vietnamese government reopened its discussions with the IMF in 1998, and subsequently obtained pledges of significant increases in aid and loans from the annual donor meeting in Paris in December 1998. About US$2.2 billion was pledged for 1999 and US$2.8 billion for 2000 which helped to offset the danger to the balance of payments, although Vietnam's absorptive capacity was far from strong enough to ensure disbursement of all the money pledged. Fears for the balance of payments seemed somewhat overstated, and in 1998 and 1999 the trade balance actually improved as a result of reduced imports. Delayed necessary imports, however, brought a dramatic rise in the first months of 2000, leading to new worries for the balance of payments.[30]

Pressures for structural reform

Representatives of multilateral and bilateral donors during the 1990s became an important pressure group in Vietnamese politics. After the Soviet aid ended, Vietnam turned to the IMF and adopted an economic stabilization programme drawn up in consultation with its macroeconomic experts. In late 1994, the IMF approved a three-year Enhanced Structural Adjustment Facility of US$530 million. It disbursed two-thirds of this money during 1995–96, which contributed to saving Vietnam from the type of crisis that Cuba suffered, and provided for a smooth transition to a position as an integral part of the East Asian growth zone. In the first half of the 1990s Vietnam was generally believed to be a new Asian tiger. At this time a great number of prospective investors, mainly from other East Asian countries, came to Ho Chi Minh City and Hanoi to explore possibilities. Already in 1996–97, however, before the Asian crisis, foreign investors in Vietnam complained about red tape, corruption, slow handling of licence applications, failure to implement announced reforms, maintenance of protectionist policies and other matters. The complaints were reflected in the international press, which had earlier been enthusiastic about Vietnam's economic prospects.

In the vanguard of gloomy reporting was the *Financial Times*.[31] Gloom was enhanced by IMF's representative in Hanoi at the time, Erik Offerdahl, who went public with his critical views after the IMF suspended disbursements of its enhanced structural adjustment facility in 1997.[32] The World Bank representative, Andrew Steer, made statements indicating a more sympathetic attitude to government policies.[33] This reflected a general difference between the IMF and the World Bank on the world scale, where the former insisted on rapid macroeconomic adjustments with little concern for social consequences, and the latter took a broader and more patient approach. However, later the World Bank also became concerned about lack of progress in reforming the financial sector and the state-owned enterprises. An unprecedented meeting of donors was called in Vietnam in June 1998 to discuss the impact of the Asian crisis, and that same month Deputy Prime Minister Nguyen Tan Dung also met with a representative of the IMF.[34] Later in 1998, the World Bank eagerly joined the complaining chorus: '...over the past three years the vigour of the reform program has slackened, and the growth impact of the earlier reforms has been fading', said its website by the end of 1998 which also mentioned the difference in point of view concerning the speed of reforms: 'Differences exist in our views on the pace of reform, with the Bank Group urging an accelerated program, especially in the crucial inter-linked areas of financial sector and state enterprise reform. The Authorities are concerned about the social costs of dramatic reform.' To resolve these differences, the World Bank's Vietnam office was strengthened, and it launched a major programme of 'advisory and technical assistance services' to support 'the needed policy actions and social programs'.[35]

As noted by a Western correspondent, foreign donors, investors and Western ambassadors were falling over themselves urging Hanoi to avoid the mistakes that had swept other Asian countries into misery. And the advice was unanimous: 'accelerate reform of the banking sector and state-owned firms, improve transparency, cut red tape and give the private sector room to bloom.'[36] When making pledges at their annuel coordination meeting in Paris in December 1998, the donors went further than usual in urging the Vietnamese government to take action. In the first months of 1999, Vietnam and the IMF continued discussions begun in November 1998 about a new Enhanced Structural Adjustment Facility. At the same time the World Bank worked on a fresh Structural Adjustment Credit facility for the country. On 18 March 1999, however, negotiations were broken off both with the IMF and the World Bank, because of failure to agree on a 'policy framework paper'.[37] In June, after the annual bilateral discussions between the IMF and Vietnamese authorities, the Board of Directors of the IMF published a report which, surprisingly, revealed internal disagreement in the IMF over Vietnam's approach to reform. The majority stuck to their warnings against Hanoi's apparent inaction, predicting that GDP growth in 1999 would remain a mere 3.5 per cent, that there would be continued high inflation, and a widening of the current account deficit. A minority of the Directors 'continued to see some merit in a more gradual approach to reform, stressing the need to maintain social and political stability'.[38]

In late 1999, the IMF appointed the former country director of the World Bank in Indonesia, Dennis de Tray, as its new representative in Vietnam. He expressed more understanding for Vietnam's cautious approach than his predecessor: 'In a sense, they have done remarkably well: They're not North Korea and they're not Cuba. They've really begun to understand the need to integrate, but they're also cautious, and for that you can't really blame them.'[39] Thus the attitude of the IMF and the World Bank tended to converge.

It is difficult to judge to what extent the Vietnamese government was influenced by pressure from foreign donors and investors. Prime Minister Phan Van Khai said in January 1999 that Vietnam must decide for itself how to shore up its economy, suggesting that conditions imposed by the IMF in exchange for aid had fuelled unrest in other countries.[40] Still the measures advocated by Vietnam's own reformers were similar to those urged by the foreigners. The latter tended to emphasize removal of restrictions on foreign and domestically-owned private companies, financial sector reform, dissolution of the cosy relationships between state banks and state-owned enterprises, tariff reductions and measures to make credit available to the private sector. The government was not against these, but also had other priorities: agricultural development, the country's infrastructure, special investment zones, the competitiveness of key industries, channelling investments to backward regions, obtaining access to export markets, and reducing corruption. This was also a reform programme, albeit with its own priorities. To the Vietnamese leaders, social and political stability were probably more important than rapid growth.

It is clear, however, that the government took the donors' views seriously. A resolution from the first session of the 6th Plenum of the VCP Central Committee in October 1998 stated: 'Economic development has slowed down. Our economic efficiency and competitiveness are low. Our financial and monetary activities are still weak.'[41]

In early February 1999, at a two-day government meeting to discuss a plan to readjust the investment structure, Prime Minister Phan Van Khai said the country could not go its own way while the rest of the world was globalizing. Pointing to the 'natural trend' of international and regional integration, he maintained that Vietnam should prepare carefully to integrate into the region and the world. In preparation for the integration process it was an urgent task to alter investment priorities. With a view to raising the efficiency of the economy, he stressed that it was essential to define sectors and products that could fully utilize the country's natural resources. The stated aim was to turn Vietnam into an industrialized country by 2020.[42]

Evidently, Phan Van Khai's intention was neither to create a liberal, non-interventionist state nor to rely on protectionism and import substitution. He sought to engage the state in a national enterprise of global integration. This was the Vietnamese version of the Asian developmental state. However, for Vietnam to realize its potential, many obstacles would have to be overcome, such as infrastructural development, fiscal reform, the introduction of a more efficient banking system and state enterprise reform. And in their struggle to carry out change within each of these domains, the younger party leaders would meet continuous opposition from entrenched interest groups and sceptical party elders.

The lack of an appropriate infrastructure was generally recognized as an impediment to economic growth in Vietnam. The state received aid and loans to build roads and bridges, construct systems for water supply, repair railways and ports, build dams, a national electricity grid and a modern telecommunications system. Interestingly enough, though, among Vietnam's main donors it was only Japan and the Asian Development Bank who were focusing on infrastructure. The World Bank and its affiliate, the International Finance Corporation, were waiting on private sector initiatives and reform in order to enter into Build-Operate-Transfer (BOT) projects. Thus the great majority of foreign investors preferred to locate their investments in the Ho Chi Minh City region or a few other privileged zones; the cost of doing business outside the main growth zones was deemed too high. It was estimated at the beginning of 1998 that only about 85 per cent of Vietnam's towns and 50 per cent of its villages were electrified, and there were frequent cuts even in the major cities. In May 1998, because of a lack of water in reservoirs, the government was forced to cut the power supply in Hanoi and Haiphong, such that only one of the two cities would have full power at any time.[43] Electricity Viet Nam (EVN) planned to produce 24.38 billion kWh in 1999, 2.72 billion more than in 1998, and to achieve this it would invest US$929 million, mainly in new power stations.[44] (Early rainfall in 1999 provided a respite from the energy problem.) However, access to potable water seemed an even greater problem, at least in the long term. No one foresaw a quick solution to Vietnam's infrastructure problems; they could, it was said, only be solved through a sustained effort involving the construction of an efficiently organized public sector with an increased absorptive capacity for foreign aid and loans.

After the end of central planning, Vietnam had a fiscal system based mainly on customs duties. In the 1990s the government increased its revenue substantially by levying customs duties on imported machinery and raw materials for the newly-established industries. This was not popular with the business community, and also made it difficult for Vietnam to fulfil its pledges to ASEAN and the Asia Pacific Economic Council (APEC) to gradually remove tariffs.[45] Substantial tariff reductions were also necessary in order to realize the government's ambition to become a member of the World Trade

Organization. A new 10 per cent value-added tax (VAT) took effect on 1 January 1999, but time will be needed to make it function properly, and the government will continue to depend on customs duties for its income. The drop in new foreign investments decreased the imports of taxable items.

The financial sector in Vietnam showed problems similar to those in China. The state banks made cheap credit available to state-owned enterprises, and a large number of bad loans resulted.[46] Foreign banks were allowed to establish themselves in Vietnam only under strict rules; they were able to serve the foreign-invested sector, but there was no legally functioning credit system for small and medium-scale Vietnamese enterprises. Credit for these enterprises was organized through informal channels. The financial crisis in other Asian countries heightened the awareness of the need for financial reform.[47] In September 1997 the National Assembly refused to endorse the government's renomination of the central bank governor. This led to an extended quarrel within the Vietnamese leadership, and it was not till the National Assembly met in April–May 1998 that it was decided to nominate First Deputy Prime Minister Nguyen Tan Dung as Central Bank Governor.[48] This 49-year-old southerner was at the time seen by many as Vietnam's key economic reformer. Nguyen Tan Dung's nomination was therefore expected by some to create a momentum for financial reform. However, he did not have the financial expertise of his predecessor. By the summer of 1999 there was no visible progress in reforming the financial sector, and rather than applying the changes urged upon him by investors and donors, Dung focused on trying to curb the role of dollars in the Vietnamese economy. In January 2000, in connection with a government reshuffle, he was replaced as governor by a professional so that he could concentrate on his work as Deputy Prime Minister.[49]

Probably the main action that the Vietnamese government needed to take to satisfy foreign investors and donors was to streamline its financial sector and create a more level playing field for state-owned and private enterprises. There were two reasons why donors and investors payed much attention to state-owned enterprise reform. First, these companies absorbed so much credit from the state banks. Second, most foreign investors were obliged to form joint ventures with state-owned enterprises. The Vietnamese partners did not usually contribute much capital, but they navigated the joint venture through the bureaucracy, and provided user-rights to land. If Vietnamese companies were privatized, they might lose the advantage of privileged access to government decision-makers, and the foreign investors would be freer to operate on their own. This would make it easier for Vietnam to attract investments, but would reduce the government's control of the economy.

A World Bank report released at the end of 1998 said that 60 per cent of Vietnam's 5500–6000 state-owned enterprises had been unprofitable before the Asian crisis started, and that the state sector was burdened by a debt of US$7.3 billion at the end of 1997.[50] The equitization programme started as early as 1992–93, as part of a broad effort to restructure the state sector. The prime ministers were the driving force behind this, first Vo Van Kiet and later Phan Van Khai, but the provinces and municipalities resisted, preventing reforms from being effective. To manage the reform, Vo Van Kiet created a limited number of enterprise groups. They were not conglomerates in the manner of the Japanese *zaibatsu* or the South Korean *chaebol*, rather, each represented a sector. Phan Van Khai pursued the same line of reform, and in July 1998 his government formally endorsed the establishment of 18 enterprise groups,[51] which would take charge of streamlining the state commercial sector. By September 1998 about 3100 state-owned enterprises had been merged and 3500 dissolved.[52] Ten per cent of their workforce, 170 000 employees, were reported to have been sacked during 1997, and a further 68 000 lost their jobs in the first few months of 1998.[53] Prime Minister Phan Van Khai admitted in March 1999 that 30 per cent of Vietnam's state-owned enterprises were losing money and that the state sector needed a major overhaul to compete in the marketplace; and as Vietnam's protective barriers were gradually dismantled, they must prepare for global competition. The state-owned enterprises still accounted for 42 per cent of Vietnam's gross domestic product, and for nearly two-thirds of industrial output. Phan Van Khai emphasized that they must continue to play a leading role in industrialization.[54] Vietnam lagged far behind China in terms of equitization, though the process was not rapid there either. The reasons for slow progress on equitization in both countries were resistance from enterprise managers and workers, fear of unemployment and unrest, and anxiety that equitization could lead to rampant corruption of the Russian kind.[55] When Secretary General Le Kha Phieu toured China in late February 1999, he said China 'was bolder than Vietnam in this area', and that Vietnam had much to learn.[56] In 1998 the government planned to equitize 150 state-owned enterprises, but only 98 companies were fully equitized.[57] In April 1999, the total number of equitized companies reached 160, but most of them were small, and in an opening speech to the National Assembly in May 1999 deputy Prime Minister Nguyen Tan Dung refrained from fixing a target for 1999. He just said that state enterprise reform had led to some 'complicated' developments. At the beginning of 2000, there were still 5280 state enterprises left. It was planned to bring the number down to 3000 by 2003 and 2000 by 2005.[58]

Equitization was sometimes presented as a euphemism for privatization. This gave a false impression, since in Vietnam a state organization, either a provincial or local People's Committee or a military region, usually retained a majority stake in the shareholding company.[59] Equitization could actually be seen as a programme to commercialize the state itself. Companies were separated from direct ministerial control, but remained under the influence of government officials. Little information is available as to the fate of the companies after equitization; it would be important to know whether they retain privileged access to credit from the state banks, and whether they sell their products to the state.

Equitization is not the only way to make state-owned enterprises competitive, and the government tried other means. It loosened ties between the ministries and the fully state-owned corporations by introducing a system whereby a few selected companies could recruit their own directors, trade directly with other enterprises, and implement self-financing schemes. In May 1998 the prime minister instructed that all state-owned enterprises should be reorganized into three groups. Group one would comprise important businesses that needed to be wholly-owned by the state.[60] Group two would include businesses that should have a new form of ownership structure, but remain under the administrative authority of the state as owner. Group three would comprise businesses that had lost money over the previous two years and would be either equitized, dissolved or declared bankrupt.[61] It is perhaps not surprising that the equitization programme was slow when only the most unprofitable and least essential companies were scheduled for equitization.

To sum up, the Vietnamese government attempted to carry out a number of reform programmes at the same time: giving key state-owned companies more flexibility; separating public utilities from other productive enterprises; dissolving unprofitable companies; and equitizing unessential but sustainable companies. Overall progress was slow, and the government received much criticism for doing too little to help the private sector and paying too much attention to keeping the state-owned enterprises alive.

In the late 1990s the state sector in Vietnam employed almost four million people, half of whom were bureaucrats and the other half working for state-owned companies.[62] Private entrepreneurs and foreign investors often complained about red tape and corruption in state offices, and in response to this the Vietnamese government took a number of measures to simplify procedures for licensing foreign investments and making government policies more transparent. The prime minister called meetings of investors to discuss their concerns, without, however, providing solutions. In December 1998 the government made an attempt to further smooth the licence procedures by giving provincial and municipal authorities the right to license small-scale projects without referring to the Ministry of Planning and Investment.

The attempt to reform the state-owned enterprises presented a challenge to the cohesion of the Vietnamese Communist Party since the company managers were often influential within it. A great many company directors were political appointees with extensive networks and little managerial competence. The VCP was not a monolithic party, and in the 1990s there seemed to be intense conflict between a market-oriented faction led by Prime Minister Phan Van Khai, Deputy Prime Minister Nguyen Tan Dung

and Foreign Minister Nguyen Van Cam, and a faction putting more emphasis on stability, cultural traditions and security. The latter, which was apparently in overall control of the party organization through Secretary General
Le Kha Phieu, found it difficult to formulate a credible economic strategy.
The combination of a strong tradition for internal party bargaining between
regional and functional groups, and the struggle between two increasingly
hostile factions made it difficult to reach decisions or renew policies. 'Vietnam must move forward at its own pace', said the 4th Central Committee
Plenum in 1997, and this was later repeated by the prime minister in statements to impatient foreigners.[63] The signing of the trade agreement with the
USA in July 2000 was a victory for the market-oriented faction, and led to
speculations that it would further strengthen its influence in the run up to
the 9th Party Congress in 2001.

More and more often the party has preferred to resolve internal disagreements by leaving decisions to representative government institutions. One of the best examples of this trend was the fate of a proposal put
forward in the autumn of 1998 for amending the land law of 1993. The
reform faction in the party wanted to extend the maximum time limit for a
contract on land lease from 20 to 50 years, and to abolish the three-hectare
upper limit on the size of individual farms. These proposals apparently
evoked memories of the hated system of land ownership that formed a
prime target for communist agitation in the colonial period. The reformers
failed to pass their motion through the politburo in September 1998, but
managed to have it endorsed by the 170-member Central Committee in
October, only to see it rejected by a majority in the National Assembly in
November.[64]

Thus, the party's failure to resolve internal differences provided the basis
for the National Assembly's ascendancy as a decision-making body, though
virtually all of the deputees were party appointees. Since the nomination
process ahead of elections was heavily screened, it was virtually impossible
for independent candidates to win nomination. Thus, the National Assembly mainly represented the interests of well-established party cadres on the
local and intermediate level. The political system in Vietnam was in a
process of change, and for some time it seemed likely that divisions within
the VCP would provide for vibrant and more open political debates. However, there remained a strong tendency to give priority to unity over clear-
ness and action.[65] Foreign liberal commentators often assumed that the
conflict between protagonists of political stability and democratization
within the Vietnamese society and the VCP coincided with the conflict
between protagonists of a state-directed economy and market-oriented
reform. This was not always the case. Although he was an economic reformer, Prime Minister Phan Van Khai was not necessarily in favour of a more
pluralistic political system. Protagonists of democratization, on the other
hand, could sometimes be party veterans who reacted against the corruption

and moral depravation that followed market-oriented reforms, and felt nostalgia for the days of Ho Chi Minh. However, Lt General Tran Do, the party veteran who circulated several critical letters in 1998 and was expelled from the VCP in January 1999, wanted both political democratization and a more market-oriented economic policy:

> Democratisation is a must and the first condition to ensure the success of national development. As long as people don't have freedom of thinking, freedom of expression, freedom of the press, freedom to associate, and other fundamental freedoms of a democracy, all the talk about national development and modernisation is useless.[66]

His exclusion from the party seems to have been widely resented. The eventual democratization of the Vietnamese state, if it were to occur, will be a complex process, and it is not evident that all market-oriented reformers will promote it. As mentioned, Phan Van Khai seems to prefer a more authoritarian Asian developmental state.

Vietnamese advantages

We can now develop the distinction between 'reform' as a liberal package and 'reforms' as a more neutral term for intentional change carried out by a government. The Vietnamese government, despite its many decision-making problems, pursued a line of reform that was different from the package implied in the liberal term 'reform'. In the view of the most consistent liberals, the state should provide the framework for free citizens to enjoy their lives independently, and leave market forces to operate as freely as possible. Ideally the state should be a smoothly operating, incorruptible and fairly small institution, taking decisions on the basis of laws and precedents. If all states were organized in such a fashion, each government's decisions would be predictable, and they would be likely to cooperate in establishing a rule-based global order. A less liberal, more realist way of thinking about the state in the contemporary world depicts it as one among several competing actors on the global arena, utilizing national advantages to attract foreign investments, to build alliances with corporations, organizations and other states, and to target foreign markets. At the end of the twentieth century it was, as Phan Van Khai said, impossible to maintain a vision of a state directing its national economy through central planning. It remained possible, however, to engage the state in an active effort to promote its own global interests as a corporation with a territory and citizens. The government would then need to pinpoint and utilize its main advantages. The term 'advantage' is not here used in the same sense as 'comparative advantage' in economic theory, which is built on the free play of market mechanisms, but rather as an asset which a government can deliberately play upon.

Vietnam has a number of advantages, or assets, which the state can exploit in the global marketplace. There is an abundance of natural resources: oil, gas, coal, minerals, fish and tourist sites. However, the two main resources are the fertile soil and the low-cost workforce. Vietnam's fertile, irrigated land has made it possible for the people who settled in the Red river Delta, along the eastern coast of the Annamite cordillera and, eventually, in the Mekong Delta, to grow to a population of almost 80 million. The Mekong Delta is one of the world's main areas for growing rice for export. Some 80 per cent of the Vietnamese population still work in agriculture, and agricultural growth was perhaps the main success story during the *doi moi* period,[67] not in terms of annual growth figures, but in terms of social impact. The record winter harvest in 1998 did much to save the country from suffering more from the regional crisis. It was no wonder that the first session of the 6th Plenum of the Central Committee 13–17 October 1998 decided to put emphasis on further developing the country's agriculture, since this is key to maintaining a minimal balance among the country's regions. Increased emphasis on growing fruit, vegetables, coffee, cashew nuts and tea is part of an attempt to combine export growth with regional development, yet there have also been negative fallout effects of market-oriented agricultural policies. They led to a steep rise in food prices and, thus, to impoverishment of the unemployed and the landless. The regime, still at least rhetorically committed to socialist ideology, has problems with its legitimacy when it carries out policies leading to dramatic cleavages between rich and poor. This may have been behind the reform faction's failure in November 1998 to further liberalize the agricultural land law.

The reason most often cited abroad for investing in Vietnam has been the country's skilled, disciplined and low-cost workforce. Vietnam has a literacy rate among the highest in the world, including rich, industrialized countries.[68] Vietnam not only uses its workforce to attract foreign capital, to reduce unemployment and gain foreign currency, the government also encourages the export of labour. This is a tradition from the colonial period when many Vietnamese worked in France, and during the central planning period when some 300 000 Vietnamese worked in Eastern Europe and the Soviet Union. At the end of the 1990s there were approximately 11 000 Vietnamese workers in South Korea and 4000 in Japan.[69]

Comparatively speaking, Vietnam is a homogenous nation, which may be seen as an asset. The great majority of the population are ethnic Viet (Kinh), who dominate the densely populated lowlands both in the southern and northern deltas and along the coast in between. A French attempt in 1946 to divide the country by the creation of an independent Cochinchinese state in the Mekong Delta got little local support and was abandoned. During 1954–75, North and South Vietnam were rival states both claiming to represent the whole nation. Although the dialects in north, centre and south differ, the Viet have basically the same language and build on the same historical tradition, and are not divided by religion. Although there are more Christians in the south (since the exodus from the north in 1954–55) and the Cao Dai church is a uniquely southern phenomenon, Buddhism, Confucianism and ancestor worship contribute to drawing the country together. Although there are multiple ethnic minorities in the highlands they are not in a position to threaten the unity of the state. Thus, the ethno-national situation in Vietnam is not as difficult to manage as in Malaysia, Burma, Indonesia or the Philippines. Both for historical reasons and because of heavy repression in the 1970s–80s, Chinese businessmen are not as powerful in Vietnam as in other Southeast Asian countries. This means that Vietnam can adopt national reform programmes without negotiating ethnic compromises. It also means that the government can be generous to its minorities without putting national cohesion at risk.

However, Vietnam suffers from a weak balance between its main regions – Vietnam has no Paris or Bangkok, no obvious centre. The country is divided into three regions, each with a town that at some point was the capital of a state – Hanoi, Hue and Ho Chi Minh (HCM) City (Saigon). Economic growth in the 1990s favoured the regions around HCM City and Hanoi. The relationship between north and south remains difficult, and most of the central region has lagged behind which might lead to the emergence of protest movements. This is a prospect which is difficult for foreign advisors to appreciate, but which has to be taken seriously by any responsible Vietnamese leader.

For Vietnam it may also be an advantage to have China in the forefront of socialist economic reform.[70] The Vietnamese can study the Chinese experiences before designing their own programmes. 'Viet Nam has learnt from many experiences, but China's is the most applicable,' said Prime Minister Phan Van Khai when receiving a Chinese visitor in late February 1998.[71] In the following month, during his first briefing for foreign journalists, Phan Van Khai said reform in Vietnam would be gradual and that China was now a suitable model to follow.[72] Le Kha Phieu gave the same message when visiting China in early 1999. In May of that year, when Vietnam and China were united in their opposition to NATO's war against Yugoslavia, first a delegation of the Vietnamese Communist Party's Commission for Ideology and Culture made a week-long visit to China, and then Deputy Prime Minister Nguyen Tan Dung, a member of the VCP politburo, headed a delegation to Beijing to study Chinese experiences with reform and open-door policies.[73]

There is, however, a basic difference between the Chinese and the Vietnamese development patterns. China has allowed and stimulated the emergence of a productive and export-oriented private sector alongside the public sector, whereas in Vietnam the state-owned enterprises, often through joint ventures with foreign investors, have played the leading role in promoting industrial growth. As far as the relationship between the public and private sector is concerned, the Chinese model converges with the World Bank's vision for Vietnam. Throughout the 1990s the World Bank urged Hanoi to allow the role of state-owned enterprises to 'slowly shrink in a rising pond of emergent private-sector firms'[74] At the beginning of the twenty-first century, China seemed to be better positioned than Vietnam for growth potential; but, as Barrett McCormick has argued, the smaller size of Vietnam and the greater domestic legitimacy of its regime might leave it with better prospects for 'an incremental transformation of the existing institutions' without violent social conflict.[75]

Economically it is of paramount importance for Vietnam to integrate its economy in the greater Chinese business network. Links with Singapore, Taiwan and Hong Kong are essential. Singapore is Vietnam's greatest foreign investor and trading partner, with about 200 licensed investment projects worth almost US$7 billion, and bilateral trade in 1997 of more than 3 billion.[76] Vietnam's economic dependence on Singapore increased significantly in the 1990s, but this should be seen as dependence on regional Chinese business networks rather than on Singapore as such. When Vietnamese President Tran Duc Luong visited Singapore in March 1998, his host, President Ong Teng Cheong, urged him to continue reforms aiming for 'a transparent and conducive business environment', using the same key words as Western economic advisers. Luong replied that he was fully aware of the need to 'develop the economy in a more effective and sustainable manner'.[77]

Japanese goodwill represents another of Vietnam's advantages. Japan is the main destination for Vietnamese exports and, at the same time, the main prospective source of foreign investment from outside the greater Chinese business network. For strategic reasons the Japanese government prefers its companies to invest in Taiwan and Vietnam rather than China. The smaller countries are viewed by the Japanese as potential buffers against Chinese expansion. However, Japan has not invested as much in Vietnam as the Vietnamese government had hoped. By mid-1998 Japan ranked only fourth on the list of investors, though Japanese investments were mainly in projects with a long gestation period. In the 1990s the reduced value of the yen and the stagnation of the Japanese economy contributed to a general reduction in Japanese investments abroad. This worried the Vietnamese government, and when Prime Minister Phan Van Khai visited Tokyo in late March 1999, he obtained an agreement with the Japanese government to 'conduct negotiations for the signing of an agreement on investment protection and promotion between the two countries'.[78] For Vietnam there was little doubt that the development of economic relations with Japan was crucial. Japan was Vietnam's main aid donor, and most of the Japanese aid went to infrastructure facilities related to energy, ports and communications.[79] Even in the middle of the Asian crisis, Japan decided to increase its aid to Vietnam.

In 1998, when Japan introduced a new aid programme to crisis-ridden countries in Asia, Vietnam was initially not included. The Vietnamese government applied strong pressure to gain access to the crisis fund despite Vietnam's apparent lack of 'crisis'. Japan yielded to the pressure, and in December 1998 promised to include Vietnam under the programme. On 26 May 1999, Japan and Vietnam finally exchanged 'most favoured nation' status.[80]

Another economic asset for Vietnam is the 2.5 million emigrants and refugees who settled abroad during and after the Vietnam War (the *Viet Kieu*). In May 1998, Nguyen Ngoc Ha, president of HCM City's Committee for Vietnamese living abroad, said that the *Viet Kieu* were 'part of Vietnam's strength'. They sent US$400–500 million each year to relatives in HCM City, he said, and invested in many projects.[81] In May 1998, the Vietnamese National Assembly adopted a new citizenship law after a long debate on the status of the *Viet Kieu*. The law declared them part of the nation, but although the law established a right to dual citizenship, foreigners of Vietnamese origin would not qualify.

The factors listed above are only some of the advantages that Vietnam has utilized and may continue to utilize to attract foreign capital, open markets for products abroad, and achieve rapid economic growth. Progress on these goals has been only a part of the Vietnamese government's programme. Its main preoccupation has been to ensure the regime's survival by preserving social and political stability. This presents an apparent contradiction which, if not resolved, could prevent Vietnam from realizing its potential.

Conclusion

After this sympathetic account of the Vietnamese attempt during 1997–2000 to emerge as unscathed as possible from the regional crisis, and after having pointed to some of Vietnam's main assets in a globalizing world, we must now return to the three initial stories: the warning from the liberal, financial press; the anti-liberal endorsement from frustrated Thais and Russians; and the qualified, pragmatic optimism of *Xinhua* and the *Vietnam News Agency*. It is far from simple to pick the story that best accounts for the facts. The better explanation must be one that takes into consideration the pertinent role that states play, and will continue to play, in economic affairs. In the 1990s, this role became more outward-oriented than in earlier periods, when many suffered from the illusion that it was possible to achieve rapid, sustainable growth in a protected economy. In the 2000s, the successful state seems to be one who actively promotes the national interest, utilizing its main advantages in the global marketplace.

The outcome of the regional crisis, which cannot yet be fully gauged at the moment of writing this chapter, is likely to influence the relative strengths of the three stories. If Thailand and South Korea (the main followers of IMF advice) had exited the crisis with renewed vigour, while the Vietnamese and Malaysian economies remained in a backwater, then the plausibility of the first story would have been enhanced.[82] Malaysia, however, who during the crisis applied currency controls that were extremely unpopular in liberal circles, achieved rapid growth again by late 1999 and early 2000, just like South Korea and Thailand. If Vietnam continues to grow while a second crisis hits more open countries, then the second story will gain strength. And if Vietnam once more achieves significant economic growth through gradual but consistent reforms, while the rest of the region also grows, then the balanced view of *Xinhua*, *Vietnam News Agency* (and this author) will seem the most reliable. Whatever the future reveals, such stories are themselves consequential. During 1998, the international financial press recounted only the first of them, thus perhaps contributing to fulfilling the prophecy by frightening away investors. The negative image of an immobile, bureaucratic Vietnam resisting 'reform' may itself have contributed to Vietnam's economic slowdown.

Future events might conceivably confirm the veracity of the liberal story of Vietnam's inability to respond adequately to the regional crisis. In a globalized world the government of a poor country must attract foreign investments to have any probability of growing out of poverty. To attract investment, Vietnam was – and will probably still be – obliged to endorse the basic rules of the international liberal order, and compete with other governments for the favours of transnational corporations.[83] Thus, the Vietnamese government needs to build the necessary legal infrastructure, create banks with normal capitalist practices, construct a stable and predictable fiscal system, and apply appropriate macroeconomic policies. On the other hand, the slowdown of the Vietnamese economy from the second half of 1998 was not caused primarily by changes within the country, but by crises elsewhere in the region. It may be argued that Vietnam's leaders failed to utilize the occasion to implement drastic changes, but the crisis as such was not caused by political failures.

It was certainly an exaggeration when it was claimed that reform in Vietnam came to a halt during 1997–99. Market-oriented reformers remained influential and sought to implement their agenda, but there was a shift in the type of reforms. One might argue that the reform process passed from a mainly deconstructive to a predominantly constructive stage, and that construction requires patience. In the first ten years of *doi moi* (1986–96) the main task was to dismantle the prohibitions and inhibitive structures of the central planning system, reinforced by pressures from below. *Fence-breaking* was the term used by researchers to describe this process: people in some areas began to ignore official restrictions, after having ascertained through informal channels that the party leaders might tolerate some disregard for the rules if the perpetrators did so discretely.[84] When the new practices proved successful, the government and National Assembly legalized what was *de facto* practice. Reforms included opening the country to foreign investment, permission for establishing private enterprises, decollectivization of land, more flexibility for the media, a more independent National Assembly, and somewhat more competitive elections. All of these were relatively easy measures to implement once ideological constraints were overcome, and they unleashed social and entrepreneurial forces which created a momentum for growth and optimism. New laws contributed to making market practices more widespread, and thus boosted economic growth.

Then, Vietnam passed into another phase in which it seemed dangerous to just dismantle existing institutions, since new structures were not yet in place. Further reforms required the construction of new institutions, *implementation* of the newly-adopted laws, and the emergence of an indigenous entrepreneurial class. Construction, implementation and class formation cannot be done overnight, but require years of effort. The reform faction in the government strove to achieve this, but it had to train new personnel, overcome resistance from incompetent civil servants, work its way through disagreements in the party, and reconfirm its authority. The impatience of the donors, investors and the IMF was enhanced by the Asian crisis which reduced international credits and directed the attention of new investors to other parts of the world. The impatience of foreign advisers could have provoked a hardening of the attitude of the Vietnamese Communist Party, but could also have tempted the most market-oriented members of the government to seek quick solutions, such as a rapid equitization of state-owned enterprises that might have led to large-scale corruption of the Russian kind.

Instead came a little of each. Some aspects of the government's policies hardened, while others softened, and all the time Vietnam moved closer to China. Some commentators have claimed that Vietnam needs an independent vision to guide its reform policies – implicitly thinking of a liberal vision; but if Vietnam had a vision it would not necessarily converge with the advice of the IMF. Visionary reforms might well include an industrial policy targeting specific international markets or certain sectors (the Vietnamese seem to be especially talented in the field of information technology, for example). Visionary reforms might also include policies aimed at social equity, environmental sustainability and developing backward regions, all areas that the Vietnamese leadership has repeatedly emphasized in public declarations.[85] In order to carry out effective reforms in these directions. Vietnam will require a more centralized, interventionist state, To really be effective, the central administration probably needs to be more independent of domestic business interests (both public and private), while also remaining able to resist pressure from investors, lenders, prospective trading partners – and story-telling media.

Notes

1 For a survey, see Harvie and Tran Van Hoa (1997).
2 Douglas Pike, 'Viet Nam as the Quarter/Year/Decade/Millennium Ends', *Indochina Chronology*, October–December 1999.
3 *The Nation*, 25 January 1990.
4 Today's only successful Russian commercial enterprise abroad, we might add, is Vietsovpetro, a joint venture between Zarubezhneft and Petro Vietnam, which exports crude oil from Vietnam's most profitable offshore oilfield. In December 1998, Zarubezhneft also took upon itself to build Vietnam's first refinery at a location in Dung Quat Bay of Quang Ngai province which had been rejected by other foreign oil companies. Work on infrastructure for the refinery has begun.
5 Violent protests over corruption and local abuse of power swept Thai Binh, a province with strong communist traditions 80 kms south of Hanoi, from May 1997. In January 1998, there were serious clashes between demonstrators and policy in the southern province of Dong Ngai.
6 'Vietnam's history suggests you tend to get big (policy) changes when you have a big crisis and at the moment you don't have a big crisis so you're not getting big changes.' Adam Fforde interviewed by Reuters correspondent Dean Yates 24 May 1998. What Adam Fforde says here may in fact be true of any country.
7 At present, the main model is China. A Vietnamese economist told a Western journalist in May 1999: 'With China, we are always like the little brother... We don't feel we need their permission to make any moves, but we do study them very, very closely. We never do anything important unless China has tried it first. They are a guiding light-for good or bad.' Mark McDonald in *San José Mercury News*, 10 May 1999. For an excellent analysis, see Tréglodé (2000), pp. 7,18-19,27-31.
8 The top ten economic performers were: China (11.2 per cent), Vietnam (8), Chile (7.8), Singapore (7.5), Sudan (7.4), Ireland and Uganda (7.2), Malaysia (6.9), Taiwan (6.2), and South Korea (5.8). World Bank figures as reported by *China News Agency*, 31 May 1999.
9 Reuters 2 January 1999. The World Bank estimated that growth in 1998 had been around 4 per cent. Faith Keenan in *Far Eastern Economic Review*, 18 February 1999.
10 *Reuters*, Hanoi, 9 May 2000. *Agence France Presse* (AFP), Hanoi, 9 May 2000.
11 *EIU Country Report*, 1st quarter 1998.
12 *Vietnam News Agency*, 2 March 1998.
13 *Vietnam News Agency, Agence France Presse (AFP)* 9 April 1998.
14 'Despite strong competition from shoe-makers in other countries, companies such as Hiep Hung, Thuong Dinh and Thang Long have managed to diversify their products and increase their quality, resulting in increased export volumes and greater market share. In the first quarter of 1998, Viet Nam's footwear industry recorded an export volume of US$250 million, an increase of 26 per cent compared with the same period last year. New strategic moves have been projected for the second quarter including expanding the market, developing local materials and lowering costs.' *Nhan Dan* (the party organ) quoted by *Vietnam News Agency*, 6 April 1998.
15 *Vietnam News Agency*, 27 April 1998.
16 'Of course the regional crisis is having an impact...but it is now important that we develop our resources to overcome this,' said Le Kha Phieu. Reuters 5 May 1998. Prime Minister Phan Van Khai had previously given another reason for sticking to the target: 'We would lose our "militant spirit" if we adjust the target now'. *Associated Press*, 27 April 1998.

17   *The Wall Street Journal*, 29 October 1998.

18   According to the Economist Intelligence Unit, the main destinations of exports in 1995 were Japan (26.8 per cent), Singapore (12.7), Taiwan (8.1), China (6.6), Hong Kong (4.7) and South Korea (4.3). In the same year the main sources of imports were Singapore (17.5 per cent), South Korea (15.4), Japan (11.2), Taiwan (11.1), Thailand (5.4) and Hong Kong (5.1).

19   *Xinhua*, 30 December 1998.

20   *Vietnam News Agency*, 25 June 1999. *AFP* Hanoi, 9 May 2000; *Reuters*, Hanoi, 9 May 2000.

21   The EU and Vietnam conluded a new 3-year agreement on textiles and garments in June 1998, allowing Vietnam to increase exports by 30 per cent. *EIU Country Report*, 3rd quarter 1998, p. 22.

22   *BBC Summary of World Broadcasts*, 17 May 2000.

23   'We estimate that if Vietnam had MFN [most favoured nation status] now, export earnings (from the U.S.) could increase three-fold by as much as $800 million a year three years from now,' World Bank representative Andrew Steer said in June 1998. *Reuters*, 18 June 1998. 'Vietnam is one of just five countries that don't enjoy normal trading status with the U.S. – the others are Cuba, Iraq, Libya and North Korea. Two-way trade between the U.S. and Vietnam amounts to less than $1 billion annually.' Faith Keenan: 'Opening the Door. Hanoi takes major step towards a trade deal with U.S.', *Far Eastern Economic Review*, 11 February 1999.

24   This was less than the depreciation from December. 1996 to 24 July 1998 of the Japanese yen (17.6 per cent) and the Singapore dollar (18.2 per cent), and much less than that of the Thai baht (37.4 per cent), the Philippine peso (37.6 per cent), the Malaysian ringgit (38.7 per cent), not to speak of the Indonesian rupiah (83.1 per cent). EIU *Country Report*, 3rd quarter 1998, p. 32.

25   The devaluation of the Thai currency was said, however, to lead to a dramatic increase in the smuggling of cheap products from Thailand to Vietnam.

26   *Vietnam News*, 16 May 1998.

27   *Dow Jones Newswires*, 22 April 1998. According to Adam Fforde, the disbursement in 1997 was US$2.6 billion, not just 2.4. Adam Fforde, 'Remarks on the 1998 Outturn and Developments in February 1999', Newsletter on http://www.aduki. com.au.

28   *Far Eastern Economic Review*, 4 May 2000; *South China Morning Post*, 25 May 2000.

29   Nike is a significant investor in Vietnam. Its subcontractors shipped 20 million shoes out of Vietnam in 1999, 15% of Nike's total production. *USA Today*, 25 May 2000.

30   Adam Fforde, 'Remarks on the 1998 Outturn and Developments in February 1999', Newsletter on http://www.aduki.com.au. 'Private sector leads sharp rise in vietnam's industrial output'. *AFP* Hanoi, 25 May 2000.

31   In *Financial Times*, 20 April 1998, its correspondent Jeremy Grant quoted a US-based scholar to say that 'Policymaking has ground to a halt to such a degree that there's no hope of serious economic reform without some sort of major shift in the political system.'

32   One outstanding example of negative reporting was Tim Larimer's article 'Hanoi's Hard Road Ahead', *Time Magazine*, 9 March 1998, vol. 151, no. 9. IMF representative Erik Offerdahl stated in May 1998: 'There are disturbing similarities between Vietnam and Indonesia, particularly the policy-making inertia and seeming inability to put in place urgently needed policy adjustments.' He urged 'a more

flexible exchange rate, dramatic financial sector reform and a tightening of monetary and fiscal policy to combat building inflationary pressures', and remarked: 'It's a very simple choice: some pain now saves a lot of pain later.' *AFP*, 25 May 1998.

33   'The economy here has momentum. There is a real vibrancy to the economy that is caused by a momentum that has gathered over the last six to 10 years,' said Andrew Steer. *Reuters*, 13 April 1998.

34   *Vietnam News*, 8 June 1998.

35   'Evolving priorities and development strategy', http://www.worldbank.org.vn/econdev/navpd.htm. The World Bank issued an alarmist report on Vietnam before the donors' meeting in Paris in early December 1998. *Reuters*, 2 December 1998.

36   *Reuters*, 22 September 1998.

37   *Associated Press*, 18 March 1999.

38   Public Information Notice (PIN) no. 99/46, 8.6.99 (available on the IMF webpage: http://www.imf.org/)

39   Interview in the *San José Mercury News*, 12 January 2000.

40   *Associated Press*, 2 January 1999.

41   *Nhan Dan*, 19 October 1998. The first session of the 6th Plenum had been held in October 1998. This was the first time in party history that a plenary meeting was divided in two sessions. The second session was held 25 January–2 February 1999

42   *Voice of Vietnam* in Vietnamese 4 February 1999 according to BBC Worldwide Monitoring.

43   'We have to resort to power cuts as hydro-electric plants are likely to cease operation on May 20 if the dry weather continues. This is really a disaster,' said EVN deputy general director Bui Thuc Khiet in early May 1998. Khiet still forecasted that electricity supply would return to normal during the monsoon season normally starting by the end of May. *Vietnam News*, 6 May 1998. (Rain came just in time to avoid the disaster.)

44   *Vietnam News Agency*, 9 February 1990.

45   Vietnam gained membership in ASEAN 1995 and APEC 1998.

46   According to one source, Vietnam's state-run firms were burdened with debts of $7.3 billion by early 1999, and 60 per cent of them were unprofitable. *Inter Press Service* (Moscow) 1 March 1999. Lt General Tran Do, who was expelled from the VCP in January 1999, claimed in an open letter one year earlier that a 'dangerous consequence of the 'Socialist direction' is that the government generously provides credits to the state-owned sector. Many of these credits could never be collected and the banking system is on the edge of insolvency'. Tran Do: 'The state of the nation and the role of the Communist Party', 13 pp. letter to the Party, the National Assembly, the Government, and concerned friends, dated 'End of 1997 and Start of 1998', circulated on the internet in February 1998.

47   'The fourth plenum [in December 1997] took note of the Asian financial crisis and resolved to reform and strengthen the state banking system, including resolving outstanding credit cases.', Thayer (1998). We might add here that banking reform was already on the agenda in Vietnam before the regional crisis. Such reform had been necessitated by the introduction of a market economy, but was slow in forthcoming. See Román (1998).

48   This was suggested by Prime Minister Phan Van Khai to the National Assembly (*Vietnam News Agency*, 5 May 1998) and immediately accepted.

49   *Voice of Vietnam*, Hanoi 6 December 1999 (BBC Monitoring).

50   *Reuters*, 2 December 1998.

51 These were: Vietnam Oil and Gas, Vietnam Post and Telecommunications, Vietnam Chemicals, Vietnam Steel, Vietnam Garments and Textiles, Vietnam Cement, Vietnam Ship Building Industry, Civil Aviation Administration of Vietnam, Vietnam National Shipping Lines, Vietnam Papers, Northern Food, Southern Food, Vietnam Coffee, Vietnam Rubber, Vietnam Gem and Gold, Vietnam Alcohol, Beer and Beverage and the Vietnam Tobacco Corporation. See *Vietnam News Agency*, 22 September 1998.

52 *Vietnam News Agency*, 22 September 1998.

53 *Vietnam News Agency*, 28 April 1998. *South China Morning Post* Internet Edition 27 May 1998. The first 18 equitized companies had by then created 1300 new jobs. *Vietnam News Agency*, 3 March 1998. By March 1998, statistics from the Ministry of Finance said Vietnam had 5962 state-owned enterprises, of which 1953 were centrally governed and 4009 managed by local governments. They produced about 42 per cent of Vietnam's gross domestic product (GDP) and accounted for about 75 per cent of state budget revenues. *Vietnam News Agency*, 6 March 1998.

54 *AFP*, 2 March 1999.

55 '. . . the equitisation process in recent years has been fairly slow. Several obstacles remain to be overcome, including: - Directors of SOEs say that they have to seek effective production measures so as to ensure stable incomes for their workers and contribute to the State Budget. - Debt and finance have been the main obstacles faced by SOEs trying to turn into equitised companies. The SOEs in general have debts, and many SOEs in particular face a huge debt or losses in production and business. Dealing with these debts are major problem for a SOE to become an equitised company. - Many SOE directors are afraid that equitisation will take away their positions and powers because they will no longer be appointed but have to be annually elected by a board of managers. - Workers worry about their futures when their enterprise faces equitisation. They worry about the implementation of policies on social insurance and buying shares.' *Vietnam News*, 9 July 1998.

56 *Xinhua*, 28 February 1999.

57 *Xinhua*, 19 January 1999.

58 *Dow Jones Newswires*, 4 May 1999. *Vietnam News Agency*, 5 May 1999. *Thoi Bao Kinh Te Saigon*, 4 May 2000; *Voice of Vietnam*, 8 May 2000 (*BBC Summary of World Broadcasts*, 18 May 2000 and 24 May 2000).

59 'We must understand that equitisation of the state sector is not privatisation and it doesn't mean that the following stage is privatisation', said party secretary general Le Kha Phieu in April 1998. *Reuters*, 3 April 1998.

60 This group included large-scale mineral, exploitation, exploitation of rare and precious ores, oil and gas exploitation, electricity, aircraft repair, post and telecom, rail, air and sea transport, printing and publishing, beverages and tobacco and investment banks.

61 *Vietnam News Agency*, 8 May 1998.

62 *Deutsche Presse-Agentur*, 27 May 1998. See Herland (1999), p. 106 and Papin (1999), p. 122.

63 *EIU Country Report*, 1st quarter 1998, p. 12 and 3rd quarter 1998, p. 21.

64 *Far Eastern Economic Review*, 10 December 1998, p. 26.

65 For a good analysis of Vietnamese party politics in 1997, see Vasavakul 1998.

66 Tran Do: 'The state of the nation and the role of the Communist Party', 13 pp. letter to the Party, the National Assembly, the Government, and concerned friends, dated 'End of 1997 and Start of 1998', circulated on the internet in February 1998.

67 Le Cao Doan: 'Agricultural Reforms in Vietnam in the 1980s', in Nørlund, Gates and Vu Cao Dam (1995). Kerkvliet and Porter (1995). Tran Thi Que (1998).
68 The adult literacy rate in 1994 was reported as 93 per cent. *UNDP Human Development Report*, 1997, p. 165. For education, see Herland (1999), p.101.
69 *EIU Country Report*, 3rd quarter 1998, p. 29.
70 The Vietnamese government 'fears instability and is apparently following the Chinese model of more gradual reform, rather than the shock therapy approach followed in Russia'. *Dow Jones Newswires*, 22 April 1998.
71 *Vietnam News Agency*, 25 February 1998.
72 *AP-Dow Jones News Service*, 24 March 1998.
73 *Vietnam News Agency*, 12 May 1999 and 20 May 1999.
74 Fforde (1998); p. 9. Fforde also notes that 'what is strikingly absent [in Vietnam], is a dynamic small-scale private or quasi-private sector' (p.8). This absence may to some extent be explained by the fact that small-scale private enterprises are not included in the statistics. On 17 May 2000, General Secretary of the VCP Le Kha Phieu said it was the government's policy to encourage the development of the private sector, which represented 50 per cent of GDP. *Nhan Dan*, 18 May 2000.
75 McCormick (1998); p.122.
76 Vietnam's main foreign investors are Singapore with 21.4 per cent of all approvals up to July 1998, Taiwan with 12.7 per cent, Hong Kong 11.7 per cent. These three 'Chinese' countries thus account for 45.8 per cent of all foreign investments in Vietnam. If we include Japan (10.7 per cent), South Korea (9.6 per cent), Malaysia (4.2 per cent) and Thailand (3.4 per cent), we get to and East Asian share of 73.7 per cent. *EIU Country Report*, 3rd quarter 1998, p. 18.
77 *Reuters*, 18 March 1998.
78 *Vietnam News Agency*, 29 March 1999.
79 *Vietnam News Agency*, 4 March 1998.
80 *Vietnam News Agency*, 27 May 1999.
81 *Vietnam News*, 26 May 1998.
82 This is what the Economist Intelligence Unit (EIU) expected. Its country report for Vietnam in the 3rd quarter 1998 (p. 10) included a table showing that Vietnam's GDP growth was more than double the Asian average in 1998, but the EIU expected the Vietnamese growth to slow down whereas the Asian average would rise from just above 2 to as much as 4 per cent.
83 According to *Reuters*, 3 April 1998, Party Secretary General Le Kha Phieu had just declared: 'In no place can people close the door themselves. If the door is closed, then it will open later itself and this is the same for Vietnam...In this situation closing the door and carrying out modernisation and industrialisation...is an illusion.'
84 Fforde and de Vylder (1996).
85 The first session of the 6th Plenum of the VCP Central Committee 13–17 October 1998 set the following tasks for 1999: 'Concentrating heavily on agriculture and rural development to create a foundation for socio-economic stability; effectively mobilising and using all investment resources; broadening the market for our products; developing and stabilising our state financial system; renovating the production process; settling all urgent social issues; reforming our administration and state mechanism; strengthening national defence and security; improving democracy together with social order and discipline.' *Nhan Dan*, 19 October 1998.

11
Trade and Industrial Policy Reform: The Challenge of Continuous Change

Ari Kokko

Introduction

During the two decades since the reunification of the country in 1976, the Vietnamese economy underwent more or less continuous change. In three major stages of reforms, Vietnam went from stagnation under orthodox central planning to double-digit growth rates in the industrial sector and an increasingly market-oriented economic system.

The first steps from plan to market were taken in 1979, when an acute economic crisis forced the Central Committee to stimulate production by introducing an individual contract system in agriculture and decentralizing decision-making in state enterprises (Dollar and Ljunggren, 1995; Ljunggren, 1996). Other cautious reforms were introduced during the following years, such as price adjustments and a reorientation of production from heavy industry towards agriculture and consumer goods, but the second significant step was not taken until 1986. An inflation rate of 775 per cent that year demonstrated that the limited reforms of the command economy had not been sufficient and that more radical action was needed. Hence, the Sixth Party Congress in December 1986 decided that *doi moi*, a thorough renovation of both the political and economic systems, was necessary. The renovated economy would still be dominated by the state, but the role of a supplementary private sector was acknowledged and the country was opened up to foreign investment and foreign trade. The third stage commenced in 1989 when the need to achieve macroeconomic stabilization motivated abolishment of the dual-pricing system and administrative prices, liberalization of the exchange rate, and increases in nominal interest rates to make real interest rates positive. Gradual reforms and fine-tuning of the legal and institutional framework have continued since that time, although the state sector remains firmly in control.

The progress and accomplishments of the Vietnamese economy since the abandonment of central planning were undoubtedly impressive. The country moved from stagnation and macroeconomic instability in the mid-1980s to reasonably stable prices and rapid growth a decade later. The annual GDP growth rate has averaged over 8 per cent from the early 1990s. Exports expanded even faster, and inflows of foreign products, technology and investment have also been accompanied by improvements in many social indicators. Poverty was reduced by a third during the first ten year of *doi moi*, various health services became more generally available, an increasing share of the population had access to safe water and sanitation, and primary school enrolment rates rose (UNDP, 1996).

However, from the second half of the 1990s it became increasingly well-understood that it might not be possible to sustain the gains of *doi moi* unless a fourth stage of reforms was introduced, since serious structural imbalances had begun to endanger the stability of the economy. Firstly, the development of the state-owned industrial sector was significantly weaker than what the aggregate growth data implied. Most state-owned enterprises (SOEs) were reported to face financial difficulties, and the large debt burden of the SOE sector became a threat to macroeconomic stability. It was therefore clear that SOE reforms were called for. Secondly, the trade deficit grew rapidly, exceeding 10 per cent of GDP since 1995. Although most developing countries incur significant trade deficits because of the need to import machinery, equipment and intermediate products for the emerging industrial sector, it was obvious that imbalances of this magnitude could not be sustained. Hence, trade reforms were necessary.

In this chapter, we argue that these weaknesses were related to the development strategy of the government, which was largely based on import substitution under state leadership. Considering what has been said above about rapid export growth and outward orientation, it may appear contradictory to claim that Vietnamese policies were import-substituting. Yet, looking at trade and foreign exchange regulations, it can be demonstrated that there was an overall bias in favour of import-competing sectors. The ambition to develop a domestic import-substituting industry led to excessive imports of capital goods and intermediates, driving up the trade deficit. At the same time, it also encouraged domestic production in sectors where Vietnam lack comparative advantages, contributing to the financial problems of the SOE sector.

That import substitution was largely carried out through state-owned enterprises added further problems. In addition to the generic problems of SOEs, related to weak incentive structures, multiple objectives and weak monitoring of performance, there was a risk that the Vietnamese SOE sector would become an obstacle to further change. The SOEs represented an important interest group with close ties to various levels of political decision-making. To the extent that they grew accustomed to import protection, they might use some of their political influence to oppose reforms that would increase competition and reduce their privileges. In the late 1990s, Vietnam might have reached the stage in which external commitments to liberalize trade, for example, through membership in the AFTA (Asean Free Trade Area) were almost impossible to fulfil because they were contrary to the interests of large SOEs.

Given the impressive economic achievement of the past decade, it would be unwise to suggest that Vietnam could have recorded higher growth rates by moving even faster towards a market economy. The argument made in this chapter is therefore not that the gradualist approach to economic reform up to the mid-1990s was misguided; instead, the main point is that transition and transformation are continuous processes. Policies and solutions that might have been appropriate at the early stages of the transition process, when markets were weakly developed and entrepreneurial and managerial talent were in short supply, did not remain the optimal ones. The traditional, central role of the state was not self-evident once the emerging private sector began to challenge the dominance of SOEs. Import substitution was not the correct strategy when the investment and import requirements of industry grew far larger than foreign currency earnings and caused heavy dependence on foreign sources of financing. Vietnam reached a stage of development where a fourth round of reforms, with further liberalization, outward orientation and more private enterprise, was needed to sustain high growth rates. It could be argued that the recent experience of Vietnam suggests at least two lessons for other countries in transformation, namely Cuba. The first was the need for continuous reform; the second was a caution against policies that might create interest groups that make continuous reform difficult.

The remainder of this chapter examines the problems discussed above in some more detail. We first focus on SOEs, before discussing the problems related to the trade deficit, and the contradiction between the present protectionist policy environment and the promises of future liberalization. The final section provides concluding remarks.

Inefficiency and indebtedness in the SOE sector

The state sector dominated the Vietnamese economy in the 1990s in spite of gradual liberalization and market orientation. Unlike in many other transition economies, Vietnamese SOEs were able to respond positively to economic reforms, for several reasons. The most important explanation might have been that the Vietnamese social, economic and political institutions did not collapse as a result of the reform process, but the structure of the SOE sector itself was also important. There were relatively few large, centrally-controlled SOEs in Vietnam, and provincial and municipal authorities instead controlled most enterprises in the state sector. In most cases it was even possible to identify the specific owners of the SOE – a ministry, a local Peoples Committee, an army division, and so forth. The decentralization of decision-making gave considerable managerial autonomy in plant operations as well as financial matters. This included the right to decide how profits were to be used, and was an important reason why many SOEs were able and willing to respond to the opportunities opened up as a result of the economic reforms (see Mallon, 1996).

Consequently, official statistics indicated that the state sector responded forcefully to the economic reforms, and the state share of GDP from 1986 to 1996 fell only marginally, from 44.7 per cent to 42.0 per cent. For industrial output, the data suggest that SOEs outperformed non-state enterprises. It has been estimated that SOEs produced 68 per cent of industrial output in the mid-1990s, while the share of the SOE sector in 1986 had been around 56 per cent of (Mallon, 1997, p. 5). However, this very positive description of the state of affairs in the SOE sector was misleading. One of the main explanations for the rapid growth rates of SOE output was that most joint ventures with foreign firms were included in the figures, since Vietnamese joint venture partners were almost always state enterprises. Wholly or partly foreign-owned firms were reported to account for about 13 per cent of GDP and 22 per cent of gross industrial output in 1995 (CIEMH, 1997). Once these production shares are deducted from the totals, the performance of the purely domestic state enterprises appears weaker than that of the private sector, although SOEs still accounted for approximately half of output.

Most SOEs were reported to operate with obsolete machinery and equipment. A survey in the mid-1990s indicated that perhaps one-third of the capital stock was more or less useless (Doanh, 1996). In combination with poor management and capital shortages, this contributed to very weak technical performance.[1] Some examples are instructive. The labour productivity of Vietnamese SOEs in vegetable oil processing was reported to be around 10 per cent of the leading foreign firms, while major industries like textiles, garments, plastics and pulp and paper might reach 30 or 40 per cent of international standards. The financial performance of the SOE sector at large was also remarkably weak. CIEMH (1997) reported that most SOEs ran at a loss, and that only 300 enterprises accounted for 80 per cent of SOE contributions to the state budget.

Other signs of the weaknesses of the SOE sector were found in reports on the debt of state enterprises. Due to their low profitability, many SOEs were forced to borrow from other state enterprises, the banking sector and other sources, which created a complex maze of cross-subsidization and indebtedness. There are no reliable data on how large the aggregate debt of the SOE sector was in the late 1990s. Tu (1997) argues that the government itself did not have detailed data on the financial situation of SOEs, but a survey by the Ministry of Finance gave an indication of the magnitude of the problem. At the end of 1995, the aggregate debt of the SOE sector was estimated at 279 000 billion dong, or about 20 per cent more than the turnover of the sector (Ministry of Finance, 1997). Although the survey did not reveal to whom these sums are owed or how old the debts were, it was clear that heavy indebtedness threatened the stability of the banking system (Leung and Doanh, 1998). It might also constitute a burden for the state budget; as the ultimate owner, the state might eventually be accountable for the liabilities of failed SOEs. Moreover, the loss-making SOEs were weakening the few efficient firms in the state sector. About a third of the total debt was internal to the SOE sector, and this internal debt alone was reportedly nearly seven times larger than the aggregate value of the sector's working capital. It should also be noted that Vietnam's external hard currency debt exceeded 35 per cent of GDP by 1996.[2] Although most of the SOE debt was domestic, it was likely that some of the larger SOEs, in aviation, oil production, tele-communications and other advanced industries, held significant amounts of foreign debt.

Given the inefficiency and financial weakness of much of the state enter-prise sector, there was no doubt about the need for reforms, and there appeared to be somewhat of a consensus among Western observers about the content of these reforms (Kokko and Sjöholm, 1997; Mallon, 1997; Riedel and Tran, 1997). Firstly, changes in the regulatory environment for business were needed to reduce disincentives to private sector development. These would include measures to strengthen property rights and contract enforcement, simplification of various registration and licensing require-ments, and a reduction of the remaining privileges of SOEs such as prefer-ential access to credits, land and foreign investment contacts. Reforms of the financial sector also belonged to this group of institutional changes. Sec-ondly, restructuring of state enterprises was essential. Mallon (1997) ident-ified five particularly important measures: (1) agencies responsible for regulating business should not be allowed to own enterprises; (2) SOEs should be incorporated under the Company Law under the same rights and obligations as private enterprises; (3) most smaller SOEs should be divested or leased to private individuals; (4) a significant number of large and medium-sized SOEs should be privatized (or equitized, which is the more commonly used term in Vietnam); and (5) corporate government and incentive structures should be improved for the remaining SOEs.

Thirdly, changes in macroeconomic policies were needed to avoid misal-location of resources. For example, trade and exchange rate policies should be formulated in such a way that domestic relative prices, for factors of production as well as for outputs, did not encourage investment in areas where the economy had no prospect of establishing competitive production. High trade barriers might be particularly harmful from this perspective. Import protection encouraged domestic production, but it also put a high premium on smuggling, which undercut the profitability of legal domestic producers.

By the end of the 1990s, the reforms of the SOE sector only touched upon some of the areas discussed above, and the disincentives facing the private sector remained significant (Mallon, 1997). Only about a dozen relatively small SOEs had been equitized by the end of 1997, and there did not appear to be a serious ambition to reduce the role of the state sector further in the near future. On the contrary, the Eight Congress of the Vietnamese Communist Party in June 1996 restated the objective that the state sector should hold a central role in the country's development. The establishment of 18 General Corporations and 70 Special Corporations – large conglomerates incorporating some 2000 SOEs operating in various strategic industries or specific geographical areas – was a step in this direction. Yet, it was not obvious how centralized management and monopolization of important industries would lead to the necessary improvements in technical and financial performance. It was also notable that trade and exchange rate policies remained biased in favour of import-substituting industries.

Trade and current account deficits

Although Vietnam's exports grew rapidly and became more diversified after the early 1990s, import growth was even faster, resulting in growing trade and current account deficits. These deficits drew attention to two potential problem areas. Firstly, could the large gap between the foreign exchange earnings of Vietnamese exporters and the foreign exchange requirements of importers be financed in a manner that does not endanger growth and macroeconomic stability? Secondly, were the imports used in such a way that they will contribute to balancing the country's external accounts in the future? In other words, did the imports improve Vietnam's capacity to earn or save foreign exchange? A look at some statistics on the country's balance of payments (BoP) and trade structure provides a starting point for a discussion about these two issues.

As illustrated in Table 11.1, Vietnam's trade and current accounts showed large negative balances after 1993, with the trade deficit exceeding 10 per cent of GDP after 1995. In principle, a trade deficit can be financed in the short run with inflows of foreign currency, foreign direct investment, official development assistance or private transfers. Short-run financing can also be achieved by building up new foreign debt, accumulating arrears on scheduled amortization and interest payments, or by drawing on the country's international reserves. All of these might, to varying degrees, have significant future costs, even when the deficit is temporary. The risks connected with debt financing are obvious, as illustrated by the Latin American debt crisis of the early 1980s. Accumulation of external debt may impose a heavy repayment burden on the country, with serious negative consequences for macroeconomic stability and growth prospects.

Similarly, drawing on the country's international reserves is undesirable since it increases the vulnerability to temporary demand and supply shocks. Foreign direct investment and official transfers are less risky, but may nevertheless have negative effects. Inflows of investment mean that foreigners

Table 11.1   Balance of payments of Vietnam, 1990–97 (US$ millions)

	1990	1991	1992	1993	1994	1995	1996	1997
Trade balance	−41	−63	−60	−547	−1190	−2345	−3150	−3 157
exports f.o.b.	1731	2042	2475	2985	4054	5198	7330	8798
imports	−1772	−2105	−2535	−3532	−5244	−7543	−10480	11 955
Factor services (net)	−411	−339	−382	−560	−297	−236	−407	
receipts	28	42	43	30	27	96	140	
payments	−439	− 381	−425	−590	−324	−332	−547	
of which:								
schedules interest	−237	−248	−282	−330	−198	−262	−363	
Non-factor services (net)	55	179	311	76	19	159	−61	
receipts	55	450	724	772	1283	2074	2243	
payments	0	−271	−413	−696	−1264	−1915	−2304	
Transfers (net)	138	90	123	264	302	290	1200	
private	0	35	59	70	170	140	1050	
official	138	55	64	194	132	150	150	
Current account excl. official	−259	−133	−8	−767	−1166	−2132	−2418	−2361
transfers	− 397	− 188	−72	−961	−1298	−2282	−2568	
Foreign direct investment	120	220	260	300	1048	1780	1803	1930
Medium- and long-term loans	−47	−191	52	−597	−275	93	279	751
Disbursements	233	65	487	54	272	433	939	
Schedules amortization	− 280	−256	−435	−651	−547	−340	−660	
Actual payments	− 166	−198	−206	−290	−119	−272	−547	
Short-term capital net	48	−88	−41	117	124	311	224	130
Capital account	1214	−59	271	−180	897	2184	2306	2811
Errors and omissions	−4	142	4	−109	140	125	125	
Overall balance (incl. official transfers)	−142	−50	268	−1056	−409	52	13	450
Change in net foreign assets (increase -)	−156	−282	−464	430	−117	−357	−293	
Memorandum items: trade deficit as per cent of GDP	<−1	<−1	<−1	−4.4	−8.0	−11.5	−15	−13

Source: IMF (1995), table 31 for 1990–92; unpublished data from the State Bank of Vietnam for 1993–97. The 1997 figures are estimates.

assume control over some of the country's assets, which is sometimes perceived as a violation of the sovereignty of national decision-makers. Moreover, present inflows of foreign investment will eventually lead to outflows of resources in the form of profit repatriation. Even inflows of ODA in the form of grant aid, without repayment obligations, may have negative effects on development by providing perverse incentives, since weaker economic performance may sometimes motivate donors to provide more aid, and aid dependency, as well as triggering Dutch Disease symptoms.[3]

The problems related to financing are most serious if deficits persist over time and are financed by borrowing. Arrears begin to mount and international financial markets begin to doubt the country's repayment capacity. In the worst case, some of the main lenders and foreign investors might withdraw, resulting in an abrupt reduction in the inflows of foreign capital, dramatically reduced import capacity, and severe problems for industry and commerce. In essence, this is what happened in several Asian countries in 1997 (Kokko, 1998). However, costs would start to build up before any acute crisis could be seen. It is enough if some major actors on the international market begin to question the sustainability of the deficits and require an interest premium to compensate for the higher risk.

In the Vietnamese case, all of the financing measures mentioned above were used to some degree to cover the trade deficit.[4] According to the data presented in Table11.1, foreign direct investment has recently been the most important source of foreign currency to cover the trade deficit, with remittances from overseas Vietnamese and Vietnamese guest workers abroad and official transfers providing most of the remaining finance. Although foreign borrowing increased over the period, and some accumulation of arrears on medium and long-term debt took place, these types of financing were apparently of relatively small importance. This suggests that the vulnerability to fluctuations in international capital markets was relatively small. It is also notable that the foreign direct investment inflows and transfers were large enough to allow significant increases in Vietnam's international reserves. Looking only at the statistics, one might draw the conclusion that there are no serious problems in Vietnam's external accounts.

However, the heavy reliance on foreign sources of financing made Vietnam dependent on foreign creditors and investors, and the Asian financial crisis had the potential to reduce all the main sources of financing. International lenders became more cautious as a result of the collapses in several of the Southeast Asian markets, and the inflow of foreign direct investment was expected to diminish as many of Vietnam's main investors struggled with severe financial problems. The depreciation of the yen and the won against the US dollar resulted in a reduction of the real value of foreign investment flows. Even if the structure of financing were sound, it appeared that the deficit was too large to be sustainable. Vietnam was likely to face severe balance of payments constraints, perhaps of crisis proportions (Leung and

Doanh, 1998, p. 3). The problems were not only caused by external factors, serious problems would have occured even if the turbulence in the Asian financial markets had not precipitated a turning point at that time. The reason, we will argue, is that the deficits incurred in recent years did not contribute much to Vietnam's ability to avoid future imbalances.

The other important question about the Vietnamese balance of payments position concerns the causes of the trade deficit. For the import surplus to be sustainable, it is necessary that the investments be directed to sectors in which they would contribute to long-term growth and facilitate a reduction of future deficits. Hence, it is relevant to examine what was imported and where these imports were used. The structure of imports presented in Table 11.2 was what one would expect in a country with an ambitious development programme. The bulk of imports was capital goods and raw materials for investment and production, and the most important individual import items were fuel, steel and fertilisers. However, the imports of semi-finished products such as electronic components and textiles also grew rapidly. Consumer imports were remarkably small, representing only 10 per cent in 1996 (see IMF, 1996, p.20). However, it should be noted that the structure of imports was determined by trade policy rather than by pure market forces: tariffs were higher and licence requirements more stringent for consumer goods than for machinery, equipment and intermediates. Vietnamese trade

Table 11.2   Structure of imports in Vietnam, 1991–96 (US$ millions and %)

	1991	*1992*	*1993*	*1994*	*1995*	*1996*
Total imports (US$ millions)	2 338.0	2 535.0	3 924.0	5 825.8	8 155.4	11 143.0
Product categories (% of total imports)						
machinery equipment and auxiliaries	21.8	21.6	23.5	31.1	25.7	33.2
materials and fuel	64.3	62.0	60.9	56.8	57.8	56.1
consumer goods	13.9	16.6	15.6	12.0	16.5	10.8
Major products (US$ millions)						
electronic components	29.7	39.7	116.9	104.0	113.8	184.8
steel	25.0	85.0	233.0	211.0	365.0	529.2
fertilisers	236.0	237.0	205.0	247.0	339.0	341.1
refined petroleum	485.0	615.0	687.4	701.0	830.0	1 079.0
textile fibres	42.0	13.8	60.0	81.0	199.0	158.0

Source: Unpublished data provided by the Ministry of Trade, Socialist Republic of Vietnam. It should be noted that the data for total imports differ slightly from the revised figures in Table 11.1.

policy explicitly aimed to restrict consumer imports in order to provide a captive market for local producers.[5] One consequence of this policy structure was substantial illegal imports of consumer goods, and some observers have suggested that the total value of illegal imports may have reached well over US$1 billion, but all estimates of smuggling are uncertain and should be interpreted with caution.

While the structure of imports appeared to be healthy in the sense that the trade deficit was generated by imports of investment rather than consumer goods, it remains to be determined whether these imports were invested in a sustainable fashion. Obviously, one of the fundamental questions must be whether the import boom was used to finance investment in import-substituting or export-oriented industries. In the latter case, there should not be much reason for worry, since the investments would contribute to the country's capacity to earn foreign exchange. However, if the bulk of investments were directed to import-substituting sectors, the situation is more serious. In most countries it proved difficult to graduate from import-substitution and infant-industry production. International experience shows that the protected industries rarely managed to reduce their dependence on imported inputs and capital goods, nor did they manage to become internationally competitive and generate significant export revenues (Kokko, 1997). Instead, import-substituting industry typically remained highly import-intensive for long periods, because the demand for foreign raw materials and intermediates remained more or less permanent. That import substitution was often accompanied by overvalued or at least highly valued exchange rates to support the necessary imports of investment goods exacerbated the problems. Even in cases where import substitution was intended to be selective, this generated a bias that promoted imports in general and discouraged exports in general, with further negative effects on the trade balance and the current account.

The Vietnamese authorities did not systematically collect or publish data on how imports were distributed among different end-users, so there was no direct way to examine whether import-competing or export-oriented industries were responsible for the trade deficit. We must therefore look for various kinds of indirect evidence to find the answer.

Beginning with the most positive developments, the investment boom facilitated rapid growth and diversification of Vietnamese exports. The balance of payments data in Table 11.1 show that the value of exports more than quadrupled between 1990 and 1996, with the most remarkable export increases during 1996, while Table 11.3 outlines some of the changes in export structure between 1991 and 1996. Export growth was most rapid in food products and other light manufacturing. While only two products, crude oil and rice, accounted for nearly half of exports in the early 1990s, their share fell to less than a third by 1995. Concurrently, exports of textiles, clothing and footwear has grown rapidly, approaching the value of oil

Table 11.3   Structure of exports in Vietnam, 1991–96 (US$ millions)

	1991	1992	1993	1994	1995	1996
Total exports (US$ millions)	2 042.0	2 571.0	2 985.2	4 054.0	5 448.9	7 255.0
Product categories (% of total exports)						
agriculture	30.0	32.1	30.8	31.7	32.0	34.1
forestry	9.0	5.4	3.3	2.7	2.8	1.9
aquaculture	14.0	11.9	14.3	13.6	11.4	9.0
industry and mining	18.6	19.2	23.3	30.6	34.8	36.4
crude oil	28.5	31.3	28.3	21.4	19.0	18.5
Major products (US$ millions)						
rubber	50.0	61.0	74.6	134.5	193.5	163.3
cashew nuts	26.0	41.0	44.0	72.5	97.7	95.0
coffee	74.0	92.0	110.6	328.2	595.5	333.8
rice	225.0	300.0	363.0	425.0	546.0	854.6
marine products	285.0	307.0	427.2	551.0	621.4	651.0
coal	48.0	62.0	51.9	75.1	88.9	114.2
crude oil	581.0	806.0	843.9	866.8	1 033.0	1 345.7
textiles and clothing	158.0	220.0	335.0	554.0	850.0	1 150.0
footwear	10.5	16.8	68.0	115.4	296.0	530.0

Source: Unpublished data provided by the Ministry of Trade, Socialist Republic of Vietnam. It should be noted that the data on total exports differ slightly from the revised figures in Table 11.1.

exports. The exports of marine products grew to be larger than rice exports by 1991, and coffee exports surpassed rice in 1995. These developments were commendable, and it was likely that trade deficits caused by investments in the export sector were sustainable, since the resulting production capacity could be used to generate much needed foreign currency. Yet, import growth was even faster than export growth, with imports in 1997 almost seven times larger than in 1990. Considering that several of Vietnam's major export products, rice, coffee, marine products and light industrial goods, were intensive users of local raw materials and labour rather than imported inputs and capital goods, it is unlikely that the export sector was the main destination for imports.

A look at some characteristics of the main actors in the Vietnamese economy suggests a similar conclusion. We have noted the central position of state-owned industry, which was not only dominant in production but also in imports and investment. With the exception of the oil sector and, to some extent, the garment and footwear industries, most SOEs focused on the production of consumer goods and some important intermediates such as steel, paper, fertilisers, cement and coal for the local market. These firms were expected to remain dominant in the future, and the state sector was directly or indirectly involved in nearly 80 per cent of all planned investment during the period of 1996–2000, according to the current Public Investment Programme (SRV, 1996a; UNDP, 1996). Although detailed data on the use of imports are missing, it is reasonable to assume that many of the intermediates and capital goods imported by SOEs were directed to the local rather than the export market.

Thanks to their knowledge of foreign markets and their international contacts, foreign multinational corporations should be in a better position to engage in export-oriented activities. Yet, many multinationals were attracted to Vietnam by the rapidly growing local market, and a large share of incoming FDI focused on import substitution, often in joint ventures with Vietnamese SOEs. The best examples were the several auto-assembly plants established in 1997 and 1998. One of the few assessments of the market orientation of foreign investment suggested that only about a quarter of the direct foreign investment in the industrial sector was intended mainly for exports (UNDP, 1996, p.27). Moreover, the high capital intensity of the FDI sector should be stressed. The United National Development Programme (1996, p.25) reported that the investment cost per foreign investment-related job was over US$66 000, indicating that this investment was directed to capital-intensive import substitution rather than labour-intensive export production. In other words, both of the main actors in Vietnamese industry, SOEs and multinational firms, seemed heavily biased towards the local market.

The observation that Vietnamese trade policies encouraged investments in import-substituting activities points in the same direction. The trade regime remained complex and highly-restrictive, although subject to significant reforms after the early 1990s. In order of decreasing transparency, the instruments for import restrictions included tariffs, reference prices, excise taxes and surcharges, quotas, other quantitative restrictions, import licences and foreign exchange controls. Several studies (CIE, 1997; Kokko, 1997; SRV, 1996b) provided detailed descriptions of the Vietnamese trade regime, and a very brief summary of the trade environment will therefore be sufficient.

A first layer of protection was provided by tariffs. These were not high in comparison with other developing countries, but they provided very high rates of effective protection to Vietnamese producers of consumer goods. Tariffs on final goods were systematically much higher than tariffs on raw materials and intermediates.[6] However, formal tariffs only made up a limited part of Vietnam's trade restrictions, and various types of opaque non-tariff barriers were often more important. For instance, the tariffs for most consumer goods were levied on reference prices established by the Vietnamese authorities rather than on the prices declared by the importers. Licensing and import quota requirements were the main trade barriers in many industries and during 1997 and 1998 foreign exchange controls were particularly important in restricting consumer imports. Apart from the difficulties of assessing how much protection these measures provided, there was also the risk that trade policy would become more discretionary and unpredictable when informal quotas and exchange controls were more important than tariffs and quotas. As noted by Chambas and Geourjon (1996), the resulting uncertainty might encourage firms with political connections to lobby decision-makers for more protection or slower liberalization of their industries. This was likely to complicate any reform process, as we will discuss below.

Hence, the available evidence on the use of imports suggests that the country's balance of payments position was not merely a necessary consequence of sound development policies. The large trade deficit was instead an early warning sign, admittedly in stark contrast to the impressive record in growth and stabilization, calling attention to the need to reform trade policy and industry structure. A reduction of the bias in favour of import-substituting industries was necessary to avoid persistent current account imbalances and related macroeconomic problems.

Trade policy reform

The Vietnamese government repeatedly declared that trade liberalization was a central element of the country's continuing economic reforms, and several important steps in the direction of increased outward orientation were taken. Most significantly, as a consequence of its membership in the ASEAN Free Trade Area (AFTA) 1996, Vietnam made a commitment to eliminate most tariff and non-tariff barriers *vis-à-vis* the other member countries. Vietnam also sought for membership in the World Trade Organizaton (WTO), which required a commitment to simplify import controls and reduce the level of import protection. In addtion, the country introduced unilateral trade reforms with support from the IMF, the World Bank and other donors (see PFP, 1996).[7]

To the extent that these commitments to trade reform were credible, it might be futile to complain about the weaknesses of the prevailing trade regime: the necessary changes were already on the agenda. However, in the late 1990s it was too early to take the promised reduction of Vietnamese trade barriers for granted. The Vietnamese authorities realized few of the trade reforms required by the AFTA, since the country was given an adjustment period until 2006 to eliminate non-tariff barriers, to reduce tariffs on regional trade below 5 per cent, and to harmonize tariff structures and customs procedures to ASEAN standards. Moreover, there was no timetable to indicate how soon different industries would have to meet their liberalization requirements. This created considerable uncertainty about the future competitive environment for most producers that enjoyed tariff protection.

It was not known if individual industries would remain protected until 2006, or if significant tariff reductions would be initiated earlier.

Moreover, some aspects of the country's economic policies contradicted comprehensive trade liberalization. Arguments highlighting the need for import substitution and infant-industry protection were common in the Vietnamese debate, and it was easy to find examples of individual interest groups calling for continued or higher protection of their specific industries. A typical example was a demand by the Vietnam Machinery Association that import tariffs on machinery be increased by 20 to 30 per cent to protect domestic production.[8] Such arguments were only to be expected in a situation in which many firms and perhaps entire industries were likely to encounter serious problems if liberalization was carried out. It was more serious that the calls for continuing protection, at least to some extent, found support among the highest level of policy-makers. For example, the Vietnamese AFTA Secretariat noted that one of the objectives in the continuing reforms process was to manage tariff reductions in a way that would 'assure the highest degree of protection possible' to Vietnamese industry (Ministry of Finance, 1996, p.3).

Another sign of continuing reliance on import substitution was provided by the objectives regarding the country's import structure. The explicit aim of the Vietnamese import-licensing system was, until 1996, to restrict import of consumer goods below 20 per cent of total export revenue. However, a new objective for the period 1996–2000 was decided during the Eighth National Congress of the Communist Party in June 1996. The aim changed, to restrict consumer goods imports to 9 per cent of total imports. Even if the total quantity of imports were estimated to more than double between 1996 and 2000, from about US$10 billion to over US$20 billion, this proposed change in import structure meant that the real value of consumer imports would only be allowed to increase marginally. This made it obvious that development would require a very restrictive import regime for consumer goods until at least 2000.

While it could be argued that these policies were only temporary and would not interfere with the planned trade liberalization process after 2000, there were other elements of Vietnamese policies that had obvious long-term implications. For example, the consolidation and merger of SOEs in strategic sectors into 18 general corporations would lead to a near-monopolization in several important industries, including steel, coal, paper, cement, chemicals and petroleum. In addition, the Vietnamese government established about 70 special corporations by merging small SOEs operating in the same sectors or the same geographical area.[9] Together, these general and special corporations absorbed approximately 2000 of the 2300 industrial SOEs that existed at the end of 1994, and they were estimated to account for some 80 per cent of the resources and production capacity of Vietnam's SOE sector (Doanh, 1996). These developments suggest that foreign firms aiming to export to Vietnam would face local competitors with significant market power, who also control the local distribution networks. Foreign firms that were not prepared to collaborate with the incumbents might face high entry barriers even if nominal trade restrictions are removed. The costs of setting up alternative distribution channels might even involve a more difficult obstacle than the tariff barriers.

Similarly, the physical production targets for state-owned enterprises for the period 1996–2000, presented in the current Public Investment Programme (SRV, 1996a), stressed import substitution and indicated a clear ambition to reach self-sufficiency in several key areas. Domestic output of cement, coal, steel, fertilizers and paper was projected to more than double over this period, with even higher growth rates for light consumer goods industry. Some of these industries would probably be competitive after the intra-regional trade barriers were removed, so outlined in the AFTA agreement. But the investment strategy did not appear to be based on a detailed analysis of Vietnam's comparative advantages with respect to the rest of the region. Hence, there was no doubt that some of the industries earmarked for expansion would fail if they were left without protection. This meant that the Public Investment Programme was not fully consistent with the Vietnamese trade liberalization objectives. More specifically, a programme that directed investment into import-substituting industries up to 2000, when significant trade liberalization was planned to begin, might create a situation in which the costs of liberalization became prohibitive.

Why reforms were not sufficient

There was a risk that the discordance between policies that were still largely import-substituting and the commitment to liberalize trade in the future might cause serious problems. The measures agreed upon under the AFTA agreement were highly relevant and important, and they are likely to have a positive impact on Vietnam's economic development if they are fully implemented. Yet, the long adjustment period and the lack of a firm time schedule for the realization of Vietnam's AFTA commitments has created uncertainty and might provide inappropriate and inconsistent incentives. Perhaps the most serious contradiction in the country's policy environment stemmed from these inconsistent incentives. While rules and regulations were biased in favour of large import-substituting SOEs, it was imperative that this policy regime should not be the foundation for long-term investment decisions. If this contradiction was not recognized, there was a risk that Vietnam would not be able to fulfil its AFTA commitments.

To the extent that private investors recognized the uncertainty caused by the lack of a firm time schedule for the AFTA agreement, they were likely to reduce investments and, in particular, to avoid long-term investments. The common complaint that the Vietnamese private sector was only interested in short-term projects in which it would be possible to recoup the investment in a few years might well have been evidence of this uncertainty. An obvious consequence was relatively low private investment in industrial production, and an investment structure sub-optimal from a development perspective. These problems provided reasons to consider pushing reforms further.

However, even more serious problems might occur if investors were to disregard the contradictions and continue investing into import-substituting industry. One reason for committing resources to investments that were not likely to be profitable in the long run could be that the investors in question were more concerned about fulfilling political objectives than commercial success. Another could be that the investors believed that their investment decisions might have some impact on trade policy. Both these possibilities pointed to SOEs rather than private investors. SOE managers were appointed by and reported to political decision-makers rather than private capital owners, and SOEs were often so large that their investment decisions might have some impact on policies. The problem with these import-substituting investments was that many of them would collapse if trade liberalization were realized. Consequently, if substantial new resources were invested into import substitution, the costs for liberalization would become very high. In such a case, the government might face a serious time inconsistency, when trade barriers to major industries were to be reduced or removed. While a commitment to trade reform was desirable *ex ante*, it might be optimal to default on some or all of these commitments *ex post* if enough resources had been placed into the old production structure. There was no doubt that the interest groups supporting import substitution were aware of this, and knew that their actions might influence policy decisions.

The problems arising because of the uncertain and drawn out trade liberalization process were probably more serious in Vietnam than in many other countries. The main reason was that the interest groups backing import substitution were remarkably strong. The main beneficiaries of protectionism were SOEs, sometimes in joint ventures with foreign firms, as noted above. These enterprises were not only large and powerful, but also intimately connected with various levels of political decision-making, and in a position to use their political influence to oppose trade liberalization or other reforms that might reduce their privileges (see Kokko and Zejan, 1996). The lack of an independent bureaucratic technocracy that could ignore the pressure from industry and eventually manage an orderly retreat from import substitution was a solid argument against Vietnamese import substitution (World Bank, 1993, chapter 4).

In this context, it is worth repeating that more than half of the planned investment spending in Vietnam during the period 1996–2000 was expected to be connected with SOEs, often in import-substituting industries (UNDP, 1996, p. 20ff). These investments were likely to provide strong incentives for SOEs to use their political power to press for continued protection and a retraction of liberalization promises. It should not be forgotten that the uncertainty surrounding the liberalization schedule facilitates this lobbying task – the lack of a credible and publicized time plan for tariff reductions might suggest that the scheme for trade reform was open for negotiation.

It can also be argued that the Vietnamese government itself had vested interests in protectionism. Import substitution accounted for perhaps three-quarters of the Vietnamese government's budget revenues in the mid-1990s, through taxes on international trade and remittances of rents from pro-tected SOEs and multinational firms. The system was convenient, both because import protection allowed SOEs to generate surpluses, and because it was easier to extract surpluses from SOEs than from independent private firms. The longer fiscal policy relied on import substitution, the more diffi-cult and painful it would be to carry through the reforms that were needed. Comprehensive trade liberalization would disturb the congenial situation and necessitate a much more thorough reform of the institutional environ-ment than what was often recognized. It would not be enough to establish a broader tax base and make collection more effective; it would also be neces-sary to provide a business environment in which all economic agents, private firms as well as SOEs, have the same tax obligations and equal opportunities to engage in industry and commerce.

In summary, established trade reforms were not sufficient at the end of 1990s because the long adjustment period and the uncertain time schedule for the AFTA commitments would make liberalization more costly than what most people expected. These costs might force Vietnam to abandon parts of the agreement. Further reforms were needed. Given the progress towards a market economy during the 1990s and the commitment to AFTA, the chal-lenge facing Vietnamese policy-makers was no longer whether or not to liberalize the trade regime; the main challenge was to manage the transition from import substitution to a more liberal trade regime.

Transition to freer trade

As in the case of SOE reform, there was some agreement among outside observers about what Vietnam should do to manage the transition to free trade (CIE, 1997; Kokko, 1997; UNDP, 1996). In the short run, the most important tasks for the Vietnamese authorities were to restate the commit-ment to liberalize foreign trade and to make the policy environment more predictable. This was necessary in order to reduce the costs of trade reform and to promote private long-term investment by domestic as well as foreign firms in sectors where the country has comparative advantages. To confirm the commitment to liberalize trade, the Vietnamese government could, for example, declare its intent to meet the AFTA targets earlier than agreed. A decision to move forward the date for the fulfilment of AFTA commitments by one or two years would not complicate policies; rather, it would constitute a clear signal to domestic and foreign producers and investors about the future policy environment. In addition, it seemed clear that the reduction of non-tariff barriers to trade deserved more attention than it was given in the AFTA agreement.

To make the policy environment more predictable, Vietnamese authorities would also need to explicitly address questions concerning the timing and sequencing of tariff reductions for different product groups. It was of great importance that a schedule for tariff reductions be specified, and that this schedule be made public. Information on the sequencing of tariff reductions was essential for domestic and foreign investors deciding how and where to invest their funds.

More attention should also be given to the export sector. The costs of trade reform, in terms of unemployment, lower budget revenues and slower growth, would be unacceptably high if the export sector were not able to employ some of the capital, labour and entrepreneurial skills released from shrinking import-substituting industries. High and sustainable export growth would be necessary to achieve a smooth transition to free trade, and Vietnamese authorities would need to engage in active export promotion during the coming decade.[10]

Trade liberalization and export promotion alone would probably not guarantee Vietnam a position among the highly successful Asian tiger economies. Summarizing a comprehensive study of trade policy reform in developing countries, Rodrik (1993, p. 2972) concluded that removing trade barriers would only be a step:

> Genuine reform requires the creation of a new set of interactions between government and the private sector, one that provides for an environment of policy stability and predictability, that discourages rent-seeking activities, and that improves the government's ability to discipline the private sector. In other words, the change that is needed is not only in policy, but also in policy *making*.

In the present context, this meant that trade reform was closely connected to reforms of the relations between the state, the SOEs and the private sector. The serious weaknesses in the technical and financial performance of state-owned industry, as well as the related problems in the financial sector, might well undermine any advances made in the field of trade policy. Somewhat crudely, it could be argued that if SOEs continued to dominate Vietnamese industry, there was a risk that politically motivated choices would eclipse economically rational decisions. This might contribute to many of the objectives of the Vietnamese leadership, but a very significant cost in terms of forgone economic growth and welfare. Considering the pragmatic approach that characterized Vietnamese economic policy after 1990, there was little doubt that the necessary reforms would eventually be achieved.

The main cause of concern was that things might become worse before they improved. It was possible that the need for further reforms would not become evident to all Vietnamese decision-makers until the problems discussed above were manifest in significantly weaker economic performance.

Summary and conclusion

Although Vietnam's macroeconomic performance after the introduction of *doi moi* in 1986 was remarkably successful, this chapter argued that further reforms were needed to sustain stability and high growth rates. Some of the policies that contributed to the success of the gradual transition from the command economy to a more market-oriented environment, such as protection of domestic industry and promotion of the SOE sector, outlived their purpose. The weakness of many SOEs and the large trade and current account deficits indicated that the strategy of SOE-led import substitution was no longer viable. To overcome structural problems, it was necessary that the next round of reforms focused on further deregulation, promotion of private enterprise and exports, and trade liberalization. Some reform commitments, in particular related to trade, were officially announced. For example, Vietnam's membership in AFTA and the application for WTO membership required significant trade liberalization.

However, the necessary reforms will not be easily implemented. Many SOEs, as well as many of the foreign firms that entered Vietnam, have benefited from the protectionist policy regime, and might oppose reforms that reduce their privileges and expose them to tougher competition. The complex and sometimes contradictory policy environment, with frequent changes in tariffs, quotas and other trade policies, makes this lobbying task easier. Even if these interest groups are not able to interfere directly in the policy-making process, they might still influence the outcome through their investment decisions. There will be an adjustment period of several years before the protectionist policies which encouraged investment in import-substituting industry give way to more a more neutral environment. It could be argued that the more resources SOEs might invest in advanced import-substituting industries during the adjustment period, the higher will be the cost of trade liberalization, and the more likely that significant trade barriers are retained.

It is possible that the Vietnamese experience of economic transformation illustrates the continuous character of the transition process. Flexibility and ability to adjust to a changing environment are perhaps neglected aspects of successful long-term policies. Policies and strategies that work well at the early stages of reforms, when markets are underdeveloped, may become obstacles to growth at later stages of development. In particular, there may be reason to be cautious with policies that establish interest groups whose objectives, current or future, may differ from those of the economy at large.

If Cuba decides that a gradual transition to a market economy is desirable, these will be very relevant concerns for its policy-makers as well.

Notes

1   Kokko and Sjöholm (1997) and Tu (1997) provide more extensive discussions of the reasons for the weak performance of SOEs.
2   In addition, Vietnam owes around 10 billion rubles to the former Soviet Union, much of which is related to SOEs. It is not known whether the figures on aggregate SOE debt include also the ruble debt. The exchange rate at which the ruble debt will be valued for repayment purposes has not been determined, but the burden may be substantial. In the mid-1990s, Russia argued for an exchange rate of 0.56 rubles per US dollar, which appears quite unreasonable. A more reasonable rate would perhaps be similar to the 5–6 rubles per dollar at which Vietnam's ruble debts to Hungary and Germany were rescheduled. However, this would still leave a very significant debt burden.
3   The bulk of ODA in Vietnam is made up of soft loans, which will eventually have to be repaid.
4   However, it is hard to provide an exact description of the structure of financing, since data collection is imprecise and official statistics are frequently revised. While some of the BoP items can be registered fairly accurately – for instance, data on exports and imports are collected by customs authorities and the disbursement of ODA is closely monitored by the government – others are not clearly visible and have to be estimated in various indirect ways.
5   Until August 1996, the objective was to limit consumer goods imports to a level corresponding to 20 per cent of export revenue. Since then, authorities have talked about the stricter objective to restrict consumer goods to 9 per cent of total imports.
6   The formal tariff structure includes about 3200 tariff lines and 28 tariff rates ranging from 0 per cent to 100 per cent. The average tariff (weighted as well as unweighted) has been 15–20 per cent in recent years. See Kokko (1997).
7   The donor agencies have played an important role for the realization of some of these reforms. For instance, disbursements of the World Bank's SAC have been conditional on the introduction of specific trade policy-related reformos, such as reductions of the maximum tariff (see PFP, 1996).
8   See *Viet Nam News*, Thursday, 20 March 1997, p. 2.
9   The general corporations are established under Prime Minister's Decision No. 91-TTg, dated 7 March 1994, while the establishment of special corporations is based on Decision No. 90-TTg of the same date.
10   World Bank (1993) summarizes much of what is known about the design of successful export-promotion programmes in Asia.

12
Global Subcontracting and Women Workers in Comparative Perspective

*Angie Ngoc Tran**

Introduction

This chapter provides a comparative analysis that examines the impact of the global subcontracting system on Vietnamese women workers in relation to other Asian countries, namely the Philippines, South Korea and Taiwan. The insights from workers' experiences in a socialist country contribute to a framework which studies women workers in labour-intensive industries such as textile and garment industries. The methodology employs both statistical and narrative analysis. Sharing a concern with Benmayor, I provide an analytical framework and at the same time give voice to the Vietnamese women workers (Benmayor, 1987, p. 10), the experiences of whom are presented through their own narratives within the conceptual framework of a global gender division of labour. I provide concrete examples from in-depth interviews with four women garment workers and two women directors from several state-owned and private garment firms (see Annex for list of interviewees).

At the time of the fieldwork in 1997 and 1998, a multilevel piecework subcontracting system was dominant in the garment industry of both Vietnam and the Philippines. The countries shared the characteristic of the system that the workers were at the bottom of the subcontracting ladder. In the Philippines, supplier firms in large cities, such as Manila, subcontracted jobs to provincial manufacturers or agents who, in turn, farmed out the work to rural households (Ofreneo, 1994, pp. 172–3). In Vietnam, relationships at the highest level of the subcontracting system were consistent with the concept of triangle manufacturing (Gereffi, 1995b, pp. 118–19)

---

* I would like to thank Melanie Beresford and Nguyen Huong for their invaluable comments on this chapter, and the interviewees whose narratives provide significant and moving insights into this global industry. This chapter is dedicated to My Mother who encourages me to bring a human face to my analysis, and to all garment and textile workers who toil everyday in Vietnam.

central to the buyer-driven commodity chains. This concept provided a snapshot of the relationships between the three main actors in the Vietnamese garment industry: the Vietnamese garment producers; foreign buyers primarily from the EU, Japan, Canada, Norway and the USA; and the middlemen, usually from Taiwan, South Korea, Hong Kong and Singapore. Foreign buyers either set up offshore production networks in developing countries directly, or place their orders via middlemen who can assure competitive pricing, quality and delivery schedules. In Vietnam at the beginning of its global integration most of those foreign buyers placed garments orders through Taiwanese and South Korean intermediaries with whom they might have worked for many years. These middlemen supplied inputs, or fabrics and garment accessories such as buttons, thread, sold machinery to Vietnamese producers, and provided management. Their specialists stayed in Vietnam for weeks or months to monitor all stages of production, especially the finishing stages, including quality control and packaging. Vietnamese workers then assembled these imported inputs, applied clothing patterns to fabrics, cut and sewed them into clothes. After the quality-control process, these workers packaged and shipped the final products to middlemen or directly to buyers.

While the ownership structure was more complex in the case of socialist Vietnam with state-owned enterprises (SOEs) and non-state firms, which include both domestic firms and foreign-invested firms (more details in the next section), the multi-level structure was not dissimilar to that of the Philippines. Work orders were subcontracted to Vietnamese workers at many levels, both in factory and at home. Large state firms produced only portions of their garment orders 'in house', and subcontracted the rest to either local state firms or private firms. Private firms, in turn, either fulfilled the contracts by themselves or further subcontracted out simple assembly tasks to household units to meet delivery dates. These household networks are very small and involve people working on their own low-tech sewing machines at home.

The garment industry in both countries was almost totally dependent on foreign imported machinery, input supplies and accessories. In the Philippines, overseas interests, mostly from the USA, dictated the fabrics, machinery and clothing designs to be used, and the quantity of orders to be completed (Ofreneo , 1994, pp. 170–1). The process of technology transfer requires elaboration. To both countries, there was transfer of 'know- how', the manner to operate the imported machinery, in most cases used machinery, and not 'know-why', the technological expertise and creation of research and development facilities. In the Philippines, the majority of machinery and associated technology came from the United States; ten of the top 20 garment exporters in 1990 were US wholly-owned firms (*ibid.*, p. 171). Vietnamese producers, on the other hand, typically bought used sewing or embroidery machines from Japan, South Korea and to a lesser extent Germany, but not the designs of clothing and embroidery products which would provide much more value-added to the producers.

However, over time, more foreign firms dealt directly with Vietnamese producers to cut out the middleman's costs. Also, more East Asian middlemen became buyers and placed their own orders directly with Vietnamese firms. The triangle manufacturing system did not capture these changes.[1] Most recent data show that four East Asian countries – Taiwan, Japan, Hong Kong and South Korea – ranked at the top in investment in textile and garment industries.[2]

Vietnam, too, had the potential to move up the subcontracting ladder by developing domestic integration, through fostering forward and backward linkages (Tran, 1997). Domestic integration, in conjunction with global integration, can be a way in which the Vietnamese garment industry could contribute to national development, and perhaps growth with equity. There is a relationship between value-added and backward and forward linkages in both trade networks, the one with Western Europe, the other with Eastern Europe. Specifically, Vietnamese producers did *not* receive the entire price of a product in the richer EU markets. In the less affluent Eastern European markets they were able to use Vietnamese-made fabrics and other accessories (backward linkage), and directly distributed garment exports to the Eastern European consumers (forward linkage). This underscores the significance of Vietnam's historical link to Eastern European countries. This relationship made Vietnam unique among other Southeast Asian countries (Dang Phong *et al.*, 2000). On the other hand, in the links with the European Union, inputs were imported and controlled by the East Asian middlemen.

Production and employment in the garment industry

The garment industry played an important role at the beginning of the industrialization process in the newly-industrializing countries, for example Taiwan and South Korea in the 1970s. In those countries the majority of workers in the garment industry, especially in export-processing zones and/ or in garment firms for export, were women (Amsden, 1989, pp. 250, 252; Bello and Rosenfeld, 1992, pp. 215–6; Ofreneo, 1994, p. 164). The same was true in Vietnam. Overall, the Vietnamese garment industry employed about 560 000 workers, at least 17 per cent of the manufacturing labour force (General Statistical Office, 1997, p. 10),[3] and of this amount over 80 per cent were young women (US Consulate HCMC, March 1998; General Statistical Office, 1997, p. 11). Most private garment firms were medium-scale, employing between 100–300 workers. However, there were some large firms in Ho Chi Minh city, such as Huy Hoang and Sai Gon May Xuat Khau, which employed between 1500 and 3000 workers (Ministry of Industry, 1997, p. 27).

Table 12.1   Firms and labour in the VTGI by ownership type, (1993, 1996, 1997)

Sector	State-owned firms		Domestic non-state (coop, limited, household)	Firms with foreign investment*	
	(1993)	*(1997)*	*(1997)*	*(1996)*	*(1997)*
Textiles	75	52	227 units and 10 000 rural households (total 40 000 workers)	58 units with 32 324 workers	129 units with 36 687 workers
Garments	100	122	384 units and 30 000 households (total 100 000 workers)	88 units with 17 730 workers	176 units with 40 906 workers

* Joint-ventures, business cooperation, and 100 per cent foreign-owned.
Sources: VINATEX (1999); Ministry of Industry (1997), pp. 5–6, 25, 28, Appendix, p. 16; Ministry of Planning and Investment (1998).

The Vietnamese garment industry grew rapidly in the 1990s, and subcontracting work played an important role in a substantial increase in garment-workers employed in all types of foreign-invested firms. The state sector employed about 60 per cent, or about 342 000 in the textile and garment industries (Table 12.1). However, between 1993 and 1997, there was a drop in the number of state-owned textile firms from 75 to 52. At the same time, the number of state-owned garment firms increased from 100 to 122. The garment sector employed more workers than textiles. In the non-state sector in 1997 there were 100 000 garment workers and 40 000 textile workers employed. Between 1996 and 1997, there was a substantial increase in garment workers in foreign-invested firms in both absolute and relative terms; the garment workforce more than doubled, while there was a mere 13 per cent increase in textiles (Table 12.1).

In terms of production structure, the state sector produced at least half of the total textile and garment output, and more textiles proportionally than garment products (General Statistical Office, 1997, pp. 166–202). In shares of output by types of ownership, the state sector produced 50.6 per cent, the Vietnamese non-state sector 33.6 per cent, and the foreign-invested sector 15.9 per cent.[4] By sector, state firms produced 60 per cent of textiles, but only 35 per cent of garment output.

Rural women workers

Many women workers in Southeast Asia came from rural areas. These semi-skilled workers relied on home villages for social security and reproduction, and their wage earnings formed a supplement to cash crops (Ong, 1990, p. 433). Enloe found cases in which women recruited from rural areas to work in urban textile and garment factories experienced hopes, frustrations and risks from removal from their families. They faced low wage payments, textile dust, job layoffs, crowded boarding houses, tension from piecework payment, and loneliness (Enloe, 1983, p. 409). Women workers from rural areas also played an important role in the garment industry in Taiwan and South Korea in the 1970s, and the Philippines and Vietnam in the 1980s and 1990s. Except for the different time frame, the similarity was striking in these countries: most of these young migrant women stayed in squalid company-owned dormitories within walking distance of the workplaces, which were under male hierarchical management (Bello and Rosenfeld, 1992, pp. 215, 218; Amsden, 1989, p. 252). Due to the existence of large numbers of rural women workers, employers could pit them against urban women workers.

In the Philippines, the garment industry was the largest employer of homeworkers, whose ages ranged from four to over 70. The women and girls lived in squalid housing in both rural and urban areas, and fulfilled household chores and childcare as well as garment subcontract work to supplement their husbands' incomes (Ofreneo, 1994, pp. 174–5). While there existed no statistics on the percentage of workers coming from rural areas, two of the four Vietnamese women workers that I interviewed came from two northern villages, and from their accounts many women workers in their factories came from nearby villages. They had to rent accommodation, which cost at least US$10 a month. In crowded and unsanitary boarding houses up to eight women shared four two-level bunk beds in a small room. The four women workers interviewed for this study confirmed that many rural women, including two interviewees, would often go back to their villages obtain rice supplies for their meals. However, more research would be needed to examine the relationships between rural workers and their families in the countryside, in terms of their dependence on rice and the need to earn money in the cities to send home.[5]

Gender division of labour in global subcontracting

Gender differentiation is used to deliver flexibility and raise productivity for global production. In particular, docility, dexterity, passivity and flexibility on the shopfloor are expected of women for higher productivity. Aihwa Ong (1983, 1990) discussed the 'biological attributes' or manual dexterity expected of women workers so they can withstand low-skilled and unstimulating assembly work. Japanese managers in Malaysia link these 'female attributes' as necessary to cost considerations and productivity (Ong, 1990, p. 396). In the context of patriarchal culture, Lim (1983) argued that women are conceived as having certain feminine social and cultural attributes that make them suitable for detailed and routine work such as sewing garments and assembling electronic gadgets. They are expected to be conscientious and patient workers who can endure long hours of repetitive work (Lim, 1983, p. 78). Managers of garment factories and Export Processing Zones (EPZs) in the three countries preferred young women workers to male workers; they were perceived to have greater manual dexterity, to be less likely to rebel than men, and willing to work long hours and accept lower earnings than male workers doing comparable jobs (Bello and Rosenfeld, 1992, pp. 25, 216; Lee and Song, 1994, p. 150; Gereffi and Pan, 1994, p. 142).

The multilevel subcontracting system affords flexibility for buyers and contractors, but requires workers, women in particular, to bear the burden of all adjustments and lose control over their own labour. In a piecework system, the manufacturing process is broken into very small, monotonous manual tasks. Workers must be effective in these tasks, for the more they produce the more income they earn. As clothing fashions change continuously in minute details, workers must learn to manufacture these new styles and patterns without direct compensation for this learning process. The tasks are fragmented: each worker would know only a small part of the whole production process. When they are laid off, they have no marketable skills for jobs other than these same low-paying assembly tasks (Tran, 1997 and 1998).

The piecerate system relieves management of the need to directly control the output of workers. Philippine management used this system and avoided the complications of organized labour (Hutchison, 1992, p. 482). Ong (1990, p. 431) demonstrated that these low-skilled, exhausting jobs in Malaysia do not provide workers with any other skills if they want to leave these factories in hope of a better job. Ong argued that a common management strategy to ensure fresh labour capable of intensive factory work at low wage rates is to offer them short term, six-month contracts so that they can be released and rehired at the same low wage rates. Nash characterized these labour-intensive industries as 'footloose' in that they do not generate long-lasting employment. Enloe (1983, pp. 414, 416) also argued that women workers who are laid off from these firms have limited skills or few options to find jobs in other sectors. Moreover, quality control of subcontracted production on the factory floor relies on not paying for work judged as unsatisfactory, or by requiring that it be corrected in workers' free time (Hutchison, 1992, p. 483).

Vietnamese contractors and foreign managers expected docility and obedience from their workers, and offered no compensation for insecurity of employment. Tran explained:

We must go to the factory even when there is no work for us. This scenario happened many times: there was no job order for the whole month but the management kept telling us that there will be work on Monday, and we must be there. When we arrived at the factory at 7:30 am on Monday, they told us that there will be work to do on Wednesday or Thursday. But we cannot leave the factory. We must stay locked inside to practice on garment patterns. They told us to practice sewing different patterns so we can make good products, and our jobs will become easier when we have orders. We earn no money while sitting there assembling those patterns. Also, Japanese managers are extremely careful about cleanliness. They don't allow us to bring any books or newspapers to read while we are in the factory; our lunch bags must be kept in a separate cabinet downstairs since they are afraid that our belongings might soil their machines or materials. Then came Wednesday or Thursday when there were not always jobs for us!

Another similarity among the countries listed above was a clear gender division of labour within the garment industry. Almost invariably in Vietnamese factories that I visited, men were in charge of higher-skilled, hence higher-paid tasks, including fabric cutting, pressing, supervision and quality control. The majority of women workers were assigned the lower-paid, tedious, monotonous, manual, assembling tasks on the assembly lines (Tran, 1997 and 1998). The situation was almost identical in the Philippine garment industry (Ofreneo, 1994, p. 173), and it is interesting to find that this gender division of labour also prevailed in Taiwan's garment production. Men were not engaged in sewing tasks and usually held management jobs, while women sewed and earned, on average, four-fifths of the pay of male workers in the same functional category (Gereffi and Pan, 1994, p. 142). In Korea male workers carried out most cutting tasks and held the managerial positions, while female workers worked the assembly lines (Lee and Song, 1994, pp. 153–4).

Beneficiaries of the subcontracting system

There is an intrinsic contradiction within national development which entails providing incentives such as low-wage labour in export-processing zones or subcontracting to attract foreign investment, and defending workers' rights. Power differentials between corporations and workers are clear when corporations can diversify risk by relying on international wage differentials and capital mobility to control workers' demands for higher wages and fringe benefits (Nash, 1983, vii–xv). That would also limit workers' ability to organize (Bonacich *et al.*, 1994, p. 370).

The one characteristic common not only in Vietnam and the Philippines, but also in other newly-industrialized countries was that the burden of adjustments to fashion seasons and market fluctuations was borne dispro-portionately by workers. Producers and contractors, be they foreign, state or private, used multilevel subcontracting to accommodate world market volat-ility. As part of this accommodation, garment workers at all levels of the subcontracting ladder worked long hours, or over 12 hours per day, to ensure on-time delivery. Their jobs were insecure primarily due to dependence on foreign production orders.

Differences among countries were in degree rather than kind. During high-demand seasons, Taiwanese garment workers laboured on average 10 overtime hours per month (Gereffi and Pan, 1994, p. 142); South Korean garment workers were assigned overtime work on Saturdays and Sundays. The companies during overtime work provided meals, and workers were permitted to have a break every other week (Lee and Song, 1994, p. 155). During the peak season, from September to December, Philippine workers laboured up to 15 hours per day, while off-season workloads dropped to one-third of peak levels (Ofreneo, 1994, p. 166). Vietnamese garment workers during the winter clothing season, between May and October, and the spring, from November through January, operated either two 12-hour shifts or three 8-hour shifts per day, with no overtime pay. The management did not provide meals. During the three-months off-season, workers suffered from short hours and entire days without work (Tran, fieldwork in 1997 and 1998).

Piecework arrangement was uncertain and guaranteed no steady employ-ment. Tran explained:

> We can never tell when we will have jobs to do. Everything must depend on the Japanese contractors/buyers; if they sign contracts with us then we will have garment orders. Normally, contracts are signed at the end of the month and to be delivered next month, so we only know about work order one month at a time. For example, at the end of December we are contracted to make 1000 pillow cases, which are to be delivered on a certain date in January. Since there is no long-term contract, in some months we were under-employed or earned nothing; some months we must work overtime from 7:30 am to 11 pm. If we were to know about work order in advance or if imported garment materials arrived as sched-uled, we can spread out work more evenly, and not have to work like that.

Constant changes in clothing styles put a further burden on workers who must use their own time to learn and be efficient at assembling these new products. For example, the interviewees had to learn new styles of jackets, pillowcases and bedspreads, and this learning process slowed down their productivity. As explained above, they did not receive wages while learning new styles; rather, they would remain in the factories after paid hours to learn these styles. In the words of Vu:

We make a lot of jackets, which require constant change in patterns. Normally, jackets are 'hot' items which require on-time delivery. As a result, we work three shifts to make sure on-time delivery. We don't work by the hours; if we are not done with our work, we must stay overtime to finish our work.

The subcontracting piecework arrangement also led to worker self-exploitation. Workers chose not to take breaks for various reasons, either because of limited access to water, since tap water in one large state garment corporation was only available during lunch time and not during working hours, or because they sought to assemble as many pieces as possible. Tran explained:

We work from 7:30–noon, and 1–5 pm. Normally there are two 15-minute breaks, one at 10 am and one at 3 pm, but most of us don't take break and continue to work. Our salary is too low already; if we take break, our monthly take-home wage is even lower.

Vu, who had worked in a state-owned garment company for 29 years (at the time of the interview), said that even when she and her family lived in the housing area of the company, she packed her lunch early every morning so that she could quickly eat for 15 minutes, then return to her sewing machine. She could not afford the time to go home, which was about a five-minute bicycle ride from the factory, to have lunch with her family, because that would take away valuable time to assemble more garment pieces.

Trade unions in Vietnam

While not attempting to theorize on labour unions or organization, I will briefly mention some general concepts about Vietnamese trade unions in order to raise questions about challenges to equitable national development goals. In Vietnam, there is a long history of the interconnection among trade unions, the Communist Party and enterprise management, which was mainly in SOEs before the more comprehensive and consistent market reform process in the mid-1980s.[6]

Vietnamese trade unions have had two main functions: the first was to mobilize workers for production, including educating workers about production, management and ideology; the second was to defend workers' interests and ensure their rights against management (Nørlund, 1998, p. 89). Within such a framework, it has been difficult for the union leadership, which was part of the management apparatus of central planning at the enterprise level, to promote the realization of state production targets as well as to defend workers' rights and social needs (Beresford and Nyland, 1999, pp. 15,

18). The outcome of tension arising from these conflicting interests was dependent on relations between the individuals involved and their links with decision-makers at higher levels.

In principle, the new Labour Code, effective since 1 January 1995, offers more protection for workers and sanctions strikes to protect their rights except under circumstances that could jeopardize national security . While the Vietnam General Confederation of Labour, a state agency with over four million members as of 1995, encouraged independent trade unions, at the time of writing there existed very few non-state trade unions. Moreover, this code requires companies to allow the formation of labour unions especially in 100 per cent foreign-owned firms and joint ventures. There was an increase in the number of unions established in firms with foreign investment, from 20 per cent of foreign-invested companies in 1995 to 60 per cent in 1997 (*ibid.*, p. 23),[7] but more research is required on the extent to which workers were represented and protected by these unions.

Even in firms with labour unions, workers did not have a safe space to voice their concerns or ask for their benefits for fear of losing their jobs. All workers that I interviewed confirmed this lack of real labour representation or protection on the factory floor. They were afraid to voice their dissatisfaction, and instead found that the unions and management in both state-owned and private firms were co-opted to serve the interests of foreign buyers or contractors. The lack of labour representation abounded on the factory floor. Ngo said:

> Physical abuse does happen on the factory floor. There is one incident in our factory that the two Vietnamese women in the quality control team beat a woman worker for a minor mistake that she made. Many of us separated them; the woman worker was bruised badly. This happened in the afternoon when the supervisor was not there. After the incident, there was no one from the labour union to protect or represent that poor worker. We signed on a petition letter, prepared by the supervisor, to be forwarded to the Vietnamese vice president of this joint venture between Vietnam and Japan. It turned out that the Vietnamese vice president defused it by transferring one of the two Vietnamese offenders to another department of the company. That was all they did to resolve that incident!

Special stipulations on women workers

There are special stipulations on behalf of women workers in Vietnamese labour laws (Su That, 1996, pp. 48–51). One can assert, however, that these stipulations are ways in which the state attempts to ensure the status quo of gender expectations that women fulfil *both* a reproductive role in the home and a productive function in the workplace. Moreover, there is a wide gap between policies and their implementation in real life as evidenced from Vietnamese workers' narratives and other secondary sources. Subcontracting piecework appeared to be one of the main factors preventing labour policies, especially on behalf of women workers, from being implemented: labour contracts were not offered to workers in a specified time frame; union representatives often did not provide real representation or protection on the factory floor; overtime work was not compensated; and most textile and garment firms with foreign investment did not have labour unions.

The state had policies to create jobs, to prioritize the hiring of women workers if they matched the qualifications for a particular position, to ensure healthy and safe working conditions, to improve job skills through vocational training, to provide good health care coverage and promote good remuneration and benefits in order for women workers to work efficiently and be able to balance responsibilities at work and at home (*ibid.*, p. 48). Also, decisions about raising salaries should prioritize women workers if they have the same qualifications as men (*ibid.*, p. 164). *De jure*, women continue to receive full pay while not working full-time in the following situations: pregnant women are not allowed to work overtime; in their 7th month of pregnancy, they have one hour off per workday and still receive full pay; they are guaranteed to have their jobs back after their maternity leave; women have a 30-minute respite every day when they have their monthly menstruation; and women nursing infants less than 12-months-old have a one-hour respite every day (*ibid.*, p. 50). In factories where the majority of employees are women, the management must provide proper and sanitary rest-room facilities; they must consult with representatives of women workers before making decisions or policies that affect the rights and welfare of women workers and their children; and they must maintain a proper percentage of women supervisors to better meet the needs of women workers (*ibid.*, p. 51).

De facto, firm owners did not provide a clear time-frame to offer labour contracts to workers. Workers, especially rural women, were not aware of various stipulations of labour laws and did not dare to ask for labour contracts due to fear of being harassed or laid off. This was doubly difficult for rural workers since they were totally dependent on their monthly income to pay for rent and basic necessities. As of January 1998, Tran, Ngo and Thuy were not offered labour contracts even after working for those companies for over six months. Tran explained:

> Who are we to ask for the contracts when more experienced workers who were there before us have not yet been offered labour contracts? Also, even when the management offers the contract to me, I would think twice about signing the labour contract, because it means that I am

obligated to work for this company for several years without guarantee of a full-time job.

In terms of labour contract and training, in principle both employees and employers must agree on these general terms: the 'try-out' or probationary period must not exceed 60 days for people with college degrees; 30 days for technicians or semi-skilled workers; six days for other types of workers. At the end of those periods, employers must inform the workers whether or not they will be hired (*ibid.*, p. 126). If trainees produce goods, they should be compensated according to mutual agreement, but it must be at least 70 per cent of the rates paid to other workers doing the same jobs (*ibid.*, pp. 162–3).

Tran explained how she was trained for her tasks in a joint venture between a Japanese corporation and a Vietnamese SOE, while not being paid for what she made:

> We are assembling embroidered pillowcases. There are four main tasks: embroidering flower patterns using Japanese machines; assembling the flower patterns at four corners of the pillow case; sewing the corners; assembling all these parts to make the whole pillow case. We must practice a lot to make sure that the thread lines are perfectly parallel, consistent and smooth. If the thread lines are bulky, we must undo them by hand and sew it again at our own time. There is no set time period for training: It can be several weeks or several months. They never tell you you how long the training will last. My training process has two parts: first, I was trained for three months in the Labour Union Job Training Centre; second, I was trained for two months on the shop floor of DTD Centre. During this whole process, I must pay 550 000 dong [or about US$55 at the time she paid it] before I was allowed to work on the line to earn some money from piecework. I was *not* paid for what I made during this whole training period. During training, I must learn all four tasks of assembling these pillow cases, but when I actually work in the line, I can only do one task which is to assemble the whole pillow case. (Emphasis added)

Factory control and discipline

There were many explicit and implicit forms of management control on the shopfloor in both private and state enterprises in order to increase productivity and just-in-time delivery. These forms of control greatly affected the working conditions on the shopfloor. Shift manipulation, in particular, had many adverse effects on women workers. For example, most women workers sat at their sewing machines continuously for at least 9 to 10 hours per day, which was especially difficult when they had their monthly menstrual periods. Vu explained:

In the garment industry, we women must sit at least 8 consecutive hours. This is very difficult, especially on our 'women's days'. Can you believe that in this day and age there are many women who cannot afford sanitary napkins? Our workday starts from 6 am to 2:45 pm. We only have 45-minute lunch break. Within that break, we quickly go to the bathroom, eat our lunch, and hurry back to the workstation to make more pieces. During work hour, we cannot go to the bathroom since there is no water available. We are told that water is only pumped on certain hours during the day. Can you imagine how difficult it is during 'women's days'? Before 1994 when we started subcontracting for Japanese and German firms, we had longer breaks: we worked from 5:00 am to 10 am, then we had a long lunch break between 10 am and 2:15 pm; we resumed working from 2:15 pm to 5 pm. The long lunch break was very helpful since most of us live right on the factory premises. We can go home, cook our lunch, and rest a little bit before we go back to work in the afternoon. That work schedule was very good for women workers since we can take care of our personal hygiene during our women's days at home. Now, we have three continuous shifts throughout 24 hours (6 am–2 pm; 2 pm–10 pm; 10pm–6 am). The reason we have three shifts is to make sure on-time delivery: if we must deliver assembled clothes by 7 am in the following morning, then we must work overnight to finish them and make sure on-time delivery by 7 am.

An owner of a small private garment factory in the North shared this concern, and expressed concerns about the health issues of women workers who were mostly in their early 20s. She said these women experienced irregular monthly menstrual cycles, especially when they had to work overtime during high-peak seasons, or more than 12-hour workdays.

Controlling the supply of essential materials for sewing activities such as needle heads can directly affect workers' income. Tran explained:

Assembling pillowcases for Japanese is a very difficult job. If you break a needle, you must find that broken piece to trade for a new one. If you cannot find it, then you basically lost a whole workday searching for it since you cannot resume work without a new needle. If you still cannot find it, then on the following day you must sign on a paper attached to that garment piece stating that you cannot find the broken needle, then they will give you a new one. We were given the explanation that the Japanese managers are afraid that the needle may be attached somewhere in the product and might injure Japanese consumers. So when the products are transported back to Japan, they will detect that broken piece with a special machine. Only then can we get paid for our work.

Quality control (QC) was an explicit form of control on the factory floor, which also had a direct impact on workers' incomes. It took the form of demanding perfection for the minute details of the products, or cleanliness of raw materials such as fabrics. In their own time, workers must redo their pieces time and time again on the assembly line until approved by Japanese QC personnel. Moreover, Japanese managers were extremely strict about cleanliness of fabrics to ensure the quality of final products. Workers were penalized for stains in fabrics, regardless of any reasons. Tran explained:

> The stains in fabrics can be caused by many reasons: the fabric itself was dirty to start with. Since the fabric was passed through many hands: it must first be cut, embroidered, then sewn together, etc., and it is bound to get dirty. However, this incident happened to my group of ten people: two workers were identified as causing the stains on fabrics, but the whole group was penalised to wash cloth for the whole company for two weeks, with *no* pay. We basically earned nothing during those two weeks since we were not allowed to assemble any products hence earning nothing. (Emphasis added)

The hierarchical working relationship with distinctive power differentials was very prevalent in firms with Japanese management. Most Vietnamese superiors, including line-leaders, supervisors or interpreters, were women who enjoyed privileges in relation to the rest of the women workers. This led to division and conflict between them, a classic case of divide-and-conquer. In the context of working in the quality-control stage, Ngo explained:

> In our company, the Japanese hired twelve Vietnamese in the quality control and interpreter levels; most were women: ten worked in quality control team led by two Japanese managers; two were interpreters but they sometime checked the quality of final products when their Japanese bosses left for Japan. The Japanese managers rotate their stay in Vietnam: each stays for 3–4 months. There are two tiers of quality control in both embroidery and assembling processes: most mistakes are detected and corrected in the first tier, which is run by the Vietnamese staff. After passing the first tier, the final products are then moved to the second tier, which is run by the Japanese managers. Only when the Japanese sign off on the products then we get paid for our work. Those Vietnamese staff have special privileges including obtaining higher education to advance their career. They can get off work early to go to night classes in English, business, management and finance. Of course, their salaries are much higher than ours. There are times when the Vietnamese staff is even stricter than the Japanese managers in monitoring our work. We must please and obey the Vietnamese staff to pass the first tier; if not

they will give us a hard time by making us correct the products again and again so we can never get to the second tier to get paid. We think our fellow Vietnamese women are afraid of being criticized by the Japanese managers so they protect themselves by being very critical of our work instead!

Public humiliation was another form of explicit control on the factory floor. Vu explained:

There are loudspeakers in our company. Every time when there are some workers who did something wrong on the job, their names are announced on these loudspeakers to the rest of the company. It is such an embarrassment to be singled out publicly like that!

Responses of workers

Workers responded to those forms of exploitation and control in various ways in Vietnam, the Philippines, South Korea and Taiwan. Strikes were waged by Philippine workers in big exporting firms, mostly owned by the USA and some non-US firms, in the late 1970s; Philippine homeworkers also organized to engage in nationwide consciousness-raising, skills training, research and advocacy work (Ofreneo, 1994, pp. 173–4, 176). The struggle for workers' rights in South Korea and Taiwan was fomented in the 1970s. Faced by unhealthy working conditions in textile factories, young South Korean rural women workers in textile and garment factories formed the base of the union organizing drive in the 1970s. The most significant labour struggle was the Chonggye Garment Workers' Union (CGWU), the symbolic centre of the nascent Korean labour movement characterized by tenacity, self-sacrifice and confrontational tactics. They engaged in demonstrations, sit-ins and hunger strikes that finally brought the employers to the negotiating table and led to the working-class explosion in the summer of 1987 (Bello and Rosenfeld, 1992, pp. 34–5, 40). While not as confrontational as Korea's labour uprising, Taiwanese workers also went on strikes in the 1970s against the Kuomintang (KMT) martial law ban on strikes. In 1977, the winning of independent candidates in the union elections at the Far East Textile Company gave birth to Taiwan's first free, non-KMT union (*ibid.*, pp. 223, 230).

About two decades after the rise of labour struggles in those two Newly Industrialized Economics (NIEs), tension on Vietnamese factory floors was also on the rise. It appeared that some Korean and Taiwanese big corporations also applied repressive management cultures and hierarchical and centralized discipline to Vietnamese workers; and there was a consistent rise in labour grievances especially in many textile and garment joint-ventures between Vietnam, Taiwan and South Korea (Tran, 1995, pp. 1, 2,

11, 22). Since 1996, there have been several cases of work stoppages in foreign-invested firms. For two days in December 1996, about 1000 workers in a 100 per cent Taiwanese-owned company in Tan Thuan EPZ, an export-processing zone in the South manufacturing high-quality gloves for export, were on strike. They were not compensated for working overtime on weekdays and weekends, and their piecerates were reduced if they disagreed to work overtime with short notice and no compensation (Tuoi Tre newspaper, 28 December 1996). Also, at the beginning of 1997, workers in another company in the South, a joint-venture between Vietnam and South Korea, engaged in a work stoppage to protest against management pressure to make them use their sick leave or personal vacation time during company slack time (Lao Dong newspaper, 15 January 1997).

In-depth interviews with the four workers in the North already mentioned provided some concrete forms of worker's protests. Women workers themselves and their spouses engaged in several forms of direct and indirect resistance on the factory floor, with *de facto* work stoppage as one form of resistance. Vu explained:

> It might be a hyperbole to say that we had a work stoppage, but our fellow women workers did refuse to work for one hour, with a reason that we were exhausted and fatigued from hard work. When that happened, the management immediately contacted and negotiated with our line-leaders/supervisors about some monetary compensation such as bonuses for us. We were, however, not included in this negotiation process. I think that the management was able to suppress such effort almost immediately. The main reason is that workers' livelihoods are absolutely attached to this company so no one can afford to sustain such work stoppage. If you don't assemble clothes, you don't earn anything!

The husbands of these women workers had an interesting reaction on behalf of their wives; in solidarity they voiced their concerns to a state-owned TV station about their wives' poor working conditions. Vu explained:

> My husband and my friends' husbands wrote a complaint letter to a local TV station to be broadcast publicly about the harsh working conditions and the exploitation that their wives are subject to in this company. They liken the exploitation to 'a lime being squeezed to the last drop'. Unfortunately, this complaint received no response from the management at our company.

Voting with their feet by moving to other garment firms was another form of indirect protest, and job fluctuation has been a common phenomenon in the VTGI with its flexible subcontracting structure. Workers constantly search for other garment companies in the hope that they might offer them higher piecerates, better working conditions and more steady work, instead of not having enough work for several months, and working over 12 hours per day during the nine-month clothing seasons (Lao Dong newspaper, 25 January 1997). Three of my interviewees moved to other garment companies in search of better wage rates and better working conditions for themselves, or to protest against unfair treatment of their friends. Ngo left a private company for her current workplace after the unjust lay-off of her friend.

However, the vicious circle continued when women workers who voted with their feet recognized that their new salaries were as low as in previous textile/garment firms. Piecerates were equally low throughout Vietnam given the competitive nature of the VTGI in a market framework. Therefore, realistically, workers could not find a better deal elsewhere. The wage rates of all four interviewees who were employed in a joint venture, a private company and a state firm, were between US$30 and US$60 per month.

On the other hand, employers complained that these worker movements created difficulties for them, since they had to train new worker to replace those skilled ones who had left in search of higher wages. However, according to all interviewees, at the beginning they paid a fee between US$50 and 100 to be trained for three months. So, in effect, they paid for their own job-training, and if they were to leave before the end of the training period, they would lose all the training fees. Furthermore, the disadvantages to managers of labour turnover were more than compensated for by maintaining competition in the workforce, thereby creating a powerful incentive which drove a large supply of workers who were willing to pay for training and to engage in self-exploitation in order to earn enough money for rent and basic living expenses.

Towards a framework for analysis

There were some differences in degree and time-frame of occurrences in these four countries, Vietnam and the Philippines in the 1980s and 1990s respectively, South Korea and Taiwan in the 1970s. Workers in these countries faced quite similar impacts of the global subcontracting system in terms of the exploited working and living conditions and gender expectations to increase productivity in this global industry. Clearly, the multilevel subcontracting piecework system afforded flexibility for contractors and buyers to deal with global market volatility, but it placed all the burden of adjustments onto workers. These women's voices are loud and clear: they all expressed their sense of hopelessness, low morale and frustration. At the time of the interviews they could not find any alternatives to this type of low-skilled and monotonous job. They felt that their total labour was controlled; they could not do anything when they got home at night; they were totally exhausted, just wanted to eat and sleep to get ready for work the next day.

In terms of gender expectations for productivity such as docility, dexterity and flexibility in this global industry, these workers' narratives are a powerful reflection of how they were subject to these demands on the factory floor. The expectation of docility was enforced on the shopfloor to the extent that workers felt fearful to voice their dissatisfaction at the labour conditions, or even to inquire about labour contracts – they felt hopeless and stayed locked up in the factory to practise on garment patterns during slack times; and they performed extra jobs with no pay when being disciplined by foreign and domestic managers. Dexterity was required to complete the minute details of garment products. This, however, did not come 'naturally' as expected under patriarchal culture, but was achieved through countless hours of practice without any monetary compensation. Workers were expected to be flexible to work very long hours when there were garment orders to ensure on-time delivery, but also had to be flexible to find additional work to earn enough money for rent and basic living expenses during slack times. Hence, flexibility benefited corporations, owners, contractors and buyers, but denied workers control over their own labour.

Moreover, these cases show that many forms of control and discipline led to some types of protests from women workers and their spouses, and that concerted effort can bring some positive results – at least in the case of Vu's one-hour work stoppage since they did get some compensation, although they were not consulted. Experiences from this learning process may be valuable in the future. There was also a sense of solidarity among the workers and their husbands, but without better organization and collective action as in the cases of South Korea and Taiwan, and to some extent the Philippines, these efforts in Vietnam can be futile as management turns a blind eye knowing that workers cannot resist for long and that they need work to survive.

In looking at the larger picture, one must consider major challenges to national development policies; there may be an incompatibility between global production and equitable national development. Bonacich *et al.* have argued that the volatile and unpredictable nature of the global garment industry, which is subjected to constant changes in the rules of various international institutions such as the Generalized System of Preferences, the General Agreement on Tariffs and Trade and the Multi-Fiber Arrangement, may be incompatible with national development goals (1994, p. 366).

There are two sides to these challenges. From workers' experiences, there were contradictions between policies promoting cheap, compliant and docile labour to attract foreign investment, and promoting real representation from labour unions to protect workers' rights. Another trade-off has to do with economic growth generated from the global subcontracting system in exchange for low-paid, low-skilled, uncertain and demeaning jobs for the people. However, from the Vietnamese state perspective, VINATEX[8] in collaboration with other ministries has proposed a long-term development plan to focus on developing backward linkages and higher value-added innovations. These were intended to support the more export-oriented garment industry, by investing in textile production and growing cotton, much more so than garment production (VINATEX, 1997, pp. 30, 35–6, appendix p. 26). One must also consider the fact that Vietnam has been caught in a bind of capital shortage and the need for global integration to attract more capital from foreign investment in order to carry out long-term plans.

In this exploratory effort, I hope to have brought forth the perspectives of women workers in their own voices, to conceptualize their concrete experiences within a comparative and analytical framework in the context of the labour-intensive garment industry to understand the global gender division of labour and production.

Annex

The table below lists the names and positions of officials interviewed, and the dates of those interviews. In the case of workers interviewed, the names are pseudonyms, assigned for clarity of presentation.

Name	*Position/organization*	*Date*
Do Thi Binh	Women's Studies Centre	January 1998
Hoang Thi Lich	Women's Studies Centre	January 1998
Le Dao	European Union Department of the Ministry of Trade	January 1998
Bui Gia Le	Director of Ha Noi Knitting Company	December 1997
Nguyen An Lich	Sociology Department, Ha Noi University	January 1998
Nguyen Thuy Huong	Foreign Investment Management Department, Ministry of Planning and Investment	January 1998
Tran Van Kinh	Strategic Planning Department, Ministry of Industry	January 1998
Tran Loc	Assistant to the President, Vietnamese Chamber of Commerce and Industry	January 1998
Tran Van Quyen	Planning and Investment Department, VINATEX	January 1998
Trinh Van Tien	Industrial Department, Ministry of Planning and Investment	January 1998
Ms Minh (pseudonym)	Owner of a private garment firm	1997 & 1998
Ms Ngo (pseudonym)	A worker in a private garment firm	1997 & 1998
Ms Oanh (pseudonym)	A director of a state garment firm	1997 & 1998
Ms Thuy (pseudonym)	A worker in a state garment firm	1997 & 1998
Ms Tran (pseudonym)	A worker in a state garment firm	1997 & 1998
Ms Vu (pseudonym)	A worker in a state garment firm	1997 & 1998

Notes

1   Triangle manufacturing offers an opportunity for these East Asian newly-industrial-izing countries (NICs) to move from their declining sectors, such as garment manufacturing, to activities that accumulate higher value-added, such as serving as intermediaries for foreign firms, and providing textiles for Vietnamese pro-ducers. Over time, they invested in textile plants in Vietnam to cut down on transportation and labour costs.

2   The top four countries that invested in the Vietnamese Textile and Garment Industries (VTGI) were from East Asia, mostly in 100 per cent foreign-owned textile enterprises. They were Taiwan with 18 projects, totalling over US$45 million; Hong Kong with 11 projects totalling over US$15 million; South Korea with 9 projects totalling over US$14 million; and Japan with 6 projects totalling over US$7 million (Vo Dai Luoc, 1998).

3   However, the total VTGI output is only about 10.2 per cent of total manufacturing output in 1997 (General Statistical Office, 1997, pp. 166–202). More research is needed to examine the primary causes of this apparently low productivity of the VTGI in relation to other manufacturing sectors in Vietnam.

4   One can deduce from Table 12.1 that in 1997, 60 per cent of the VTGI workforce in the state sector produces only 50 per cent of the output, while the foreign-invested sector produces 15.9 per cent of output with only 14 per cent of the workforce, and interestingly the non-state sector produces 33.6 per cent of output with only 25 per cent of the workforce. At least statistically, it seems that the domestic non-state sector is more productive than even the foreign-invested sector. However, more research is needed since these statistics are based on gross values of output, not value-added. I'd like to thank Melanie Beresford for pointing out this interesting deduction.

5   Again, I thank Melanie Beresford for sharing insights from her field research in the Philippines. She found women workers in the Philippine textile and garment industries who said they could not afford the bus fare to go home regularly, and that there were other workers who said they sent money home to their families.

6   For a more nuanced analysis of Vietnamese 'bottom-up' reforms that started much earlier than the commonly-cited Sixth Party Congress in 1986, see Dang Phong *et al.* (2000).

7   According to the Labour Minister, Tran Dinh Hoan, only a fraction of these com-panies have signed collective-bargaining agreements with workers.

8   VINATEX, the Vietnam Textile and Garment Corporation, is a state-owned cor-poration which oversees all state textile and garment firms at the central level. All local state textile/garment firms are managed by provincial people's committees. For an in-depth discussion of this topic, see Tran (1997).

13
The Social Impact of the Reform Process

Adam McCarty

An economic success story

The economic performance of Vietnam in the 1990s would be classified as a 'miracle' if such achievements were not so common in Asia in the latter half of the twentieth century. GDP growth rates between 8.1 per cent and 9.5 per cent during 1992–97 were led by industry and services, though the agriculture sector growth also increased by an impressive 4.8 per cent per annum. Transition, typically identified as 'starting' in 1986, was a relatively painless affair of structural adjustment and stabilization for the first decade. The state sector was never large in Vietnam, where 80 per cent of the population lives in rural areas, mostly growing rice. By 1986 the planned part of the economy was thoroughly undermined, and inflation had eroded any monetary overhang. The collapse of the Council of Mutual Economic Assistance (CMEA) trading relationship forced restructuring in the state-owned enterprise sector, which shed almost one-quarter of its workforce (see below). However, institutional reforms created a boom in the urban household economy that absorbed the unemployed. The shift in employment was relatively easy, without the burden of a large military-industrial complex, and Vietnam's exports to the CMEA found new Western buyers with relative ease.

Therefore, Vietnam did not experience a transitional crisis in trade or even in the rate of GDP growth. The only exception to the 'costless' scenario was in industry, which slumped between 1988–89, but at the same time the agriculture and services sector boomed, which allowed GDP to rise over the period. This success was largely because the planning system declined to a residual by 1988. The failure to rigorously implement the central-planning model in the ten years after 1976 became a virtue for transition. Consequently, comparisons with other transitional economies, for example, Cuba, China and Eastern Europe where planning was much more extensive, must be undertaken with caution.

The 1990s were not without their problems. Many of these, such as rural–urban income inequality and migration, were more typical of a fast-growing developing economy than a transitional one. There would be little point in trying to distinguish the 'transitional' from other causes of changes, but one should bear in mind that Vietnam was both a fast-growing developing country *and* an 'economy in transition'. The social consequences of transition were due to fundamental changes in incentive structures and regulations. This chapter considers these consequences in several areas: food, poverty, land, employment, social protection systems, health and education.

Food, land and poverty

A rise in gross food output was a key feature of Vietnam's success story; total food production increased by 50 per cent in ten years (and 30 per cent on a per capita basis). Livestock numbers and industrial crop production increased even faster (GSO, 1998, p. 42). This extraordinary performance has enabled Vietnam to become a major rice exporter and caused a steady decline in poverty. The performance was not even across the country.

The growth in rice output (which constituted over 90 per cent of total food output) was despite controls on exports for reasons of food security. The food security argument for rice export quota controls weakened every year, as per capita output increased. Such security concerns in 1999 focused on distributional constraints and the possibility of localized shortages. In this context, the rationale for quantitative controls on exports was unclear, but nevertheless they remained and were a source of economic rents. In the second half of the 1990s, the International Food Policy Research Institute (IFRI) carried out research which, on bold assumptions, estimated that without quotas paddy production would rise by about 12 per cent, with rice exports increasing to about 5.7 million tonnes. The IFPRI calculated that the domestic rice price would rise by around 20 per cent, and farm income per capita by about 28 per cent (UNDP, 1998, p. 32).

However, rice exports were liberalized substantially during 1997–98. Restrictions on domestic trading were removed in 1987, and local governments were allocated greater shares of export quotas. In 1998, more companies were allowed to participate in the rice export trade. These institutional changes stimulated competition and convergence between export and domestic market prices. The Asian financial crisis brought a fall in the cost of fertilizer imports, part of which was passed on to farmers. Possibly for the first time in Vietnam's economic history there was a divergence between input costs, notably fertilizer, and output prices. In the prior environment of powerful local purchasing and national export monopolies, farmers were paid on a cost-plus basis. This changed, and farmers with a surplus to sell benefited greatly. By November 1998, the FOB export price for 5 per cent broken rice, at US$273 per tonne, was equal to the domestic price of white rice. The subsequent four months saw a fall in export prices to US$236 per tonne, but the domestic rice price rose from 3750 dong per kilogram to 3900 dong. It seemed unlikely that domestic rice prices would continue to rise, unless export prices recovered.

Liberalization of markets and a strengthening of property rights generated strong supply responses in the agriculture sector during transition. The benefits, as may be expected, were not spread evenly. Those farmers who grew only enough to survive were bypassed by the reforms. The bottom strata of the poor remained very poor, and the task of lifting these households out of poverty was more complex than it was for those who were capable of producing a surplus for markets.

The definition of a household in poverty was a subject of some controversy in Vietnam, after the World Bank anounced that 51 per cent of Vietnamese households were in poverty according to the 1992–93 living standards measurements survey (LSMS). Alternative definitions (see Table 13.1), which generally did not account for non-food needs, produced estimates ranging from 19–22 per cent, with an apparent gradual decline during 1992–96.

A second LSMS, conducted during 1997–98, indicated a remarkable decline in overall poverty in Vietnam; using a consistent methodology, it appeared that the 51 per cent measure of 1992/93 declined to about 27 per cent.[1] Official Vietnamese estimates put the population in poverty at about 18–20 per cent during 1997–98 (*Vietnam Investment Review*, 23 May 1999, p. 4). The World Bank planned to produce a new poverty report in December 1999. One interesting question would be how income inequalities had

Table 13.1   Poverty lines used in Vietnam

1   *The hunger poverty line*, used by MOLISA (Ministry of Labour, Invalids and Social Affairs) identifies 'hungry households' in rice equivalents. An 'urban poor household' consumes less than 25kg of rice capita per month, and rural households less than 20kg in lowland/midland areas, and 15kg in highland areas. MOLISA estimates that households below the poverty line have declined from 22% in 1994, to around 20% in 1995, and to 19% in 1996.

2   *The very poor or starvation poverty line*, used by GSO, defines hunger poverty by the income needed to secure a minimum daily calorie intake of 2100 per capita. A monthly per capita income of dong 50 000 (1993 prices) identified a rural poverty household, dong 30 000 a 'very poor' or 'starving' rural household, dong 70 000 an urban poor and 70 000 a very poor urban household. GSO also projects VLSS data to estimate that around 19% of households were below the poverty line in 1996.

3   *The basic needs poverty line*, employed by the World Bank, is based on the 2100 calorie intake criterion but also makes allowance for non-food basic needs, including education, health care, travel and cultural expenses. It was estimated that the minimum basket in 1995, would need an annual income of VND1.1 million per capita (or US$100 equivalent p.c. per year). For 1995 (based on VLSS 1992/93 survey data), the World Bank estimates that 51% of Vietnam's households were below the poverty line.

Source: UNDP (1998).

Table 13.2   Poverty households in rural areas of Vietnam by region, 1992/93 (based on various definitions, as percentage of total rural households in each region)

Major Regions	*Average household consumption expenditures (dong 000 p.a.)*	*Poverty line ('hungry') households (<dong600 th.) (%)*	*Very poor ('starving') households (<dong360 th.) (%)*	*Basic needs deficit households (<dong 1.1m) (%)*
1 North Central Coast	974	26.4	5.1	70.9
2 Northern Uplands	1007	28.8	5.2	58.6
3 Central Highlands	1159	34.7	7.7	50.1
4 Red River Delta	1349	15.9	2.7	49.0
5 South Central Coast	1457	19.6	4.1	48.5
6 Mekong River Delta	1506	18.5	5.4	42.7
7 South East	2008	14.0	3.0	32.8
Vietnam	1373	22.3	4.4	50.9

Source: UNDP (1998).

developed: regional, rural–urban, and intra-rural. Table 13.2 uses the 1992–93 LSMS data to examine regional differences in poverty. Average household consumption expenditures in the South East (Ho Chi Minh City) were double those of the North Central Coast. The Red River delta ranked in the mid-range in average expenditure, which reflected the basic needs rankings, but had low percentages of 'hungry' and 'starving' households. This suggested a relatively 'flat' income distribution in the Red River delta, possibly due to land distribution policies. The South East had a marginally higher percentage of 'starving' households.

Anecdotal evidence suggested that income distributions within urban centres were increasingly skewed as commercial middle and upper classes developed. State employees, including doctors and teachers, as well as many public officials and Party cadre, were left behind, as most of the new income opportunities came from trading, small-scale production and other service activities. The new LSMS data would reveal greater income inequalities in urban areas and, more importantly, identify the 'persistently poor' in rural areas. The trends towards greater inequality were to be expected in a rapidly growing developing economy. The interesting analysis would be on how these trends will develop and influence political and social stability.

Land scarcity appeared to be increasing in most regions of the country in the 1990s and land use and changes in land use are summarized in Table 13.3 for 1985–94. An average farm family of five cultivated about one-half hectare of land, with farmers in the Mekong and Central Highlands averaging one hectare. The People's committees had less scope to reallocate land or to find unused land for newly-formed families, and families with three or more children, often the poorer families, could not expect to receive more land.

Table 13.3 Land use and changes in land use, Vietnam, 1985–94

	1985		1994		Change 1985 to 1994	
	000 ha	*%*	*000 ha*	*%*	*000 ha*	*% change*
A.Land classification						
agricultural land	6 942	20.9	7 367	22.2	+425	+6.1
forestry land	9 642	29.1	9 915	30.0	+273	+2.8
other land use	16 520	49.8	15 822	48.8	−698	−3.9
Total land area	33 104	100	33 104	100	0	0
B. Agricultural land use						
rice	4 297	13.0	4 230	12.8	−67	−1.2
other food crops	1 130	3.4	1 210	3.7	+80	+7.1
annual industrial crops	1 007	3.0	1 192	3.6	+185	+18.4
perennial industrial crops	470	1.4	811	2.5	+341	+72.5
Total sown area	6 904	20.9	7 443		+539	+7.8

Note: 'Total agricultural land' and 'total sown area' are not identical as land classified as agricultural may not be used, and land classified for other purposes may be used for agriculture. Ambiguities can also arise from mixed land uses, such as 'agro-forestry'.
Source: Choeng Hoy Chung (1997).

There were reports of land consolidation, through purchase of user rights, by larger commercial farmers, especially in the South. At the same time, developers converted land to industrial, residential or recreational use, though information on the extent of this was not available (UNDP, 1998). A new class of landless families was being created which worked for wages on other people's land, who might find off-farm activities, or might join the increasing flow of people seeking work in urban areas.

The strengthening of land-use rights was one factor 'pushing' farmers off land. As of July 1997, agricultural land-use certificates had been issued nationwide to about 43 per cent of farm families, with completion dates for land allocation and certification in most areas announced for late 1997 (UNDP, 1998). There was legitimate concern that land reforms would create a landless and unemployed peasantry that could not be easily absorbed into other economic activities. The pace of off-farm and urban sector employment growth would be crucial to solving this problem. The issue required more empirical investigation, but it seemed unlikely that land reform had been a significant cause of rural–urban migration. More important were the pressures of rural population growth rates and the 'pull' factor of rapid urban-sector development.

In 1996, at least two million rural residents were officially estimated to have migrated to cities looking for work, equal to 7 per cent of the nation's working-age population. An estimated 23 000 arrived in Hanoi seeking casual work, compared to an estimated 9 000 in 1992. Ho Chi Minh City reported a rural influx of 700 000 in 1996. Six out of seven of these did not have permanent registration permits, and data did not show how many were seasonal, rather than permanent migrants (UNDP, 1998).

Employment generation

The early years of economic transition, 1986 through 1991, saw substantial structural change in Vietnam's labour force. Total state sector employment fell by about 250 000 per year during 1989–91, and in addition about 500 000 soldiers were demobilized. Workers returning from abroad added to the supply. The demographic profile aggravated the situation by increasing the number of people of working age by 3.7 per cent per year. During this 'first phase', the booming household sector absorbed the growing supply of workers. Unemployment and underemployment, while severe, were not at socially dangerous levels. Unemployment was estimated at between two and six million persons.

In the 'second phase', beginning around 1992–93, change in the structure of employment was less dramatic, though the threat of large-scale unemployment and underemployment remained a serious problem for Vietnam. The sustained growth of the household production sector absorbed some of this labour-force growth, but the ability of the economy to generate jobs with higher value-added remained problematical.

The 1989–91 fall in employment was largely due to the collapse of CMEA trade, and due to a tightening of state enterprise budget constraints during the 1989 stabilization period. At the same time, removal of internal trade barriers and official decrees supporting the development of the private sector created incentives and opportunities for Vietnam's household businesses. This process of coordinated reform allowed state enterprise employment to fall from 8.7 per cent of total employment in 1989 to 6.2 per cent in 1991, without a huge rise in unemployment. It was estimated that the private sector created jobs for 4 369 000 workers (Table 13.4).

However, the capacity for the private sector to absorb more employment was limited without further institutional change. Value-added and profit margins in private household activities were low, though the enterprises were very competitive. Vietnam remained an economy with much of its GDP coming from agriculture, and, as Tables 13.5 and 13.6 show, the state sector as a whole employed only 9 per cent of Vietnam's workforce, and that percentage varied considerably across economic sectors. About one-quarter of industry sector workers were employed by the state during 1991–97. In commercial service areas the share of state employment fell from 26 per cent in 1991 to 13 per cent in 1997, and it has also fell, but less quickly, in other sectors. Despite the slowly falling share of total employment, the number of people in the state sector rose during 1991–97. The workforce increased by six million during 1991–97, of whom the state sector absorbed 155 000 (3 per cent) and the non-state the remaining 5 865 000, largely in agriculture (two million) but also in industry (898 000), trade (1.38 million) and across other sectors.

Table 13.4 Employment trends by sectors, Vietnam, 1989–91 (thousands of persons)

	1986	*1989*	*1990*	*1991*
Total employed labour force	27 398	28 941	30 294	30 974
state sector	4 027	3 801	3 421	3 144
cooperatives	19 730	19 750	20 414	18 071
private	3 641	5 390	6 459	9 759
State enterprises	2 658	2 506	2 180	1 916
central	1 278	1 188	1 091	1 018
local	1 380	1 318	1 089	898
Share of total employment (%)				
state sector	14.7	13.1	11.3	10.2
state enterprises	9.7	8.7	7.2	6.2

Source: World Bank (1995b).

Table 13.5 Employed population by sectors and employer, Vietnam, 1991–97 (thousands of persons and %)

	1991	*1992*	*1993*	*1994*	*1995*	*1996*	*1997*
Total	30 974	31 815	32 718	33 664	34 590	35 792	36 994
Per cent state sector	10.1	9.4	9.0	8.7	8.8	8.8	8.9
Agriculture. forestry & fisheries	23 122	23 160	23 425	23 565	24 106	24 776	25 444
Per cent state sector	1.7	1.5	1.4	1.3	1.2	1.0	1.0
Industry	3 736	3 847	4 140	4 326	4 493	4 629	4 634
Per cent state sector	27	25	24	23	23	23	25
Trade, transport, hotels, services	2 485	2 833	3 033	3 363	3 493	3 773	4 291
Per cent state sector	26	21	18	16	15	15	13
Health and education	1 010	1 094	1 143	1 218	1 259	1 287	1 295
Per cent state sector	85	75	73	68	69	71	72
Others	623	881	975	1 191	1 238	1 327	1 334
Per cent state sectors	41	30	27	23	25	24	27

Sources: MOLISA (1997) *Statistical Yearbook of Labour-Invalids and Social Affairs, 1996*, Statistical Publishing House, Hanoi, for data to 1994, and GSO (1998) *Vietnam Statistical Yearbook*, Statistical Publishing House, Hanoi, for 1995–97 data.

Table 13.6   Employed population by sectors and employer, Vietnam, 1991 and 1997 (thousands of persons)

	Total employment		State sector employment	
	1991	*1997*	*1991*	*1997*
Total	30 974	36 994	3 136	3 291
Agriculture and forestry	22 841	24 814	371	243
Fishery	281	630	12	9
Industry	3 736	4 634	999	1 160
of which:				
Mining	325	211	89	99
Manufacturing	2 727	3 293	560	672
Electricity, gas and water supply	104	153	48	61
Construction	579	977	302	328
Wholesale and retail trade, repairing	1 292	2 672	278	209
Hotels and restaurants	519	519	44	45
Transport, storage and communication	533	856	191	208
Finance, credit	73	126	74	52
Science and technology	45	41	45	33
Property business and consulting services	23	77	14	31
State management, defence and social security*	295	411	144	252
Training and education	770	999	674	768
Health and social work	240	296	186	170
Culture and sporting activities	56	96	28	33
Activities of party, mass organizations	82	100	57	59
Activities of personal and public service	135	595	24	19
Others**	55	132	0	0

* The total employment data for 'State management, defence and social security' differs between sources. MOLISA (1997, p. 35) data is reported to 1995, and GSO (1998) thereafter. These two sources overlap in reporting 1995 data for this sector. MOLISA reports 307 200 persons, while GSO report 392 500 persons. Similar changes in the data for 'Activities of party and mass organisations' account for the difference, so it would seem that some employment groups under the latter heading are now counted as state employees.
** What MOLISA (1997) describes as 'others' (datea to 1994) is explained as mostly 'Private households with employed persons' by GSO (1998).
Source: GSO (1998).

In terms of employment, the state sectors stagnated. This was despite the priority given to state sector development, and a reported rising state sector share of GDP in recent years (Table 13.6). The state sector and its enterprises, even with protection and access to state funds, foreign investment, land and bank credit failed to produce jobs.

Table 13.7   GDP by ownership, Vietnam (US$ and %)

	US$ millions*			Percentage shares	
	1995	*1996*	*1997*	*1995*	*1997*
Total	20 076	22 488	22 855	100	100
State	7 535	8 574	8 887	37.5	38.1
Household	7 547	8 280	8 309	37.6	36.8
Collective	2 168	2 301	2 217	10.8	10.2
Private	615	751	791	3.1	3.3
Mixed	888	948	983	4.4.	4.2
Foreign invested sector	1 321	1 634	1 709	6.6	7.3
(dong per US$)	(11 100)	(11 500)	(12 938)		

* Current GDP data divided by average exchange rate.
Sources: *GSO (1998) Vietnam Statistical Yearbook,* Statistical Publishing House, Hanoi; World Bank (1998b) *Vietnam: Rising to the Challenge,* Hanoi, for exchange rate data.

Vietnam faced an imperative to create jobs. To achieve this, it would be necessary to remove biases towards capital-intensive development, reform and privatize state enterprises, and strengthen competition. A set of policy reforms, for example, that enabled the private corporate sector to develop and to compete with state enterprises would precipitate a bout of employment-creating restructuring. Employment creation would also be fostered by policies that enabled state enterprises to compete against each other. Such a package would have the potential to increase overall employment, even if unemployment-creating state enterprise restructuring was actively pursued.

Social protection

Vietnam's system of social security could be best understood with a dualistic model that classifies persons and households into the formal or informal sector. 'Informal' in this sense means outside of the government-designed social security mechanisms (pensions, unions, health insurance, etc.). Households outside of these relied on village-level income transfers and other mechanisms, such as extended family and community networks. Most 'formal welfare system' households were employed in the state sector, though not all. For example, larger non-state enterprises came under the scope of the Labour Code.

Land distribution in the Red River Delta was traditionally a mechanism to ensure the basic needs of the population (Van de Walle, 1998), but markets and the strengthening of property rights gradually undermined land distribution as a 'social safety net', and use of land as loan collateral led to foreclosures. Extended family and village networks of informal social security also came under pressure, particularly as labour mobility has increased. In short, a more efficient use of factors of production undermined existing social security mechanisms. We argue the solution was not to weaken factor markets, but to develop financial alternatives to the social security mechanisms which operated under planning. The government emphasized the need for 'community solidarity funds' to finance its poverty alleviation and hunger eradication campaign. Scholarships and subsidies were provided for 'poor households' to access health and education services. Financial decentralization accompanied these initiatives. Communes collected land taxes, production taxes, water charges, electricity charges, road building contributions, school and health clinic maintenance fees, charges for people's committee salaries and administration expenses, and numerous other levies. In many localities, this appeared to result in greater public awareness and involvement in local government (UNDP, 1998).

Extended family associations traditionally existed as important mutual assistance networks in Vietnam, and appeared to be flourishing during the 1990s. The networks could be quite small, a few related families, or quite large, including relatives overseas. They functioned as sources of informal credit; provided connections in finding jobs or interceding with the authorities. They also offered support to people or whole families when travelling or migrating. They might help care for childlren and assist elderly relatives. Further, they served as information networks on business opportunities, potential marriage partners, scholarships and educational opportunities. The family networks provided a multi-purpose safety net, and greatly extended the possibilities for social and economic advancement for those recognized as 'members in good standing'.

Voluntary community organizations have also been encouraged to develop, with financial and technical support from the government and donor agencies. These include the outreach activities of the Women's Union, the Peasant's Association, the Youth Union, the Veteran's Association, and the Fatherland Front. Special purpose cooperatives, savings and credit circles, charitable agencies targeting specific disadvantaged groups, environmental awareness groups, extensions of parent-teacher associations, medical volunteers, and literacy-improving groups are examples of the range of new associations coming into existence.

The revised 1992 Constitution laid the foundation for a new Labour Code, which came into effect on 1 January 1995. The Labour Code and a long list of implementing decrees provided a comprehensive regulatory framework for the state management of the labour market. The authority of employee unions was clarified and strengthened under the Labour Code, which also specified Vietnam's formal system of social security. Health care, retirement, housing, child-care, education and other benefits were linked to state enterprises before the reform period, but under the Labour Code many of the same links were established within the larger non-state enterprises (i.e., those with ten or more employees).

This linkage was important for several reasons: (1) by addressing the needs of workers in these other sectors as well; (2) making it more difficult to restructure state enterprises when this would imply the need to reduce excess labour; and (3) such linkage interfered with the ability of workers to take advantage of alternative employment opportunities and with the great general development of flexible labour markets.

The social insurance system is funded by obligatory payment of social insurance premiums by the employer (15 per cent of the wage fund) and the employee (5 per cent of the wage) in all enterprises with ten or more employees. For all other arrangements involving hired labour, the social insurance allowances shall be included in the salary paid by the labour user so that the worker can join a social insurance scheme of his choice or look after his own insurance. The social insurance fund provides pensions for workers, as well as benefits for childbirth, sickness, disabilities related to work-related accidents or occupational diseases. Workers become eligible for pensions at 60 for men and 55 for women, if they have paid social insurance premiums for at least 15 years. The benefit is equal to 45 per cent of the salary earned in the previous five years, with an additional 2 per cent payable for every additional year worked up to 30 years. Therefore, the maximum pension is 75 per cent of the salary over the previous five years. More favourable pension benefits are available to the disabled and to those in especially heavy or noxious jobs.[2]

Workers who did not qualify for pensions, but who contributed to the system, were entitled to a one-off payment by the government equal to one month of salary for each year of contributions.[3] Some 146 000 of the 236 000 retirees receiving benefits in 1996 were given lump-sum payments. The coverage of the social insurance system was limited by the unwillingness of many employers and employees to make the required payments, and such payments could be legally avoided if the employment were in enterprises or operations with less than ten employees. These enterprises accounted for the vast majority in agriculture, fisheries and the private sector in other sectors of the economy. It was estimated that the vast majority of workers, 30 million out of a workforce of 37 million, did not pay insurance.[4] In 1995, the turnover on Social Insurance premiums was US$315 millions.[5]

There were important issues that required solution if the social insurance system was to be effective. Two of particular importance were (1) the level of benefits and financial viability of the social insurance fund; and (2) the effect on labour mobility and the growth in employment opportunities, particularly for small private sector firms. A sound social security system should be financially sustainable over the long run, and although the government covered the cost of the benefits provided to state workers, the long-term financial viability of the social security system required further examination for several reasons. First, the levels of benefits relative to contributions claimed were generous by Asian standards, more comparable to developed countries, for example Canada and the United States.[6] Second, the system was vulnerable when the average wages over the previous five years rose above the average wages during which payments were made into the system, or would have been made given the coverage provided to workers based on years worked prior to the introduction of the system. The system was also vulnerable when payments could be claimed in circumstances that might be difficult or costly to control, for example, sickness allowances paid by the social insurance fund on the basis of a medical certification. Finally, the surplus funds being accumulated at the end of the 1990s were deposited with state banks at a very low interest rate of three-tenths of a per cent per month.[7]

Without nationwide coverage, the social security system could become a substantial barrier to labour mobility. Moving from less productive to more productive employment is an important ingredient in making markets efficient, but workers would be unlikely to move if they were unable to transfer pension rights and other benefits. Labour mobility between the state and non-state sectors would be considerably constrained by the lack of a universal social insurance system. In this context, many of the problems with the Vietnamese social insurance system would be reduced if the system were based directly on past contributions, and if the rights to pension funds were fully vested with the worker. These changes would solve both the financial viability and the constraint on the labour mobility problem. Social insurance accounts could be based on direct contributions; if the worker moved out of a job covered by the social insurance system, he or she would still retain a claim on the funds accumulated at the time of retirement. Contributions up to 20 per cent of wages could still be invested in the fund if the worker were employed in a firm with less than ten workers. This would eliminate the disincentive to leave jobs in insured sectors of the economy for fear of losing all benefits, or having to take lump-sum payment rather than a pension if the worker left prior to reaching retirement age.

The Compulsory Health Insurance System (CHIS), like the Social Insurance Scheme, represented an attempt to provide a universal 'safety net' for workers, with a large part of the costs shifted to enterprises. Both systems required contributions from workers to be matched by employers, and both were intended to be nationwide and have transferable coverage, although in practice there were problems achieving this. The problems with the systems resulted from the poor quality of service, or the reluctance of health centres to provide services. In particular, health insurance beneficiaries could only claim for locally-provided services; reimbursement for health services remained city or province-specific so that, for example, a worker from Hanoi could not claim for health expenses incurred in Ho Chi Minh City.

Health insurance beneficiaries cannot easily choose the health facility they want as the provincial Health Insurance Authority (HIA) often has a private deal to send all its beneficiaries to a specific health facility which, consequently, tend to be overcrowded. The HIA holds hospitals and their personnel responsible for wrong medical acts, and pays only for a specified list of medicines and services at fixed prices. Hospital management has sometimes made medical personnel pay if they over-prescribe medicines to health insurance patients so that, consequently, medical personnel are reluctant to deal with such patients. In addition, payments to service providers by the HIA are slow and inefficient. Disputes, delays and refusals to pay certain items undermine hospital care of CHIS patients. Although it is intended to be a universal health system, these problems result in a very limited coverage.

Regulatory control of enterprises in Vietnam has been very weak. If enterprises, even state enterprises, do not perceive advantages from joining the pension and health systems, they often avoid doing so. Further, at the central level, record keeping and research are so weak that knowledge about the extent and nature of coverage is vague. The health insurance system covers only 10 per cent of the population, and expansion is slow because both the health institutions and those covered are both dissatisfied. Even people with health insurance cards avoid using them if they can afford private health. A 1996 survey of 100 enterprises paying health insurance benefits found that 80 of them considered the system 'inefficient and did not know the rates and conditions of compensation . . .', and 70 'were willing to buy complementary health insurance if premiums were reasonable' (NQH, p. 121).

Health insurance premiums are equal to 3 per cent of the gross salaries of workers in enterprises covered by the system. In theory, 1 per cent came from workers and the other 2 per cent was contributed by the enterprise, in practice enterprises often paid the full 3 per cent. In 1995, premiums totalled only US$36.5 million, and claims paid totalled US$28.6 million (NQH, p. 110). Consequently, the system provided only 11 per cent of public health revenues in 1995. Given the problems of the health system, it is not surprising that ministries and some state enterprises maintain their own health facilities. The oil and gas, coal, rubber, road and transport sectors, and the Ministry of Defence all operate their own private health insurance networks (NQH, p. 69).

It would not be difficult to develop a system in which costs are shifted to firms, but the attempt to force such a system on enterprises would be likely to discourage investment and growth in such enterprises. It would be more realistic to finance costs of public health programme through taxes that would subsidize healthcare for low-income groups without access to higher quality alternatives. Participation in the existing health system might be voluntary, an outcome of negotiations between enterprises, workers and their unions, and efforts could be made to improve the attractiveness of the compulsory health system, perhaps by including private providers. A low fee per service paid directly by the patient would help to cover costs and discourage excessive claims on the system where expected benefits are low. Competition from other health insurance schemes might also be allowed and even encouraged.

A reported literacy rate of 93 per cent puts Vietnam on a par with Thailand and above most low-income Asian countries in literacy. Some health indicators have also been overall higher than for countries like Bangladesh, India and Indonesia. However, during the transition there was a reported decline in health and education services (World Bank, 1993, p.170). The early years of transition put public services, particularly those in rural areas, under enormous pressure; non-monetary incomes such as payment in rice were abolished, and the newly-monetized salaries failed to keep pace with inflation. A doctor received the equivalent of about US$18 per cent month in the early 1990s. Teachers were similarly affected, and in the 1991–92 academic year, 20 per cent of teachers quit their jobs or retired (*Vietnam Investment Review*, 13 September 1992). Further, the number of pupils undertaking primary education declined as parents withdrew them to work on the land or in household production.

The fall in official wages and salaries led to the institutionalizing of inefficient work practices throughout the public sector. Routine permissions and information had to be purchased, doctors sold their medicines and neglected

Table 13.8   Social sector indicators, Vietnam and other countries

	Vietnam	Indonesia	Thailand	China
Human Development Index (HDI), 1993	0.523	0.641	0.832	0.609
GDP per capita at PPP*, 1993 (US$)	1040	3270	6350	2330
Life expectancy at birth, 1993 (yrs)	65.5	63	69.2	68.6
Average calorie supply, 1992 (per day)	2250	2755	2443	2729
Adult literacy rate, 1993 (%)	92.5	82.9	93.6	80
Years of schooling, 1985 (average yrs)	3.2	3.1	3.5	4.8
Enrolment rates, 1988–90: primary & secondary (%)	69	84	58	83
Primary drop-out rate, 1985–87 (%)	50	20	36	32
Educational attainment index	57.3	48.9	61.6	47.1
HDI rank (out of 174 countries)	121	102	52	108
Real GDP rank (out of 174 countries)	148	89	49	111

Notes: * PPP refers to a Purchasing Power Parity index that attempts to measure the 'real' purchasing power of nominal incomes across countries. 1989 PPP per capita for Myanmar, Bangladesh and India were US$595, US$820 and US$910 respectively.
Source: GSO (1998); UNDP Human Development Report (1996).

saw a deterioration in education and health services, a trend which began to be reversed.

Future prospects remained bright, so long as incomes continued to rise and jobs to be created. The spectre of a steady rise in the numbers of unemployed remained. Rural–urban migration increased. This 'employment imperative' was not addressed through policies promoting capital-intensive import substitutes, nor by protection of the state enterprise sector. Development of a private corporate sector was painfully slow, though it would be central to sustained long-term development, and to the ability to generate increasing levels of income transfers to achieve welfare goals.

Notes

1 From informal conversations with GSO staff.
2 Workers with 61 per cent disability (in heavy or noxious jobs) can get pension benefits ten years earlier (at any age) if they have had 20 years of contributions.
3 The monthly salary is calculated as the average of the past five years of employment.
4 *Vietnam Investment Review*, issue 277, 2 March 1997.
5 NQH & Associates (1997) 'Preliminary Report on Health and Personal Line Insurance Market Survey in Vietnam', unpublished, April, p. 137.
6 OECD (1996) *Labour Market Aspects of State Enterprise Reform in Viet Nam*, Technical Paper no. 117, Paris, p. 34.
7 Molisa interview.

preventative health care, and teachers used school time to undertake second jobs. Salaries were generally regarded as retainers, with normal work often requiring additional payment. The transaction costs and efficiency losses of this incentive structure were substantial. As a result, the inability of the government to meet recurent expenditures reduced the availability of low cost services. The growth of private sector activities covered the demands of middle and upper urban income groups, but services for low income groups declined without a commensurate improvement in employment.

Table 13.9 shows various indicators of the health and education sector decline, until about 1992–93 when increased government spending, development assistance and selective policy liberalization reversed the declines. The number of grade-school teachers declined after 1988–89, as did the numbers of students; the number of primary school students fell by 8 per cent to 11.7 million during 1987–90. Numbers of both students and teachers increased in the 1990s, though secondary school students did not rise until 1992–93. The teacher–student ratio had been steady at 1:27, but rose subsequently to 1:31 in 1997–98. The number of kindergarten teachers stagnated until the late 1990s, when liberalization, allowing private kindergartens, prompted a boom in teacher numbers and schools.

Health data show a less clear picture of slump and recovery. Although the numbers of doctors increased each year, the numbers of nurses fell sharply. The number of hospital beds showed an increase from 1994, after falling steadily from 224 000 beds in 1987. But these and other aggregate data disguise important trends. For example, although the number of hospital beds was 198 000 in both 1992 and 1997, the number in rural areas fell from 69 600 to 63 800. The slump in health services, particularly in rural areas, may have continued in the late 1990s, but this was not a priority concern in the central government budget.

Central budget education expenditures rose steadily as a percentage of GDP from 1 per cent in 1991 to about 2.4 per cent in 1997. Health sector expenditure trends were less consistent: rising from 0.8 per cent of GDP in 1991 to 1.3 per cent in 1994, but subsequently dropping to about 1 per cent (World Bank, 1998b, p. 97). These education and health sector shares were low by international standards. The increases did not compensate for substantial falls in local government funding during transition. Further, expenditures were inequitably targeted in favour of urban areas.

Prior to transition, Vietnam's basic education and health services were commendable for a country with such a low level of development. One consequence was that human development indicators were on a par with or better than richer neighbouring countries, even in the early 1990s. However, the first years of transition placed Vietnam's education and health services under extreme pressure, essentially 'privatizing' many aspects of social assistance which citizens had previously looked to the government to provide. User fees came to be charged for education, health care, child

Table 13.9 Health and education indicators for Vietnam, 1990–98

	1990–91	1991–92	1992–93	1993–94	1994–95	1995–96	1996–97	1997–98
No. of kindergarten teachers (000)		69.8	69.3	66.3	69.3	75	84.4	94.9
No. of grade school teachers (000)	435	424	427	446	467	493	521	551
No. of grade school children (000)	11 883	12 344	12 911	13 653	14 529	15 561	16 348	17 074
% of population attending grade school	17.9	18.3	18.5	19.1	20.1	21	21.7	22.3

	1990	1991	1992	1993	1994	1995	1996	1997
Population of Vietnam (000)	66 233	67 744	69 405	71 026	72 510	73 962	75 355	76 710
No. of doctors (000)	23.3	25.9	27.4	28.5	29.7	30.6	31.9	32.9
No. of nurses (000)			55.2	53.7	50.8	47.6	45.8	46.2
No. of Hospital beds (000)	205	206	198	195	191	192	197	198

Sources: GSO (1998); Tran Hoang Kim (1996).

care, and levies were established for many other types of community services. Rural areas suffered most. The education sector recovered in the late 1990s, but the health sector, aside from user-paying services for the urban elite, remained in relative crisis.

Conclusion

Without doubt, Vietnam's transition was a success. Incomes rose, poverty fell and farmers gained. That success, however, was largely due to the failure to implement central planning in depth after 1976. Further, that Vietnam was a poor developing country, with largely unprocessed agricultural exports and a labour force willing and able to work at wages slightly above subsistence made it very different from most transitional economies.

Structural transformation of Vietnam's 'residual element' of central planning was achieved during the first decade of transition without crisis, with the exception of industrial production for a couple of years. However, it would seem that social services and support systems experienced a slump before gradual recovery. The collapse of subsidies and in-kind payments from the planning system was not immediately replaced by monetary equivalents, which were constantly eroded by high inflation until about 1992. Teachers left schools, and dropout rates rose. Health services declined particularly in rural areas.

Recovery after 1992 was notable but incomplete. Education services improved markedly. There were still teacher shortages, but dropout rates fell, and government funding of the sector rose. Government funding of health services was less generous. De facto privatization of education and health services allowed services to increase in line with rising household incomes, but those in poverty found access to health and education services worse than in 1985.

Informal and formal social security systems also came under pressure to adapt to a more market-based economy. Increased factor mobility, of capital and workers, undermined traditional systems of welfare support. Extended family ties proved important through this transitional phase, as welfare systems became monetized and community organizations developed. A formal social security system changed less. The Labour Code was essentially an attempt to expand the existing system to cover the non-state sector. It did not address the fundamental design and delivery problems that remain. Health financially unsustainable and an obstacle to labour mobility. Health insurance remained in crisis.

The social consequences of transition have been overwhelmingly favourable. Increased income inequality has been the main negative consequence, and that may be more attributable to a rapidly growing developing economy than a transitional one. However, transition did place social and welfare systems under pressure to change. This process of cha

14
Alternative Responses to Globalization

Claes Brundenius and John Weeks

The 1930s was a decade of world depression, followed by turmoil with a devastating world war. The last decade of the century witnessed equally dramatic events, including the collapse of the so-called Socialist Bloc. This collapse of a geopolitical bloc ushered in a period of spectacular and appalling economic chaos, which at the end of the century continued to wax and wane. This volume has considered in detail two countries which have tried to manage their economies to avoid such chaos, Cuba and Vietnam. Looking back at the contributions, one can ask, are there lessons to be learned from the experience of these two countries?

An analytical consideration of lessons requires answering a prior question: for what purpose are the lessons being identified? There are at least four possibilities:

1 the experiences of Cuba and Vietnam provide insight into the causes of the transition disasters in other countries;
2 they provide a positive guide to current and future policy in countries whose transitions have been disastrous;
3 each experience provides policy guidelines relevant only to the country in question and to each other; and
4 their experience is quite generally relevant, not just to transitional economies, but also to other underdeveloped countries seeking solutions to the problems of global integration.

Looking back at the Introduction, our answer to the first question should be obvious. The experiences of Cuba and Vietnam indicate that the appalling social costs during transition in Central Europe, and especially the former Soviet Union, could have been mitigated. Even more, future generations will look back upon the 1990s as a decade of incredible callousness to human suffering in the Former Soviet Union (FSU) much in the way that subsequent generations found the indifference to the Irish Potato Famine or mass starvation in colonial India so incomprehensible. Cuba and Vietnam, despite the severe costs of the crisis in the former country, show that it was not necessary for poverty in Russia to increase from 2 to 50 per cent, nor male life-expectancy to decline by over 10 years. Policies, well-known and practised, could have prevented such tragedies, just as in Ireland in the nineteenth century importing food could have prevented the starvation of tens of thousands and the emigration of millions. A different sequencing of policy changes (Stiglitz, 1994, chapter 15) combined with provision of social welfare services could have saved the lives and health of millions. This adds to the analytical indictment of the policy framework applied in Central Europe and the FSU countries.

However, Cuba and Vietnam offer limited, if any, guidance to policy in the disaster countries. Consciously, if not purposefully, most governments of transitional countries dismantled the state institutions through which a growth strategy could be developed (as in Vietnam) or social costs minimized (as in Cuba). As most clearly shown in the case of Russia, the orthodox strategies tended to create great concentrations of wealth and power, such that the government had little interest and less political commitment to protecting the population from the social costs of transition.

We can conclude that the experiences of Cuba and Vietnam have historical-analytical importance, but little or no relevance to ongoing policy in other transitional countries. However, it is of considerable relevance to analyse the relationship between past and future policy in each country, and several of our authors have done exactly that. Perhaps the clearest presentation was in Kokko's chapter which agrees with the other authors that the Vietnamese government managed the transition with remarkable success (compare to Weeks, Mallon and Irvin, and Tønnesson). Then, he goes on to argue that this very success, *via* a relatively managed economy, required a radical change in policy at the end of the 1990s to much greater market orientation and dramatically less state intervention. Whether or not one agrees with the conclusion, which is highly proscriptive, it highlights the subtlety of the transition process, and that transition is not a question of creating a once-and-for-all policy framework.

A true alternative transition strategy, which seeks to establish a long-term policy framework substantially different from the so-called free market economy, needs clarity of exposition. The 'Washington Consensus' view might be summarized as follows: a moderate pace of 'reform',[1] even reform delayed, can provide for a more economically and socially functional transition, but the ultimate outcome should be the free market model. If one does not endorse this long-term goal, how is the alternative outcome specified? If anything is clear from the experiences of Cuba and Vietnam, it is that the alternative outcome cannot merely be a marginal reformulation of the antediluvian central planning framework. Even the Cuban government, despite its rejection of the term 'transition', in favour of 'special period', explicitly accepts that central planning must undergo radical reformulation. The government's emphasis on foreign investment as a source of growth and structural change in itself rules out a reconstruction of the old framework.

Then, what is the alternative long-term framework? The first step to answer this question requires exposing what Stiglitz calls 'The Myth of the Two Ways':

> [T]he seeming failure of market socialism has led many to conclude that there is no third way between the two extremes of markets and state enterprises... [T]his way of framing the question is misleading. The fact of the matter is that governments play a prominent role in all societies. The question is not *whether* there will be government involvement in economies, but what that role should be.
>
> (Stiglitz, 1994, p. 253)

With the Myth in mind, the alternative framework could be specified according to the following general principles: (1) there are negative outcomes of relatively unregulated capitalist development, particularly acute in underdeveloped countries; (2) the role played by the state would be determined by the goal of minimizing these outcomes; and (3) the quantitative size of the state sector and qualitative character of the state's role should vary according to political, social and historical factors. Thus, the first step towards concrete policy alternatives is to specify the negative outcomes of capitalism that a society would seek to avoid.

Another important matter is the question of property rights in a market economy. In the past, systemic change towards a market economy has become almost synonymous with property rights, primarily implying privatization of SOEs. But SOEs do not necessarily have to be privatized in order to be restructured, or reformed. A private sector can flourish parallel with an expanding state sector or a non-state collective sector, as the Chinese example clearly shows. With hindsight, it is clear that what went wrong in Russia was not the insufficient speed of privatizing SOEs, but rather the contrary. Or in Stiglitz's words:

> Yes, Russia has succeeded in 'privatizing' much of its industry and natural resources, but the level of gross fixed investment – a far more important sign of a burgeoning market economy – had fallen dramatically over the last five years. Russia was fast becoming an extractive economy, rather than a modern industrial economy. Standing in marked contrast with these failures has been the enormous success of China, which created its own path of transition (rather than just using a 'blueprint' or 'recipe' from western advisors). It succeeded not only in growing rapidly, but in creating a vibrant, non-State owned collective enterprise sector.
>
> (Stiglitz, 1999)

Perhaps first and foremost, relatively unregulated capitalism tends to generate concentrations of economic power which become loci of political domination over the rest of society. Unregulated capitalism also easily leads to 'virtual economies' like the emergence in Russia of 'a new kind of economic system with its own rules and its own criteria for success and failure' (Gaddy and Ickes, 1998). The danger of monopoly, and anti-competitive behaviour in general, is not primarily its impact on consumers, but that, as in Russia, it tends to undermine democratic institutions.[2] This danger is particularly important in Cuba. A relatively open and unregulated Cuban economy might quickly become dominated by US business interests, supported by the US government. As the chapter by Figueras shows in detail, it would be a foolish Cuban government indeed that allowed its policy framework to become heavily influenced by US interests. This is all the more the case given the political influence of Cuban exile groups on US policy towards Cuba. In this context, restricting foreign investment for the most part to joint ventures with state enterprises (as in both Cuba and Vietnam) was an instrument to limit the concentration of political power. While observers might bemoan the absence of liberal electoral democracy in both countries, this political form would be unlikely to facilitate effective democratic institutions if economic power were highly concentrated.

Second, relatively unregulated capitalism tends to generate extreme inequalities of income and wealth. This tendency can be magnified exponentially during a rapid transition process. As with concentration of economic power in general, the more important negative effects of inequality in individual or household income are political and social, not economic. Were it the case that the rich had no more political power than the poor, inequality would be a relatively benign problem. In his chapter, Kokko argues that a major problem of institutionalizing state enterprises is that this may solidify a political constituency in opposition to certain types of policy changes. Similarly, from an initial position of very low inequality, a government of a transitional country, if it facilitates a rapid increase in inequalities, creates a strong political constituency opposed to active poverty reduction by state policies. Thus, state action to prevent rapid growth of inequalities may be a necessary measure to achieve a future economic system that spreads the benefits of growth throughout the population. The sustainable outcome would require a degree of inequality considerably greater than prevailed before the transition, a necessity highlighted by the extremely low level of public sector salaries in both Cuba and Vietnam at the end of the 1990s. However, economic theory, even in its most orthodox form, does not dictate how great inequalities need be to achieve allocative efficiency. In particular, greater inequality does not imply greater efficiency, nor is the reverse the case.

In a capitalist economy with great inequalities there may be a 'trade-off' between growth and equity, though recent literature casts this into doubt (see Van der Hoeven, 1999). There is no theoretical reason to conclude that Cuba and Vietnam societies must achieve the inequalities of neighbouring capitalist countries to sustain rapid growth. To a great extent these levels of inequality, especially in Latin America, are not derivative from allocative efficiency, but reflect an even greater inequality in the distribution of assets. Much of asset distribution derives from historical legacies that have no efficiency rationale. Public ownership represents one vehicle for preventing the concentration of assets in private hands, though there are many others, such as cooperative ownership.[3]

Third, a relatively unregulated capitalist economy tends to produce a pattern of trade based upon static (current) relative costs. In orthodox trade theory, this tendency is eulogized as conforming to 'comparative advantage'. It is beyond the scope of this conclusion to enter into a critique of the Heckscher–Ohlin–Samuelson model upon which the neoclassical version of comparative advantage is based. We can merely note that under empirical test the model performs quite poorly, both in terms of its predictions about the composition of trade,[4] and its predictions about the behaviour of exchange rates and trade balances (Shaikh and Antonopoulos, 1998). A relatively unregulated trade regime may in some circumstances result in export diversification. If so, this would be the result of a country's structural characteristics, such as skills and geographic position, rather than the operation of relative prices. An alternative framework would attempt to use a range of policies to avoid entrapment within a primary-product-based export structure. However, as the new century began, the scope for governments to pursue industrial policy was substantially less than it had been a decade before.[5]

Clearly, there are lessons from the experiences of Cuba and Vietnam which are relevant for other developing countries. The assertion that socialist, even interventionist policies were anachronisms in the 'age of globalization' can be seen as an ideological counteract by neoliberals in the face of growing unease at the social and economic costs of less-regulated trade and capital flows. Cuba and Vietnam certainly did not provide any panaceas, nor did they represent a blueprint for the reconstruction in other countries of a more developmentally-focused policy package. However, their policies indicate that countries need not accept the one-size-fits-all orthodoxy of the Washington Consensus.

Notes

1 After reading Tønnesson's chapter one hopes that the word 'reform' would only be used with clear definition and explicit value judgements.
2 In a now forgotten, but fundamentally important article in the *American Economic Review* in 1948, Rothchild argued that oligopoly power tended to engender fascism in the political sphere.

3   Stiglitz reaches a strong conclusion on ownership and incentives, 'If each farmer owned the land he or she worked, or if each worker owned the capital goods with which he or she worked, there would be no incentive problem' (Stiglitz, 1994, p. 49).
4   There is a considerable empirical literature that casts doubt on the generalization that freer trade tends to foster exports of labour intensive products in developing countries (Yeats, 1989).
5   Lall concludes pessimistically: '... [T]he scope for selective interventions has been considerably narrowed by the new rules of the game of international trade and finance. This constitutes... the single most important constraint to the use of the tools that were deployed as successfully by [Korea and Taiwan]' (Lall, 1997, p. 52).

References

Abbassi, J. (1997) 'The Role of the 1990s Food Markets in the Decentralization of Cuban Agriculture', *Cuban Studies*, vol. 27, pp. 21–39. Pittsburgh & London: University of Pittsburgh Press.

Adaman, F. and P. Devine (1996) 'The Economic Calculation Debate: Lessons for Socialists', *Cambridge Journal of Economics*, no. 20.

——and——(1997) 'On the Economic Theory of Socialism', *New Left Review*, no. 221, Jan.–Feb.

Adler Lomnitz, L. (1988) 'Informal Exchange Networks in Formal Systems: A Theoretical Model', *American Anthropologist*, vol. 90, no. 1, pp. 42–55.

Aduki Pty Ltd (1999) *Study on the Effects of the East Asian Economic Crisis on Agriculture and Rural Development in Vietnam*. Ausaid research paper, 9 February.

Akyüz, H., Ha-Joon Chang and R. Kozul-Wright (1998) 'New Perspectives on East Asian Development', *Journal of Development Studies*, vol. 34(6).

Amsden, A. (1989) *Asia's Next Giant: South Korea and Late Industrialisation*. New York: Oxford University Press.

——(1994) 'Why isn't the Whole World Experimenting with the East Asian Model to Develop?', *World Development*, vol. 22, April.

Asian Development Bank (ADB) (1996) *Asian Development Outlook: 1996 and 1997*. Hong Kong: Oxford University Press.

——(1997a) *Asian Development Outlook: 1997 and 1998*. Hong Kong: Oxford University Press.

——(1997b) *Emerging Asia: Changes and Challenges*. Manila: ADB.

——(1999) *Asian Development Outlook 1999* Hong Kong: Oxford University Press

——(2000) *Asian Development Outlook 2000*, Hong Kong: Oxford University Press

Bahro, R. (1973) *The Alternative in Eastern Europe*. London: New Left Review Books.

Bairoch, P. and Kozul R. Wright (1996) *Globalization Myths: Some Historical Reflections on Integration, Industrialization and Growth in the World Economy*. Geneva: UNCTAD Discussion Papers, no. 133.

Banco Nacional de Cuba (1995) *Informe Económico 1994*. Havana.

——(1996) *Informe Económico 1995*. Havana.

——(1999) *Informe Económico 1998*. Havana.

Bello, W. and S. Rosenfeld (1992) *Dragons in Distress: Asia's Miracle Economies in Crisis*. San Francisco: The Institute for Food and Development Policy.

Benmayor, R. (1987) 'For Every Story There Is Another Story Which Stands Before It', in R. Benmayor (ed.), *Stories to Live By: Continuity and Change in Three Generations of Puerto Rican Women*. Hunter College of the City University of New York.

Beresford, M. and C. Nyland (1999) 'The Labour Movement of Vietnam', *Labour History*, Sydney.

Bienefeld, M. (1994) 'Capitalism and the Nation State in the Dog Days of the Twentieth Century', in R. Milib and L. Panitch (eds), *Between Globalism and Nationalism*, Socialist Register, 1994. London: The Merlin Press.

Bonacich, E., N. Hamilton, L. Cheng, N. Chinchilla and P. Ong (1994) 'The Garment Industry, National Development, and Labour Organizing', in E. Bonacich, L. Cheng,

N. Chinchilla and P. Ong (eds), *Global Production: The Apparel Industry in the Pacific Rim*. Philadelphia: Temple University Press, pp. 365–73.

Bowles, P. and Xiao-yuan Dong (1994) 'Current Successes and Future Challenges in China's Economic Reforms', *New Left Review*, no. 208.

Brenner, R. (1998) *The Economics of Global Turbulence*. London: New Left Review, Special Report.

Brundenius, C. (1982) 'Development Strategies and Basic Needs in Revolutionary Cuba', in C. Brundenius and M. Lundahl (eds), *Development Strategies and Basic Needs in Latin America – Challenges for the 1980s*. Boulder: Westview Press.

——(1984) *Revolutionary Cuba: The Challenge of Economic Growth with Equity*. Boulder: Westview Press.

——(1998) 'Globalization, Long Waves and Convergence Theories' (in Swedish), *Den Ny Verden*, no. 3. Copenhagen: Centre for Development Research.

——(1999) 'Economic Restructuring and Implications for Science and Technology in Transition Economies', in C. Brundenius *et al.*, *Reconstruction or Destruction? Science and Technology at Stake in Transition Economies*. Hyderabad: Universities Press (Longman).

Bryson, L. (1996) 'Revaluing the Household Economy', *Women's Studies International Forum*, vol. 19, no. 3, pp. 207–19.

Buber, M. (1977) (1952) 'On the Suspension of the Ethical', in M. Buber, *Eclipse of God. Studies in the Relation between Religion and Philosophy*. Westport, Conn: Greenwood Press.

Cao, Y., Qian and B. Weingast (1997) 'From Federalism, Chinese Style, to Privatization, Chinese Style', Center for Economic Policy Research, Discussion Paper no. 1838, pp. 1–38.

Carranza Valdés, Julio, L. Gutiérrez and P. Monreal González, (1995) *Cuba. La Restructuración de la economia. Propuesta para un debate*. Editorial de Ciencias Sociales, Havana.

Carranza Valdés, Julio L. Gutiérrez Urdaneta and P. Monreal González (1996) *Cuba: Restructuring the Economy – A Contribution to the Debate*, Institute of Latin American Studies, University of London.

Carranza Valdés, Julio (1998) *Las finanzas externas de Cuba entre 1994 y 1997*. Centro Estudios de la Economia Cubana, Havana.

Chambas, G. and A.-M. Geourjon (1996) 'Les incitations fiscales et douanières dans une économie en transition: le cas du Vietnam', paper prepared for conference on *L'économie vietnamienne en transition: les facteurs de la réussite*, Paris, May.

Chan, A., B. J. Tria Kerkvliet and J. Unger (eds) (1999) *Transforming Asian Socialism, China and Vietnam Compared*. St Leonards and London: Allen & Unwin.

Chan, K. W. (1996) 'Post-Mao China: A Two-Class Urban Society in the Making', *International Journal of Urban and Regional Research*, vol. 20, no. 1, pp. 134–50.

CIE (1997) *Vietnam's Trade Policies 1997*. Canberra and Sydney: Centre for International Economics.

CIEM (Centro de Investigaciónes de la Economía Mundial) (1998) *Economía cubana – Boletín informativo*, publicación trimestral, no. 33, January–February–March, Havana.

CIEMH (1997) *Vietnam's Economy in 1996 – A Policy Analysis* (mimeo). Hanoi: CIEMH.

——(Central Institute of Economic Management: Hanoi) (1999) *Vietnam's Economy 1998*. Hanoi: CIEMH.

Comisión Económica para América Latino y el Caribe (CEPAL) (1985) *Economic Survey of Latin America and the Caribbean 1984*. Santiago de Chile.

——(1991) *Economic Survey of Latin America and the Caribbean 1990*. Santiago de Chile.

——(1996) *Cuba: Evolución Económica durante 1995*. Mexico City.

——(1997a) *La Economía Cubana. Reformas estructurales y desempeño en los años noventa*. Ciudad de México: Fondo de Cultura Económica.

——(1997b) *Economic Survey of Latin America and the Caribbean 1996–1997*. Santiago de Chile.

——(1997c) *Cuba: Evolución Económica durante 1996*. Mexico City.

——(1998a) 'Seminario de CEPAL sobre la Evolución Económica de Cuba y sus Perspectivas', Mexico City, 20–21 October 1997. Havana: Ministerio de Economía y Planificación.

——(1998b) 'Tablas Estadísticas', *Boletín Informativo de Economía Cubana*, no. 33. CIEM. Havana, Cuba.

Comité Estatal de Estadísticas (1989) *Anuario Estadístico de Cuba 1989*. Havana: CEE.

Commander, S. (1993) 'Unemployment in Eastern Europe: Social Disease or Economic Necessity?' *Transition*, World Bank newsletter (December).

CONAS, (1997) *Cuba: Investment and Business, 1996/1997*. Habana: CONAS.

——(1995) Consultores Asociados S.A., *Investment and Business – Cuba, 1994–1995*. Havana: CONAS.

Cornett, L. (1997) Review: 'International and Domestic Causes of Economic Policy Reform', *Studies in Comparative International Development*, vol. 32, no. 1, Spring. Penn: Transaction Publishers.

Cronologías (1989) *Agresiones de Estados Unidos a Cuba Revolucionaria*. Havana: Editorial de Ciencias Sociales.

Cuervo, M., H. Friñas and A. Hernandez (1987) 'Análisis conjunto de la sustitución de importanciones y el proceso de evaluación de inversones', *Cuba Economia planificada*, año 2, no. 1. Havana: Junta Central de Planificación.

Dang, P. and M. Beresford (1998) *Authority Relations and Economic Decision-Making in Vietnam: An Historical Perspective*. Copenhagen: NIAS-Report no. 38.

Dang, P. and M. Beresford, *et al.* (2000) *Opening the Door: Two Centuries of Markets in Vietnam*. Hanoi: Vietnam National Center for Social Sciences and Humanities Publishing House.

Dapice, D. O. (1998) 'Facing the New Reality: Can the Economic Crisis become an Advantage for Vietnam?', Harvard Institute for International Development, 1 May.

de Vylder, S. and A. Fforde (1988) *Vietnam: An Economy in Transition*. Stockholm: Swedish International Development Agency.

Deere, C. D. (1997) 'Reforming Cuban Agriculture', *Development and Change*, vol. 28, no. 4, October.

Desai, P. (ed.) (1996) *Going from Plan to Market in the World Economy*. Cambridge, Mass: MIT Press.

Devine, P. (1992) 'Market Socialism or Participatory Planning?', *Review of Radical Political Economics*, vol. 24., no. 3.

Díaz-Briquets, S., Casals and Associates (1994) 'Emigrant Remittances in the Cuban Economy: Their significance during and after the Castro Regime', *Cuba in Transition*, vol. 4, proceedings of the fourth annual meeting of the Association for the study of the Cuban Economy (ASCE), 13–14 August 1994, Miami, Florida, USA, http://lanic.utexas.edu/la/cb/cuba/asce/cuba4/diaz.htm.

Doanh, L. D. (1996) 'State-Owned Enterprise Reform and its Implications for Industrialization in Vietnam', paper presented at the Senior Policy Seminar on *Industrialization and Integration: Vietnam and the World Economy*, Hanoi, 20–22 November 1996.

Dodsworth J. R., E. Spitaller *et al.* (1996) *Vietnam: Transition to a Market Economy.* Washington, DC: International Monetary Fund, Occasional Paper no. 135.

Dollar, D. (1992) 'Outward-Oriented Developing Economies Really Do Grow More Rapidly: Evidence from 95 LDCs, 1976–1985', *Economic Development and Cultural Change*, vol. 40, no. 3, pp. 523–44.

Dollar, D. (1994) 'Macroeconomic Management and the Transition to the Market in Vietnam', *Journal of Comparative Economics*, vol. 18(3), pp. 357–75.

Dollar, D., P. Glewwe and J. Litvack (eds) (1998) *Household Welfare and Vietnam's Transition*, Washington, DC: The World Bank.

Dollar, D. and B. Ljunggren (1995) 'Macroeconomic Adjustment and Structural Reform in an Open Transition Economy: The Case of Vietnam', paper presented at Conference on Participation of Reforming Economies in the Global Trading and Financial System, UNU/WIDER, Helsinki, May.

Drucker, P. (1995) *Managing in a Time of Great Change.* New York: Truman Talley Books/ Dutton.

Echevarría, O. (1988) 'Principales aspectos del desarrollo de la industria mecánica nacional en el período revolucionario', *Cuba Economies planificada*, no. 2, April–June. Havana: Junta Central de Planificación.

Economist Intelligence Unit (EIU) (various years) Country Report Cuba (quarterly), London: EIU.

——(1997) *Reassessing Cuba – Emerging Opportunities and Operating Challenges*, Research Report. London: EIU and Arthur Andersen.

——(2000) *Cuba, Country Profile 1999–2000.* London: EIU.

Ellison, C. and G. Gereffi (1990) 'Explaining Strategies and Patterns of Industrial Development', in G. Gereffi and D. I. Wyman (eds), *Manufacturing Miracles. Paths of Industrialization in Latin America and East Asia.* Princeton, N J: Princeton University Press.

Elson, D. (1988) 'Market Socialism or Socialization of the Market?', *New Left Review*, no. 172, Nov.–Dec.

Enloe, C. (1983) 'Women Textile Workers in the Militarization of Southeast Asia', in *Women, Men, and the International Division of Labour.* New York: State University of New York Press, Albany.

European Commission (1994) 'An Industrial Competitiveness Policy for the European Union', *Bulletin of the European Union*, Sup. 3–94. Brussels-Luxembourg: EC.

——(1994) 'Crecimiento, Competitividad, Empleo. Retos para Entrar en el Siglo XXI'. Brussels-Luxemburgo: EC.

Everleny Pérez, O. (1998) 'La inversión extranjera en Cuba. Peculiaridades', Centro de Estudios de la Economía Cubana, Havana (mimeo).

Fernándex, M. (1998) 'Algunas Reflexiones sobre el Período Especial', *Revista Bimestre Cubana*, No. 8. SEAP, C. Havana. Cuba.

Ferreira, F.H.G. (1997) 'Economic Transition and the Distributions of Income and Wealth', World Bank working paper (May).

Ferriol, A. and V. Pérez. (1989) 'La eficiencia de los factores de producción en las ramas de la industria (1975–1985)', *Cuba Economía Planificada*, año 4. no. 2. Havana: Junta Central de Planificáción.

Ferriol Muruaga, A. (1998) 'Política social cubana: situación y transformaciones', in *TEMAS* no. 11, July–September, pp. 88–99, Havana.

Fforde, A. (1995) 'The Level Playing Field Problem and Rural Development in Vietnam', paper presented to the Conference on Rural Development: An Exchange of Chinese and Vietnamese Experiences, Hanoi, 28 February–2 March.

——(1998) 'Vietnam – Culture and Economy: Dyed-in-the-Wool Tigers?', paper for the Asia Update, Canberra, December.

——(1999) 'Vietnam: Monthly Economic and Social Analysis', various months, to be found at http://www.aduki.com.au

——and S. de Vylder (1996) *From Plan to Market: The Economic Transition in Vietnam.* Boulder: Westview Press.

——, ADUKI website. http://www.aduki.com.au/

——and A. Goldstone (1995) *Vietnam to 2005: Advancing on all Fronts.* London: Economist Intelligence Unit.

Figueras, M. A. (1998) 'El acuerdo multilateral de inversiónes', Havana: Cuba Socialista, no. 11.

Figueroa Albelo, V. M. (1997) *Los procesos cooperativos en la transformación agricula cubana.* Havana.

Font, M. (1997) 'Crisis and Reform in Cuba', M. A. Centeno and M. Font (eds) *Toward a New Cuba? Legacies of a Revolution.* Boulder and London: Lynne Rienner Publishers.

Forbes, D. K. *et al.* (eds) (1991) *Doi Moi: Vietnam's Renovation and Performance. Political and Social Change*, Monograph 14, Research School of Pacific Studies, Canberra: ANU.

Frank, N. and P. J. Cook (1996) *The Winner-Take-All Society.* New York: Martin Kessler Books.

French-Davies, R. (1997) 'Alcances Económicos de la Globalización', *Revista Nueva Sociedad*, no. 147. Caracas, January–February.

Friedman, E. (1996) 'Review Article: Learning from East Asian Economic Success: Avoiding the Pitfalls of Soviet-Style Developmentalist Dead Ends', *Economic Development and Cultural Change*, vol. 44, no. 4, July.

Fuentes, A. and B. Ehrenreich (1988) *Women in the Global Factory.* Boston: South End Press.

Fukuyama, F. (1992) *The End of History and the Last Man.* London: Hamish Hamilton.

Gaddy, C. G. and B. W. Ickes (1998) 'Russia's Virtual Economy' *Foreign Affairs*, vol. 77, no. 5, September/October.

Galasi, P. and E. Sik (1988) 'Invisible Incomes in Hungary', *Social Justice*, vol. 15, nos. 3–4, issues 33, 34, Fall-Winter, pp. 160–177.

Gates, C. (1995) 'Enterprise Reform and Vietnam's Transition to a Market-Oriented', *ASEAN Economic Bulletin*, vol. 12, no. 1 (July), pp. 29–52.

General Statistical Office (1995) *Social Indicator Guidebook for Vietnam.* Hanoi: Statistical Publishing House.

——(1996) *Impetus and Present Situation of Vietnam Soiety and Economy after Ten Years of Doi Moi.* Hanoi: Statistical Publishing House.

——(1998) *Major Social and Economic Information obtained from the Large Scale Surveys in Period of 1990–1996.* Hanoi: Statistical Publishing House.

——(1999) *Statistical Yearbook*, 1998. Hanoi: Statistical Publishing House.

——(1990) 'Paths of Industrialisation: An Overview', in G. Gereffi and D. L. Wyman (eds), *Manufacturing Miracles: Paths of Industrialisation in Latin America and East Asia.* Princeton, NJ: Princeton University Press.

——(1995a) 'Contending Paradigms for Cross-Regional Comparison: Development Strategies and Commodity Chains in East Asia and Latin America', in P. H. Smith (ed.), *Latin America in Comparative Perspective: New Approaches to Methods and Analysis.* Boulder, Colo: Westview Press.

——(1995b) 'Global Production Systems and Third World Development', in B. Stalings (ed.), *Global Change, Regional Response: The New International Context of Development*. New York: Cambridge University Press.

——(1997) 'Contending Paradigms for Cross-Regional Comparison: Development Strategies and Commodity Chains in East Asia and Latin America', in P. H. Smith (ed.), *Latin America in Comparative Perspective. New Approaches to Methods and Analysis*. Boulder: Westview Press.

——and M. Korzeniewicz (1994) *Commodity Chains and Global Capitalism*. Westport, Conn: Greenwood Press.

——and M.-L. Pan (1994) 'The Globalization of Taiwan's Garment Industry', E. Bonacich, L. Cheng, N. Chinchilla, N. Hamilton and P. Ong (eds), *Global Production: The Apparel Industry in the Pacific Rim*. Philadelphia: Temple University Press.

González, A. (1993) *Modelos económicos socialistas: Escenarious para Cuba en los años noventa*. Instituto Nacional de Investigaciones Económicas, Havana: editora JUCE-PLAN.

Government of Vietnam (1996) *Development and Official Development Assistance in the Period of Strongly Promoting Industrialisation and Modernisation in Vietnam*, Government Report to Consultative Group Meeting, Hanoi.

Granma (1996) 'Informe sobre los resultados económicos de 1996 y el plan económico y social para 1997 presentado ante la Asamblea Nacional por José Luis Rodríguez, ministro de Economía y Planificación', *Granma*, 26 December 1996, pp. 4–5.

——(1998) *Panorama agropecuario de fin de año. Los alimentos a debate*. http://206.130.183.230/1998/98-ene1/50dic5e.html

Griffin, K. (ed.) (1995) *Social Policy and Economic Transformation in Uzbekistan*. Geneva: International Labour Organization, ILO.

Hart, J. A. and A. Prakash (1997) 'Strategic Trade and Investment Policies: Implications for the Study of International Political Economy', *The World Economy*, vol. 20, no. 4, July. Oxford: Blackwell.

Harvie, C. and Tran Van Hoa (1997) *Vietnam's Reforms and Economic Growth*. London: Macmillan.

Herland, M. (1999) *Le Vietnem en mutation*, Paris: la documentation française.

Hiebert, M. (1996) *Chasing the Tiger*. New York: Kodansha International.

Hirst, P. and G. Thompson (1996) *Globalization in Question*. Cambridge: Polity Press.

Hopkins, T. K. and I. Wallerstein (1996) *The Age of Transition. Trajectory of the World System, 1945–2025*. London and New Jersey: ZED Books.

Horne, J. (1995) 'The Economics of Transition and the Transition of Economics', *Economic Record* (Australia), vol. 75, no. 2 (December), pp. 379–92.

Hutchison, J. (1992) 'Women in the Philippine Garments Exports Industry', *Journal of Contemporary Asia*, vol 22(4).

Institute for European–Latin American Relations (1998) *The World Opens up to Cuba: Towards Full Membership of the International Community*. Madrid: IRELA.

International Labour Organization (1998) *The Social Impact of the Asian Financial Crisis*, technical report for discussion at the High-Level Tripartite Meeting on Social Responses to the Financial Crisis in East and South-East Asian Countries, Bangkok, 22–24 April 1998. Geneva: ILO.

International Monetary Fund (1995) *Vietnam. Statistical Tables*, IMF Staff Country Report no. 95/92, Washington, DC: IMF.

——(1996) *Vietnam – Recent Economic Developments*, (mimeo), Washington, DC: IMF, November.

——(1996a) *Vietnam: Transition to a Market Economy.* Washington, DC: IMF.

——(1996b) 'Vietnam – Recent Economic Developments', IMF Staff Country Report no. 96/145, Washington, DC, December.

——(1999) *World Economic Outlook*, Washington, DC: M.F. (October 1999).

Irvin, G. W. (1994) *Vietnam: Some Macroeconomic Dimensions of Doi Moi.* The Hague: Institute for Social Studies.

——(1995) *Vietnam: Will Market Transition Increase Poverty?* ISS Working Paper no. 200, May.

——(1996) 'Emerging Issues in Vietnam; Privatisation, Equity and Sustainable Growth', *European Journal of Development Research*, vol. 2, no. 8, December.

Jefferson, G., T. Rawski and Y. Zheng (1992) 'Growth Efficiency and Convergence in China's State and Collective Industry', *Economic Development and Cultural Change*, vol. 40(2), pp. 239–66.

——, ——and——(1996) 'Chinese Industrial Productivity: Trends, Measurement Issues, and Recent Developments', *Journal of Comparative Economics*, vol. 23, pp. 146–80.

Jerneck, A. and Nguyen Thanh Ha (1995) 'The Role of Enterprise Unions in the Shift from Central Planning to Market Orientation', in Nørlund *et al.* (eds), *Vietnam in a Changing World.* London: Curzon Press, pp. 159–80.

Karshenas, M. (1995) 'Development Theory and Intersectoral Resource Flows', in *Industrialization and Agricultural Surplus. A Comparative Study of Economic Development in Asia.* Oxford: Oxford University Press.

Keidel, A. 'China: Analysis of Selected Enterprise Reform Trends', *SOE Monitoring note 1, World Bank Resident Mission,* (mimeo).

Kerkvliet, B., J. Tria and D. J. Porter (eds) (1995) *Vietnam's Rural Transformation.* Boulder: Westview/Singapore: ISEAS.

Knowles, J., J. R. Behrman, B.E. Diokno and K. McInnes (1996) *Key Issues in the Financing of Viet Nam's Social Services.* Report for ADB TA no. 2135-VIE, December.

Kokko, A. (1997) 'Managing the Transition to Free Trade: Vietnamese Trade Policy for the 21st Century', *Macroeconomic Report*, 1997:4. Stockholm: Sida.

——(1998) 'Asienkrisen: ett nordiskt perspektiv', in *Asiatiska vägval. Delstudier för en svensk Asienstrategi*, Ds 1998: 34 Stockholm: Ministry of Foreign Affairs.

——and F. Sjöholm (1997) 'Small. Medium, or Large? Some Scenarios for the Role of the State in the Era of Industrialization and Modernization in Vietnam', *Macroeconomic Report*, 1997:6. Stockholm: Sida.

——and M. Zejan (1996) 'Vietnam 1996: Approaching the Next Stage of Reforms', *Macroeconomic Report*, 1996: 9. Stockholm: Sida.

Kuilwijk, K. J. (1997) 'Castro's Cuba and the U.S. Helms–Burton Act. An Interpretation of the GATT Security Exemption', *Journal of World Trade*, vol. 31, no. 3.

Lall, S. (1997) 'Selective Policies for Export Promotion: Lessons from the Asian Tigers', *Wider Research for Action*, no. 43. Helsinki: Wider.

Latin American Caribbean and Central America Report (LACCAR) (1998) RC-98-08, 29 September 1998. London: Latin American Newsletters.

——(1999) RC-99-01, 19 January 1999. London: Latin American Newsletters.

Lavigne, M. (1995) *The Economics of Transition: From Socialist Economy to Market Economy.* London: Macmillan.

Le Dang Doanh (1990) *Economic Renovation in Vietnam: Achievements and Prospects*, paper presented at the conference on Doi Moi, Vietnam's economic renovation held at the Research School of Pacific Studies, Australian National University, 19–21 Sept. 1990; reprinted in Forbes *et al.* (1991).

——(1999) *Recent Economic Developments in Viet Nam*, presentation at CIEM/UNIDO Conference on Governance, Globalisation and Stability. Hanoi.

——and A. McCarty (1995) 'Economic Reform in Vietnam: Achievements and Prospects', in S. Naya and J. Tan (eds), *Asian Transitional Economics: Challenges and Prospects for Reform and Transformation*. Singapore: Institute of Southeast Asian Studies.

Lee, S. H. and K. S. Ho (1994) 'The Korean Garment Industry: From Authoritarian Patriarchism to Industrial Paternalism', in E. Bonacich, L. Cheng, N. Chinchilla, N. Hamilton and P. Ong (eds), *Global Production: The Apparel Industry in the Pacific Rim*. Philadelphia: Temple University Press.

Leipziger, D. M. (1992) *Awakening the Market: Viet Nam's Economic Transition*. Washington: World Bank.

Leung, S. and Le Dang Doanh (1998) 'Country Case Study: Vietnam', paper presented at Conference on East Asia in Crisis: From Being a Miracle to Needing One?, Australian National University, Canberra, 4–5 May 1998.

Lim, L. (1983) 'Capitalism, Imperialism, and Patriarchy: The Dilemma of Third-World Women Workers in Multinational Factories', in *Women, Men, and the International Division of Labour*. New York: State University of New York Press, Albany.

Ljunggren, B. (1996) 'Doi Moi in the Year of the Eighth Party Congress: Emerging Contradictions in the Reform Process', (mimeo), Hanoi.

Maddison, A. (1995) *Monitoring the World Economy, 1820–1992*. Paris: OECD Development Centre.

Malinowitz, S. (1997) *Public and Private Services and the Municipal Economy in Cuba*, Cuban Studies. no. 27, pp. 68–89. Pittsburgh and London: University of Pittsburgh Press.

Mallon, R. (1996) *State Enterprise Reform in Viet Nam: Policy Developments, Achievements and Remaining Constraints*, paper prepared for the Asian Development Bank, (mimeo), Hanoi (May).

——(1996a) 'Review of State Enterprises: Policy Developments, Achievements and Remaining Constraints', draft report prepared for the Asian Development Bank, Hanoi, May.

——(1996b) *Doi Moi and Economic Development in Vietnam: Some General Comments*, discussion paper presented at the Vietnam Update Conference, Australian National University, (Canberra), December.

——(1997) *Mapping the Playing Field: Options for Reducing Private Sector Disincentives in Viet Nam*, discussion paper for Swedish Embassy, Hanoi (November).

——and G. Irvin (1997) *Is the Vietnamese Miracle in Trouble?*, Institute for Social Studies Working Paper, The Hague (August).

Marquetti, H. (1996) *Cuba desempeño del sector industrial en 1990–1995*. Havana: Centro de Estudios de la Econocía Mundial.

Marshall, J. H. (1998) 'The Political Viability of Free Market Experimentation in Cuba. Evidence from Los Mercados Agropecuarios', *World Development*, vol. 26, no. 2.

Martínez Carrera, R. (1990) 'Cuba, crecimiento económico e inestabilidad externa', *Economía y Desarrollo*, no. 1. Havana: Facultad de Economía, Universidad de la Habana.

McCarty, A. (1993) 'Enterprise Reform in Vietnam, 1986–91', in M. Than and J. Tan (eds), *Vietnam's Dilemmas and Options: The Challenge of Economic Transition in the 1990s*. Singapore: Institute of Southeast Asian Studies.

McCormick, B. L. (1998) 'Political Change in China and Vietnam: Coping with the Consequences of Economic Reform', *The China Journal*, no. 40, July, pp. 121–43.

McKinnon, R. (1994) 'Financial Control in the Transition from Classical Socialism to a Market Economy', *Journal of Economic Perspectives*, vol. 5, no. 4 (Fall).

Meier, G. M. (1995) *Leading Issues in Economic Development*, 6th edn. Oxford: Oxford University Press.

Mesa-Lago, C. (1995) 'Prospective Dollar Remittances and the Cuban Economy', in A. Ritter and J. Kirk (eds) *Cuba in the International System – Normalization and Integration*. New York: St Martin's Press.

——(1998) 'Assessing Economic and Social Performance in the Cuban Transition of the 1990s', *World Development*, vol. 26, no. 5, pp. 857–76.

——, C. Quijano, A. Recarte, J. J. Ruiz and C. Solchaga (1999) 'La economía cubana: hipótesis de futuro', *Encuentro de la Cultura Cubana*, no. 11, Winter 1998/1999, pp. 103–28, Madrid.

Milanovic, B. (1998a) *Explaining the Growth in Inequality During the Transition*, World Bank Working Paper (February).

——(1998b) *Income, Inequality, and Poverty during the Transition from Planned to Market Economy*, Washington, DC: The World Bank Regional and Sectoral Studies.

Ministerio de Educación Superior (1996) *Boletin Informativo*, no. 2, Havana.

Ministerio de Finanzas y Precios (various years) *Anuario Estadístico*, Havana.

Ministerio de Justicia (1996, 1997) *Gaceta Oficial de la Republica de Cuba*, no. 16, 21 May 1996 and no. 22, 30 June 1997, Havana.

Ministerio de Trabajo y Seguridad Social (1996) *Resolución conjunta no. 1 MTSS-MFP sobre el ejercicio del trabajo por cuenta propia*, April 1996, Havana.

Ministry of Economy and Planning (1997) *Cuba: Economic Report Year 1996*, Havana.

——(1998) *Cuba: Economic Report Year 1997*, Havana.

Ministry of Finance (1996) 'Vietnam towards AFTA; Challenges, Advantages and Expected Developments', paper presented at Senior Policy Seminar on *Industrialization and Integration: Vietnam and the World Economy*, Hanoi, 20–22 November 1996.

——(1997) *State Enterprises: Small Capital, Big Debt*, (mimeo), Hanoi.

Ministry of Industry (1997) *The General Plan of VTGI Development to Year 2010*, Hanoi.

Ministry of Planning and Investment (1997) *Law on Foreign Investment in Vietnam*, Hanoi.

——(1998) *Documentation on Foreign Investment in Textile and Garment Industries*, Hanoi.

Ministry of Trade and Ministry of Industry (1997) *Inter-Ministerial Memorandum on European Union Export 1997 List of Import/Export Tax rates 1997 Guidelines for Procedures to Implement Foreign Investment Projects*, Hanoi.

Monreal Gonzáles, P. (1999) *Migraciones y Remesas Familiares: Notas e Hipótesis Sobre el Caso de Cuba*, Havana: Centro de Investigaciones de Economía International (CIEI), (mimeo).

Moock, P. and S. Venkataraman (1998) *Education and Earnings in a Transition Economy: The Case of Vietnam*, World Bank Working Paper (January).

Morales, A. (1997) 'Epistemic Reflections on the "Informal Economy"', *International Journal of Sociology and Social Theory*, vol. 17, nos 3/4, pp. 1–17.

Morris, E. (1997, 1998) 'Country Risk Service: Cuba', *EIU Country Risk Service*, 2nd quarter. London: Economist Intelligence Unit.

Mosley, Paul (1991) 'Structural Adjustment: a general overview', in V. Balasubramany and S. Lall (eds) *Current Issues in Development Economics*. London: Macmillan.

Myers, R. (1995) 'Chinese Debate on Economic Reform. Can China Create a Socialist Market Economy?', *Asian-Pacific Economic Literature*, vol. 9, no. 2 (November).

Naisbitt, J. (1995) *The Global Paradox*. London: Nicholas Brealey.

Nash, J. (1983) 'Introduction', in *Women, Men, and the International Division of Labour*. New York: State University of New York Press, Albany.

Naya, S. and J. Tan (eds) (1995) *Asian Transitional Economies: Challenges and Prospects for Reform and Transformation*. Singapore: Institute of Southeast Asian Studies.

Negocios en Cuba (1999) no. 3, Havana (journal).

Nguyen Van Ngai (1996) *The Impact of Price Intervention on Vietnamese Agriculture*, paper presented at AusAID/NCDS Vietnam Economics Research Conference (July).

Nolan, P. and Xiaoqiang Wang (1999) 'Beyond Privatization: Institutional Innovation and Growth in China's Large State-Owned Enterprises', *World Development*, vol. 27(1), pp. 169–200.

Nørlund, I., C. L. Gates and Vu Cao Dam (eds) (1995) *Vietnam in a Changing World*. London: Curzon/NIAS.

——(1998) 'Democracy and Trade Unions in Vietnam: Riding a Honda in Low Gear', in *The Copenhagen Journal of Asian Studies*. Copenhagen, Denmark: NIAS.

Nove, A. (1983) *The Economics of Feasible Socialism*. Boston: George Allen, and Unwin.

——(1987) 'Markets and Socialism', *New Left Review*, no. 161. Jan.–Feb.

NQH & Associates (1997) 'Preliminary Report on Health and Personal Life Insurance Market Survey in Vietnam', unpublished, April.

Núñez Moreno, L. (1998) 'Más alla del cuentrapropismo en Cuba', *TEMAS*, no. 11, July–September, pp. 41–50, Havana.

OECD (1996) *Labour Market Aspects of State Enterprise Reform in Viet Nam*, Technical Paper no. 117, Paris.

——(1999) *OECD Economic Outlook*. Paris: OECD (December 1999)

Oficina Nacional de Estadísticas, (ONE) (1995) *Cuba – Transición de la Fecunidad. Cambio Social y Conducta Reproductiva*. Havana.

——(1998) *Anuario Estadístico de Cuba 1996*. Havana.

——(1999) *Anuario Estadístico de Cuba 1997*. Havana.

——(2000) *Anuario Estadístico de Cuba 1998*. Havana.

Oficina National de Administración Tributaria (1997) *Declacación Jurada. Impuesto sobre ingresos personales – Moneda nacional modelo DJ-04. Instrucciónes para su confección*, Havana.

Ofreneo, R. P. (1994) 'The Philippine Garment Industry', in E. Bonacich *et al.* (eds), *Global Production: The Apparel Industry in the Pacific Rim*. Philadelphia: Temple University Press.

Ohmae, K. (1990) *The Borderless World. Power and Strategy in the Global Marketplace*. London: HarperCollins.

Ohno, I. (1996) 'Ownership, Performance, and Managerial Autonomy: A Survey of Manufacturing Enterprises in Viet Nam', *Journal of Development Assistance*, vol. 1, no. 2 (March) pp. 65–90.

Oman, C. (1996) *Los Desafíos Políticos. Globalización y Regionalización*. Fundación Friedrich Ebert, Lima, Perú, June.

Ong, A. (1983) 'Global Industries and Malay Peasants in Peninsular Malaysia', in *Women, Men, and the International Division of Labour*. New York: State University of New York Press, Albany.

——(1990) 'Japanese Factories, Malay Workers: Class and Sexual Metaphors in West Malaysia', in *Power and Difference: Gender in Island Southeast Asia*. Stanford: Stanford University Press.

Panitch, L. (1994) 'Globalisation and the State', in R. Miliband and L. Panitch (eds), *Between Globalism and Nationalism*, Socialist Register, 1994. London: The Merlin Press.

Papin, P. (1999) *Vietnam, Parcours d'une nation*, Paris: La documentation française.

Partido Communista de Cuba (1997) 'Resolución Económica del V Congreso del Partido Comunista de Cuba', *Granma*, 7 November 1997.

Pastor Jr., M. and A. Zimbalist (1987) *The International Monetary Fund and Latin America: Economic Stabilization and Class Conflict*. Boulder: Westview Press.

——(1996) 'Cuba and Cuban Studies: Crossing Boundaries during a "Special Period"', *Latin American Research*, vol. 31. No. 3.

——(1997) 'Has Cuba Turned the Corner? Macroeconomic Stabilization and Reform in Contemporary Cuba', *Cuban Studies*, vol. 27, pp. 1–19. Pittsburgh and London: Pittsburgh University Press.

Pérez, C. (1989) 'Technology, Crisis and Opportunities for Development', Central Bank of Brasilia, Brasil, (mimeo).

Pérez-López, J. F. (1995) *Cuba's Second Economy. From Behind the Scenes to Center Stage.* New Brunswick (USA), London (UK): Transaction Publishers.

Pérez Rojas, N. and D. Echevarria (1998) *Participación y producción agraria en Cuba: las UBPC, TEMAS*, no. 11, July–September, pp. 69–75, Havana.

People's Republic of China (1998) *China Statistical Yearbook 1998*. Peking.

——(1998) *'Report on the Implementation of the Central and Local Budgets for 1997 and on the Draft Central and Local Budgets for 1998'*, delivered by Finance Minister Liu Zhongli, First Session of the Ninth National People's Congress, 6 March.

——National Bureau of Statistics (1999) *Statistical Communiqué on the 1998 National Economic and Social Development.* China Statistical Information Net, 26 February.

Perkins, F. C. (1996) 'Productivity Performance and Priorities for the Reform of China's State-Owned Enterprises', *Journal of Development Studies*, vol. 32(3), pp. 414–44.

Peters, P. (1998) *Cuba's Small Business Experiment: Two Steps Forward, One Step Back*, Cuba Briefing Paper Series, March, Georgetown University.

Pham Bich San (1995) *Social Implications of the Economic Renovation in Vietnam*, paper for Vietnam – Reform and Transition Conference, Stockholm University, September.

Pike, D. (1999) 'Vietnam as the Quarter/Year/Decade/Millennium Ends', *Indochina Chronology*, October–November.

Poirine, B. (1994) 'Rent, Emigration and Unemployment in Small Islands: The MIRAB Model and the French Overseas Departments and Territories', *World Development*, vol. 22, no. 12.

——(1997) 'A Theory of Remittances as an Implicit Family Loan Arrangement', *World Development*, vol. 25, no. 4.

Pollitt, B. H. and G.B. Hagelberg (1994) 'The Cuban Sugar Economy in the Soviet Era and After', *Cambridge Journal of Economics*, vol. 18, no. 6.

Porter, M. (1990) *The Competitive Advantage of Nations*. London: Macmillan.

Prescott, N. (1997) *Poverty, Social Services, and Safety Nets in Vietnam*. World Bank Discussion Paper no. 376.

Quintana Mendoza, D. (1995a) 'Mercado Agropecuario: Apertura o Limitación?', *Investicación Económica*, INIE (December) no. 4, pp. 21–54, Havana.

——(1995b) 'La seguridad social y la distribución de los ingresos en Cuba. Un enfoque para la situación actual', *Investigación Económica*, INIE (December), no. 4, pp. 55–69, Havana.

——(1997) 'El sector informal urbano en Cuba: Algunos elementos para su caracterización', *Investigación Económica*, INIE (April–June), no. 3, Havana.

Rana, P. B. and N. Hamid (eds) (1994) *From Centrally Planned to Market Economies: The Asian Approach.* New York: Oxford University Press.

Ranneberger, M. (1998) 'Statement before the House International Relations Committee, Subcommittee on International Economic Policy and Trade'. Washington, DC: US Congress, 12 March.

Riedel, J. (1993) 'On the Trail of the Tigers', *World Economy*, vol. 16, no. 4 (July), pp. 401–22.

——and C. S. Tran (1997) 'The Emerging Private Sector and the Industrialization of Viet Nam', (mimeo), report on the project The Emerging Private Sector and the Industrialization of Viet Nam, VCCI, Hanoi, April.

Ritter, A. R. M. (1995) 'The Dual Currency Bifurcation of Cuba's Economy in the 1990s: Causes, Consequences and Cures', *Cepal Review*, no. 57, December.

——(1998) *Cuba's Economic Reform Process, 1998: Paralysis and Stagnation?*, paper presented to the symposium 'Reintegration into World Society: Cuba in International Perspective', 27–28 September, New York.

Rodríguez, J. L. (1997) 'Informe sobre los Resultados Económicos de 1997 y el Plan Econónico y Social para 1998', *Trabajadores* (weekly), Havana, 15 December.

Rodrik, D. (1995) 'Trade and Industrial Policy Reform', in J. Behrman and T. N. Srinivasan (eds), *Handbook of Development Economics*, vol. III. Amsterdam: Elsevier Science.

Román, L. (1998) *Institutions in Transition: Vietnamese State Bank Reform.* Amsterdam: Kluwer Academic.

Ronnås, P. and Ö. Sjöberg (1990) *Doi Moi: Economic Reforms and Development Policies in Vietnam.* Stockholm: Norstedts Tryckeri.

——(1995) 'Economic Reform, Employment and Labour Market Policy in Viet Nam', *Labour Market Papers*, no. 9. Geneva: ILO.

Roosevelt, F. and D. Belkin (eds) (1994) *Why Market Socialism?* New York: M.E. Sharpe.

Rosendahl, M. (1992) 'The March of History. Revolution as Development in Cuba', in G. Dahl and A. Rabo (eds), *Kam-ap or Take-off. Local Nations of Development.* Stockholm: Stockholm Studies in Social Anthropology.

——(1997a) *Inside the Revolution. Everyday Life in Socialist Cuba.* Ithaca: Cornell University Press.

——(1997b) 'The Ever-changing Revolution', in M. Rosendahl (ed.) *The Current Situation in Cuba: Challenges and Alternatives.* Stockholm: Institute of Latin American Studies.

Rostowski, J. (1997) 'Comparing Two Great Depressions, 1929–33 and 1989–93', in S. Zecchini (ed.) *Lessons from the Economic Transition: Central and Eastern Europe in the 1990s.* Paris: OECD.

Rowthorn, R. and Kozul-Wright, R. (1998) *Globalization and Economic Convergence: An Assessment.* Geneva: UNCTAD Discussion Paper Series no. 131.

Sampson, S. (1987) 'The Second Economy of the Soviet Union and Eastern Europe', *The Annals of the American Academy of Political and Social Science*, September, pp. 120–37.

Sanger, D. E. (1999) 'How Push by China and U.S. Business Won over Clinton', *The New York Times*, 15 April.

Scheper-Hughes, N. (1992) *Death Without Weeping. The Violence of Everyday Life in Brazil.* Berkeley, Los Angeles, Oxford: University of California Press.

Schumpeter, J. (1943) *Capitalism, Socialism and Democracy.* New York: Harper and Brother.

Schwartz, A. (1995) 'The Honeymoon is Over', *Far Eastern Economic Review*, 13 July.

Serbin, A. (1997) 'Globalización y Sociedad Civil en los Procesos de Integración', *Revista Nueva Sociedad*, no. 147. Caracas, Venezuela.

Shaikh, A. and R. Antonopoulos (1998) 'Explaining Long Term Exchange Rate Behavior in the United States and Japan', working paper no. 250, Jerome Levy Economics Institute.

Shutt, H. (1998) *The Trouble with Capitalism. An Enquiry into the Causes of Global Economic Failure*. London: ZED Books.

Sik, E. (1992) 'From the Second to the Informal Economy', *Journal of Public Policy*, vol. 12, part 2, April–June, pp. 153–75.

——(1994) 'From the Multicoloured to the Black and White Economy: The Hungarian Second Economy and the Transformation', *International Journal of Urban and Regional Research*, vol. 18, no. 1, pp. 46–70.

Singh, A. (1994) 'Openness and the Market Friendly Approach to Development.: Learning the Right Lessons from Development Experience', *World Development*, vol. 22, no. 12. London: Elsevier Science.

Socialist Republic of Vietnam (1996) 'Memorandum on the Foreign Trade Regime of the Socialist Republic of Vietnam', (mimeo). Hanoi: Ministry of Trade.

——(1996a) *Public Investment Program 1996–2000*, Hanoi: Government of the Socialist Republic of Vietnam.

Solchaga, C. (1997) 'Cuba, Perspectivas Econónicas', *Encuentro de la cultura cubana*, no. 3. Madrid.

Soros, G. (1998) *The Crisis of Global Capitalism*. London: Little, Brown & Co.

State Planning Committee (1994) *Report on the Living Standards Measurement Study*. Hanoi: Statistical Publishing House.

Stiglitz, J. E. (1997) *Whither Socialism?* Cambridge, Mass: The MIT Press.

——(1998) *More Instruments and Broader*. Helsinki: WIDER.

——(1999) *Whither Reform? Ten Years of the Transition*, paper presented for the Annual Bank Conference on Development Economics, Washington, DC, 28–30 April.

Su That (1996) *Van Tan Huong Dan Thi Hanh* Bo Luat Lao Dong (*A Guiding Document for the Implementation of the Labour Code*), Hanoi: Su That Publisher, Hanoi: National Political Publishing House.

Than, M. and J. Tan (eds) (1993) *Vietnam's Dilemmas and Options: The Challenge of Economic Transition in the 1990s*. Singapore: Institute of Southeast Asian Studies.

Thayer, C.A. (1998) 'Keeping an Even Keel', *Vietnam Business Journal*, vol. vi, no.2

Togores González, V. (1997) *El trabajo por cuenta propia. Desarollo y peculiaridades en la economía Cubana*, (mimeo). Havana: Centro de Estudios de la Economía Cubana (CEEC).

Tran, A. N. (1995) 'The Vietnamese Textile and Garment Industries in the Global Economy', *The Bridge* (Spring). Washington, DC: Southeast Asia Resource Action Center Publication.

——(1997) 'Through the Eye of the Needle: Vietnamese Textile and Garment Industries Rejoining the Global Economy', *Crossroads: An Interdisciplinary Journal of Southeast Asian Studies*, vol. 10(2), Center for Southeast Asian Studies, Northern Illinois University.

Tran Hoang, K. (1992) *Economy of Vietnam: Reviews and Statistics*. Hanoi: Statistical Publishing House.

——(1996) *Vietnam's Economy in the Period 1945–1995 and its Perspective by the Year 2020*. Hanoi: Statistical Publishing House.

Tran Thi Que (1998) 'Economic Reforms and their Impact on Agricultural Development in Vietnam', *ASEAN Economic Bulletin*, vol. 15, no. 1 (April), pp. 30–46.

Tréglodé, B. de (2000) 'Un théâtre d'ombres: Le Vietnam entre La Chine et l'ASEAN au lendemain de la Crise asiatigue', *Les Études du CERI* (Centre d'études et de recherches internationales), no. 68 (August).

Triana, J. (1997) *Cuba: Tranformación económica y conflicto vs Estados Unidos*. Havana: Centro de Estudios de la Economía Cubana.

——*et al.* (1998) *La Economía Cubana*. Havana: Centro de Estudios de la Economía Cubana.

Truong, T.-D. (1997) 'Uncertain Horizon: The Women's Question in Vietnam Revisited', in B. Beckman, E. Hansson and L. Roman (eds), *Vietnam: Reform and Transformation*. Stockholm: Stockholm University Press.

——and C. Gates (1992) 'Effects of Government Policies on the Incentive to Invest, Enterprise Behaviour and Employment: The Case Study of Vietnam', *World Employment Programme Research Paper* no. 57, Geneva.

Tu N. M. (1997) 'Reforming State-owned Enterprises in Vietnam', *Saigon Times*, 21–27 June.

Turras, R. and I. Hizástegui (1988) 'Potencialidades de un balance intersectorial inter-complejo en las proyecciones a largo plazo en Cuba', *Cuba, Economía Planificada*, año 3, no. 3 July–September. Havana: Junta Central de Planificación.

Ugarteche, O. (1997) *El Falso Dilema. América Latina en la Economía Global*, Editorial Nueva Sociedad – Fundación Friedrich Ebert (Perú). Caracas, Venezuela.

Unanue, A. and R. Martínez Carrera (1989) 'El desbalance financiero en el desarrollo de la economía cubana', *Cuba, Economía Planificada*, año 4, no. 3 (July–September). Havana: Junta Central de Planificación.

UNDP/UNICEF (1996) *Catching Up: Capacity Building for Poverty Alleviation in Vietnam*. Hanoi: UNDP.

United Nations (1995) *Poverty Elimination in Viet Nam*. Hanoi: UN.

——(1997) *The World Economy at the Beginning of 1998*. New York: Department of Economic and Social Affairs.

United Nations Conference on Trade and Development (UNCTAD) (1997) 'Informe sobre las Inversiones en el Mundo, 1997. Empresas Transnacionales Estructura de los mercados y Políticas en Materia de Competencia. Panorama General'. New York and Geneva: UN.

United Nations Development Programme (UNDP) (1997a) *Human Development Report 1997*. New York: UN.

——(1997b) *Investigación sobre el desarollo humano en Cuba 1996*. Havana: UNDP.

——(1998) *Expanding Choices for the Rural Poor: Human Development in Viet Nam*. Hanoi: UNDP.

——(1999) 'Globalisation, Governance and Stability: Key lessons from East Asia', *Staff Paper*, working draft, March.

United States Trade Representative (1999) 'Market Access and Protocol Commitments', USTR Web Page, 8 April.

US Bureau of the Census (1997) *Selected Characteristics of the Foreign-born Population by Year of Entry and Selected Countries of Birth* (1996): Table 6 (Cuba). Washington, DC.

Van Bergijk, P. A. G. and N. W. Mensink (1997) 'Measuring Globalization', *Journal of World Trade*, vol. 31, no. 3.

Van de Walle, D. (1998) 'Protecting the Poor in Vietnam's Emerging Market Economy', *World Bank Policy Research Working Paper* no. 1969 (September).

Van der Hoeven, R. (1999) *Poverty and Labour Markets in a Context of Structural Adjustment and Liberalization: Some Remarks on Tradeoffs between Equity and Growth*, invited paper for the Inaugural Workshop on the Development Studies Association on 'New Poverty Strategies', University of Reading, 8–12 April.

Vasavakul, T. (1998) 'Vietnam's One-Party Rule and Socialist Democracy?', *Southeast Asian Affairs* (yearbook). Singapore: ISEAS.

Vietnam Economic Times (VET) (1996) 'Corruption: Vietnam Clamps Down', issue 35, March, and the various issues.

Vietnam Investment Review, weekly, various issues.

Vietnam News Agency website: http://www.vnagency.com.vn

Vietnam News List: vnnews-l@coombs.anu.edu.aul

Vietnam, Socialist Republic of (1993) *Viet Nam: A Development Perspective: Prepared for the Donor Conference*. Hanoi.

VINATEX (1997) *Quy Hoach Tong The (:) Phat Trien Nginh Nganh Cong Nghiep Det May Viet Nam 2010 (The General Pen of VTGI Development to year 2010)*. Hanoi: Ministry of Industry.

Vo Dai Luco (1998) *Vietnam's Policies on Trade and Investment and the Development of Some Key Industries*. Hanoi: Social Science Publishing House.

Von Mises, L. (1935) 'Economic Calculation Debate in the Socialist Commonwealth', in F. Hagek (ed.), *Collectivist Economic Planning*, London.

Wade, R. and F. Venerosos (1998) 'The Asian Crisis: The High Debt Model vs. the Wall-Street-IMF Complex', *New Left Review*, no. 228 (March/April).

Weeks, J. (1997) 'Social Policy for Uzbekistan: Analytical Guidelines', paper prepared for the UNDP Conference *Economic Policy in Uzbekistan after Five Years of Independence*. London: SOAS.

——(1998) *A Contribution to the Human Development Report for Mozambique*, paper prepared for the International Labour Organization and the United Nations Development Programme. London: SOAS.

——(1998) *Finance Capital and Myths of Globalisation*. London: SOAS Department of Economics Working Paper.

Welfens, P. J. J. (1992) 'The Socialist Shadow Economy: Causes, Characteristics, and Role for Systemic Reforms', *Economic Systems*, vol. 16, no. 1.

Woo, W. T., W. Hai, Y. Jin and G. Fan (1994) 'How Successful has Chinese Enterprise Reform been? Pitfalls in Opposite Biases and Focus', *Journal of Comparative Economics*, p. 410.

World Bank (1993a) *Historically Planned Economies – A Guide to the Data*, Washington, DC.

——(1993b) *The East Asian Miracle: Economic Growth and Public Policy*. Oxford: Oxford University Press.

——(1993c) *Viet Nam: Transition to the Market, An Economic Report*. Washington, DC.

——(1995a) *Viet Nam: Economic Report on Industrialization and Industrial Policy*. Washington, DC.

——(1995b) *Viet Nam: Poverty Assessment and Strategy*. Washington, DC.

——(1995c) *Vietnam: Environmental Program and Policy Priorities for a Socialist Economy in Transition*, Report no. 13200-VN, Washington, DC, 27 February, vol. 1 of 2.

——(1996a) *China: Reform of State-owned Enterprises*. Washington, DC.

——(1996b) *Vietnam: Fiscal Decentralisation and the Delivery of Rural Services*, Report no. 157435-VN, Washington, DC, 31 October.

——(1996c) *Vietnam: Education Financing Sector Study*. Washington, DC.

——(1996d) *World Development Report 1996 – From Plan to Market*. Oxford: Oxford University Press.

——(1996e) *The Chinese Economy: Fighting Inflation, Deepening Reform.* Washington, DC.

——International Monetary Fund and the Socialist Republic of Vietnam (cited as PFP) (1996f) *Vietnam. Policy Framework Paper, 1996–1998.* Hanoi.

——(1997a) *China Engaged: Integration with the Global Economy.* Washington, DC.

——(1997b) *China's Management of Enterprise Assets: The State as Shareholder.* Washington, DC.

——(1998a) *East Asia: Road to Recovery.* Washington, DC.

——(1998b), *Advancing Rural Development from Vision to Action,* Report for Donor Consultative Group meeting (December). Washington, DC.

——(1998c) *Viet Nam: Rising to the Challenge* (December). Washington, DC.

Yeats, A. J. (1989) 'Developing Countries' Exports of Manufactures: Past and Future Implications of Shifting Patterns of Comparative Advantage', *The Developing Economies*, vol. xxvii(2).

Zimbalist, A. and C. Brundenius (1989) *The Cuban Economy – Measurement and Analysis of Socialist Performance.* Baltimore and London: The Johns Hopkins University Press.

Index

Acronyms used in the index:
FSU   former Soviet Union
GDP   gross domestic product
MAI   Multilateral Agreement on Investment
SOEs state-owned enterprises
WTO World Trade Organization